Culturally Responsive Instructional Supervision

Leadership for Equitable and Emancipatory Outcomes

Edited by
Dwayne Ray Cormier,
Ian M. Mette, and Yanira Oliveras

Foreword by Mark Anthony Gooden
Afterword by Geneva Gay

TEACHERS COLLEGE PRESS
TEACHERS COLLEGE | COLUMBIA UNIVERSITY
NEW YORK AND LONDON

Published by Teachers College Press,® 1234 Amsterdam Avenue, New York, NY 10027

Copyright © 2024 by Teachers College, Columbia University

All rights reserved. No part of this publication may be reproduced or transmitted in any form or by any means, electronic or mechanical, including photocopy, or any information storage and retrieval system, without permission from the publisher. For reprint permission and other subsidiary rights requests, please contact Teachers College Press, Rights Dept.: tcpressrights@tc.columbia.edu

Library of Congress Cataloging-in-Publication Data is available at loc.gov

ISBN 978-0-8077-6948-5 (paper)
ISBN 978-0-8077-6949-2 (hardcover)
ISBN 978-0-8077-8228-6 (ebook)

Printed on acid-free paper
Manufactured in the United States of America

Contents

Foreword Mark Anthony Gooden   v

Introduction: Delivering Equitable Outcomes
    Through Instructional Supervision   1
    Ian M. Mette, Dwayne Ray Cormier, and Yanira Oliveras

1. A Primer for Culturally Responsive Instructional Supervision   11
    Dwayne Ray Cormier, Ian M. Mette, and Yanira Oliveras

2. Confronting the Lack of Diversity in Supervision Frameworks   31
    A. Minor Baker, Ann Marie Cotman, and Patricia L. Guerra

3. Race-ing Instructional Supervision: Plantation Traditions
    and Instructional Supervision   52
    Noelle Arnold and Rhodesia McMillian

4. Toward a Praxis Orientation for Teacher Candidate Supervision   79
    Megan Lynch and Rebecca West Burns

5. Rethinking Teacher Evaluation as Professional
    Development for Culturally Responsive Pedagogy   97
    Helen M. Hazi

6. Using Cultural Knowledge to Develop Structures and
    Systems That Lead to Equitable and Emancipatory Outcomes   112
    Ian M. Mette, Dwayne Ray Cormier, and Yanira Oliveras

7. The Role of Equity Audits in Culturally Responsive
    School Leadership   124
    Bodunrin O. Banwo, Kashmeel D. McKoena,
    Coy Carter Jr., and Muhammad Khalifa

8. Culturally Responsive Instructional Supervision and
   Mindfulness: A Somatic, Embodied Practice ... 149
   Steve Haberlin

9. Using Classroom Observation and Schoolwide Supervision
   Data to Facilitate Culturally Responsive Conversations
   About Diversity, Equity, Inclusion, and Belonging ... 166
   Sally J. Zepeda, Sevda Yildirim, and Salih Cevik

10. Building Bridges for Change: Culturally Responsive
    Instructional Supervision for Indigenous Students ... 188
    Hollie J. Mackey, Cailen M. O'Shea, and Sashay Schettler

11. Applying the Supervisory Behavior Continuum to
    Determine a Plan of Action and Support When
    Teaching Isn't Culturally Responsive ... 201
    Patricia Virella

12. Developing Supervisors' Critical Consciousness ... 214
    Shannon R. Waite

13. Black Women as Instructional Leaders: Historical
    and Contemporary Perspectives ... 231
    Terri N. Watson and Linda C. Tillman

14. Supervision Redux: Leaders With Teachers Activate
    Culturally Responsive Practices ... 251
    Lynda Tredway and Matt Militello

15. Supervision of Guerrilla Pedagogies ... 273
    Armen Álvarez and Mariela Rodríguez

Afterword   *Geneva Gay* ... 287

Author Index ... 290

Subject Index ... 301

About the Editors and Contributors ... 306

Foreword

What is instructional supervision, and who is responsible for it? How do we make it more culturally responsive? Is the process of becoming more culturally responsive in instructional leadership hindered by historical, structural, and institutional forces that challenge the development of an equity-focused and culturally responsive approach? While I do not intend to answer all these questions in this foreword, I assure readers that the answers found in this rich and valuable volume will provide enlightening answers to these questions and challenge you to be more culturally responsive globally.

The content here reminds those interested in instructional supervision that traditional approaches, often led by predominantly White institutional supervisors, may have cultural and knowledge gaps. While not ideal, these gaps present opportunities for improving instructional supervision by observing and leveraging cultural knowledge endemic to minoritized, marginalized, and otherized student populations. Accordingly, you will find rich discussions that will push the field forward as the student population of the public schools becomes more racially and culturally diverse, which is consistent with the world majority. To that end, I shun "majority-minority" language to describe the still growing majority of students of color. However, it is well-known that as the student population diversifies, teachers and principals will continue to be predominantly White despite the growing challenge of recruiting and retaining Black and Brown educators. While connections to race and culture are not absolute, it is essential to recognize that more work is needed to address this "cultural mismatch" in the short and long term. One approach that falls in the latter category is to continue educating the predominantly majority White workforce about what it means to be culturally responsive within the work of instructional supervision.

Instructional supervision is the critical process in which principals support teachers through various actions, such as managing curriculum and observing and coaching teachers to enhance the success of every student in the school. Therefore, a crucial part of America's charge should be making instructional supervision more culturally responsive, if in fact we aim to be as "woke" as resistors in this country claim. I believe being "woke" can still be seen as productive when grounded in an educational component aimed at reforming schools to improve students' sense of belonging and enhance their social and economic mobility. Of course, this critical work must be supported by the kind of theory, research, and practice presented in this volume.

In this volume you will find arguments for why scholars and practitioners should start with embracing the work of developing the critical consciousness of instructional leaders, something I have generally championed with colleagues and coauthors when arguing for more Culturally Responsive School Leadership (CRSL) being applied more broadly to school systems (Khalifa et al., 2016). CRSL requires leaders to recognize that being unaware increases the danger of facilitating and promoting the status quo in so many important school functions, from monitoring curriculum to assessing how teachers deliver it. If a leader does not reflect on what it means to promote current school policies and practices as if they are racially and culturally neutral, then they will surely fail to reform the school. Moreover, failing to examine inequities in supervision will not automatically make the school environment more equitable. Therefore, the instructional supervisors must be willing to examine all levels of inequity that surely impact the instructional process. However, the efforts of instructional supervision moving forward must be underpinned by the kind of scholarship in this volume.

So, if one supports the idea that instructional supervision should be more culturally responsive, then it is an easy logical jump to explore Culturally Responsive Instructional Supervision (CRIS) practices. If that is the goal, then this is the place to start a powerful and enlightened exploration. And as scholars and practitioners, we should be curious about what this process is exactly and how it might look, especially as it sets out to disrupt the common and troubling way of doing instructional supervision.

For example, one chapter in this volume highlights that a widely used and foundational supervision textbook neglects to delve into a deeper examination of race, culture, or other areas of marginalization. This is a problem. Although it may be somewhat surprising, given the conditions I described earlier, it is not entirely unexpected. Historically, research and content creation have occurred for many years without sufficient attention to critical consciousness or the researcher's positionality. As a result, we are currently saddled with the same challenges of neglecting issues of equity. However, this volume highlights the need to address these challenges. It emphasizes the importance of integrating our efforts to disrupt the influential, normalized, yet harmful methods of training future leaders in instructional supervision.

Embracing CRIS generates excitement and possibilities for individuals who often feel there is untapped potential for instructional supervision. It pushes us to consider, how could we be more sensitive to needs of marginalized students and staff? As such, CRIS should be thoroughly studied and widely shared with both professors and practitioners. Then, in that process where principals have pre- and post-conferences with teachers, they can start or expand efforts to empower teachers to become leaders themselves as they engage in equity-focused endeavors that will beckon them to redistribute the weight of the school's responsibilities more equitably, thereby providing a model of teamwork for students to look upon and observe the true changes that can result. I look forward to expansions on this topic and other relevant learning that will spring forward because of the exciting contributions in this book.

—Dr. Mark Anthony Gooden
Christian Johnson Endeavor Professor in
Education Leadership and Director of the
Endeavor Antiracist & Restorative
Leadership Initiative (EARLI)
Department of Organization and Leadership
Teachers College, Columbia University

Introduction
Delivering Equitable Outcomes Through Instructional Supervision

Ian M. Mette, Dwayne Ray Cormier, and Yanira Oliveras

Education in the United States has never been ahistorical or apolitical. Since the inception of public-school systems in the United States, our society has used the schoolhouse to leverage power and privilege to determine who education is intended to serve. The classroom has always functioned as a cultural battleground to whitewash our violent racialized history, as well as to oppress marginalized students based on a variety of sociocultural identities, including but not limited to race, ethnicity, socioeconomic status, birth sex, LGBTQIA+ identity, ability, and other lived experiences (Mette et al., 2023a). Most recently, we have witnessed the use of policy to codify privileged sociocultural identities through anti-critical race theory legislation (Waxman, 2023), anti-immigration policies (Mehta & Blazer, 2023), and anti-gay and anti-trans legislation (Peele, 2023). These efforts are a direct attempt to deliberately prevent educators from teaching historical truths and accuracies that contribute to our modern U.S. society, which is anti-Black, xenophobic, patriarchal, classist, and hegemonic in a variety of ways that are nuanced and effective in perpetuating an "us versus them" paradigm.

Just as concerning is the proliferation and resurgence of White Christian nationalism that is willing to use violence to maintain consolidation of power and privilege based on the hierarchy of whiteness (Burden-Stelly, 2023). These ideologies have effectively perpetuated white supremacy ideologies and have continually influenced U.S. policies over the last half of the 20th century and into the 21st century, most recently with the packing of a conservative Supreme Court, the overturning of *Roe v. Wade*, and the gerrymandering of congressional districts (Lieb, 2022). Perhaps most disturbing, through ongoing and aggressive media campaigns, the conservative political agendas of White Christian nationalists have aggressively attacked efforts to address racial violence and inequities through policy efforts *and* through cultural outlets, such as podcasts and various news media (Jones, 2023). This includes the vast spread of disinformation about election fraud, and anti-Black/anti-gay/anti-trans ideologies—among other efforts.

As such, White Christian nationalism actively attempts to maintain an identity, rather than increase self-consciousness, about what people racialized as White in the United States imagine a nationalist identity *should be* (Anderson, 1991). In doing so, they have maintained a pseudo sociocultural identity—one that is conceived and actively reinforced by various social systems, including legal, political, medical, and education systems.

U.S. society has been a source of great possibilities; however, we have failed to provide care for all students, particularly those from marginalized, minoritized, and otherized communities in schools and broader society. Throughout this book, the terms *marginalized, minoritized,* and *otherized* are employed to encompass a range of oppressions and their intersections perpetuated by systems of whiteness. These systems affect not only non-White individuals but also those who are economically disadvantaged, based, among other factors, on race, class, gender, sexual identity, geography, language, religion, and political affiliation. It is important to note that individuals subjected to these forms of oppression did not choose to be marginalized, minoritized, or otherized; rather, it is a systemic consequence of the entrenched system of whiteness shaped by historical, cultural, legal, social, economic, and educational factors and mechanisms. As such, education systems in the United States have a moral obligation to reckon with our violent racialized and discriminatory foundations and to close knowledge and sociocultural gaps that continue to persist in our modern society (Ladson-Billings, 2022). To honor the racial and cultural identities of all students, as well as their vast array of lived experiences, educators—specifically instructional leaders—must reimagine what can occur in the schoolhouse and how instruction can serve to enact equitable and emancipatory outcomes.

WHY THIS BOOK IS IMPORTANT

As schools struggle to implement culturally responsive instructional practices, we need to provide educators with new frameworks to examine how they contribute to instructional inequities, as well as how they can reimagine outcomes for all students that contribute to a more equitable U.S. society. Currently, the ecosystem of the U.S. education system is dysfunctional on many levels. Since the implementation of *No Child Left Behind* (NCLB), schools have become increasingly reliant on the education industry that produces an incredible amount of prepackaged curricula and teacher evaluation systems (NCES, 2017)—none of which are, or claim to be, culturally responsive. Moreover, education systems have continuously implemented technorational school improvement efforts in this era (Mette et al., 2020), which center whiteness and deficit-oriented ideologies. Feedback about how teachers might improve instructional practices has also been based on hierarchical perspectives that empower the principal as an enforcer of high-stakes accountability practices, all of which contributes to a continuation of sociocultural gaps and structural inequities (Mette et al., 2023a).

When schools function in this way, they fail to consider and implement asset-based approaches that center the identities and lived experiences of students (Yosso, 2005). In order to decenter whiteness and other privileged sociocultural identities, educators must re-envision how to best serve students who have been historically marginalized, minoritized, and otherized (Milner, 2017). This requires instructional supervisors—including but not limited to principals, instructional coaches, and teacher leaders—to increase cultural competence, critical consciousness, and culturally responsive practices through ongoing training and professional development about instructional practices that center anti-oppressive education within the classroom (Mette et al., 2023a). As such, there is a huge need for instructional supervision to be reconceptualized in a way that centers the voice of the marginalized and allows a conscious change about teaching practices that can in turn lead to more liberatory outcomes (Cormier & Pandey, 2021; Guerra et al., 2022).

To accomplish these shifts in how educators think about delivering culturally responsive pedagogies will require patience, persistence, and practices to address, mitigate, and close sociocultural gaps. Through formative feedback structures, instructional supervisors can help develop a community of culturally responsive teachers, which is particularly important given that 80% of the teaching force is racialized as White (Taie & Lewis, 2022) and often perpetuate middle-class ideologies and orientations, among other deficit-oriented perspectives about whom education is supposed to serve (Khalifa, 2020). However, to support school systems in this philosophical reimagination of what the schoolhouse *could be*, we must develop new paradigms and frameworks that detach and unmoor our education systems from the failed accountability experiment that started with NCLB and has continued through the first quarter of the 21st century.

UNDERSTANDING THE HISTORICAL CONTEXT OF INSTRUCTIONAL SUPERVISION

Currently, most instructional supervision frameworks lack criticality and fail to address the factors that contribute to the sociocultural gaps that persist in the United States. Historically, these instructional supervision frameworks have focused on the idea of being clinical, objective, and neutral—concepts that maintain and protect whiteness as well as fail to acknowledge positionality in how feedback about instructional practices is delivered and perceived (Guerra et al., 2022). Additionally, many traditional supervision paradigms fail to center the lived experiences of marginalized, minoritized, and otherized students and often reify inequitable outcomes based on privileged sociocultural identities (Cotman et al., 2023). In short, these instructional supervision frameworks lack the development of critical consciousness that is needed to implement culturally responsive school leadership (Waite, 2021).

Not only are these instructional supervision paradigms and practices culturally unresponsive, but they also fail to utilize various methods, observation tools, and techniques that could be adapted to better support reflection and implementation of culturally responsive instructional practices. For example, there are a variety of instructional supervision tools that could be updated to ensure teachers connect learning objectives to cultural identities, empower students to address social inequities through their learning, and engage students in rigorous and validating pedagogy that affirms cultural identities (Mette et al., 2023b). Additionally, small tweaks to developmental supervision approaches (Glickman et al., 2018) could be updated to help educators reflect upon and improve their cultural competence through data generated with classroom observations.

As an education profession, we cannot simply wait for cohorts of newly trained teachers to enact culturally responsive instructional practices. We need to be able to support teachers—now—with developmentally appropriate feedback that helps them develop cultural competence and critical consciousness, center the identities and lived experiences of their students in their instruction, and empower students to address social inequities to help contribute to a more democratic society. Over the last several years, we have worked to develop an instructional supervision framework that is more culturally responsive. Many of the chapters in this book started as ideas shared during presentations at the Council of Professors of Instructional Supervision (COPIS), University Council for Educational Administration (UCEA), and American Educational Research Association (AERA) annual meetings. It is from these presentations, critical conversations, and discussions that a new, reimagined form of instructional supervision has emerged to help create more inclusive learning experiences for all students.

ORGANIZATION OF THIS BOOK

In this book, we bring together influential scholars from across the fields of educational leadership and instructional supervision to develop an evolving and visionary framework of Culturally Responsive Instructional Supervision (CRIS). We offer three parts to this book that span 15 chapters, addressing foundations for CRIS, practical approaches of CRIS, and examples of CRIS praxis. The book opens with a Foreword by Mark Anthony Gooden, a leader in the field of Culturally Responsive School Leadership (CRSL), and the book ends with an Afterword by Geneva Gay, a foundational and distinguished scholar of culturally responsive teaching. This incredible lineup of transformative scholars helps to decenter whiteness in the field of instructional supervision and provide a framework for CRIS that leads to more equitable and emancipatory outcomes for all children in the United States.

The first five chapters focus on developing the foundations for CRIS. Chapter 1, authored by Dwayne Ray Cormier, Ian M. Mette, and Yanira Oliveras, serves as a primer and introduction to CRIS within the culturally responsive ecosystem, encompassing culturally responsive teaching (CRT; Gay, 2018) and Culturally Responsive School Leadership (CRSL; Khalifa, 2020; Khalifa et al., 2016). Furthermore, the introduction of CRIS integrates instructional supervision into the culturally responsive discourse community. By critically examining traditional instructional supervision paradigms, the authors offer an overview of how instructional leaders can implement CRIS practices to effectively leverage students' cultural capital, employing high levels of cultural competence and critical consciousness to enhance instructional outcomes and student achievement. Most importantly, this chapter lays the foundation for key roles and functions within schools (e.g., school leadership, instructional supervision, teaching) to align with cultural responsiveness and intended praxis, promoting greater adoption of culturally responsive practices and improving student achievement and academic outcomes.

A. Minor Baker, Ann Marie Cotman, and Patricia L. Guerra, the authors of Chapter 2, offer a much-needed critique of the lack of criticality in traditional instructional supervision frameworks. By examining how instructional supervision has often reified race-evasive and culturally neutral practices, the authors provide a foundation for how educators might conceptualize CRIS to better support students with socioculturally diverse identities. Readers will be excited to see how the authors provide an in-depth analysis of knowledge, skills, and dispositions needed to apply CRIS in practice, as well as the work that remains to better develop instructional leaders, to ensure that culturally responsive instructional practices occur throughout the schoolhouse.

In Chapter 3, Noelle Arnold and Rhodesia McMillian deconstruct the historical legacies of instructional supervision, specifically the racialized policies and practices of the U.S. education system that can be tied to plantation traditions. Through a powerful critique of the (mis)application of supervision, the authors detail how plantation traditions help contribute to the control of what is taught through the surveillance of a white enterprise. Arnold and McMillian analyze how supervision is an enactment of political ideologies and oversight of labor to produce a standardized product that does little to address the influence of race within U.S. society. By centering race in instructional supervision, the chapter details the concept of *Race-ing Instructional Supervision* that details the way racial identities influence how the supervision process is enacted, but also how educators might move the field of instructional supervision theoretically and practically out of the plantation.

Megan Lynch and Rebecca West Burns, in Chapter 4, provide the reader with a framework for a transformational teacher candidate supervision approach that is influenced by Freirean ideologies and perspectives. Through a critique of neoliberal capitalism, Lynch and Burns detail how teacher candidate supervision is devalued, deskilled, and deprofessionalized, leading to compliance-ordered tasks that leverage hegemonic power dynamics. To reimagine how a more culturally responsive form of teacher candidate supervision might function, the chapter details how to center humanizing and liberatory practices in pre-service teacher development that supervisors must enact through social justice–oriented inquiry stances.

In Chapter 5, Helen M. Hazi details how the summative function of teacher evaluation serves as a lever to control how and if teachers can engage in historically accurate conversations with students about race, immigration status, and LGBTQA+ identity. By reimagining teacher evaluation as a tool for professional development, Hazi attempts to democratize the definition of "good teaching" by engaging in a discourse analysis about the current limitations of teacher evaluation. In this chapter, the author discusses what is needed systematically to support the development of Culturally Responsive Teaching, specifically how education systems can empower teachers to engage in self-evaluation and peer-evaluation and shift away from the damaging effects of the current approach to teacher evaluation. Through a reimagining of this process, readers can envision what is needed to develop a more critical mindset about how to engage in ongoing school improvement efforts that value asset-based approaches to instruction.

The next six chapters provide a variety of practical approaches for how CRIS might be implemented in the schoolhouse. In Chapter 6, Ian M. Mette, Dwayne Ray Cormier, and Yanira Oliveras provide an overview of the CRIS framework (Mette et al., 2023a), specifically the current hierarchical feedback loop that uses technorational approaches to tightly control classroom instruction. Leveraging the creation of intentionally representative supervision teams, the chapter details how teacher leaders can use observation practices to inform the presence of culturally responsive practices and what to do when instruction is observed to be culturally destructive. Through the development of structures to close sociocultural gaps, CRIS can be used to support the growth of teachers individually and through critical colleagues.

Bodunrin O. Banwo, Kashmeel D. McKoena, Coy Carter Jr., and Muhammad Khalifa, the authors of Chapter 7, offer important insights into how equity audits can be used to identify inequities in academic-based outcomes. Through a connection of CRSL to CRIS, the authors detail a critical analysis for practitioners to use regarding the use of equity audits to inform the development of culturally responsive curriculum and pedagogical practices. By examining critical self-awareness, educators can target professional development that leads to more inclusive school environments as well as higher levels of student engagement. Specifically, this chapter highlights how CRIS and CRSL can complement each other in ways that lead to more culturally affirming practices at the building level and within individual classrooms.

In Chapter 8, Steve Haberlin creates a framework for how instructional leaders can leverage meditative practices to become more aware of their values, beliefs, and privileged sociocultural identities. As a powerful tool for practitioners to consider, the framework provides insights into how teachers can engage in critical self-reflection to change at the *individual level*. Using meditation practices, Haberlin details how educators can become more aware of their own internalized sensations and the embodied mindfulness that is required to break unconscious cycles and raise awareness of implicit biases—a concept that should be of great interest for educators as they attempt to further develop their own critical consciousness.

Sally J. Zepeda, Sevda Yildirim, and Salih Cevik, in Chapter 9, provide a detailed description of how teacher leaders, instructional coaches, and principals can use classroom observations to determine conversations about how to improve instructional practices through a culturally responsive lens. By focusing on how to frame culturally responsive classroom observations, the authors go into great depth to detail how these data can inform the pre-observation conference, drive the classroom observation, and influence the post-observation conference. From this, practitioners can help target professional learning development, deepen understanding and application of Culturally Responsive Teaching practices, and leverage asset-based pedagogies to reimagine how school improvement efforts might contribute to a more inclusive schoolhouse.

In Chapter 10, authors Hollie J. Mackey, Cailen M. O'Shea, and Sashay Schettler give the reader important questions to grapple with when considering embedded colonized structures in the schoolhouse, specifically as the structures relate to understanding the history of erasure in the United States around Indigenous being and knowledge. By problematizing how CRIS might serve as a bridge to build authentic relationships with Indigenous students and parents, educators can develop an authentic curiosity and commitment to engage responsibly with Indigenous curriculum and instruction. In doing so, educators can begin the process of mediating the colonized systems that have repeatedly rendered Indigenous knowledges invisible. As such, the authors offer great insights for practitioners to consider that will benefit both Native and non-Native students.

Patricia Virella, the author of Chapter 11, details her approach to the implementation of Culturally Responsive Instructional Supervision Practices (CRISP). Leveraging the Supervisory Behavior Continuum (Glickman et al., 2018), the author astutely marries this work with the Cultural Proficiency© Continuum. Through the development of developmentally appropriate feedback, Virella details how supervisors can structure and facilitate dialogue which allows teachers to receive feedback that helps deconstruct hegemonic structures that are often replicated through classroom instruction. Readers should take note of the specific CRISP detailed based on the observed level of Cultural Proficiency© and the corresponding supports required from supervisors.

The final four chapters provide examples of CRIS praxis. In Chapter 12, Shannon R. Waite summarizes the core concept of instructional supervisors developing critical consciousness, which is necessary for CRIS to help deliver equity-oriented instructional improvement efforts. To help liberate the schoolhouse from remaining a system of oppression, educational leaders must interrogate the hegemonic structures and practices that have been replicated in U.S. education systems and support teachers in the enactment of liberatory efforts through teaching. Through internal reflection, supervisors can enact CRIS through self-reflection that challenges white supremacy, which in turn leads to greater awareness of how to transform beliefs into practice.

Terri N. Watson and Linda C. Tillman, authors of Chapter 13, describe the important contributions of Black Feminism and Black Feminist Theory in the ongoing development of CRIS. Through the tenets of dialogue and the ethic of care, the authors provide the reader with recommendations of the praxis of CRIS and how it can inform academic success for Black students. Readers will be excited to read how traditional scholarship of instructional leadership is problematized, as well as how Watson and Tillman connect Black Feminist Theory to culturally responsive teaching to identify how CRIS can apply a standard of care and meaningful instruction that centers the voices of Black women educational leaders to help transform educational leadership preparation programs.

In Chapter 14, authors Lynda Tredway and Matt Militello ground CRIS practices through the Community Learning Exchange (CLE) process (Guajardo et al., 2016). Through a humanistic lens, the authors provide a reimagination of evidence-based supervisory practices with an eye toward culturally responsive and rigorous instruction. Tredway and Militello detail how CRIS can be used as a vehicle for cultivating more student-centered instruction using deprivatized, evidence-based supervision feedback structures. Specifically, the authors highlight the use of the CLE axioms and how this can relate to greater relational trust among teachers and the supports needed to engage teaching in ongoing self-improvement.

Armen Álvarez and Mariela Rodríguez, the authors of Chapter 15, challenge instructional supervisors to engage in Guerrilla Pedagogies to resist the assimilation and oppressive practices that are often reified in the schoolhouse. To dismantle the logic of white supremacy, the authors provide a critical analysis of how supervisors can produce instructional practices that support the eviction of settler colonizer epistemologies, empower a renewed vision of democracy that values equality and justice, and counter the Eurocentric history so often reinforced in U.S. schools. Readers will especially appreciate the framework Álvarez and Rodríguez provide to help CRIS to decenter whiteness and help implement instruction that is affirming of all students in the United States.

INSTRUCTIONAL SUPERVISION FOR EQUITABLE AND EMANCIPATORY OUTCOMES

This book is published with the notion that to enact culturally responsive school systems, the work must transpire within individual classrooms themselves. As such, teachers need support—ongoing formative feedback through CRIS—to critically explore their own privileged sociocultural identities and privileges so they can create learning opportunities that center the identities of their students (Villegas & Lucas, 2002). Teachers also need ongoing professional development to challenge ahistorical and apolitical approaches to education that continue to prevent addressing social injustices from a historic and contemporary perspective (Brooks & Watson, 2019). It is through the development of the CRIS framework that we hope to provide teacher leaders, instructional coaches, and principals with the tools necessary to reimagine and recreate a schoolhouse that allows all children to see themselves in the curriculum and in daily instruction.

Through this collection of chapters, we also hope educational leaders understand that the greatest form of accountability school systems can enact is in service to the local community. If the schoolhouse is to ever contribute to a more equitable society, it must occur through the decentering of whiteness and the (re)centering of the various sociocultural identities and lived experiences that education has traditionally marginalized, minoritized, and otherized. This is not to say that all students racialized as Black, non-White, or identify as part of the LGBTQA+ community will require the same instructional supports. However, our collective hope is that instructional leaders enacting CRIS will help teachers understand how education systems produce ongoing inequities based on race, ethnicity, class, birth sex, orientation/identity, ability, and other lived experiences, as well as the responsibilities we all have as educators to mitigate and eliminate those inequities. As such, in order for CRSL to ensure CRT occurs, CRIS must be embedded in these practices.

As with any book, the ideas we offer here are only as powerful as the practices they influence. Moreover, the concepts presented here come from a coalition of people who are comprised of a variety of sociocultural identities and lived experiences and are committed to reimagining and recreating a schoolhouse that is more equitable and inclusive for all students. As editors, we hope to follow the tradition of Fred Hampton through the creation of rainbow coalitions to support people in the active engagement of naming, addressing, mitigating, and eliminating social inequities in the United States. Through this common cause, we offer this book as part of our efforts to contribute to a more democratic society and world.

REFERENCES

Anderson, B. (1991). *Imagined communities* (2nd ed.). Verso.

Brooks, J. S., & Watson, T. N. (2019). School leadership and racism: An ecological perspective. *Urban Education, 54*(5), 631–655. https://doi.org/10.1177/0042085918783821

Burden-Stelly, C. (2023). *Black scare / red scare: Theorizing capitalist racism in the United States*. University of Chicago Press.

Cormier, D. R., & Pandey, T. (2021). Semiotic analysis of a foundational textbook used widely across educational supervision. *Journal of Educational Supervision, 4*(2). https://doi.org/10.31045/jes.4.2.6

Cotman, A. M., Guerra, P., & Baker, A. M. (2023). Culturally responsive instructional supervision: Further analysis of a leading textbook. *Journal of Educational Supervision, 6*(1), 45–63. https://doi.org/10.31045/jes.6.1.4

Gay, G. (2018). *Culturally responsive teaching: Theory, research, and practice* (3rd ed.). Teachers College Press.

Glickman, C. D. Gordon, S. P., & Ross-Gordon, J. M. (2018). *Supervision and instructional leadership: A developmental approach* (10th ed.). Pearson.

Guajardo, M., Guajardo, F., Janson, C., & Militello, M. (2016). *Reframing community partnerships in education: Uniting the power of place and wisdom of people*. Routledge

Guerra, P. L., Baker, A. M., & Cotman, A. M. (2022). Instructional supervision: Is it culturally responsive? A Textbook analysis. *Journal of Educational Supervision, 5*(1). https://doi.org/10.31045/jes.5.1.1

Jones, R. P. (2023, August 31). The roots of Christian nationalism go back further than you think. *TIME*. Retrieved from https://time.com/6309657/us-christian-nationalism-columbus-essay/

Khalifa, M. (2020). *Culturally responsive school leadership* (4th ed.). Harvard Education Press.

Khalifa, M. A., Gooden, M. A., & Davis, J. E. (2016). Culturally responsive school leadership: A synthesis of the literature. *Review of Educational Research, 86*(4), 1272–1311. https://doi.org/10.3102/0034654316630383

Ladson-Billings, G. (2022). *The dreamkeepers: Successful teachers for African American children* (3rd ed.). Jossey-Bass.

Lieb, D. A. (2022, July 3). *Abortion ruling puts spotlight on gerrymandered legislatures*. PBS News Hour. Retrieved from https://www.pbs.org/newshour/politics/abortion-ruling-puts-spotlight-on-gerrymandered-legislatures

Mehta, S., & Blazer, J. (2023). *White supremacy is fueling extreme anti-immigration policy in Texas*. ACLU. Retrieved from https://www.aclu.org/news/immigrants-rights/white-supremacy-is-fueling-extreme-anti-immigrant-policy-in-texas

Mette, I. M., Aguilar, I., & Wieczorek, D. (2020). A 30-state analysis of teacher supervision and evaluation systems in the ESSA era. *Journal of Educational Supervision, 3*(2), 105–135. https://doi.org/10.31045/jes.3.2.7

Mette, I. M., Cormier, D. R., & Oliveras, Y. (2023a). *Making a difference: Instructional leadership that drives self-reflection and values the expertise of teachers*. Rowman & Littlefield.

Mette, I. M., Cormier, D. R., & Oliveras-Ortiz, Y. (2023b). Culturally responsive instructional supervision: (Re)Envisioning feedback for equitable change. In A. Lavigne & M. L. Derrington (Eds.), *Actionable feedback for PK–12 teachers* (pp. 75–87). Rowman & Littlefield.

Milner, H. R., IV. (2017). Where's the race in culturally relevant pedagogy? *Teachers College Record, 119*(1), 1–32. https://doi.org/10.1177/016146811711900109

National Center for Education Statistics. (2017). *2017 digest of education statistics*. https://nces.ed.gov/programs/digest/d16/tables/dt16_236.10.asp?%20current=yes

Peele, C. (2023). *Roundup of anti-LGBTQ+ legislation advancing in states across the country*. Human Rights Campaign. Retrieved from https://www.hrc.org/press-releases/roundup-of-anti-lgbtq-legislation-advancing-in-states-across-the-country

Taie, S., & Lewis, L. (2022). *Characteristics of 2020–21 public and private K–12 school teachers in the United States: Results from the National Teacher and Principal Survey. First look. NCES 2022–113*. National Center for Education Statistics.

Yosso, T. J. (2005). Whose culture has capital? A critical race theory discussion of community cultural wealth. *Race Ethnicity and Education, 8*(1), 69–91. https://doi.org/10.1080/1361332052000341006

Villegas, A. M., & Lucas, T. (2002). Preparing culturally responsive teachers: Rethinking the curriculum. *Journal of Teacher Education, 53*(1), 20–32. https://doi-org.tc.idm.oclc.org/10.1177/0022487102053001003

Waite, S. R. (2021). Towards a theory of critical consciousness: A new direction for the development of instructional and supervisory leaders. *Journal of Educational Supervision, 4*(2), 65–79. https://doi.org/10.31045/jes.4.2.4

Waxman, O. B. (2023). New data shows the anti-critical race theory movement is 'far from over.' *Time*. Retrieved from https://time.com/6266865/critical-race-theory-data-exclusive/

CHAPTER 1

A Primer for Culturally Responsive Instructional Supervision

Dwayne Ray Cormier, Ian M. Mette, and Yanira Oliveras

In the field of instructional supervision (i.e., instructional leadership), a misalignment in objectives exists when compared to the objectives of Culturally Responsive Teaching (CRT; Gay, 2018; Villegas & Lucas, 2002) and Culturally Responsive School Leadership (CRSL, Khalifa, 2020). Over the last 50 years, culturally responsive praxis,[1] which is the intersection of theory and practice, has yielded a host of comprehensive theories, research, and approaches that correspond with key functions or roles (e.g., school leadership, instructional supervision, teaching) within the PK–12 schooling enterprise. This evolution underscores the critical need for supervision practices to align with and actively promote the principles of culturally responsive praxis, ensuring that educational leaders are equipped to foster schooling environments that are culturally affirming across key functions within PK–12 schools. Furthermore, incorporating culturally responsive practices into instructional supervision is paramount for developing pedagogical strategies that are inclusive, equitable, and socially just, reflective of the growing diversity in student populations and overwhelmingly White PK–12 educator workforce.

CRT, in principle, equips educators with developmental pathways, metacognitive frameworks, and an ethics of care to aid in fostering and leveraging students' cultural capital. Yosso (2005) introduced the concept of Community Cultural Wealth, which encompasses aspirational, familial, social, navigational, resistant, and linguistic forms of cultural capital, serving as essential entry points for addressing and eliminating opportunity gaps in PK–12 educational settings. Gay (2018), Ladson-Billings (2006), and Milner (2020) stress the importance of developing a professional disposition that not only fosters culturally relevant and responsive educational outcomes for minoritized, marginalized, and otherized students but also values the cultural capital that these students and their families

---

1. Culturally responsive praxis refers to theory and practice that leverages students' cultural capital to eliminate observed opportunity gaps in PK–12 school systems. This form of praxis encompasses high levels of cultural competence and critical consciousness aimed at actively addressing disparities and creating more equitable and empowering schooling environments for all students.

contribute to the educational environment, as characterized by Yosso (2005). Conversely, CRSL seeks to organize and operate PK–12 educational settings in a way that respects and actively leverages the cultural capital, resources, and assets brought by students and their families into the school building. Noted CRSL scholars (Gooden & Dantley, 2012; Khalifa, 2020; Khalifa et al., 2016) advocate for a praxis that uses data to identify opportunity gaps and create avenues that utilize students' and families' cultural capital to foster school renewal. As such, CRSL employs instruments like equity audits to evaluate and enhance the cultural competence, as well as develop critical consciousness and professional dispositions of PK–12 educational stakeholders to inform how to better serve students and families who are minoritized, marginalized, and otherized in school.

Ladson-Billings (2006) introduced the concept of missed learning opportunities in PK–12 schooling contexts as "opportunity gaps," which are a result of the economic and human resources that are not afforded to minoritized, marginalized, and otherized students. Milner (2020) added that opportunity gaps as systemic deficiencies within a school system, particularly in financial capital, human resources, and curricular offerings, lead to diminished educational opportunities. Freire (1970) discussed that these gaps are particularly harmful and often irreparable when exacerbated by social, political, and economic factors. Sociocultural gaps are the social and cultural distance between students and families and the educational settings they encounter (Gay, 1993). We assert that these sociocultural gaps—stemming from a lack of cultural competence and critical consciousness—give rise to opportunity gaps within PK–12 schools and classrooms. Moreover, addressing sociocultural gaps, knowingly or unknowingly held by instructional supervisors or leaders, is the ideal starting point for transforming their problematic assumptions and instructional supervision practices (Mette et al., 2023a). Please note that in this chapter we will use the terms "instructional supervisor" and "instructional leader" interchangeably. Addressing sociocultural gaps head-on will not only improve instructional supervisors' cultural competence and critical consciousness but will also lead to culturally appropriate supervision, corresponding instructional practices, and improved student achievement (Mette et al., 2023b). Up until recently, culturally responsive teaching (CRT) and culturally responsive school leadership (CRSL) have not explicitly focused on the pivotal role instructional supervision plays in addressing opportunity gaps, which result from a host of sociocultural gaps (e.g., cultural competence, critical consciousness) that consequently negatively impact student achievement in PK–12 schools.

To help bridge the gap between CRT and CRSL, we focus our efforts on developing a supervision paradigm that can help all educators in the classroom reflect on being more culturally responsive through the pedagogies enacted in the school building. Supervision is a theory, practice, and field of study focusing on how teachers implement curriculum and assess subsequent instruction. However, traditional conceptions of supervision problematically rely on Eurocentric frameworks of ontology, epistemology, axiology, and teleology to define and evaluate instruction (i.e., instructional behaviors) and its impact on student achievement.

The historical emphasis on Eurocentric ways of knowing and practicing in supervision has resulted in missed learning opportunities for minoritized, marginalized, and otherized students. As such, the field of supervision has historically leveraged Eurocentric frameworks, which correspondingly have resulted in the continuation of opportunity gaps for minoritized, marginalized, and otherized students. It is long overdue for the field of instructional supervision to make the transformative shift toward more culturally responsive and equitable practices within the field to address and eliminate opportunity gaps in PK–12 schools.

This chapter offers a primer for Culturally Responsive Instructional Supervision (CRIS), an emergent framework being situated within the PK–12 culturally responsive ecosystem and the field of instructional supervision. We aim to advocate for the necessity of CRIS within higher education, such as instructional supervision and teacher education programs, as well as within the U.S. PK–12 school systems for instructional supervisors. First, we critically examine the origins of supervision. Second, we highlight efforts aimed at helping educators achieve culturally responsive praxis. Third, we make the case for the explicit development of a CRIS framework. Fourth, we introduce and situate CRIS within the culturally responsive ecosystem and discuss the value CRIS aims to contribute within the field of instructional supervision. Last, we discuss future directions for CRIS within higher education and PK–12 educative contexts. Ultimately, this chapter is purposed to equip the field of instructional supervision with a framework for delivering contextual, formative, and summative assessments, leveraging the cultural knowledge and assets inherent to minoritized, marginalized, and otherized students, and establishing a system for codifying and evaluating student achievement based on culturally responsive principles.

CRITICAL EXAMINATION OF THE ORIGINS OF SUPERVISION

From its origins in the early 1900s, instructional supervision (i.e., instructional leadership) by way of a school principal primary aim is to manage curriculum and subsequent instruction to control teachers' instructional behaviors. The origins of supervision, from an epistemological standpoint, can be traced back to essentialism and perennialism (Gordon, 2020). These philosophical approaches indicate that the curriculum in the United States seeks to distill academic knowledge, skills, rigor, relevance, and achievement into forms that closely conform to Western societal norms and objectives (Bagley, 1938; Hutchins, 1952; Khalifa et al., 2016). Inherently, the theories mentioned above are grounded in ideologies of whiteness (Lynch, 2018). From a sociocultural perspective, these theories employ curriculum and subsequent instruction to facilitate student outcomes (e.g., student achievement, socialized assimilation) that maintain White racial dominance and common sense (Leonardo & Manning, 2017). Consequently, ideologies rooted in whiteness, influenced by power dynamics shaped by politics, economics, race, and geography, are not inclusive of ways of knowing and doing beyond ideologies of whiteness. Effectively, supervision largely fails to leverage the cultural capital of students and families who belong to minoritized, marginalized, and otherized groups within the U.S. PK–12 school systems, particularly through curriculum and subsequent supervision.

Contemporary scholars focusing on school renewal have redefined supervision as instructional supervision. This model for school change predominantly incorporates principles from developmental psychology and andragogy to offer transformative pathways for the supervision of curriculum, subsequent instruction, and observational feedback provided to teachers (Glickman et al., 2018). Institutional supervision practices privilege collaborative practices and the distribution of power beyond the school principal, which includes teacher leaders and teacher(s) of record, who are subject to teacher observation, evaluations, and student achievement objectives (Sergiovanni & Starratt, 2007). This contemporary approach contrasts with traditional instructional supervision models that position school principals as the sole individuals responsible for instructional supervision and teacher and student outcomes. Conversely, contemporary approaches to supervision have yet to capitalize on the opportunity to foster developmental protocols that systemically support supervisors in building teachers' capacity to execute culturally responsive praxis aimed at redressing opportunity gaps observed in curriculum, instruction, and teacher observational feedback.

To put it plainly, contemporary forms of supervision still hold on to the spirit of essentialism and perennialism (Guerra et al., 2022). Fundamentally, the above-mentioned philosophies were not designed to employ cultural and critical epistemologies (e.g., cultural competence, critical consciousness) that identify and mitigate social, political, and economic contradictions observed and felt by students who are minoritized, marginalized, and otherized by U.S. PK–12 schools and broader society (Freire, 1970). Current and progressive forms of instructional supervision, which are designed for broader application and political flexibility, tend to rely on ahistorical and apolitical discourses. These discourses often promote calls to action for the adoption of democratic practices that employ epistemologies devoid of context and race considerations, ultimately centering on whiteness (Cormier & Pandey, 2021). Consequently, current and progressive forms of instructional supervision subvert notions of diversity, equity, inclusion, and belonging (DEIB) in curricula, subsequent instruction, and teacher feedback aimed at improving academic outcomes for PK–12 students who are minoritized, marginalized, and otherized.

This critical examination of contemporary and progressive forms of instructional supervision is warranted. Moreover, the notion of controlling teachers' instructional behaviors within the present U.S. sociopolitical educational context is significant and extremely relevant, evident by the passing of legislation, primarily in conservative states (e.g., Florida, Texas), that prohibits the use of culturally responsive praxis (e.g., CRT, CRSL, CRIS). Consequently, laws prohibiting culturally responsive praxis have led to increased control over teachers' instructional behaviors within U.S. PK–12 schools and classrooms. Essentially, this moment in

U.S. educational history denotes a return to educational ideologies and epistemologies that essentialize academic knowledge, skills, rigor, relevance, and achievement to socially assimilate students into embodying and performing Western societal norms grounded in whiteness, honoring white fragility. Further, these laws enable state and district leaders to whitewash curricula products, often removing representation to facilitate inclusivity and increase the sense of belonging for minoritized, marginalized, and otherized students in U.S. PK–12 schools. As many have theorized, since the enactment of these laws, students from racially and ethnically minoritized populations have experienced a decline in their sense of belonging, and had to navigate schools with increased opportunity gaps.

FOSTERING THE CAPACITY OF EDUCATORS TO ACHIEVE CULTURALLY RESPONSIVE PRAXIS

Teleologically, the primary objectives of CRT, CRSL, and CRIS are to enhance teachers', school leaders', and instructional leaders' capacity to recognize, utilize, and leverage minoritized, marginalized, and otherized students' cultural capital within the schooling context. However, the capacity to leverage students' cultural capital is linked with educators' understanding of, assumptions about, and relationships with students from diverse ethnic and racial backgrounds. These understandings, broadly, are understood as educators' funds of knowledge and frames of reference. Banks (1993) offered that fundamental funds of knowledge, including personal/cultural, popular, mainstream academic, transformative academic, and school-based, are needed to effectively leverage students' cultural capital. Banks (1993) added that developing such capacity requires educators to undergo a transformative and reflective experience, enabling them to divest themselves from ideologies of whiteness and reorient their positionality, thus reducing problematic assumptions and biases. Yosso's (2005) expansion on Bourdieu's work, achieved through a critique of Bourdieu's use of deficit perspectives to explain why students of color lag behind White students in academic success, resulted in a conceptual framework that identifies the various forms of cultural capital educators must leverage to achieve culturally appropriate and responsive educative outcomes. These outcomes broadly encompass school leadership, instructional supervision, and teaching. The cultural capital, levers, or funds of knowledge that Yosso (2005) presented are rooted in the various forms of cultural knowledge students bring into the school community, including aspirational, navigational, social, linguistic, familial, and resistant capital. Milner (2020) categorized problematic dispositions (i.e., deficit perspectives) into an explanatory framework for opportunity gaps. This framework highlights various forms of cognitive dissonance that should be addressed within the schooling context, including color blindness, cultural conflicts, the myth of meritocracy, deficit mindsets, low expectations, and context-neutral mindsets. The combination of Banks's (1993), Yosso's (2005), and Milner's (2020) insights into the precise knowledge or lever points to engage learners from racially and ethnically diverse backgrounds effectively is closely tied to the ideologies that are either centered (e.g., whiteness) or not centered (e.g., minoritized, marginalized, and otherized) within PK–12 schooling enterprises. Cormier (2019) emphasized that such capacity must be developed through educational policy, with andragogical processes and tools to enhance educators' effectiveness in delivering culturally responsive praxis.

KEY EMBODIMENTS: CULTURAL COMPETENCE AND CRITICAL CONSCIOUSNESS

CRT, CRSL, and CRIS argue that educators should embody high cultural competence and critical consciousness levels to educate students from diverse backgrounds and lived experiences effectively. These embodiments translate into tangible efforts that humanize minoritized, marginalized, and otherized students within PK–12 schools and classrooms. Approaches that leverage students' cultural assets, such as CRT and CRSL, consistently yield culturally appropriate outcomes in PK–12 education. As previously mentioned, school contexts that achieve these outcomes prioritize access, equity, and diversity in education within their accountability systems (Villegas & Lucas, 2002). Equity-minded accountability systems are characterized by high levels of cultural competence and critical consciousness, resulting in observed and felt culturally responsive praxis. In such systems, equity-minded educators are empowered to recognize, navigate, and resist the social, economic, and political forces contributing to oppressive environments for these students. Equity-minded accountability systems are mechanized by equity-minded educational policies (Dowd et al., 2015).

Educators must engage in developmental processes that yield metacognitive tools and capacity to counter the social, economic, and political forces within U.S. PK–12 schools. Subsequently, these tools enable educators to engage in critical self-reflection, which aids in developing their cultural competence and critical consciousness. This skill set, in turn, leads to culturally responsive praxis (e.g., leadership, teaching), which is observed and experienced by minoritized, marginalized, and otherized students and their families. Educators can effectively identify, navigate, and resist social, economic, and political forces in educational systems committed to equity and culturally responsive praxis. To guide students along pathways leading to social and economic mobility, educational stakeholders must be supported by equity-minded policies, curricula, practices, and beliefs. An equity-minded framework fosters equitable school environments and promotes student achievement through asset-based approaches such as culturally responsive praxis.

From our perspective, developing the field of instructional supervision capacity to co-curate culturally responsive praxis, with minoritized, marginalized, and otherized students, hinges on their willingness to embody two foundational professional dispositions: cultural competence and critical consciousness. These dispositions are potent mediators of the social, economic, and political forces that significantly impact minoritized, marginalized, and otherized students within U.S. PK–12 schools.

Cultural Competence

Cultural competence connotes an educator's ability to teach students from cultures other than their own effectively (Moule, 2011). Lindsey et al. (2019) detail cultural competence as a mindset and worldview that informs how educators make assumptions and respond to issues in diverse schooling contexts. Howard (2019) posits that enhancing teachers' cultural competence increases their capacity to acquire and leverage students' and families' cultural capital to facilitate transformative learning experiences. Therefore, culturally competent educational stakeholders, such as school leaders, instructional supervisors, and teachers, are self-aware, reflective, and dedicated to enhancing their understanding of their students' cultural backgrounds, leading to observable and tangible culturally responsive praxis through creating inclusive and effective learning environments. Correspondingly, endowing instructional supervisors with tools to develop cultural competence can improve curriculum and teaching assessments and foster formative feedback that supports CRT and student achievement.

Critical Consciousness

Within culturally responsive praxis, critical consciousness represents a form of awareness that enables educators to problematize and be responsive to social, political, and economic contradictions observed on behalf of minoritized, marginalized, and otherized students within U.S. PK–12 schools. This form of consciousness empowers educators to examine, embody critically, and challenge observed acts of oppression, inequality, and injustice. This form of embodiment is not surface level but one that comes from a place of deep empathy (Warren, 2018). To cultivate instructional supervisors, developing systemic capacity and transformative consequences is crucial, enabling leaders to co-create culturally responsive praxis with minoritized, marginalized, or otherized students. This process hinges on their commitment to two vital professional dispositions: cultural competence and critical consciousness. These dispositions serve as powerful social mediators that actively counter the ongoing social, economic, and political harms that negatively affect minoritized, marginalized, and otherized students daily in U.S. PK–12 schools. However, researchers and practitioners in instructional supervision must establish equity-minded accountability systems and measures that disrupt the status quo, challenge biases, and advocate for policies and practices that yield culturally responsive praxis. Critical consciousness in instructional supervision is essential for realizing culturally responsive praxis across the field. This involves implementing an equity-minded curriculum, instruction, and formative teacher-feedback protocols, all instrumental in creating inclusive and socially just learning environments that support the success of minoritized, marginalized, and otherized student groups.

Cultural competence and critical consciousness are crucial in promoting culturally responsive praxis in instructional supervision. Instructional supervisors must value and leverage diverse student groups' cultural and experiential knowledge to eliminate opportunity gaps in curriculum, instruction, and teacher-feedback protocols. Praxis, in this spirit, fosters emancipatory futures that reflect the aspirations of minoritized, marginalized, and otherized student groups. However, equity-minded policies must be cultivated to develop a collective disposition in field instructional supervision and the broader educational context. Such policies will challenge systemic inequities and empower instructional supervisors to develop high levels of cultural competence and critical consciousness, thereby becoming agents of change and ensuring academic success for all students.

MAKING THE CASE FOR CULTURALLY RESPONSIVE INSTRUCTIONAL SUPERVISION

Culturally responsive practices since the early 1970s (e.g., Erickson & Mohatt, 1982; Gay & Abrahamson, 1972; Villegas, 1988) have offered an approach for bridging sociocultural gaps between students' home and community culture and the cultural system of U.S. PK–12 schools. Gay (1993) asserted that sociocultural gaps create an "alarming schism in the instructional process" (p. 287). Building on Gay's (1993) bold proposal for teacher development, Cormier (2022) offers educational sociocultural gaps as the root cause for the observed and felt social and cultural disconnections between PK–12 systems and minoritized, marginalized, and otherized student groups. Sociocultural gaps are a distancing phenomenon that materializes into many human actions (e.g., minoritizing, marginalizing, and otherizing) due to racial and economic disparities along with factors associated with sex, geography, generation, politics, religion, gender identity, sexual orientation, and/or education levels.

Complicating sociocultural gaps are subsequent opportunity gaps, which in most cases are a result of educational stakeholders not having lived experiences, values, and aspirations analogous to their minoritized, marginalized, and otherized students. Correspondingly, the lack of lived experience or cultural competence relevant to the student population being served results in the lack of critical consciousness praxis or the lack of capacity to recognize and redress social, political, and economic contradiction observed within the PK–12 schooling process with human action that yields remediation for the observed contradiction. The combination of cultural competence and critical consciousness is most often remedied with fostering effective educator–student relationships. However, ongoing research on the development of educator–student relationships demonstrates a significant gap in fostering effective relationships with minoritized, marginalized, and otherized student groups, particularly those intersecting with Black and Brown racial identities, in PK–12 schools and classrooms (Castro, 2010; Rudasill et al., 2023). As such, culturally responsive praxis is intended to address sociocultural friction endemic to students from minoritized, marginalized, and otherized student groups and communities.

Over the last 50 years, culturally responsive praxis has yielded a host of comprehensive theories, research, and practices that correspond with critical functions (e.g., school leadership, instructional supervision, teaching) within the PK–12 schooling enterprise (Gay, 2018; Hammond, 2015; Khalifa, 2020; Muhammad, 2020; Villegas & Lucas, 2002). Despite this progress, a comprehensive framework incorporating the principles of culturally responsive praxis into the field of instructional supervision has not been definitively established—a notable omission given the centrality of instructional supervision and leadership to PK–12 education. Correspondingly, this chapter and the accompanying edited chapters are designed to serve as a primer to establish a trajectory for cultivating and enhancing CRIS.

CULTURALLY RESPONSIVE ECOSYSTEM OF TEACHING, SCHOOL LEADERSHIP, AND INSTRUCTIONAL SUPERVISION

In this section of the current chapter, we introduce and situate CRIS within the culturally responsive ecosystem, which for this chapter includes CRT and CRSL. We recognize that there are various conceptions of culturally responsive praxis, yet our focus is on the three that correspond with the critical functions in U.S. PK–12 public schools, namely: school leadership, instructional supervision, and teaching. These key functions are our focus because they are each tied to high-stakes accountability measures or expectations, such as School Accountability Report Cards, Learning Standards/Objectives, and Teacher Assessment and Evaluation. Opportunely, this chapter highlights shared goals for facilitating culturally responsive praxis at the nexus of school leadership, instructional supervision, and teaching. Accordingly, in this section, we will provide a brief overview of CRSL and CRT, discussing their key objectives and opportunities for alignment with CRIS. Lastly, we will introduce and situate CRIS within the culturally responsive ecosystem and discuss the value CRIS aims to contribute within the field of instructional supervision.

Culturally Responsive Teaching

Within the culturally responsive ecosystem, CRT serves as the foundation (e.g., Gay, 2018; Hammond, 2015; Villegas & Lucas, 2002) for developing the ontological, epistemological, axiological, and teleological aspects necessary to develop educators' capacity to facilitate culturally responsive praxis. At its core, CRT is about employing a form of teaching that effectively leverages "comprehensive knowledge [i.e., cultural competence], unshakable convictions [critical consciousness], and high-level pedagogical skills" (Gay, 2018, p. xxvi) to improve academic achievement for students who are minoritized, marginalized, and otherized in PK–12 schools. Moreover, adopting culturally responsive instructional and pedagogical approaches to improve student achievement is a shared objective of both CRT and CRIS (see Figure 1.1).

Thus, understanding the significant role of teachers, who not only spend the most time with students but also make numerous impactful decisions daily, is crucial in recognizing how their beliefs and dispositions, influenced by various social, economic, and political factors, play a pivotal role in influencing the educational experiences and outcomes of students, particularly those who are minoritized, marginalized, and otherized in PK–12 schools. It is essential for culturally responsive researchers and practitioners to recognize that teacher beliefs and dispositions, particularly during their induction years, are greatly influenced by their sociocultural construction, which includes family, friends, media, geography, and teacher professional training/development (Gay, 1993, 2018; Villegas & Lucas, 2002). This understanding underscores the importance of addressing sociocultural gaps in PK–12 education, particularly within instructional supervision.

Addressing sociocultural gaps in instructional supervision necessitates developing and implementing protocols that utilize adult learning approaches (i.e., andragogy), such as transformational learning, professional learning communities, and research–practice partnerships, to build teachers' capacity for executing CRT. These protocols should assist teachers in redressing problematic assumptions and meta-cognitive processes that lead to biases and subsequent prejudices against minoritized, marginalized, and otherized students within U.S. PK–12 schools, particularly through curricula products, instructional supervision, and teacher feedback. In the forthcoming section, we will delve deeper into how CRIS acts as a pivotal resource for instructional supervision, guiding the development and adoption of equity-minded curricular products, instructional supervision strategies, and teacher-feedback methods to enhance student achievement through culturally responsive praxis effectively.

Culturally Responsive School Leadership

Gay (2018), through her seminal work *Culturally Responsive Teaching: Theory, Research, and Practice*, contends that the renewal, reform, or transformation (i.e., [re]imagining) of PK–12 school buildings should not rest solely on the work of culturally responsive teachers. The fact of the matter is that if teachers are expected to adjust their teaching practices to effectively attend to students' sociocultural needs in the classroom, then school leaders, including district leaders, school leaders, and instructional leaders, must be tasked with creating a school culture, climate, and capacity that supports and delivers culturally responsive praxis. Gay (2018) underscored the necessity of reforming and transforming every facet of the educational enterprise, including funding, policymaking, administration, curriculum, and instruction, to ensure they are also aligned with culturally responsive praxis. As such, culturally responsive school leaders are crucial in promoting and sustaining an environment that attracts, retains, and supports the continuous development of culturally competent and critically conscious teachers. These teachers and other educational stakeholders (e.g., school counselors, school resource officers, community partners) are essential for effectively serving all learners, particularly those from minoritized, marginalized, otherized, and economically disadvantaged student groups and backgrounds. Moreover, district and school leaders must value the importance of recruiting and nurturing culturally responsive teachers and other stakeholders, engaging with the community, and ensuring the necessary financial resources are in place to realize culturally responsive praxis.

Distinguished school leadership theorists and researchers have responded to calls for action from Gay and others (Ladson-Billings, 1998; Villegas & Lucas, 2002) by reimagining and conceptualizing school leadership in ways that leverage students' cultural capital to facilitate culturally responsive praxis. This evolution has given rise to CRSL, which complements Gay's seminal work (2018), emphasizing a holistic approach to educational reform. CRSL has become a focal point in research on culturally responsive education, reform, and social justice education. Notably, it has developed into a model that actively promotes and embraces culturally responsive praxis (e.g., CRSL), Gay (2018) highlighting that culturally responsive leaders prioritize developing and supporting school staff while fostering a school climate that is welcoming, inclusive, and accepting of minoritized, marginalized, and otherized students. As a result, CRSL has broadened the scope of culturally responsive praxis to encompass the entire school ecosystem, emphasizing the pivotal role school leaders play in scrutinizing and addressing systemic inequities within PK–12 school systems (Khalifa, 2020). Furthermore, Khalifa (2020) underscores the importance of incorporating community-engaged praxis into CRSL. Employing community-engaged praxis enables school leaders to leverage students' cultural capital, including aspirational, familial, linguistic, resistant, and navigational assets. By actively working to dismantle systemic inequities rooted in ideologies of whiteness and utilizing students' cultural capital, CRSL aims to cultivate a more inclusive and equitable school culture.

PK–12 public education is predominantly administered through top-down approaches that problematically rely on Eurocentric ontologies, epistemologies, axiologies, and teleologies to define and determine school, teacher, and student outcomes. To counter Eurocentric ways of knowing and doing, CRSL offers ways of knowing and doing within the PK–12 ecosystem that are informed by high levels of cultural competence and critical consciousness to yield culturally responsive praxis. This approach leverages the cultural capital of students and their families, along with school resources (e.g., financial, human) and data (e.g., student achievement, teacher effectiveness, school climate, equity audits). For culturally responsive school leaders as well as culturally responsive instructional leaders (see Figure 1.1), these data are crucial to facilitate culturally responsive praxis aimed at understanding and eliminating sociocultural gaps and subsequent opportunity

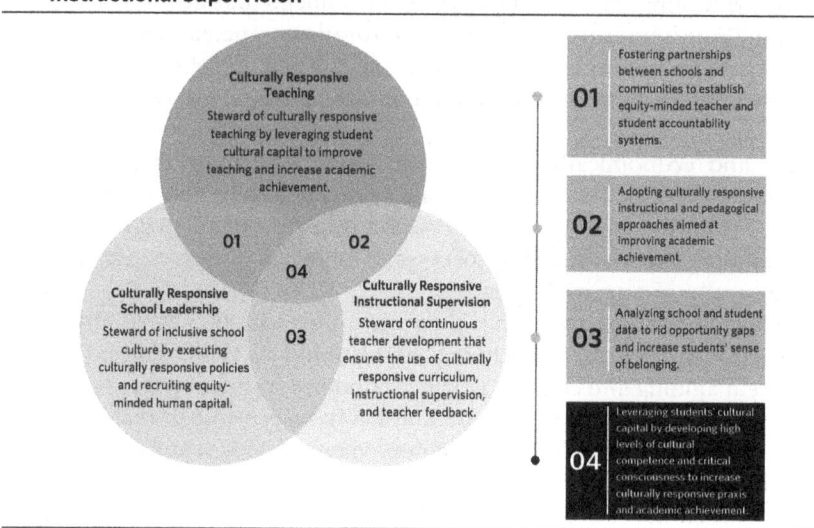

Figure 1.1. Culturally Responsive Nexus: Teaching, School Leadership, and Instructional Supervision

Venn diagram with three overlapping circles:

- **01 Culturally Responsive Teaching**: Steward of culturally responsive teaching by leveraging student cultural capital to improve teaching and increase academic achievement.
- **02 Culturally Responsive Instructional Supervision**: Steward of continuous teacher development that ensures the use of culturally responsive curriculum, instructional supervision, and teacher feedback.
- **03 Culturally Responsive School Leadership**: Steward of inclusive school culture by executing culturally responsive policies and recruiting equity-minded human capital.
- **04** (intersection of all three)

Accompanying list:

01. Fostering partnerships between schools and communities to establish equity-minded teacher and student accountability systems.

02. Adopting culturally responsive instructional and pedagogical approaches aimed at improving academic achievement.

03. Analyzing school and student data to rid opportunity gaps and increase students' sense of belonging.

04. Leveraging students' cultural capital by developing high levels of cultural competence and critical consciousness to increase culturally responsive praxis and academic achievement.

---

gaps observed and felt within PK–12 schools. Findings from school data, sourced by culturally responsive school leaders, are used to make decisions that impact the quality of education, which most often correlates with the allocation of financial resources available to students by way of their teachers.

CRSL also advocates for the continuous development of culturally responsive curricular products, instructional leadership, and teacher feedback. However, it is important to note that CRSL, much like CRT, has not fully addressed the specific instructional supervision skills needed to support ongoing development and reflection of teachers through formative feedback structures. This gap in culturally responsive praxis highlights the need for a more focused approach, which can be accomplished through CRIS. Thus, in the next section, we will detail how CRIS can expand the culturally responsive ecosystem by drawing on the traditions of CRT and CRSL and merging them with equity-minded instructional supervision strategies to enhance academic achievement through effective culturally responsive praxis.

Culturally Responsive Instructional Supervision

CRIS is a conduit connecting CRT and CRSL, empowering PK–12 school instructional leaders to develop cultural competence and critical consciousness to foster culturally responsive praxis in instructional supervision. From a CRT perspective, Gay (2018) and Villegas and Lucas (2002) have indicated the necessity of instructional leaders to embody culturally responsive approaches and dispositions for supervising the development of teachers' capacity to facilitate culturally responsive teaching. Hammond (2015) offered a practitioner-oriented text that provides practical concepts drawing on neuroscience for classroom teachers, instructional coaches, and instructional leaders to promote and foster CRT for culturally and linguistically diverse students. Likewise, CRSL scholars Khalifa et al. (2016) have signaled the need of instructional supervision to foster culturally responsive praxis to "develop and improve teachers' craft in ways that result in improved student outcomes" (p. 1275). As such, with the observed gap in culturally responsive praxis within the PK–12 schooling enterprise via instructional supervision, we respond to the call to action and the need to extend the culturally responsive ecosystem by providing a primer for CRIS.

This work, specifically this section of this chapter, serves as a primer for CRIS. As discussed above, the ideation of CRIS is not a new concept (e.g., Gay, 2018; Hammond, 2005; Khalifa et al., 2016; Villegas & Lucas, 2002), but its conceptualization is. Cormier (2019) introduced the concept of Culturally Responsive Supervision, which was aimed at centralizing culturally responsive praxis within the Glickman et al. (2018) textbook and framework, *SuperVision and Instructional Leadership: A Developmental Approach*. Glickman et al.'s foundational text addressed the needs of instructional leaders from curriculum, instructional supervision, and teacher feedback perspectives. However, when it came to culturally responsive praxis, it was positioned as an add-on in the last chapter rather than embedded across all aspects of instructional supervision, as presented by Cormier and Pandey (2021) and Guerra et al. (2022). Most recently, Mette et al. (2023a), building on the work of Cormier (2019) and Cormier and Pandey (2021), introduced the concept of CRIS in a practical text. Thus, this section provides instructional leaders with the core features of CRIS to facilitate the development of theory, practice, and research that support the ongoing development of instructional supervision approaches as well as the PK–12 culturally responsive ecosystem and praxis.

Correspondingly, in this section, we position CRIS within PK–12 culturally responsive ecosystems. This provides instructional leaders, school leaders, and teachers with a comprehensive and dynamic foundation to foster culturally responsive praxis by leveraging students' cultural capital, together with high levels of cultural competence and critical consciousness across all key functions of PK–12 schooling. Moreover, the addition of CRIS provides the PK–12 schooling context with a comprehensive, culturally responsive ecosystem to address all students' social and cultural needs from school leadership, instructional supervision, and teaching perspectives. This primer will begin to solidify CRIS's role in bridging sociocultural gaps and eliminating opportunity gaps in the PK–12 curriculum, instructional supervision, and teacher feedback to support the broader cultural response ecosystem.

Curriculum

Curriculum is broadly defined "as what students have the opportunity to learn" (Milner, 2012, p. 713) and materializes in many forms: explicit (e.g., Written Curriculum, Taught Curriculum, Supported Curriculum, Assessed Curriculum, Learned

Curriculum) and implicit (e.g., Hidden Curriculum, Null Curriculum); in this section, we focus on the implicit forms. As such, the PK–12 schooling enterprise is a sociocultural process powered by the curriculum it employs, which serves as a socially mediated tool that privileges the few and disadvantages the majority. This disadvantage is so significant that leading scholars coin and describe this sociocultural phenomenon as opportunity gaps (e.g., Howard, 2019; Ladson-Billings, 2006; Milner, 2020). Conversely, curriculum "should be seen as a tool to help students assert and accentuate their present and future powers, capabilities, attitudes, and experiences" (Gay, 2018, p. 142). However, we, along with many others, understand that curriculum will never fully serve all students, particularly those who are minoritized, marginalized, otherized, and come from economically disadvantaged backgrounds. This reality will persist as long as schools continue to be organized around ideologies of whiteness (Banks, 2013; Ferguson, 2000; Gay, 2010; Jay, 2003; Ladson-Billings & Tate, 1995; Leonardo & Manning, 2017). Ideologies of whiteness are deeply ingrained in the United States' cultural fabric, which is deeply embedded in the structures, ethos, programs, and practices that govern our PK–12 school systems (Ferguson, 2000; Gay, 2010). Correspondingly, we believe instructional leaders must be acutely aware of the hidden forces that enable curriculum to privilege the few and disadvantage the masses.

The implicit curriculum we believe instructional supervisors and leaders must be aware of is the hidden curriculum of hegemony. Jay (2003) explained that the hidden curriculum of hegemony acts as a normalizing discourse within U.S. PK–12 school systems. Put practically, the hidden curriculum of hegemony is a bigger sociocultural force that maintains ideologies of whiteness and subsequent sociocultural gaps and corresponding opportunity gaps. A novice instructional leader may be led to believe the hidden curriculum of hegemony to be sound pedagogical approaches or strategies to enhance student achievement. Yet, for instructional leaders whose aims are not emancipatory, the hidden curriculum of hegemony is used to overtly teach students what they must learn, practice, and embody to thrive in a U.S. society, which is grounded in Eurocentric ways of thinking and doing—in simpler terms, to teach students how to assimilate into the world socially mediated by ideologues of whiteness (Leonardo & Manning, 2017).

However, we offer that instructional leaders who leverage students' cultural capital and possess high levels of cultural competence and critical consciousness are well equipped to identify and navigate the sociocultural forces endemic in the hidden curriculum, making them more effective in serving students who are minoritized, marginalized, or otherized within the PK–12 school system. Such instructional leaders possess and embody subversive praxis (Freire, 1970; Givens, 2021; Love, 2019). These types of instructional leaders are needed within PK–12 schools to develop improved curriculum products for both teachers and students. Furthermore, this type of instructional leadership will result in curriculum products that better reflect the cultural capital that students and their families bring into the schooling environment, ultimately leading to increased student achievement and a heightened sense of belonging.

Instructional Supervision

Glickman et al. (2018) think of instructional "supervision as the glue of a successful school" (p. 9). We believe this metaphor for success is analogous to CRIS with respect to its situatedness within the PK–12 culturally responsive ecosystem. CRIS represents a form of praxis where instructional leaders collaborate to leverage students' cultural capital; these leaders, including supervisors, teacher leaders, mentor teachers, and peer teachers, facilitate culturally appropriate instruction for all students, especially minoritized, marginalized, or otherized student groups within PK–12 school systems.

However, to observe such culturally responsive praxis, instructional supervisors must embody and model the same culturally responsive praxis they expect from their supervisees, such as instructional leaders and teachers. Moreover, such supervisors must possess qualitative attributes that put them in the ideal cognitive and emotional position to leverage students' cultural capital with high levels of cultural competence and critical consciousness, ultimately fostering improved instruction and academic achievement. Gay (2018) provides a character profile that outlines the essential qualities an educator must possess to achieve culturally responsive outcomes, particularly for instructional leaders seeking to create culturally appropriate and equity-minded student learning environments.

First, culturally responsive instructional supervisors know that the curriculum, instructional supervision, and teacher feedback chosen must validate and affirm all students. Denoting that this CRIS is a form of praxis that validates and affirms students' cultural capital (e.g., aspirational, familial, social, navigational, resistant, linguistic). At the same time, this form of praxis ensures that instructional activities are comprehensive, academically rigorous, and inclusive, and consider various forms of cultural representation related to students' racial and ethnic backgrounds and other social and identity groups, such as gender, geography, politics, religion, and sexual orientation.

CRIS also demands that instructional leaders recognize the multidimensional nature of their role within the school environment. As Gay (2018) points out, multidimensional, culturally responsive instructional leaders must be attuned to all the factors influencing the function and effectiveness of school, including "curriculum content, learning context, classroom climate, student-teacher relationships, instructional techniques, classroom management, and performance assessments" (p. 39). The multidimensional nature of engaging in culturally responsive praxis that validates and affirms students and supervisees' sense of belonging is ultimately empowering. Culturally responsive instructional supervisors empower their supervisees, such as instructional leaders and teachers, to translate their practice into culturally competent and critically conscious actions that effectively and safely leverage students' cultural capital. Subsequently, culturally responsive praxis in specific forms enables instructional leaders to leverage students' cultural capital dynamically and responsively to the social, economic, and political factors and forces observed in PK–12 curriculum, instructional supervision, and teacher feedback.

The cognitive and emotional work to execute culturally responsive praxis is transformative. Transformation within CRIS occurs as instructional leaders leverage students' cultural capital with high levels of cultural competence and critical consciousness. This transformative process is akin to empathy, which is a socioemotional force that compels human action (Warren, 2017). Warren (2017) discusses the development of educators' empathy as an iterative process that involves both high cognitive functioning (perspective-taking) and emotional functioning (empathic concern). In culturally responsive praxis, perspective-taking aligns with cultural competence, while empathic concern aligns with critical consciousness. Lindsey et al. (2019) detailed how culturally competent leaders have the capacity to effectively and ethically leverage cultural capital from the students and communities they serve. Similarly, critical consciousness leaders possess deep insights into their own sociocultural backgrounds and construction, understanding how this knowledge and experience base informs the assumptions and biases they bring into the school (Gay & Kirkland, 2003; Khalifa et al., 2016; Villegas & Lucas, 2002). Most important, culturally responsive instructional leaders recognize how their actions, influenced by sociocultural phenomena, can, negatively or positively, impact the instructional process and student achievement, particularly for students who are minoritized, marginalized, or otherized in PK–12 schools and classrooms.

Culturally responsive instructional supervisors understand that their work is emancipatory in nature. In other words, CRIS serves as an instructional leadership framework that enables leaders to critically assess and take action to rectify social, economic, and political contradictions within the curriculum, instructional supervision, and teacher feedback. These leaders accomplish this by leveraging students' cultural capital, which includes aspirational, resistant, and navigational elements, to eliminate sociocultural and opportunity gaps present in the curriculum, instructional supervision, and teacher feedback (Villegas & Lucas, 2002). This form of praxis embodies a form of humanistic altruism that is both observed and felt by its recipients.

Ultimately, CRIS aspires to be normative and ethical and create an environment in which PK–12 educators create a context that seeks to execute the collective aims of CRSL, CRIS, and CRT. In this way, they can denote that culturally responsive praxis is actualized in PK–12 policies and practices establishing culturally responsive curriculum, instructional supervision, and teacher feedback as the standard, rather than the exception. Culturally responsive instructional leaders who effectively demonstrate this form of affective praxis do so based on their values, professionalism, and ethical principles. When CRIS praxis and its embodiment is internalized by instructional leaders, it becomes a strong sense of their professional identity and personhood (Gay, 2018). This, in effect, creates a PK–12 schooling context that significantly enhances student and academic achievement because of the collective praxis across and within the ideal culturally responsive ecosystem, which includes CRSL, CRIS, and CRT.

Teacher Feedback

At its core, CRIS focuses on how principals, instructional coaches, and teacher leaders can provide developmental support to teachers using feedback structures to increase cultural competence and help support the expansion and evolution of teachers' reflective stances. Through the rejection of ahistorical and apolitical ideologies about instruction, CRIS positions instructional leaders to be equity leaders first and foremost (Mette et al., 2023a). Moreover, CRIS focuses on supporting teacher development that does not (and should not) need to occur as a power dynamic, meaning instructional supervisors should also focus on increasing self-awareness at the individual level, learning with critical colleague groups to engage in vulnerable reflections to drive growth. This in turn empowers large groups of faculty members to explore formative observational data that can help target building-wide professional development opportunities.

CRIS requires that instructional supervisors acknowledge their privileged sociocultural identities when they consider how to deliver feedback by leveraging critical, cultural, and Indigenous frameworks to challenge hegemonic structures such as Eurocentric ideologies, xenophobia, Islamophobia, anti-Blackness, classism, and ableism in education systems. CRIS utilizes various formative feedback structures, including peer-led observations, equity audits, and the Cultural Proficiency Continuum, to support teachers' reflective stances and create validating and asset-based teaching practices. It also emphasizes the need for intentionally representative supervision teams committed to equity-oriented instructional practices, thus flattening the hierarchy of feedback (Guerra et al., 2022; Mette et al., 2023a; Mette et al., 2023b; Waite, 2021).

From our perspective, CRIS helps complete the culturally responsive ecosystem through increasing the capacity of teachers to co-curate culturally responsive praxis with minoritized, marginalized, and otherized students. As such, CRIS helps serve as a mediator of the social, economic, and political forces that significantly impact minoritized, marginalized, and otherized students within U.S. PK–12 schools by supporting the development of teachers to use cultural identities as assets and design lessons that are responsive to students' lived experiences, promoting social justice and inclusivity. At its core, CRIS focuses on developmentally appropriate feedback that can be provided to teachers to help develop empathy and understanding of students' identities as well as their lived experiences. Here, cognitive plasticity is required to counter sociocultural processes, namely cognitive dissonance (e.g., white fragility, deficit mindsets, low expectations) (Hammond, 2015; Milner, 2020). CRIS centers feedback and support *at the individual classroom level* to help educators create inclusive and equitable learning environments by contextualizing instruction around various aspects of students' lived experiences, including race, ethnicity, gender, class, and orientation/identity (Gay, 2018).

FUTURE HOPES AND DIRECTIONS

We believe our primer of CRIS is warranted by way of historical and future understandings of the implications of the current sociopolitical context of U.S. PK–12 schooling. Much of the work of CRIS aims to ensure the implementation of culturally responsive praxis to reform educational practices and to increase academic achievement and success for students who are minoritized, marginalized, and otherized in the U.S. education system based on race, ethnicity, sex, class, gender identity, sexual orientation, ability, and other lived experiences. However, any resulting sociocultural gaps between students and educators with similar racial and ethnic backgrounds are less than prevalent between students and educators who share different racial and ethnic backgrounds). Considering that 80% of educators are racialized as White, and when we take into account how the schoolhouse perpetuates inequities based on various sociocultural identities, it becomes imperative that educators from privileged backgrounds can reflect on and implement instructional approaches that draw from the perspectives of cultural competence and critical consciousness. This reflection is essential for effectively integrating instruction that leverages students' cultural capital and values the assets they bring with them to the classroom every day.

Gay (2018) describes CRT as a sociocultural phenomenon. As such, the phenomenon of culturally responsive praxis, teleologically, ought to be understood as being in a constant state of fluidity or as a dynamic and ever-changing process. This orientation for schooling situates educators in a constant state of responsiveness, which requires the development of empathy, understanding, validation, and affirmation of the identities and lived experiences of the students the serve. Similar to the role of a first responder, when a child reaches out for help or is struggling, the teacher must answer the call with responses that are caring and loving, and allow the child to see a future for themselves through the ingestion of instruction that is prepared by the teacher.

However, many of our fellow educators miss this call. We have found that missing the call often occurs unknowingly. We posit that this is due to the sociocultural gaps between the education system and students who are minoritized, marginalized, and otherized in U.S. society. Consequently, when sociocultural gaps remain unchecked, they compound into opportunity gaps. As a result, it is critical that instructional leaders learn how to implement CRIS to deconstruct curriculum and instruction that are the last holdovers of essentialism. Described another way, most curricula and instruction currently being implemented in the United States were never intended to emancipate students who are minoritized, marginalized, and otherized. Our job, as instructional supervisors who want to expand the culturally responsive ecosystem, is to leverage the tools of CRIS (i.e., students' cultural capital, cultural competence, critical consciousness), to identify and mitigate sociocultural gaps before they are marshaled into opportunity gaps. The tools are there. It is simply a matter of creating an educational environment where all players—students, parents, teachers, and administrators—are aware of, and attend to, the cultural needs of their communities.

REFERENCES

Bagley, W. C. (1938). An essentialist's platform for the advancement of American education. *Educational Administration and Supervision, 24*(4), 241–256.

Banks, J. A. (1993). The canon debate, knowledge construction, and multicultural education. *Educational Researcher, 22*(5), 4–14.

Banks, J. A. (2013). Multicultural education: Approaches, developments and dimensions. In *Education Cultural Diversity* (pp. 83–94). Routledge.

Castro, A. J. (2010). Themes in the research on preservice teachers' views of cultural diversity: Implications for researching millennial preservice teachers. *Educational Researcher, 39*(3), 198–210.

Cormier D. R. (2019). *The cultural proficiency continuum dialogic protocol: An emerging tool for examining preservice teachers' sociocultural consciousness concerning majority-minority schools and student populations*. The Pennsylvania State University.

Cormier, D. R. (2022). Prototyping the cultural proficiency continuum dialogic protocol with professional development school teacher interns. *Urban Education*. https://doi-org.tc.idm.oclc.org/10.1177/00420859221140405.

Cormier, D. R., & Pandey, T. (2021). Semiotic analysis of a foundational textbook used widely across educational supervision. *Journal of Educational Supervision, 4*(2). https://doi.org/10.31045/jes.4.2.6

Dowd, A. C., & Bensimon, E. M. (2015). *Engaging the "race question": Accountability and equity in U.S. higher education*. Teachers College Press.

Erickson, F., & Mohatt, G. (1982). Cultural organization and participation structures in two classrooms of Indian students. In G. Spindler (Ed.), *Doing the ethnography of schooling* (pp. 131–174). Holt, Rinehart & Winston

Freire, P. (1970). *Pedagogy of the oppressed*. Bloomsbury Academic.

Gay, G. (1993). Building cultural bridges: A bold proposal for teacher education. *Education and Urban Society*, 285–299.

Gay, G. (2018). *Culturally responsive teaching: Theory, research, and practice* (2nd ed.) Teachers College Press.

Gay, G., & Abrahamson, R. D. (1972). Talking Black in the classroom. In R. D. Abrahamson & R. Troike (Eds.), *Language and cultural diversity in education* (pp. 200–208). Prentice-Hall.

Glickman, C. D. Gordon, S. P., & Ross-Gordon, J. M. (2018). *Supervision and instructional leadership: A developmental approach* (10th ed.). Pearson.

Givens, J. R. (2021). *Fugitive pedagogy: Carter G. Woodson and the art of Black teaching*. Harvard University Press.

Gooden, M. A., & Dantley, M. (2012). Centering race in a framework for leadership preparation. *Journal of Research on Leadership Education, 7*(2), 237–253.

Gordon, S. P. (2020). Lessons from the past: Ideas from supervision books published from 1920 through 1950. *Journal of Educational Supervision, 3*(2), 51–82. https://doi.org/10.31045/jes.3.2.4

Guerra, P. L., Baker, A. M., & Cotman, A. M. (2022). Instructional supervision: Is it culturally responsive? A Textbook analysis. *Journal of Educational Supervision, 5*(1). https://doi.org/10.31045/jes.5.1.1

Hammond, Z. L. (2015). *Culturally responsive teaching and the brain*. Corwin Press.

Howard, T. C. (2019). *Why race and culture matter in schools: Closing the achievement gap in America's classrooms*. Teachers College Press.

Hutchins, R. M. (1952). *The great conversation* (Vol. 1). Encyclopedia Britannica.

Khalifa, M. (2020). *Culturally responsive school leadership*. Harvard Education Press.

Khalifa, M. A., Gooden, M. A., & Davis, J. E. (2016). Culturally responsive school leadership: A synthesis of the literature. *Review of Educational Research, 86*(4), 1272–1311.

Ladson-Billings, G. (1998). Teaching in dangerous times: Culturally relevant approaches to teacher assessment. *Journal of Negro Education, 67*(3), 255–267.

Ladson-Billings, G. (2006). From the achievement gap to the education debt: Understanding achievement in U.S. schools. *Educational researcher, 35*(7), 3–12.

Leonardo, Z., & Manning, L. (2017). White historical activity theory: Toward a critical understanding of white zones of proximal development. *Race Ethnicity and Education, 20*(1), 15–29.

Lindsey, R. B., Robins, K. N., & Terrell, R. D. (2019). *Cultural proficiency: A manual for school leaders*. Corwin.

Love, B. L. (2019). *We want to do more than survive: Abolitionist teaching and the pursuit of educational freedom*. Beacon Press.

Lynch, M. E. (2018). The hidden nature of whiteness in education: Creating active allies in White teachers. *Journal of Educational Supervision,1*(1), 18–31. https://doi.org/10.31045/jes.1.1.2

Mette, I. M., Cormier, D. R., & Oliveras, Y. (2023a). *Making a difference: Instructional leadership that drives self-reflection and values the expertise of teachers*. Rowman & Littlefield.

Mette, I. M., Cormier, D. R., & Oliveras-Ortiz, Y. (2023b). Culturally responsive instructional supervision: (Re)Envisioning feedback for equitable change. In A. Lavigne & M. L. Derrington (Eds.), *Actionable feedback for PK–12 teachers* (pp. 75–87). Rowman & Littlefield.

Milner, H. R., IV. (2020). *Start where you are, but don't stay there: Understanding diversity, opportunity gaps, and teaching in today's classrooms*. Harvard Education Press.

Moule, J. (2011). *Cultural competence: A primer for educators*. Cengage Learning.

Muhammad, G. (2020). *Cultivating genius: An equity framework for culturally and historically responsive literacy*. Scholastic.

Rudasill, K. M., McGinnis, C., Cheng, S. L., Cormier, D. R., & Koziol, N. (2023). White privilege and teacher perceptions of teacher-child relationship quality. *Journal of School Psychology, 98*, 224–239.

Sergiovanni, T. J. & Starratt, R. J. (2007). *Supervision: A redefinition.* (8th ed.) McGraw Hill.

Villegas, A. (1988). School failure and cultural mismatch: Another view. *The Urban Review, 20*, 253–265.

Villegas, A. M., & Lucas, T. (2002). Preparing culturally responsive teachers: Rethinking the curriculum. *Journal of teacher education, 53*(1), 20–32.

Warren, C. A. (2018). Empathy, teacher dispositions, and preparation for culturally responsive pedagogy. *Journal of Teacher Education, 69*(2), 169–183. https://doi.org/10.1177/0022487117712487

Yosso, T. J. (2005). Whose culture has capital? A critical race theory discussion of community cultural wealth. *Race Ethnicity and Education, 8*(1), 69–91. https://doi.org/10.1080/1361332052000341006

CHAPTER 2

Confronting the Lack of Diversity in Supervision Frameworks

A. Minor Baker, Ann Marie Cotman, and Patricia Guerra

Since the inception of schooling as a public good and the radical increase in educational access with the common school movement in the United States in the late 19th century and early 20th century, there has been a connection between school leadership and the supervision of teachers. In those 100+ years, much has changed in education and supervisory praxis, and yet many things have also remained the same. These changes, or lack thereof, continue to define the educational environments where supervisory practice occurs. This chapter examines how the past continues to inform our present, often resulting in race-, culture- and color-evasive practices (Bendixen et al., 2023; Heidelburg et al., 2022; Kohli et al., 2017; Wilt et al., 2022) despite the continuing diversification of U.S. schools and society. With an understanding of where supervision has come from, we will shift our focus to reconsider supervision, specifically the clinical supervision cycle in ways that respond to the educational realities of schools. As student populations become increasingly diverse and educator populations remain persistently less so, there is a need for supervision that helps create learning environments that respond to diverse student needs and identities.

SUPERVISION: FOUNDATION OF SCHOOL LEADERSHIP

At its inception, much supervision was merely the delegation of personnel oversight that was the responsibility of local governing councils and boards to an individual(s) serving at their behest (Burnham, 1976). As U.S. schools grew larger and supported the educational needs of an entire community, the professionalization of the role of school leader became increasingly important. With the growing ubiquity of schools came a focus on improvement and efficiency (Lucio & McNeil, 1968). Specific training to perform the roles of educational leaders increased dramatically, including the supervision of classroom instruction. As the foundational element of school leadership preparation, effective instructional supervision was positioned as the primary tool for improving classroom teaching and, thereby, schoolwide academic outcomes (Glickman et al., 2018; Mette et al., 2017). There is significant agreement within educational leader scholarship on the importance of effective instructional supervision (Glickman et al., 2018; Jacobs, 2014, Mette et al., 2017).

However, while there is consensus about the importance of supervision, particularly regarding its potential to improve instructional outcomes, how supervisory practices are conceptualized and implemented requires (re)examination. Instructional supervision, specifically the Clinical Supervision Cycle (CSC), has been positioned as the most effective way to bring about instructional improvement in schools (Glickman et al., 2018; Goldhammer, 1969; Gordon, 2016; Zepeda, 2016). Glickman et al. (2007) highlight the importance of supervision in schools as a tool to "deliver on the promise of education that promotes a better democracy for all" (p. 12). Sadly, one would be hard pressed to point out evidence that indicates anything other than a complete failure to fulfill either promise, as U.S. society has continued to find nuanced ways to create inequitable outcomes across the schoolhouse. As such, schooling continues to be experienced in disproportionately negative ways for minoritized, marginalized, and otherized students and communities. Emancipation and equality of experience are foundations of democratic experience (Biesta, 2010), but supervision has not created equitable schooling experiences for all.

HISTORY OF SUPERVISION

To understand the current supervision landscape, it is important to examine the foundations that serve as the base for current practice. For many, the work of Goldhammer (1969) and Cogan (1976) in the late 1960s into the early 1970s serves as the foundation on which many current interpretations of supervision, particularly instructional supervision, are based (Glanz, 2018). These early conceptual approaches focused on clinical supervision, specifically articulating a conceptual structure for collaborations between teachers and supervisors, usually school leaders (Goldhammer, 1969). At the time, this approach was novel because of the inherent parity or collaborative responsibility owned by both teacher and supervisor. In framing a clinical supervision model, Goldhammer (1969) specifically highlights individual human autonomy as a framework for teachers and supervisor relationships, stating:

> We are driven by images of teaching that enhance the learners' self-sufficiency and freedom to act; of supervision that facilitates such teaching and aims for a parallel condition in the teachers' own existence; and finally, of a supervision in which the supervisor's own capacities for autonomous functioning are heightened by the very practice in which [they] engage. (p. 55)

This new conceptualization of supervision from Goldhammer (1969) came at a time when schools and teacher populations were experiencing the employment shifts of desegregation. U.S. schools with majority White teacher and leader populations saw little change in their educator populations. In contrast, Black, Brown, and Indigenous educators were denied employment opportunities in the newly desegregated White schools because of the belief that White students and parents would not accept instruction or school leadership from educators of color (Tillman, 2004). Little to no acknowledgment or consideration of supervisory practices or approaches used in segregated schools serving Black, Brown, and Indigenous students informed the evolving conceptions of supervision.

The development of supervision was swept up in larger societal debates about educational bureaucracy in the 1980s when a skeptical eye was cast on the purpose of school leadership (Firth & Eiken, 1982). Still, without alternative conceptions of the leadership role, supervision lingered, although creative interpretations and manifestations of supervisory practice were becoming more visible, including supervisory approaches outside the school administrator roles (Sullivan & Glanz, 2000). Supervision continued to evolve, and the seed of instructional supervision scholarship began to emerge at the end of the 20th century.

Glickman (1992), in the aptly named *Supervision in Transition*, attempted to steer away from the top-down managerial approach that the term "supervision" implies in favor of a more collaborative and constructivist approach. This flattening of the supervisory hierarchy was made increasingly difficult as the shift in clinical supervision rode the tidal wave of attention and funding that came with the high-stakes accountability movement. At the same time that scholars of clinical supervision and instructional leadership were calling for more collaborative school improvement approaches, the accountability movement was shifting the roles and responsibilities of school leaders to improve student outcomes, as measured by high-stakes testing, particularly perceived gaps in student achievement, later to be known as educational opportunity gaps (Carter & Welner, 2013; Gorski, 2017; Ladson-Billings, 2006; Milner, 2020).

The role of supervision continues to be inextricably linked with the role of school leadership (Zepeda, 2014). Although there are increasingly diverse approaches to supervision both in role and approach, school leaders are often positioned as the foci of educational improvement and quality. It is worth noting that a common path to school leadership includes successful experiences as a teacher. However, many leaders come without successful experiences as *culturally responsive teachers* (Hines, 2016). Even as alternative approaches to supervision continue to be discussed, the reality is that supervision and school leaders remain in a tight partnership. Due to the inherent whiteness of schools (Sleeter, 2008, 2017) culturally responsive instructional leaders who engage in helping lead this work could act as a key to unlocking more equitable schooling.

The U.S. educational system is extremely complex, with many stakeholders and even more perspectives on how schooling should be done. Each countervailing element pulls on other elements. Focusing just on supervision, we propose that subtle shifts in a few areas have the potential to yield profoundly different outcomes. School leaders directly influence campus culture, climate, and teacher development, which, in turn, impact student learning and experience. If school leaders are positioned to have this outsized influence on teacher support and development, the need for a clinical supervision cycle that is also culturally responsive is critical. School leaders who are not culturally responsive can fail to recognize culturally responsive teaching or exert their views and beliefs and further marginalize the experiences, expertise, and voices of culturally responsive teachers. This is a detriment to students, particularly student populations that have long been marginalized by schooling.

CRITIQUES OF SUPERVISION

The field of supervision has seen a variety of frameworks and models. Although there is variation within the frameworks, as a general rule they share similar foundations and action steps for engaging in the supervision process. At the heart of the supervision cycle remains a supervisor and a supervisee (teacher) engaging in a multistep process starting with a pre-conference, classroom observation, data analysis, and post-conference/debrief. There are variations to that basic model, but they all have some version of these elements. It has also become increasingly clear that supervision and high-stakes accountability have become well entangled in the process (Mette et al., 2020). The challenge for supervision, and the clinical supervision frameworks, is to not allow the motivations of high-stakes accountability to drive the constructive focus of supervision. Although supervision has from time to time attempted to limit the hierarchal nature of supervisor overseeing supervisee, the act of supervision remains hierarchical. Additionally, the role of supervisor remains primarily the responsibility of school administrators (principals and assistant principals), a population that continues to be largely White (NCES, 2022).

Terms and concepts are uninterrogated and thereby in danger of reinforcing White, cishet, male, able norms as culturally "neutral." Supervision as a field has long utilized terminology such as "dominant culture," "subculture," and "Standard English," covertly signaling a racial hierarchy. Simultaneously uninterrogated culturally "neutral" terms (e.g., democratic or democracy) are employed to signal recognition of broader issues around culturally sustaining and responsive practices. These words often skim over the surface of supervisory behaviors instead of providing an anchor in culturally responsive instructional supervision (CRIS), allowing for generational inequality of outcomes and experiences to persist (Hung et al., 2020). It is not enough to define what constitutes democracy; it is also critical to understand how democracy is experienced, to understand the biases and interpretations of democracy. Democracy is meaningless outside of the human context; it must be examined in practice.

DEMOCRACY IN SUPERVISION

There is a close relationship between democracy and education (Straume, 2016). In a society that depends on collective decision-making, it helps to ensure that citizens have the knowledge, skills, and critical thinking abilities necessary to participate effectively in the political process (Dewey, 1916). In a democratic society, education is also promoted to achieve social mobility and equal opportunity (Spiel et al., 2018). If schooling is the basis for social mobility, one expects those opportunities to extend to all student identities. However, as much as schooling is trumpeted as a means to social mobility, there continues to be a well-established body of literature highlighting a "school to prison pipeline" (Morgan, 2021, para. 1). Do schools offer opportunities to students? Without a doubt. Do schools offer those opportunities equitably to all students and communities? Most assuredly, they do not. We cannot point to schools as a path to social mobility or a key element of democracy and fail to acknowledge that schools are also still, at least partially, connected to the denial of both opportunities and freedoms.

Education and schooling, much like democracy, are contested ideas that are conceptualized and experienced differently by individuals. As such, democracy and schooling need constant critique, evaluation, and reflection as they are perpetually co-created and re-created. The relationship between democracy and education is complex and multifaceted, but education plays a vital role in supporting the functioning of U.S. society. Supervision has a long history of democracy-friendly language, language that assumes beneficence in the democratic project and neglects the lived reality of so many. The practice of supervision continues to take a limited view of democracy and how it is experienced, and in doing so, it is slow to evolve to respond to the cultural identities present in increasingly diverse schools.

Democracy as a Color-Blind Proxy for Cultural Responsiveness

Scholars and other authors in supervision, as in other fields, have often imagined that true democracy and democratic schools would necessarily be culturally responsive. As a result, "democratic" has been often used as a proxy for "culturally responsive." It has been expected that democratic schools work "for the common good," recognizing "the work of individuals and the social value of community . . . celebrat[ing] differences" and "interdependence of all" (Furman & Starratt, 2002, p. 116, quoted in Glickman et al., 2018, p. 46).

However, democracy is not experienced the same way by all peoples. Although we live in a democratic country the examples of unequal experiences with democracy are too numerous to name, but a few salient examples can be pointed to now, and likely for some time to come. Women have different experiences with body autonomy and the law, with an increasing number of anti-choice laws becoming common (Klibanoff, 2022). Teachers are not allowed to mention or discuss the identities of the very students present in their classrooms (Diaz, 2022). Repeated examples of curriculum limit or altogether erase the experiences of marginalized communities (Schwartz, 2021). It was in our democracy that the red-lining and sundown towns were allowed to persist for generations, criminalizing, segregating, and generally limiting the democratic rights of people outside of the hegemonic privileged identities (O'Connell, 2019). To be clear, we are not attacking democracy, but more simply, we are highlighting that democracy, left uninterrogated or unexamined, is not a substitute for CRIS practices.

Schools as Microcosms of Societal Understandings of Democracy

Supervision scholars may use the term *democracy* liberally because they have rarely been on the losing end of democratic decision processes. Our schools are microcosms—mini versions—of society at large. The way democracy operates in our nation and states is mirrored in the way democracy operates in schools. People of color and others disenfranchised in the system are far more skeptical of democratic processes. Are the disciplinary over-referrals of Black boys (Skiba et al., 2002) and the push-out of Black girls (Morris, 2016) democratic schooling? Is the under-referral of students of color to gifted and talented programs an example of democratic schooling (Grissom & Redding, 2015)? Is the eradication of Indigenous culture and subsequent indoctrination of Indigenous children (e.g., the Carlisle Indian School) (Fear-Segal & Rose, 2016) an example of democratic schooling? These are just a few examples, but there are certainly more. The role of supervision remains connected to each of these examples, thereby highlighting the extreme urgency needed when understanding how democratic schooling and supervision are linked.

CULTURAL RESPONSIVENESS IN SUPERVISION

For years, there have been calls for cultural responsiveness to be implemented in classroom instruction—and yet people teaching supervision rarely come with a paradigm or understanding to consider how cultural values impact that work. Changing student demographics, high-stakes testing, expanding teacher evaluation systems, and an increased focus on equity have changed expectations for what school leaders need to know and do (Grissom et al., 2021). Developing cultural competence cannot rely solely on teachers and teacher preparation programs but now includes principals and leadership preparation programs (Khalifa et al., 2016; Khalifa, 2018). More than ever, leaders who heed this call must move their vision of culturally responsive leadership to understand the concrete ways that leadership tasks, including instructional supervision, can be culturally responsive. Principals must add to their current expertise in CRIS with a strong focus on transforming instruction to ensure the academic success of students from diverse racial, ethnic, cultural, linguistic, and economic backgrounds and varying abilities (Gay, 1998; Grissom et al., 2021; Khalifa, 2018; Ladson-Billings, 2009).

CRIS is grounded in recognizing the diverse backgrounds, experiences, and needs of students, teachers, and communities (Griffin et al., 2016). This approach to supervision seeks to create a supportive and collaborative environment where all stakeholders are valued and empowered to contribute to the learning process. The question then becomes, does the current framework for the clinical supervision cycle accomplish the goals of valuing and empowering educators in the learning process? CRIS emphasizes the importance of building solid relationships with teachers, students, and families and of providing support and guidance that is tailored to the unique needs and context of individual settings and identified needs (Jacobs, 2006; 2014). This approach also focuses on supporting teachers to develop their cultural competence so that they can better understand and respond to the diverse backgrounds and experiences of their students (Clayton & Goodwin, 2015).

RECONCEPTUALIZING A FRAMEWORK FOR SUPERVISION

Glickman et al. (2018) have presented a framework and model for supervision that is clear and concrete, yet some have argued as with many things in education, that it become hijacked or distorted with the high-stakes accountability-based teaching expectations (Glanz, 2018; Mette et al., 2020). We acknowledge that the clinical supervisory cycle operationalized by Glickman et al. (2018) is widely known and accepted in supervision cycles as the standard by which other approaches to instructional supervision will be compared. Many teacher evaluation tools employ the basic model laid out in the text that uses: (a) a preconference with the teacher, (b) observation of classroom instruction, (c) an analysis of observed data, (d) a post-conference with the observed teacher, and (e) a critique of previous steps (Glickman et al., 2018, p. 272). As bricoleurs (Baker, 2019) of instructional supervision, we recognize the value of this model, but also feel an obligation to highlight the limitations or blind spots that may exist with universal adoption of the approaches detailed in *SuperVision and Instructional Leadership: A Developmental Approach* (Glickman et al., 2018).

SuperVision (Glickman et al., 2018) may be the single most influential text in supervision preparation for school leaders, and certainly the most widely used (Kao, 2020). For many school leaders, the text is a foundational element of their supervisory development; and for many more the key element of the book, the clinical supervision cycle, remains the way in which instructional supervision is done. It is therefore important to interrogate the processes and underlying foundation to the supervisory process.

SuperVision's treatment of the clinical supervision cycle, a powerful means of changing instructional practices (Gordon, 2016; Gordon & Espinoza, 2020; Grissom et al., 2021), is all but devoid of references to culture (Cormier & Pandey, 2021; Guerra et al., 2022). The chapters that focus on implementing the clinical supervision cycle (Chapters 8–12 and 15) include no mention of culture within the text narrative. Without deliberate consideration of culture, race, or identities, practitioners of supervision may conclude that supervision has no role in supporting diverse identities and perspective in schools and there is no connection to student learning. This is especially the case since school leadership and teaching populations remain significantly whiter than the population of students being served in schools today, and with little sign that changes in educator populations are changing fast enough to mirror the increasing racial and ethnic representation in schools for years, if not decades to come.

SuperVision as well as other instructional supervision texts have separated the work of instructional supervision from the reality of supporting increasingly diverse students, and to a lesser degree, teaching populations. From a critical perspective, we believe the clinical supervision cycles adopt a largely color/culturally-blind approach that increasingly becomes more noticeable as the population of teachers and school leaders becomes more socioculturally representative of the general student populations in American schools. In our opinion, *SuperVision* inadequately prepares leaders for culturally responsive work in American schools. A reconceptualization of the clinical supervision cycle, undertaken through the lens of culturally responsive supervisory practices, is long overdue and this chapter's focus going forward.

SUPERVISION FOR SOCIOCULTURALLY DIVERSE STUDENTS

Supervision has long embodied many principles of whiteness (Lance, 2021). Therefore, to counter a historical indifference to issues of justice, equity, and inclusion of traditionally marginalized populations, it is important to work with a framework examining those structures. As educators increase their awareness of sociocultural identities and the delivery of asset-based instruction based on these identities, the limitations of current instructional supervision are highlighted as an increasing and persistent failure to ineffectively support the needs of all students, including those from historically marginalized or underserved groups. This can occur in a variety of ways, such as failing to provide adequate resources or support for teachers working with diverse student populations, failing to address issues of bias or discrimination within the classroom, or failing to provide appropriate accommodations or support for students with disabilities. Instructional supervision positioned as "clinical" or unbiased has nibbled around the margins of inequities, making incremental changes. However, CRIS must serve as the core ideology and practice of the clinical supervision cycle for any meaningful school improvement.

CRIS is indispensable to ensuring that all students have equitable access to high-quality education and can reach their full potential. It involves providing ongoing support and professional development for teachers, as well as ongoing evaluation and feedback so teachers can meet student needs and instructional practices are aligned with research-based best practices. Instructional supervision must address the systematic issues of marginalization that continue to occur in U.S. schools to this day. A reconceptualization of the clinical supervisory cycle, undertaken through the lens of culturally responsive supervisory practices, is long overdue and the focus of this chapter going forward.

DOMINANT VIEWPOINT INFORMS INSTRUCTIONAL SUPERVISION

As surely as schools are educational and community spaces, they are also racial spaces governed by structural inequities that disadvantage minoritized students and educators (Gordon & Reber, 2021; Kuchynka et al., 2022). Key supports for these inequitable structures are "hegemonic ideologies and practices" (Valencia, 2020, p. 30) rhetorically reinforced by color-evasive discourse (Annamma et al., 2017; Bonilla-Silva, 2003). Leonardo and Manning (2015) explain that, "White attitudes and preferences masquerade as common sense and are embedded in the language we speak and through which we teach our children" (p. 20). Creating culturally responsive school spaces requires both challenging this status quo and providing leaders with the "know *how* to properly push against oppression" (Khalifa, 2018, p. 7). Neither of these tasks can begin without making whiteness visible in our school practices and throwing out the mask of cultural neutrality within supervisory practices.

Teacher preparation and development have begun to take up the call to make explicit the previously hidden cultural underpinnings of curriculum, educational structures, and school traditions (Thomas & Dyches, 2019). The field of instructional supervision, however, has focused on how supervisors can support teachers' growth toward more culturally responsive classroom practices rather than turning the gaze inward toward culturally responsive approaches to supervising. As a result, instructional supervision developments have continued to replicate White social values as universal and natural even as they have evolved (Cormier & Pandey, 2021; Guerra et al., 2022). For example, supervisors are encouraged to match teachers' "dispositions and behaviors" (Glickman et al., 2018, p. 131) with the most appropriate supervisory approach on a continuum from explicitly directing teachers' choices to full support for teachers' autonomous decision making. Both the linearity of the continuum and placing independence at the apex, superior to collaboration, suggests values that resonate more clearly with individualistic cultures with low power distance (see Hofstede et al., 2010, and Unsworth et al., 2010, for discussions of cultural dimensions of individualism, power distance, and categorization approaches). Therefore, even as *SuperVision* offers leaders a variety of supervisory approaches, they remain grounded in a hierarchy with an emphasis on White cultural values. The implicit message communicates that a "non-directive" (Glickman et al., 2018, p. 117) individualistic supervisory relationship is the most valued approach; other approaches, including a more collectivistic "collaborative" (Glickman et al., 2018, p. 117) approach, are less valued.

More perniciously, teachers' dispositions and behaviors inextricably link with their cultural identities, and supervisors' decisions will be made through their own cultural lens. Interpreting the behavior and dispositions of others holds myriad opportunities for culture clashes, which will inevitably resolve in favor of supervisors, most of whom are White and from majoritarian cultural backgrounds (NCES, 2022). Regardless of racial and ethnic background, instructional supervisors have almost certainly been steeped in hegemonic U.S. cultural values through schooling (Tevis et al., 2022). As Milner warns education researchers, there is danger when we "do not pay careful attention to [our] own and others' racialized and cultural systems of coming to know, knowing, and experiencing the world" (2007, p. 388).

Avoiding the cultural underpinnings of supervisory practices can lead to marginalizing teachers and students, and color-evasive instructional supervision practices work directly against supporting culturally responsive teaching practices. Race-evasive practices in education limit opportunities to recognize the cultural assets (Yosso, 2005) of some teachers and students by registering only certain strengths, beliefs, and behaviors familiar in White culture as desirable. Further, a monocultural approach to supervision limits the range of epistemologies that could productively inform the work of schools, especially as they serve such a diverse population of students and communities. Lastly, as we work toward culturally responsive schools, supervision cannot be wedded to ideas about teaching and learning grounded only in whiteness and marginalize the dispositions, behaviors, and funds of knowledge (Moll et al., 1992) of teachers from other racial and ethnic backgrounds.

Misapplication of the Supervisory Continuum: A Brief Vignette

Consider, for example, Mr. Gil's high school block-scheduled chemistry class. Mr. Gil, a legally blind, Mexican-American cishet man, teaches in a large school with a high population of students with Mexican or Central American heritage. The whole department uses the same unit tests, and Mr. Gil's students always score higher on the unit test than other teachers' students. There are rumblings about students taking advantage of Mr. Gil's low vision to cheat, which have come to the attention of the principal, Mr. Avery. In a pre-conference meeting, he and Mr. Gil selected an upcoming test day to conduct an observation that would focus on student on-task/off-task behaviors.

During the observation, Mr. Avery, a White, able, cishet male, noted that Mr. Gil spent almost 20 minutes taking roll and chit-chatting with students, asked only group questions low on Bloom's taxonomy during the lesson, and allowed students collaboration time during a unit test. From Mr. Avery's perspective, Mr. Gil made poor use of valuable instructional time, failed to develop higher-order thinking, and defeated the purpose of summative student assessments by allowing students "to cheat." Based on the observation data, it was clear Mr. Gil's instruction needed to change. Subsequently, in the post-conference, using a "directive informational supervisory approach" (Glickman et al., 2018, p. 141), Mr. Avery suggested an instructional improvement goal with several activities for accomplishing it from which Mr. Gil could select (Glickman et al., 2018, p. 141).

Lacking knowledge of other cultures' worldviews, particularly cultures that value collectivism, Mr. Avery was quick to judge Mr. Gil's instructional actions as inappropriate and ineffective. His judgments minimized the value of the relationship-building evidenced in Gil's roll-call practices, instead prioritizing a White Western orientation to time efficiency (time on task). The time investment in relationship building may pay off in fewer disciplinary issues, in getting to know students' interest for teaching (i.e., funds of knowledge), in less need to convince students of a task's value because of the built trust, or in a myriad of other ways. Mr. Avery viewed Gil's roll-call practice through a deficit lens instead of recognizing the cultural assets informing his instructional practice.

Similarly, criticism of Gil's memory-centered questions relied on and privileged certain beliefs about the nature of learning and knowledge; however, other epistemologies place higher value on choral responses and memorization (Gratier et al., 2009), activities that might have particular value in the few minutes before an exam. Lastly, offering students time for collaboration during a test may limit the test's value as a measure of acquired skills and knowledge; however, it may offer advantages that are overlooked when viewing learning and testing through an individualistic lens. Given a limited time to ask one another for help, students self-assess their weaknesses, then give and receive just-in-time learning, thereby learning the bits that eluded them that can be reframed through peer language.

Enacting a directive information supervisory approach with Mr. Gil positioned Mr. Avery "as the information source for the goal and activities of the improvement plan" (Glickman et al., 2018 p. 141), resulting in decisions and recommendations congruent with his own cultural lens and little if nothing of Mr. Gil's. Mr. Avery values individualism, low-context communication, low-power distance, low-uncertainty avoidance, etc., over Mr. Gil's values of collectivism, high-context communication, high-power distance, and high-uncertainty avoidance, etc. (see Hall, 1989; Hofstede et al., 2010). Using a collaborative supervisory approach in place of the directive-informational one may have been more culturally congruent with Mr. Gil's value orientation of collectivism and afforded Mr. Avery a deeper understanding of Mr. Gil's teaching practice so that he could support his professional growth.

In reflecting on the post conference with Mr. Avery, Mr. Gil did not understand why Mr. Avery was so critical of his instruction and did not view him as a highly effective teacher. After all, his students had scored higher on the unit tests than other students and had done so for the last 5 years; students in his chemistry classes had all passed the state's end-of-course assessment with flying colors. Plus, when students needed advice or just needed to talk, they sought him out. Feeling criticized and unappreciated for his work, Mr. Gil no longer trusted Mr. Avery, because in the principal's eyes, he would always be "right" and Mr. Gil "wrong." In this case, Mr. Avery's color-evasive instructional supervision practices failed to recognize the cultural assets Mr. Gil had incorporated into his instruction to increase student learning. In failing to support Mr. Gil's culturally responsive teaching practices, the principal not only marginalized him but also damaged the supervisory relationship. This example is just one of many that occur between minoritized teachers and supervisors who are not culturally responsive.

In the preceding example, the cultural aspects of each character's behaviors are briefly described to highlight the influence of invisible culture on teaching, student learning and supervising. Since culture refers to the *tendencies* of a group, it is important to note that not every individual within a group will adhere to all beliefs or behaviors at all times (Hofstede, Hofstede, & Minkov 2010). The only way one can be certain about an individual's cultural background is to get to know that person. How this knowledge of others is gained and applied through instructional supervision requires a complex collection of purposefully acquired knowledge, skills, and dispositions. As evident in the brief exploration of Mr. Gil's supervisory experience, without these knowledge, skills, and dispositions, instructional leadership is culturally evasive, particularly when working with teachers with marginalized identities, and can result in culturally destructive instruction and instructional leadership. When teachers are disinvited to bring their diverse experiences to their work, leaders set a hegemonic standard for classroom practices, and an essential opportunity is lost to model how to embrace the cultural assets of school community members, whether they be staff, faculty, or students.

KNOWLEDGE, SKILLS, AND DISPOSITIONS NEEDED TO BECOME A CRIS

Becoming a culturally responsive instructional principal/supervisor does not happen overnight or even over several months. It does not happen from reading a book or a few articles on culture, chatting with diverse individuals, or taking educational leadership courses (Guerra & García, 2000). The reality is that most aspiring principals graduate from leadership preparation programs with less culturally responsive knowledge, skills, and dispositions than the teachers they will supervise (Marchitello & Trinidad, 2019; NCES, 2020). This is largely because many educational leadership faculty enter higher education with little to no experience teaching diverse students in public schools and/or come with a hegemonic lens and white privilege (Marchitello & Trinidad, 2019; NCES, 2020; Robertson & Guerra, 2016). Culturally responsive supervisors "have [a] deep understanding of their own culture" but also "understand cultural differences, they value cultural groups, and they avoid privileging one group over another" (Ortiz, 2014, at minute 1:00–1:18).

The transformative journey takes time, participating in long-term professional learning led by a skilled culturally responsive facilitator who assists participants in critically examining and reflecting on their own and others' identities, including race, ethnicity, culture, gender, sexual orientation, abilities, religion. This examination also covers aspects of invisible culture or one's values, beliefs, privilege, ways of relating to others, communicating, and thinking, views on power, uncertainty/change, conflict resolution, etc. (Guerra & García, 2000). Aspects of invisible culture also influence learning, teaching, parenting, leading, supervising, curriculum development, school policies, procedures and practices, and other aspects of schooling. Lacking a knowledge of invisible culture often leads to misunderstandings, conflict, deficit thinking, opportunity gaps, and less learning for minoritized students. Since groups of diverse participants discuss these sensitive topics throughout the professional learning sessions, the facilitator must also have the courage to address, deconstruct, and reframe participants' deficit beliefs, biases, stereotypes, and racist comments when they are voiced, ultimately modeling the process repeatedly for participants to learn. Finally, over time it takes engaging with individuals from other cultural identities than your own to deepen the learning acquired in professional learning. This means sharing and reflecting on one other's lived experiences to better understand how they inform and reinforce each person's worldviews.

Responding to the call to bring a critical perspective to supervision by challenging the traditional color- and culture-evasiveness of the field and imbue instructional supervision with the work of more current scholarship and scholarship from other fields, we aim to detail "how their work influences and impacts... practitioners directly" (Mette, 2019, p. 4). Although it's not exhaustive, we offer this list of critical knowledge, skills, and dispositions needed to perform CRIS to help instructional supervisors identify relevant professional learning, and eventually recognize daily opportunities to build a culturally responsive lens and develop the "supervisory identity" (Mette, 2019, p. 4) required for CRIS. Inspired and informed by the work of others (Gay, 2010; Guerra & García, 2000; Guerra & Nelson, 2006; Jacobs, 2014; Khalifa, 2016; Ladson-Billings, 2009; Moll et al., 1992; Valencia, 1997; Villegas & Lucas, 2002), we found it helpful to collect important ideas into the three categories. We also noted that this knowledge and these skills and dispositions (see Table 1) are interwoven in significant ways that must be recognized—for example, dispositions of openness and warmth help build stronger supervisory relationships (Crockett, 2011).

Looking at the field of counseling, we know that while cross-cultural supervisory relationships can be challenging, key knowledge, skills, and dispositions greatly impact the efficacy of supervisory relationships (Duan & Roehlke, 2001). Supervisor dispositions and the strength of their built supervisory relationships mitigate culture clashes and outweigh demographic differences when measuring success (Crockett, 2011).

FUTURE CONSIDERATIONS

Developing as a culturally responsive supervisor is daunting, iterative, and ongoing work. Rather than be intimidated, however, leaders can be confident being part of the work, and in the process will move their supervisory practices toward cultural responsiveness. This is not a destination but a journey. As we have shown, there are countless travelers that have already begun this journey toward a more CRIS, but there are many left to begin it. Thankfully, the roadmap to a more culturally responsive supervisory model exists, with important waypoints to consider in this process.

First, there remains a need for CRIS to be embedded in the preparation of the largest number of instructional supervisors, namely school administrators.

Table 2.1. Critical knowledge, skills and dispositions needed to perform CRIS

Knowledge of	Skills needed for CRIS	Dispositions of CRIS
• Self (identity, worldview, intersectionality) and selves of other individuals
• Culture general knowledge (i.e., dimensions of culture)
• Invisible culture and its influence on teaching, learning, and supervising
• Culture-specific knowledge, cultural responsiveness, and inclusiveness
• Culturally responsive instruction and curriculum
• Multiple perspectives/realities
• Culture clashes and alternate explanations
• Mindfulness (nonjudgmental awareness)
• Systemic inequities including practices, policies, and procedures that favor some groups over others, for example, Eurocentric hiring practices and protocols that often result in hiring White over minoritized educators)	• Engage in critical self-reflection (e.g., race, class, gender, ability, sexual orientation, etc.)
• Facilitate critical reflection in others, deconstructing aspects of their identity
• Build a safe environment where teachers of all backgrounds will feel free to talk
• Build strong supervisory relationships with teachers of all backgrounds
• Facilitate groups of teachers (e.g., develop norms and mediate conflict)
• Remain calm in conflict
• Recognize, deconstruct, and reframe deficit beliefs without humiliation
• Act as a change agent
• Speak explicitly about race and cultural issues when supervising; avoid color- and culture-evasiveness	• Believe educators are well-intentioned, caring individuals
• Every person can learn and succeed
• There is no one "right" way to supervise or teach
• Requires evolving beliefs and practices
• Benefits all educators
• Multicultural understanding is important for all educators, not just those with marginalized identities
• Perseverance
• Courage
• Openness to feedback

44

- Deficit thinking, assumptions, stereotypes, implicit bias, racism, and the role these play in inequities for minoritized educators, including not being hired, and receiving less recognition, awards, and promotion than their White peers. Examples:
  » "she can't give you a straight answer"
  » "he rambled in the interview and didn't answer the questions"
  » "get to the point"
  » "before you enter this meeting, check your passion at the door"
  » "there are few qualified minority applicants"
  » "they don't know how to write"
- Asset-based approaches (i.e., Funds of Knowledge)

- Ask tough questions when no one else will and confront resistance to create more equitable schools
- Recognize the influence of invisible culture when misunderstandings and conflict occur between individuals
- Resist making assumptions
- Explore alternate explanations to help resolve culture clashes
- Identify implicit bias, stereotypes, racism, and deficit thinking
- Continually check to determine if your practices/actions reflect your espoused beliefs. And if not, reflect on why there is a mismatch, get feedback from minoritized individuals (individuals you do not supervise like other principals or supervisors), and work toward improvement.
- Apply, integrate, and practice cultural knowledge, skills, and dispositions in all supervision work (i.e., cultural responsiveness)

- Interest in educators' personal background
- Maintain a positive attitude toward cultural differences
- Open to discussing cultural differences in supervision
- Warm and supportive

Note: Inspired and informed by the following works: Gay, 2010; Garcia & Guerra, 2004; Guerra, 2012; Guerra & García, 2000; Guerra & Nelson, 2006, 2009, 2013; Guerra & Valverde, 2007; Jacobs, 2014; Khalifa, 2016; Ladson-Billings, 2009; Moll et al., 1992; Nelson & Guerra, 2014; Valencia, 1997; Villegas & Lucas, 2002, as well as the regular contributor columns titled "Cultural Proficiency" found in the *Journal of Staff Development* by Guerra and Nelson from 2007 to 2012.

Undoubtedly, as the generation of teachers that experienced culturally responsive teaching preparation ages, more future school administrators will at least have an inkling of what culturally responsive schools are, but recognize that the need for specific and targeted ongoing development is also important. Instructors of supervision must examine their practice through the lens of CRIS now or further risk perpetuating the identity-evasive supervisory approaches of the past.

State, district, and even school cultures are insidiously resistant to change, and the longer individuals work in that resistant environment, the more inured they might become to the role schools play in marginalizing nondominant identities of both educators and students. While the ideologies of schooling remain stubbornly hegemonic, the people in our school communities embody increasingly varied sociocultural identities, bringing a rich diversity of perspectives, skills, and strengths to the learning environment. Continuous professional development in CRIS is needed to blunt the silent influence of hegemony that would dismiss, ignore, and denigrate this diversity. CRIS is needed for all school settings regardless of the diversity of student or community populations. There is a particular urgency in schools that work with racially and culturally diverse student and community populations, of which there are more each day. The accompanying dismissal and denigration can extend beyond diverse values and beliefs to be wickedly applied to the people themselves.

As is often the case with a moral imperative, there has been an increasing sense of urgency to develop CRIS. Cooper (2009) pushed school leaders toward "rejecting ideologies and practices steeped in blatantly biased or color-blind traditions to transform school" (p. 695). It is past time for instructional supervision to take up this call. As Cooper (2009) also wrote, "Principals have not adequately addressed the cultural tension and separatist politics that marginalized ethnic and linguistic minority students and their families" (p. 695). The sense of urgency noted, often by scholars with identities that schools have and continue to marginalize, has only increased over time. Supervision must follow the trailblazing educators who have long called for culturally responsive teaching and school leadership. Intervention needs to start with supervisory preparation, and professionals in instructional supervision in schools should take hope when looking around at supervision in other fields (clinical supervision/psychology), to see that meaningful change can be achieved with attention and diligence. Gaining much-needed momentum toward becoming more culturally responsive in our instructional supervisory practice is how we ensure that the schoolhouse becomes a place that values the strengths that all students bring to the classroom.

REFERENCES

Annamma, S. A., Jackson, D. D., & Morrison, D. (2017). Conceptualizing color-evasiveness: Using dis/ability critical race theory to expand a color-blind racial ideology in education and society. *Race, Ethnicity, and Education, 20*(2), 147–162.

Baker, A. M. (2019). "Straddling the Divide Between Practice and Scholarship, Tensions of School Leaders Pursuing a Social Justice Leadership Ph.D." *Journal of Leadership Studies, 13*(2), 77–82. https://doi.org/10.1002/jls.21643

Bendixen, L. D., Plachowski, T., & Olafson, L. (2023). Criticalizing teacher perceptions of urban school climate: Exploring the impact of racism and race-evasive culture in a predominantly White teacher workforce. *Education and Urban Society, 55*(8), 949–974. https://doi.org/10.1177/00131245221106724

Biesta, G. (2010). A new logic of emancipation: The methodology of Jacques Rancière. *Educational Theory, 60*(1), 39–59.

Bonilla-Silva, E. (2003). "New racism," color-blind racism, and the future of Whiteness in America. In A. Doane & E. Bonilla-Silva (Eds.) *White out: The continuing significance of racism* (pp. 271–284). Routledge.

Burnham, R. M. (1976). Instructional Supervision: Past, Present and Future Perspectives. *Theory Into Practice, 15*(4), 301–305. http://www.jstor.org/stable/1476050

Carter, P. L., & Welner, K. G. (Eds.). (2013). *Closing the opportunity gap: What America must do to give every child an even chance*. Oxford University Press.

Clayton, J. K., & Goodwin, M. (2015). Culturally competent leadership through empowering relationships: A case study of two assistant principals. *Education Leadership Review, 16*(2), 131–144.

Cogan, M. L. (1976). Rationale for clinical supervision. *Journal of Research and Development in Education*.

Cooper, C. W. (2009). Performing Cultural Work in Demographically Changing Schools: Implications for Expanding Transformative Leadership Frameworks. *Educational Administration Quarterly, 45*(5), 694–724.

Cormier, D. R., & Pandey, T. (2021). Semiotic analysis of a foundational textbook used widely across educational supervision. *Journal of Educational Supervision, 4*(2). https://doi.org/10.31045/jes.4.2.6

Crockett, S. A. (2011). *The role of supervisor-supervisee cultural differences, supervisor multicultural competence, and the supervisory working alliance in supervision outcomes: A moderated mediation model* [Doctoral dissertation, Old Dominion University]. Retrieved from ProQuest Dissertations and Theses database (3455280).

Dewey, J. (1916). *Democracy and education: An introduction to the philosophy of education*. Macmillan.

Diaz, J. (2022, March 28). *Florida's governor signs controversial law opponents dubbed "don't say gay."* NPR. Retrieved from https://www.npr.org/2022/03/28/1089221657/dont-say-gay-florida-desantis

Duan, C., & Roehlke, H. (2001). A descriptive "snapshot" of cross-racial supervision in university counseling center internships. *Journal of Multicultural Counseling and Development, 29*, 131–146.

Fear-Segal, J., & Rose, S. D. (Eds.). (2016). *Carlisle Indian Industrial School: Indigenous histories, memories, and reclamations*. University of Nebraska Press.

Firth, G. R., & Eiken, K. P. (1982). Impact of the schools' bureaucratic structure on supervision. In T. J. Sergiovanni (Ed.), *Supervision of teaching* (pp. 153–169). Association for Supervision and Curriculum Development.

García, S. B., & Guerra, P. L. (2004). Deconstructing deficit thinking: Working with educators to create more equitable learning environments. *Education and Urban Society, 36*(2), 150–168.

Gay, G. (1998). Cultural, ethnic, and gender issues. In G. R. Firth and E. F. Pajak (Eds.), *Handbook of research on school supervision* (pp. 1184–1227). MacMillan.

Gay, G. (2010). *Culturally responsive teaching: Theory, research, and practice* (2nd ed.). Teachers College Press.

Glanz, J. (2018). *Chronicling Perspectives about the State of Instructional Supervision by Eight Prominent Scholars of Supervision.* 1(1). https://doi.org/10.31045/jes.1.1.1

Glickman, C. D. (1992). *Supervision in transition: 1992 Yearbook of the Association for Supervision and Curriculum Development.* Association for Supervision and Curriculum Development.

Glickman, C. D., Gordon, S. P., & Ross-Gordon, J. M. (2007). *Supervision of instruction: A developmental approach.* Allyn & Bacon.

Glickman, C. D. Gordon, S. P., & Ross-Gordon, J. M. (2018). *Supervision and instructional leadership: A developmental approach* (10th ed.). Pearson.

Goldhammer, R. (1969). *Clinical supervision: Special methods for the supervision of teachers.* Holt McDougal.

Gordon, N., & Reber, S. (2021). Addressing inequities in the U.S. K–12 education system. In M. S. Kearney & A. Ganz (Eds.), *Rebuilding the post-pandemic economy* (pp. 106–149). Aspen Institute Press.

Gordon, S. P. (2016). Framing instructional supervision. In J. Glanz & S. J. Zepeda (Eds.). *Supervision new perspectives for theory and practice* (pp. 23–42). Rowman & Littlefield.

Gordon, S. P., & Espinosa, S. (2020). Instructional supervision for culturally responsive teaching. *Educational Considerations, 45*(3), 1–22.

Gorski, P. C. (2017). *Reaching and teaching students in poverty: Strategies for erasing the opportunity gap.* Teachers College Press.

Gratier, M., Greenfield, P. M., Isaac, A. (2009). Tacit communicative style and cultural attunement in classroom interaction. *Mind, Culture, and Activity, 16*(4), 296–316.

Griffin, L. B., Watson, D., & Liggett, T. (2016). "I didn't see it as a cultural thing": Supervisors of student teachers define and describe culturally responsive supervision. *Democracy and Education, 24*(1), 3.

Grissom, J. A., Egalite, A. J., & Lindsay, C. A. (2021). *How principals affect students and schools: A systematic synthesis of two decades of research.* The Wallace Foundation. https://wallacefoundation.org/report/how-principals-affect-students-and-schools-systematic-synthesis-two-decades-research

Grissom, J. A., & Redding, C. (2015). Discretion and disproportionality: Explaining the underrepresentation of high-achieving students of color in gifted programs. *AERA Open, 2*(1), 2332858415622175.

Guerra, P. L. (2012). Valuing diversity: A well-intended but empty promise. *Multicultural Education, 19*(3). 44–47.

Guerra, P. L., Baker, A. M., & Cotman, A. M. (2022). Instructional supervision: Is it culturally responsive? A textbook analysis. *Journal of Educational Supervision, 5*(1). https://doi.org/10.31045/jes.5.1.1

Guerra, P. L., & García, S. (2000). *Understanding the cultural contexts of teaching and learning [Series of 11 staff development modules].* Southwest Educational Development Laboratory.

Guerra, P. L., & Nelson, S. W. (2006, April). *Leadership for diverse schools: Putting tough issues on the table.* Session presented at the annual meeting of ASCD, Chicago, IL.

Guerra, P. L., & Nelson, S. W. (2009). Changing professional practice requires changing beliefs. *Phi Delta Kappan, 90*(5), 354–359.

Guerra, P. L., & Nelson, S. W. (2013). Latino parent involvement: Seeing what has always been there. *Journal of School Leadership, 23*(3), 424–455.

Guerra, P. L., & Valverde, L. A. (2007). Latino communities and schools: Tapping assets for student' success. *Principal Leadership, 8*(2), 40–44.

Hall, E. T. (1989). *Beyond culture*. Anchor Books. (Original work published in 1976)

Heidelburg, K., Phelps, C., & Collins, T. A. (2022). Reconceptualizing school safety for Black students. *School Psychology International, 43*(6), 591–612.

Hines III, M. T. (2016). The embeddedness of white fragility within white pre-service principals' reflections on white privilege. *Critical Questions in Education, 7*(2), 130–145.

Hofstede, G., Hofstede, G. J., & Minkov, M. (2010). *Cultures and organizations: Software of the mind* (3rd ed.) McGraw-Hill.

Hung, M., Smith, W. A., Voss, M. W., Franklin, J. D., Gu, Y., & Bounsanga, J. (2020). Exploring student achievement gaps in school districts across the United States. *Education and Urban Society, 52*(2), 175–193.

Jacobs, J. (2006). Supervision for social justice: Supporting critical reflection. *Teacher Education Quarterly, 33*(4), 23–39. http://www.jstor.org/stable/23478869

Jacobs, J. (2014). Fostering equitable school contexts: Bringing a social justice lens to field supervision. *Florida Association of Teacher Educators, 1*(14), 1–16. http://www.fate1.org/journals/2014/jacobs.pdf

Kao, K. (2020, June 3), *Textbook by professor emeritus reaches no. 1 on Book Authority* [Press release]. https://coe.uga.edu/news/2020/06/textbook-by-professor-emeritus-reaches-no-1-on-book-authority

Khalifa, M. A. (2018). *Culturally responsive school leadership*. Harvard Education Press.

Khalifa, M. A., Gooden, M. A., & Davis, J. E. (2016). Culturally responsive school leadership: A synthesis of the literature. *Review of Educational Research, 86*(4), 1272–1311. https://doi.org/10.3102/0034654316630383

Kohli, R., Pizarro, M., Nevarez, A. (2017). The "new racism" of K–12 schools: Centering critical research on racism. *Review of Research in Education, 41,* 182–202. https://doi.org/10.3102/0091732X16686949

Klibanoff, E. (2022, August 25). Texans who perform abortions now face up to life in prison, $100,000 fine. *The Texas Tribune*. Retrieved January 19, 2023, from https://www.texastribune.org/2022/08/25/texas-trigger-law-abortion/#:~:text=Performing%20an%20abortion%20is%20now,its%20judgment%20in%20Dobbs%20v.

Kuchynka, S. L., Eaton, A., & Rivera, L. M. (2022). Understanding and addressing gender-based inequities in STEM: Research synthesis and recommendations for U.S. K–12 education. *Social Issues and Policy Review, 16*(1), 252–288.

Ladson-Billings, G. (2006). From the achievement gap to the education debt: Understanding achievement in U.S. schools. *Educational researcher, 35*(7), 3–12.

Ladson-Billings, G. (2009). *The dreamkeepers: Successful teachers of African American students*. Jossey-Bass.

Lance, T. (2021). Chasing down the educational debt by centering race in educational supervision. *Journal of Educational Supervision, 4*(1). https://doi.org/10.31045/jes.4.1.2

Leonardo, Z., & Manning, L. (2015). White historical activity theory: Toward a critical understanding of White zones of proximal development. *Race, Ethnicity, and Education, 20*(1), 15–29.

Lucio, W. H., & McNeil, J. D. (1968). *Supervision: A synthesis of thought and action.* McGraw-Hill.

Marchitello, M., & Trinidad, J. (2019). *Preparing teachers for diverse schools: Lessons from minority serving institutions.* Bellwether Education Partners. https://bellwether.org/wp-content/uploads/2019/06/Preparing-Teachers-for-Diverse-Schools_Bellwether.pdf

Mette, I. M., (2019). The state of supervision discourse communities: A call for the future of supervision to shed its mask. *Journal of Educational Supervision, 2*(2). https://doi.org/https://doi.org/10.31045/jes.2.2.1

Mette, I. M., Aguilar, I., & Wieczorek, D. (2020). A thirty state analysis of teacher supervision and evaluation systems in the ESSA era. *Journal of Educational Supervision, 3*(2). https://doi.org/10.31045/jes.3.2.7

Mette, I. M., Range, B. G., Anderson, J., Hvidston, D. J., Nieuwenhuizen, L., & Doty, J. (2017). The wicked problem of the intersection between supervision and evaluation. *International Electronic Journal of Elementary Education, 9*(3), 709–724. https://files.eric.ed.gov/fulltext/EJ1134210.pdf

Milner, H. R. (2007). Race, culture, and researcher positionality: Working through dangers seen, unseen, and unforeseen. *Educational Researcher, 36*(7), 388–400. http://www.jstor.org/stable/30136070

Milner, H. R., IV. (2020). *Start where you are, but don't stay there: Understanding diversity, opportunity gaps, and teaching in today's classrooms.* Harvard Education Press.

Moll, L. C., Amanti, C., Neff, D., & Gonzalez, N. (1992). Funds of Knowledge for Teaching: Using a Qualitative Approach to Connect Homes and Classrooms. *Theory Into Practice, 31*(2), 132–141. http://www.jstor.org/stable/1476399

Morgan, H. (2021). Restorative justice and the school-to-prison pipeline: A review of existing literature. *Education Sciences, 11*(4), 159.

Morris, M. W. (2016). *Pushout: The criminalization of Black girls in schools.* The New Press

National Center for Education Statistics. (2020). *Annual reports: Racial and ethnic enrollment in public schools.* https://nces.ed.gov/programs/coe/indicator/cge

National Center for Education Statistics. (2022). *Characteristics of 2020–21 public and private K–12 school principals in the United States: Results from the National Teacher and Principal Survey.* https://nces.ed.gov/pubsearch/pubsinfo.asp?pubid=2022112

Nelson, S. W., & Guerra, P. L. (2014). Educator beliefs and cultural knowledge: Implications for School improvement efforts. *Educational Administration Quarterly, 50*(1), 67–95.

O'Connell, H. A. (2019). Historical shadows: The links between sundown towns and contemporary black–white inequality. *Sociology of Race and Ethnicity, 5*(3), 311–325.

Ortiz, A. A. (2014, September 16). *Why is it important to ensure instruction and interventions are culturally responsive?* National Center on Intensive Intervention. https://intensiveintervention.org/resource/why-it-important-ensure-instruction-and-interventions-are-culturally-responsive

Robertson, P. M., & Guerra, P. L. (winter 2016). The voice of one—The power of many. *Multicultural Education, 23*(2), 2–12.

Schwartz, S. (2021, June 18). Four states have placed legal limits on how teachers can discuss race. More may follow. *Education Week.* Retrieved January 19, 2023, from https://www.edweek.org/policy-politics/four-states-have-placed-legal-limits-on-how-teachers-can-discuss-race-more-may-follow/2021/05

Skiba, R. J., Michael, R. S., Nardo, A. C., & Peterson, R. (2002). The color of discipline: Sources of racial and gender disproportionality in school punishment. *The Urban Review (34),* 317–342

Sleeter, C. E. (2008). Preparing White teachers for diverse students. In M. Cochran-Smith, S. Feiman-Nemser, & D. J. McIntyre (Eds.), *Handbook of research on teacher education: Enduring questions in changing contexts* (3rd ed., pp. 559–582). Routledge and Association of Teacher Educators.

Sleeter, C. E. (2017). Critical race theory and the whiteness of teacher education. *Urban Education, 52*(2), 155–169.

Spiel, C., Schwartzman, S., Busemeyer, M., Cloete, N., Drori, G., Lassnigg, L., Schober, B., Schweisfurth, M., & Verma, S. (2018). The contribution of education to social progress. In International Panel on Social Progress (Ed.), *Rethinking society for the 21st century: Report of the International Panel for Social Progress* (pp. 753–778). Cambridge University Press.

Straume, I. S. (2016). Democracy, education and the need for politics. *Studies in Philosophy and Education, 35*(1), 29–45.

Sullivan, S., & Glanz, J. (2000). Alternative approaches to supervision: Cases from the field. *Journal of curriculum and supervision, 15*(3), 212–35.

Tevis, T. L., Martinez, J. G. L., & Lozano, Y. E. (2022). Disrupting White hegemony: A necessary shift toward adopting critical approaches within the teaching and learning environment. *International Journal of Qualitative Studies in Education, 54*(4), 341–355. https://doi.org/10.1080/09518398.2022.2035453

Thomas, D., & Dyches, J. (2019). The hidden curriculum of reading intervention: A critical content analysis of Fountas & Pinnell's leveled literacy intervention. *Journal of Curriculum Studies, 51*(5), 601–618.

Tillman, L. C. (2004). (Un)intended consequences? The impact of the Brown v. Board of Education decision on the employment status of Black educators. *Education and urban society, 36*(3), 280–303.

Unsworth, S. J., Sears, C. R., & Pexman, P. M. (2010). Cultural influences on categorization processes. *Journal of Cross-Cultural Psychology, 36*(6), 662–688.

Valencia, R. R. (1997). *The evolution of deficit thinking: Educational thought and practice*. Falmer Press.

Valencia, R. R. (2020). *International deficit thinking: Educational thought and practice*. Routledge.

Villegas, A. M., & Lucas, T. (2002). Preparing culturally responsive teachers: Rethinking the curriculum. *Journal of Teacher Education, 53*(1), 20–32.

Wilt, C. L., Annamaa, S. A., Wilmot, J. M., Nyegenye, S. N., Miller, A. L., & Jackson, E. E. (2022). Performing color-evasiveness: A DisCrit analysis of educators' discourse in the US. *Teaching and Teaching Education, 117*, 103761.

Yosso, T. J. (2005). Whose culture has capital? A critical race theory discussion of community cultural wealth. Race, *Ethnicity, and Education, 8*(1), 69–91.

Zepeda, S. J. (2016). *Instructional supervision: Applying tools and concepts*. Taylor & Francis.

Zepeda, S. J. (2014). *The principal as instructional leader: A handbook for supervisors*. Routledge.

CHAPTER 3

Race-ing Instructional Supervision
Plantation Traditions and Instructional Supervision

Noelle Arnold and Rhodesia McMillian

Studies of the education system are rife with research that chronicles schools' constantly evolving endeavors to serve an increasingly racially and culturally diverse population of students, faculty, and staff (Clayton, 2011; Irizarry, 2015; Jenlink & Townes, 2009; Shields, 2010). Although schools and districts have experienced some successes at providing greater access to individuals of color, there is now a growing need for expanded research on how to meet the needs of these individuals and the policies and practices that support this. The phenomenon of increasing numbers of groups historically excluded in education has created an opportunity and challenge for teachers and leadership. On the one hand, this diversity assumes that the presence of these marginalized groups equals the full and positive participation of these groups However, this diversity does not mean that structures, policies, and procedures in schools have become more equitable or accessible. Opportunity gaps (Hung et al., 2020; Milner, 2012) are widening and the educational debt (Ladson-Billings, 2004, 2006, 2013) is increasing.

All of these historical, economic, socio-political, and moral components of inequality that shape the contours of this nation are largely reified in education through policies and practices such as accountability, achievement, and reform (Turner, 2020). These policies and practices, which are historically raced and racialized, build on the frameworks in which race continues to be a significant factor in determining inequity in society, including schooling (Feagin, 2009, 2013). In society and education, "These frameworks carry a broad and persistent set of racial stereotypes, prejudices, ideologies, images, interpretations, narratives, emotions, and . . . racialized inclinations to discriminate" (Feagin, 2013, p. 3).

Several scholars have argued that the "history" of supervision has lacked a definitive theoretical and practical theme (Glanz, 1991, 2018). However, perhaps the "throughline" for supervision might be *race* or *the racist legacies* on which much of society and its institutions are built, including education (Anderson, 1988; Dancy et al., 2018; Mills, 2002; Omi & Winant, 2014). It is these legacies this chapter seeks to highlight by discussing the *ecology* in which instructional supervision continues to operate, embedding racist and racialized traditions in its processes. The examples provided in this chapter highlight the practices in the new accountability movement that is impacting instructional supervision once again and bringing along with it racialized understandings of instruction and supervision. These traditions can be traced to plantation and slavery, whose traditions endure to the present day. These "plantation traditions" (Sharpe, 2016; Woods, 1998) reveal analogous policies and practices between education institutions and their racist roots that migrate across time, spaces, and places, with significance in analyzing historical and contemporary practices (Beckford, 1999, 2000; McKittrick, 2013). These plantation traditions also extend across societies and institutions that create and maintain certain structures and functions (Tomich, 2011). The new accountability issues bring with them a set of notable characteristics of plantation practice(s).

Supervision cannot seem to disentangle itself from its accountability roots and its historical relationship with inspection, surveillance, and control of teaching and learning (Gordon, 1997; Waite, 1997; Zepeda, 2014). Moreover, theories of instructional leadership theory had their genesis in practices in schools in underserved communities containing mostly students of color (Edmonds, 1979). In addition, instructional supervision itself remains a white enterprise (Guerra et al., 2022; Lance, 2021). Principals or head teachers are most often responsible for instructional supervision in schools. Consequently, as the nation's population, and in turn the nation's student body, has grown more diverse, the teaching and principal force has not been consistent with the diversity, with almost 80% being racialized as white (Ingersoll. al., 2019; Schaeffer, 2021; Spiegelman, 2020; Taie & Lewis, 2022).

Researchers have explored this growing incongruity between the degree of racial/ethnic and U.S. student population and teaching and principal workforce (Albert Shanker Institute, 2015; Bartanen & Grissom, 2023; Boser, 2014; Carter Andrews et al., 2019; Easton-Brooks, 2019, 2021; Spiegelman, 2020). These statistics are not provided as an indictment against white educators or to imply that those individuals might not create positive outcomes for historically marginalized students of color (Bristol & Martin-Fernandez, 2019; Goldenberg, 2014). Nevertheless, these representational gaps foster questions in the face of accumulating evidence that the race of teachers and principals matters when the focus is on educating students of color (Egalite et al., 2015; Gershenson et al., 2016; Grissom & Redding, 2016; Lindsay & Hart, 2017).

A key characteristic of the plantation was its relationship between politics, labor regimes, and homogenous approaches to standardize, inspect, and build efficiencies. Instructional supervision is often subject to the direction of societal and political "winds" (Anyon, 2005; Apple & Aasen, 2003; Mitra, 2022; Payne, 2008; Spring, 2011). More often than not, these winds blow in an environment for supervision that often downplays, ignores, or even denies the salience of race and racism (Garman, 2020; Mette, 2020). And in 2023, it might be said that these winds are marked by increased racism, anti-democratic leaders, and neo-reform efforts (Ganon-Shiloh et al., 2022; Kafka & Wilson, 2023). Race and racism inform every facet of the experiences of PK–12 students, including school funding (Kozol, 2012), disproportionate discipline of Black children (Gage et al., 2019), and textbooks and curriculum grounded in white erasure of the Black experience (Loewen, 2008). Schooling is reduced to its plantation tradition, demonstrated in the "problematization" of education and the characterization of students *and* teachers as "lacking" and "in crisis" (Sriprakash et al., 2020).

Race "colors" the instructional supervision process, but exploring these racial realities provides opportunities to consider a practice that sees and responds to racialized realities of instructional supervision as a part of supervision's story (Hazi, 2020; Mette et al., 2016). This is a reality of the accountability movement, "which has largely ignored the impact of race . . . and has negatively impacted our ability for supervisors to serve as experts of pedagogical practices and has perpetuated the 'deficit gaze' often applied to poor students and BIPOC students throughout the American PK–20 education system" (Mette, 2020, p. 2). In this chapter, we call attention to how plantation traditions of accountability have an ability to reproduce and re-inscribe themselves in education articulations of instructional supervision that are tied to the larger historical dynamics and racial frames of schooling that continue to exclude people of color. Doing so allows instructional supervision to advance its role in equity, not just in its processes, but in its purposes, to one that "improves social and educational inequities" (Ross & Cozzens, 2016, p. 162). What follows is a critique of the traditions of instructional supervision and how they relate to plantation practices that defined chattel slavery. Following this critique, we offer insights into how race can inform culturally responsive instructional supervision (CRIS) practices.

PLANTATION TRADITIONS AND INSTRUCTIONAL SUPERVISION

According to the National Humanities Center, by 1860, there were over 46,000 plantations with 89% of all people of African descent enslaved in the United States. While the plantation might typically be viewed as a product of a long-gone period, its physical and sociocultural traditions continue to exist (Hook, 2023; Wolford 2021). According to Squire et al. (2018), "Plantations and their main form of production formed due to a colonial imperialist need for land, religious and racial superiority, and economic power" (p. 3). These plantations heavily relied on slave labor and other forms of exploited practices (Haraway, 2015). Plantation systems emerged from an inherently racialized quest for modernity and industrial advancement (Hesse, 2007) that created hegemonic distinctions between people racialized as white and people racialized as Black. The history of the plantation was long rooted in the interests of plantation owners in preserving a surveilled and coercive labor relationship that was mirrored in education. For example, rather than expanding education, plantation owners limited educational opportunity to maintain and control a supply of workers. Plantation owners and their supporters continued to oppose any educational improvements for Blacks, to relegate them to certain roles.

Much more than a big house built on big land, the plantation served material and psychic functions of control that hold over to this day. While plantations varied over time, place, and space, they set the stage for other systems and institutions that perpetuated forms of standardization, surveillance, and control. These practices are often racialized and mediated through the regulation of the work of teachers and leaders in the supervisory process. Plantations were "subject to constant experimentation, treated as laboratories" (Hook, 2023, p. 96) for new production, organizational, and managerial methods (Mitman, 2021; Purifoy, 2021).

It could be said that the largest holdover in instructional supervision was built based on the laboratories of and experiments within large urban districts and resource-disposed communities with large numbers of Black and Brown students and families (Henry & Dixson, 2016; Lipman, 2004, 2021a, 2021b; Lipman & Haines, 2007; Orfield & Eaton, 1996). Instructional leadership theory had its practical study in elementary schools of poor urban communities (Edmonds, 1979; Hallinger & Wang, 2015; Ylimaki, 2007). These schools, defined by their success or their failure, were thought to comprise a representative stage of what needed to occur in schools, or what *should happen* in schools based on white standards (Hallett, 2010; MacPherson, 1998). Instruction and supervision have been marked by the centralized regulation of teachers, and a caste system of education access, autonomy, and administration that continues to reproduce inequity and racial exclusion for students of color (Hallett, 2010; Macpherson, 1998). Instruction and supervision have also historically been among the means policymakers contrived to maximize compliance and control via standardization and uniformity of policy and procedures (Jennings et al., 2007). Through this lens, schooling is reduced to its plantation tradition as demonstrated in the "problematization" of schools and teachers as "lacking" and "in crisis" (Sriprakash et al., 2020).

Educational research literature has addressed the enduring bonds between plantation traditions and education (Beckert, 2005; Donnor, 2021). The consequence is dealing with a plantation legacy that has fostered a racialized educational system that has created socioecological hierarchies as both a cause and consequence. In a content analysis of 12 states' teacher evaluation systems (TES) policy, Arnold, McMillian, and Morrow (in progress-a) found that supervisory processes based on these systems are based on a combination of a cyclical process of supervision with foci on various state standards, formative and summative feedback, curriculum content, teacher growth or improvement, and professional development. However, all indicate a purpose of improving or quality of instruction and outcome metrics and measures, such as student achievement. While scholars have made the distinction between supervision and evaluation (Mette & Riegel, 2018; Zepeda & Ponticell, 2019), TES systems still provide the "language" and parameters of a district's instructional supervision processes (Arnold et al., in progress-a). However, preliminary findings note that many of these TES systems are devoid of language related to teaching or supervision that acknowledge and consider the ethnicity or race of the learner or the teacher in the instructional supervision process.

However, these racialized languages are often present in other ways through encoded practices that favor homogenous and colorblind practices (Allen & Liou, 2019; Diem et al., 2016; Davis et al., 2015). This seems to support Pierre's (2020) argument that policies contain a certain vernacular—a "racial vernacular" (p. 1), even if it is hidden. These vernaculars, such as those relating to instructional supervision, "sustain racial thought, index particular racial meanings, and prescribe certain practices" (p. 1). This is an interesting preliminary finding considering that 18 states have signed into law or approved legislation that bans teaching, programming, or materials specifically related to critical race theory (CRT) (*World Population Review*, 2023). In addition, another 20 states are currently considering a ban, with another eight that have tried to pass a ban that failed (Alexander et al., 2023; Wisevoter, 2023). This does not include the measures of almost 1,000 local or district measures with over 94% of all enacted measures focused on PK–12 education (Alexander et al., 2023). Of the measures targeting PK–12 schools, 73% focus on regulating classroom teaching and 75% on regulating curricular materials, with many of the measures targeting both.

This measure against CRT is one of many examples of attempts in a cultural and political landscape that seek to influence education. Much like the plantation tradition, in this way labor and learning are restricted for those who may "rise up" against oppressive conditions. Systemic and institutionalized racism and racialized policy have historically driven curricular, instructional, and supervisory processes staff training or development programs (Lopez & Jean-Marie, 2021; Sawchuck, 2021. The plantation tradition of authority, inspection, discipline, regulation, accountability, and control may be understood as an anti-Black response to agency, access, and affirmation (Dumas, 2014). These plantation traditions deny the ways education and policy reify injustice and oppression by standardizing, depoliticizing, and color-blinding educational practices (Glickman & Mette, 2020). In the case of instructional supervision, curriculum, instruction, and supervision are still reduced to universal solutions (Li, 2007; Lipman, 2015).

Although more critical approaches to supervision have been proposed, we wonder if these approaches are "theoretical" or philosophical considering that all 50 states still employ TES and supervision requirements that still have plantation traditions of observation, surveillance, inspection, and regulation. In addition, all 50 states have accountability- and deficit-based discourse and languages still embedded in TES and instructional supervision practices grounded in whiteness, privilege, and inequity (Arnold, 2016, 2018a; Garman, 2020; Mette & Glickman, 2020; Townsend et al., 2013). State education agencies still have control over instructional supervision even when some states allow for district "tweaking" of TES to include their own goals (Arnold et al., in progress-a). The continued focus on standardized test outcomes and newer measures of accountability forms a plantation-informed web in which the instructional supervision process in all its iterations have been ensnared in a "devaluation of Blackness" and a value of whiteness continues through contemporary governance and policy (Henry 2021; Woods, 2017).

Since the inception of U.S. public education over 150 years ago, the legacy of racism and white supremacy has loomed in policies and practices. In its early days, the educational structure began with principles rooted in a plantation mentality of dehumanization that prohibited enslaved Africans being educated. Even after slavery's abolition, newer plantations emerged though Jim Crow, the system of Black codes that limited the rights of Black people, many of whom had been enslaved. The last half century in education has been characterized by a continued plantation-like educational caste system through tracking, standardized testing, and a highly stratified organization. This has meant a stratified access to programs, school success, and a "stratified class of student" (Brouillette, 1997, p. 547), with little or no opportunity for certain students to thrive in this caste system (Edwards & Tomlinson, 2002).

From the time of the one-room schoolhouse to the more formalized practices of today, supervision has often lacked choate understandings but has instead followed a panoptic and autocratic approach (Nielson, 2011). It might also be said that supervision has been saturated with the key characteristics of a plantation, such as homogenization and standardization of practice (Vintimilla & Pacini-Ketchabaw, 2020). Supervision at its earliest roots was focused on instrumentality and direct application, with much of the driver of supervision driven by new plantation-isms such as managerial discourses of capitalism, investment, scalability, and quality control (Farley et al., 2021).

The role of standards for classroom teachers has not actually evolved much over the last 50 years, and these standards are still dependent upon state policies often rooted in old plantation politics of standardization and accountability (Cuban, 1990). The "highly centralized system of schooling [and] mandated curricula, add responsibilities for supervisors, and institute narrow definitions of accountability aimed at holding principals accountable for increases in student achievement" (Glanz et al., 2007, p. 1). Trujillo (2013) found that school districts oversimplify district equity, with a myopic focus on student outcomes and too little focus on mechanisms of equitable improvement, such as centering student voice in learning objectives (Holquist & Walls, 2021), evidence-informed improvement (Brown et al., 2017), or community-informed practice (Oakes et al., 2017), to name a few. Because of this, instructional supervision is maintained as an "academic policing enterprise" (Witherspoon Arnold, 2014). This is in spite of the fact that positive school outcomes can often be linked to the "culture governing of the school, the sense of belonging and community, the influence of teachers and other school personnel, and the willingness of school personnel to engage equity" (Chambers et al., 2014, p. 472). As such, the reification of plantation practices occurs through traditional instructional supervision practices and generally lacks culturally responsive paradigms to help deconstruct these vestiges.

Authority and Oversight

Webster defines supervision as "to oversee." One of the earliest models for supervision comes from the Colonial period. The lone teacher, often from a one-room schoolhouse, was often overseen by a committee of community leaders to determine his or her effectiveness in teaching "core" subjects such as religion and reading (Cornelius, 1983). Later, the locus of the plantations were certain spaces with panoptic functions such as geographies (the auction block, the big house, the fields and crops, the slave quarters, the transportation ways leading to and from the plantation, and so on). Foucault (1977) discussed how certain spaces were designed for surveillance and monitoring of the social, mental, and physical life of individuals such as prisoners or slaves (Bates, 2007; Epperson, 2000; Jefferson & Smith-Peterson, 2021; Nielsen, 2011). Other researchers have expanded on the idea that this type of control remained in continued use across society (Foucault 1977; Skerritt, 2020). The idea and realities of the panoptic plantation (Davis, 2016; Nielson, 2011) are rooted in a plantation "pecking order" and enforce a subjugated state on the slave and working populations. Even in the absence of "the master," the plantation maintained and enforced control with a series of rules and regulations that defined labor life (Browne, 2015; Delle, 2002). The power of the master was distributed, and continuous, and this same "spirit" has proliferated through institutions such as schools.

Much like what happened with the panoptic plantations, some educational researchers have argued that despite changes in the area of instructional supervision, there is still a lack of agency and autonomy in teaching and the supervision of this teaching (Skerritt, 2020). These institutions that have provided the means and mechanisms, policies, and procedures that regulate individual teaching and supervision through state and district norms for instruction are grounded in oversight and surveillance. Foucault (1977) argued that panoptic realities create "dis-individualizing power and creating an automatic and unfaltering source of both authority and punishment" (p. 202). We must ask ourselves how the plantation tradition of oversight and authority might shape and maintain racist oppression in the supervision process.

The instructional supervision process has no doubt been shaped by accountability. Although not the first policy of its kind, the No Child Left Behind Act (NCLB) (2002) was a major piece of educational reform legislation touted as a means to eliminate the achievement gap, particularly for those who were traditionally underserved. The development of NCLB increased accountability among stakeholders related to teaching, learning, and curriculum (Hull, 2013; Louis et al., 2010; NCLB, 2002; Simpson et al., 2004). In addition, NCLB also established yearly proficiency targets and attendance and graduation rates, and declared that all educators must be certified and highly qualified to continue receiving federal funds for educational improvements (Hightower et al., 2011). NCLB represented the greatest extension of the government's oversight through mandated assessments and accountability structures (Hull, 2013). Subsequent federal mandates such as the reauthorization of ESSA have offered "reform without repair" (Saultz et al., 2019) for the major issues plaguing schools. It has also failed to loosen the plantation control measures that inevitably impact supervisory practice.

Inspection and Surveillance

In her book *Dark Matters*, Browne (2015) explored how plantations attempted to standardize and regulate each instance of the laborer's being through "rules, instructions, routines, inspection, hierarchical observation, the timetable, and the examination" (p. 51). She posited that not only was this the norm of plantation life, *but also was a marker of society and the institutions within them*. On the plantation, variation was not permitted, and laborers had to adhere to strict production and labor plans to enhance inspection ease and uniformity of production. Enslaved laborers worked under a highly standardized labor structure that was quota- driven and surveilled and managed by an "overseer." Overseers were charged with the responsibility of supervising, inspecting, and monitoring all labor on the plantation (Sandy, 2012). The overseer's role was "fundamentally to maintain order and control" (Bristol, 2012, p. 110) on behalf of an owner or master who controlled the entire system. This system was a "top-down" one in which the laborer and overseers were isolated from processes in favor of simply policing a plan already set for them.

In many ways, supervision has been intimately intertwined with inspection (Bencherab & Al Maskari, 2020). This inspection is chiefly the responsibility of someone with positional power or other authority whose responsibility is to evaluate performance or compliance (Glanz, 1998). While some would argue that this type of supervision is a thing of the past, the plantation tradition of authority figure vs. subordinate is still present in instructional supervision grounded in TES. Newer movements such as neo-accountability and educational oversight have led to a reification of old practices in supervision such as inspection and accountability. In TES systems, supervisors' roles are still largely mediated by class inspection visits that include lesson plan reviews, textbook or program fidelity checks, student behavior control, and classroom grouping, etc. (Arnold et al., in progress-a; Tesfaw & Hofman, 2014).

Recent crises such as COVID-19, racial unrest, mass shootings, and other crises have become a persistent reality, impacting communities and schools (Carter & Mcintee, 2021). Schools have always been sites of surveillance; however, this increases in times of crises (Witherspoon, 2010). For example, after the events of 9/11 or Hurricane Katrina, there were tensions surrounding equity and accountability (Corbin et al., 2003). In the communities and their schools that experienced crises, there was renewed hyper-focus on accountability, including an increased focus on school reform, standardized test scores, "back to basics" curricula, new supervision requirements, and a focus on teacher quality (Arnold, 2018a; Witherspoon Arnold et al., 2015). The surveillance and inspection of teacher instruction normalized hyper-visibility in an effort to re-normalize schooling after every crisis (Arnold, 2019; Page, 2018b).

While crises can occur in any area of the world at any time, those schools and communities with already limited resources, high vulnerability, and people whose needs are considerable are the areas impacted the most in times of crisis (Arnold, 2018a, 2021; Levitt & Whitaker, 2009; Patton & Davis, 2014; Witherspoon, 2010). After a school or community crisis such as Hurricane Katrina, researchers have found that students of color experience disproportionate negative impacts in these schools (Cook & Dixson, 2013; Henry & Dixson, 2016; Patton & Davis, 2014). Under these conditions, the nature of curriculum and supervision creates a strident emphasis on data-driven instruction and test-based accountability combined with strict guidelines for principals and supervisors related to monitoring instruction (Cheng et al., 2017; Frazier-Anderson, 2008; Gross, 1998).

The more recent crisis of COVID-19 has highlighted a widening achievement gap, particularly for students of color. In response, states and legislatures are instituting neo-accountability policies to inspect and surveil teaching to address learning loss and monitor teacher productivity and curricula standards (Arnold et al., in progress-b; Brock et al., 2021). Since that time, there has been state and federal urgency to measure the pandemic's impact on student achievement by resuming high-stakes assessments (Carter & Mcintee, 2021; Sofia, 2020). As with other crises, schools serving communities of color are more keenly impacted by these changes, which make them simultaneously "hyper- and in-visible" (Turner et al., 1999).

Labor

Plantation labor was often divided by raced and gendered racialized distributions of labor relying on slave and other forms of subjugated labor (Haraway et al., 2019; Murphy & Schroering, 2020). Plantations have operated through *labor control* (Boatcă, 2017) by restricting rights, the regulation of work and bodies, and the disposability of the laborer (McKittrick, 2011). Take for example standards-based school reform movements that cyclically inform education (Cohen et al., 2018; Keegan, 2021). In the 1980s and 1990s, federal and state policy wrought a set of sweeping standards, assessments, and school and system accountability for students' performance. An outcome of these policies was a set of plantation-style practices in instructional supervision in which the very labor of teachers and supervisors was highly standardized and surveilled. Instructional and supervisory labor bore (and still bears) a plantation ethos of homogenization and controlled instructional content, teaching methods, and learning outcomes. In addition, TES and formal supervision structures are amended or created that control for metrics related to these teacher labor practices and "science"-based pedagogies that are supposedly effective for all students and measure all "good" teacher instruction (Cohen et al., 2018).

Race-ing Instructional Supervision

Plantations often standardized labor through repetitive and uniform movements in the fields to indicate conformity to rules and to show which laborers were productive or "slacking" (Littlefield, 2023; Morgan, 2017). "Lockstep, highly supervised labor replaced traditional patterns of individual work" (Littlefield, 2023, para. 3). Laborers were divided into work "gangs" determined by their physical condition and abilities with strict supervision of routines and tasks. Similarly, educational ainstruction occurs through various forms of supervision and surveillance that regulate pedagogy, via standardization, mandated curricula and textbooks, and scripted lessons that remove teacher agency. The instructional supervisor observes and evaluates to produce standardized, homogeneous work (Morgan, 2017).

In yet another example, the resurgence of the "Reading Wars" supports a "back to basics" instruction that includes phonics. Since 2019, 30 states and the District of Columbia have passed laws or implemented policies banning other literacy approaches in favor of evidence-based reading instruction, with 22 states implementing changes post-pandemic (Schwartz, 2022). All districts are required to implement instruction and supervision strategies, ranging from specific curricula and/or reading programs, focused professional development, and coaching or supervision, with half of these practices required for licensure or renewal (Education Commission of the States, 2023). Research on past reading mandates has found that these exacerbate the existing gaps between Black and Latino students and their white counterparts (Campano et al., 2013; Dee & Jacob, 2010). While these states' policies will impact all their teachers and supervisors, there are calls for "special" oversight by supervisors in those schools and classrooms considered "underperforming" and often comprised of mostly students of color. In this example and others, teacher labor and instructional supervision is standardized and surveilled with teachers' and supervisors' primary directive to "follow orders" and a mandated curriculum. In addition, much like the plantation, labor and work are regimented and instructional supervision becomes hierarchical, surveilled, and racialized.

Discipline

On the plantation, discipline or violence was often meted out based on productivity, rule adherence, and hierarchical arrangements (Littlefield, 2023). Bringing laborers "back in line" intersected with violence and other disciplinary measures designed to temper any potential uprising or disobedience and to bring about plantation "reform" (Fanon, 1961). "Slave codes dictated life on the plantation through restriction of movement, education, behavior, and also dictated behavior" on the plantation (Squire et al., 2018, p. 11). The codes translated into inhumane conditions and labor that characterized the "mundane terror of plantation life" (McKittrick, 2013, p. 9). Under each of the examples mentioned throughout this chapter have been unique documentation and surveilling requirements that have outcomes for students and teachers of color: For example, since COVID-19, students, especially Black and Brown students, have continued to suffer neo-reforms that ignore the realities that existed before the pandemic (Dron et al., 2021; Hassan & Daniel, 2020; Horsford et al., 2021). Post-pandemic curriculum, instruction, and supervision focus on "sorting [students and teachers, addition mine] and intervening without necessarily considering the context, policies, and histories that have created inequit[ies]" (Carter & Mcintee, 2021, p. 8).

Instructional supervision is still used for employment, development, promotion, tenure, or termination (Conrad & Hackmann, 2022; Fusarelli & Fusarelli, 2018; Gordon & McGhee, 2019). Instructional supervision and TES continue to incentivize based on school outcomes, which may create a racialized caste system whereby teachers of color are impacted (Irvine, 1988; Lynch, 2018; Williams, 2018). Teachers of color are disproportionately represented in high-needs schools that serve a large proportion of poor and minority students (Ingersoll et al., 2019; Mabokela & Madsen, 2005; Sun, 2018; Villegas & Lucas, 2004). These same teachers and schools more keenly experience the negative effects of plantation traditions that inform accountability or reforms that are often touted as "politically and racially neutral, progressive, beneficial, and inherently good" (Cook & Dixson, 2013, p. 1251). Teachers and schools are still judged on their ability to close the racial "achievement gap" that has resulted from state and district strategic plans based on anxiety. This creates a racialized discipline at the root of contemporary corporatized education reforms. Once again, the functions of instructional supervision are tightly tied to curriculum, assessment/testing, professional development, and students' outcomes. The processes again produce a racialized approach to curriculum, pedagogy, instruction, and outcomes and produce plantation-like foci that impact the "hiring, firing, and rewarding, and punishing" (English & Steffy, 2001, p. 289) of teachers and administrators.

FROM E/RACING TO RACE-ING INSTRUCTIONAL SUPERVISION

Historically, instructional supervision often downplays, ignores, or even denies the salience of race and racism (Farley et al., 2021). Exploring the plantation traditions of instructional supervision is more than just a provocative exercise or one that simply bemoans supervision as e/rasure. As a field, instructional supervision is still mining all the ways in which evolving concepts and practices of supervision have harmed and prevented the advancement of education and equity, particularly for students, teachers, and supervisors of color (Arnold, 2016; Garrett et al., 2001; Gordon & Espinoza, 2020; Guerra et al., 2022; McGhee & Stark, 2021; Theoharis & Haddix, 2011). Unpacking the plantation helps us further name and identify some of its normalized workings and neo-accountability, whose outcome is often deleterious for those of color. The plantation helps us reflect and respond to supervision's continued participation in and reproduction of inequitable racialized system. However, unpacking modern-day plantation traditions in educational challenges creates mere surface restructuring and overhauls in favor of equitable responses within schools (Douglas et al., 2015; Witherspoon, 2010). As such, the field must look more closely at the development of CRIS paradigms and practices.

McKittrick (2011) describes the concepts of "plantation futures" as sites of agency and resistance. It is important to hope (Garman, 2020) about the possibilities of instructional leadership in countering the racist logic of the plantation and thus advancing equity in education. Scholars of supervision are continuing to advance notions of CRIS frameworks for equity, justice, and anti-racism (Green, 2017; Ishimaru, 2020, Jacobs & Casciola, 2016; Marshall & Khalifa, 2018; Lee, 2011; Mette et al., 2023; Welton & Freelon, 2018). A future outlook for CRIS would benefit from racial equity-focused practices that emphasize structural, pedagogical, curricular, and procedural changes to ameliorate disparities for instructional feedback practices in schools. However, instructional leaders must be trained, supervised and supported in practices that address structural and systemic inequities that impact students. Leaders devoted to equity create sustained strategies and supports for racial equity that are not satisfied with school accountability outcomes alone. In educational literature, equity-related issues are largely attached to cause-and-effect relationships or treated as accountability-based outcomes, which are often only a portion of the equity story (Sleeter & Banks, 2007).

Parts of the equity story include the process and outcomes of equity (Roegman et al., 2020). This includes the creative and often subversive ways individuals and groups and the people who lead them find to work around systems to achieve equity (Khalifa et al., 2016; Witherspoon & Taylor, 2010), which can and should be addressed through various forms of CRIS practices. Another means includes correct problem identification through the analysis of historical and existing oppressions that serve as foundations of inequity (Green, 2015, 2017). Still others include interrogating existing structures of promoting and measuring in/equity that may be inadvertently grounded in deficit models that blame individuals or groups for their inequity (Green, 2017).

The following sections highlight concepts for an emerging approach for race-ing instructional supervision as an important foundation to the development of CRIS, based on a current study about the race-neutral and colorblind policies across 12 states' TES systems, and how those TES systems mediate instructional and supervisory practice, for racial equity (Arnold et al., in progress-a). An encouraging trend highlights how some districts are able to "tweak" instruction and supervision to meet their unique goals, including those related to racial equity. These 10 districts inform our concept of *race-ing instructional supervision* (Figure 3.1) by exploring the ways race "colors" the supervision process and experience, but also is put into a practice that sees, considers, and responds to race as agentic practice. In these districts, when not constrained by state legislative bans, teachers and supervisors have sought to institute anti-racist or race-conscious policies, practices, and curriculum, as well as the procedures that determine the composition and assignment of supervisor and teaching personnel. The authors have identified three thematic

Figure 3.1. Race-ing Instructional Leadership: An Emerging Approach

[Diagram: Central circle labeled "Race-ing Instructional Leadership" surrounded by four nodes: "Race-ing Development and Assesment" (top), "Race-ing Knowledge and Learning" (right), "Race-ing Supervisory Operations" (bottom), "Race-ing Supervisory Context" (left), with circular arrows connecting them.]

domains for creating sustained instructional and supervisory strategies and supports for racial justice equity and improvement. The domains bridge theories related to racial equity, but also practices—key skills for leaders in organizations and actionable domains for designing targeted interventions and strategies. These also serve as leadership domains for racial equity, for which participants will gain understandings and skills to effect change in each area.

Race-ing Knowledge and Learning

Race-responsive instructional supervisors must be able to focus on knowledge building as, and coming to a deeper understanding of, the interactive process of questioning, dialogue, and continuing improvement of instructional practices related to racial equity. We must develop greater understandings of the historical realities that have wrought racial inequities and those that redress and ameliorate negative outcomes (Gorski, 2017). This must occur through feedback about instruction that is observed in the classroom. This involves both organizational learning (and unlearning) of strategies and practices that have been harmful in the organization. Specific actions might include

- Providing teachers and supervisors with ample training, support, and time to develop racial and cultural competence and ability to lead and sustain change for equity;
- Creating racial equity plans that specifically include collaborative CRIS plans to address racial inequity; and
- Teaching and supervising using philosophies and methods that respect, value, and use positively the strengths and assets of the students based on their race, culture, contexts, language, and other sociocultural identities.

Race-ing Supervisory Operations

Race-responsive instructional supervisors must also be able to focus on re/framing operations, practices, and policies from traditional plantation practices of accountability and reform, to make racial equity the driver for teaching and supervision. In addition, there should be a focus on pervasiveness of racial equity across the organization and steps to achieve lasting changes to culture and climate. This dimension focuses on supervisors understanding and re/framing the diverse operational contexts of the organization, while building new complex and dynamic processes, procedures, and programs. Specific actions might include:

- Preparing and supporting supervisors to evaluate interventions that address the root causes of inequities,
- Preparing and supporting supervisors to improve how the principal supports teachers to use culturally responsive practices and monitor classrooms to ensure they are applied in all classrooms, and,
- Preparing and supporting supervisors in creating adjacent supervision processes (Arnold et al., in progress-b) such as wise feedback (Newton, 2021; Yeager, 2014), well-being-focused supervision (Arnold et al., in progress-b); and context-based approaches to instructional leadership (Arnold, 2018a).

Race-ing Development and Assessment

The third dimension of the development of CRIS includes assessing and evaluating readiness, progress, and outcomes at various points in the racial equity improvement process. In this process, there is focused critique that considers potential uses of evaluation and assessment, and the intended outcomes of programs. The intended goal is to set racial equity as a part of the "continuous improvement process of systems—from class to a school district or even a network of many districts—to set goals, identify ways to improve, and evaluate change" (Sparks, 2018, p. 19). Specific actions might include:

- Preparing and supporting supervisors to review students' surveys to discover whether classroom practices are inclusive and how the principal gathers feedback to inform instruction; and,

- Preparing and supporting supervisors to conduct interviews with historically marginalized students and families on instruction and supervision that consider race.

Race-ing Supervisory Context

In a race-responsive supervisory relationship, there is recognition of the power differential in the relationship and the mediation of that power. The supervisor should consider how each person's racial background, including students', might provide a strength focus in formal or informal supervisory processes. Early and recurring discussion of supervisor and supervisee expectations and orientation of how to best use supervision makes the supervision process a contextual one that considers the teacher and the students served. This also considers racialized influences on perceptions of power throughout the supervision process. Specific actions might include:

- Preparing and supporting supervisors to recognize and mediate the unequal power relationship present in supervision. Preparing and supporting supervisors to share responsibility, connection, and caring in teacher goals and that centers race responsive pedagogies.

These examples are but a few examples in response to student and school diversity (Swalwell, 2011). Through this work, districts can attempt to create race-responsive learning and CRIS practices that tease out systemic and systematic roots, causes and perpetuations of racial inequity and counter the deleterious effects of plantation traditions. In many ways, these emerging practices highlight a resistance of the teachers, educators, and students, redefining the plantation of neo-accountability to potentially become a system that is transformative and racially relevant for those who are more vulnerable.

SUMMARY

Race-ing instructional leadership is one of many emerging ideas toward more humanizing, responsive, and critical approaches to the development of CRIS. Interrogating plantation traditions that inform the ecology of supervision "encourages new methodologies, epistemologies, and methods of dissemination, while highlighting the importance of history [and] context" (Hook, 2023, p. 105). While "to return to the plantation, in the present, can potentially invite unsettling and contradictory analyses" (McKittrick, 2013, p. 9), the development of CRIS allows us to resist any plantation traditions that reproduce or resist inequity prevalent in our U.S. society (Dei & Calliste, 2000). Even more specifically, understanding the "othered" nature of supervision highlights the fact that instructional supervision is not race- or discourse-neutral but rather serves to "enslave" certain individuals and groups in racialized representations, roles, contracts, hierarchies and other hegemonic processes.

Another question in considering plantation futures is to ask, "Can the plantation be instructive in our quest for culturally responsive instructional supervision?" Brand's (2013) concept of *inventory* asks us to consider practices in which we are not mere consumers of "transparent enumeration but rather engage in cooperative human efforts and turn the practice of accounting for the brutalities of our world" (McKittrick, p. 14). In other words, how do we move beyond the plantation practice of counting/measuring student, instructor and even supervisor metrics to one that reimagines the supervisory process? Wynter (1971) argues that the "plot" of plantations is "the central narrative of the plantation novel that contextualizes its economic superstructure while developing a creative space to challenge this system" (McKittrick, 2013, 10). These plots are critical sites of opposition against, and break away from, the larger plantation structure, which should include a rejection of plantation practice. This calls for clear approaches and frames for instructional supervision that move beyond espoused philosophies of supervision alone to enacted ones that address research, preparation and training of supervisors, teachers, and even students in a dignity-honoring ecology of supervision.

As Chrobot-Mason, Gerbasi, and Cullen-Lester (2016) indicated, "In many organizations, leadership increasingly looks less like a hierarchy of authority. Instead, it is better understood as a network of influence relationships in which multiple people participate, blurring the distinction between leader and follower" (p. 298). A culturally responsive facet of supervision calls for the traditional role of the leader as a lone enforcer of curriculum to change to that of a collective of school citizens taking action on behalf of students. To be culturally responsive, it is no longer tenable for the leader to hold the position as the "superior" of the supervisory process. Instead, supervision is both "claimed and granted" (Chrobot-Mason et al., 2016, p. 298) by all in the supervisory ecology.

Another facet is advancing the interests of teachers and students in a supervisory process that is not leader-serving but creates advantage. Supervisors are most effective when they pursue purposes toward developing the collective good and ameliorating inequities (Nordentoft et al., 2013). When the supervision ecology is non-threatening and non-violent, the culturally responsive supervision process creates advantages for all involved. This is an anti-plantation approach whereby race and difference are assets and levers rather than plantation fixes. Plantations have traditionally been sites of mistrust and disconnection to individual and collective well-being. The supervision ecology should inspire, provide agency, engagement, institutional support, and citizenship in the organization (Russell & Slater, 2011).

The race-responsive supervisor values the relationship with the teacher and thus models this behavior so that it may be transferred from teacher to students. In this sense, the supervisor works to counter the plantation practices of supervision to create a school environment that affords dignity for both teachers and students. Dignity is an essential human condition, yet there are continued concerns about education where people experience multiple assaults to their sense of dignity. A race-responsive approach to supervision offers a counter to the plantation practice of race as deficit model that ignores, minimizes, or erases in education (Dei, 1996). Indeed, this approach can empower and support students and teachers, pursue justice, reduce oppression and marginalization, and foster human dignity, all of which are anti-plantation practices.

REFERENCES

Albert Shanker Institute. (2015). *The state of teacher diversity in American education.* Retrieved December 1, 2023, from http://www.shankerinstitute.org/sites/shanker/files/The%20State%20Teacher%20Diversity%20Exec%20Summary_0.pdf

Alexander, T., Clark, T. B., Reinhard, K., & Zatz, N. (2023). *CRT forward: Tracking the attack on critical race theory.* UCLA School of Law. https://crtforward.law.ucla.edu/wp-content/uploads/2023/04/UCLA-Law_CRT-Report_Final.pdf

Allen, R. L., & Liou, D. D. (2019). Managing whiteness: The call for educational leadership to breach the contractual expectations of white supremacy. *Urban Education, 54*(5), 677–705.

Anderson, J. D. (1988). *The education of Blacks in the South, 1860–1935.* University of North Carolina Press.

Anyon, J. (2005). A political economy of race, urban education, and educational policy. In W. Crichlow (Ed.), *Race, Identity, and Representation in education* (pp. 369–378). Taylor and Francis.

Apple, M., & Aasen, P. (2003). *The state and the politics of knowledge.* Routledge.

Arnold, N. W. (2021, February 9). *Confounding crises: Covid-19 and the challenge for inclusive leadership.* Keynote address at Graduate Representative Advisory Board (GRAB) Research Symposium, Texas A & M University.

Arnold, N. W. (2016). Cultural competencies and supervision. In J. Glanz & S. J. Zepeda (Eds.), *Supervision: New perspectives for theory and practice*, (pp. 201–220). Rowman & Littlefield.

Arnold, N. (2018a). Supervisory identity: Cultural shift, critical pedagogy, and the crisis of supervision. In S. J. Zepeda & J. A. Ponticell (Eds.), *The Wiley handbook of educational supervision* (pp. 575–600). Wiley.

Arnold, N. W. (2018b, December). *School/community-based health clinics.* Crane Center Lecture, Ohio State University, Columbus, OH.

Arnold, N. W., McMillian, R. & Morrow, L. (in progress-a). *Content analysis of 12 states' teacher evaluation systems (TES).* Manuscript in preparation.

Arnold, N. W., Penn, C., & McMillian, R. (in progress-b). *Racing instructional supervision: Dimensions of racial equity.* Manuscript in preparation.

Bartanen, B., & Grissom, J. A. (2023). School principal race, teacher racial diversity, and student achievement. Journal of Human Resources, *58*(2), 666–712.

Bates, L. A. (2015). Surplus and access: *Provisioning and market participation by enslaved laborers on Jamaican sugar estates.* University of Pennsylvania.

Beckert, S. (2005). From Tuskegee to Togo: The problem of freedom in the empire of cotton. *The Journal of American History*, 92(2), 498–526.
Beckford, G. L. (2000). *The George Beckford papers*. Canoe Press, University of the West Indies.
Beckford, G. L. (1999). *Persistent poverty: Underdevelopment in plantation economies of the third world*. University of West Indies Press.
Bencherab, A., & Al Maskari, A. (2020). Clinical supervision: A genius tool for teachers' professional growth. *The Universal Academic Research Journal*, 3(2), 51–57.
Boatcă, M. (2017). The centrality of race to inequality in the world-system. *Journal of World-Systems Research*, 23(2), 1–8.
Boser, U. (2014). *Teacher diversity revisited: A new state-by-state analysis*. Center for American Progress.
Brand, D. (2013). *Inventory*. McClelland & Stewart.
Bristol, L. (2012). *Plantation pedagogy: A postcolonial and global perspective*. Peter Lang.
Bristol, T. J., & Martin-Fernandez, J. (2019). The added value of Latinx and Black teachers for Latinx and Black students: Implications for policy. *Policy Insights from the Behavioral and Brain Sciences*, 6(2), 147–153.
Brock, J. D., Beach, D. M., Musselwhite, M., & Holder, I. (2021). Instructional Supervision and the COVID-19 Pandemic: Perspectives from Principals. *Journal of Educational Research and Practice*, 11(1), 168–180.
Brouillette, L. (1997). Revisiting an innovative high school: What happens when the principal leaves? *Educational Administration Quarterly*, 33(1), 546–575.
Brown, C., Schildkamp, K., & Hubers, M. D. (2017). Combining the best of two worlds: A conceptual proposal for evidence-informed school improvement. *Educational Research*, 59(2), 154–172.
Browne, S. (2015). *Dark matters: On the surveillance of blackness*. Duke University Press.
Campano, G., Ghiso, M. P., & Sanchez, L. (2013). "Nobody knows the . . . amount of a person": Elementary students critiquing dehumanization through organic critical literacies. *Research in the Teaching of English*, 18(1), 98–125.
Carter, C., & Mcintee, K. (2021). Pausing for answerability: a critical investigation of U.S. assessment and accountability decisions amidst the COVID-19 pandemic. *Beijing International Review of Education*, 3(2), 234–267.
Carter Andrews, D. J., Castro, E., Cho, C. L., Petchauer, E., Richmond, G., & Floden, R. (2019). Changing the narrative on diversifying the teaching workforce: A look at historical and contemporary factors that inform recruitment and retention of teachers of color. *Journal of Teacher Education*, 70(1), 6–12.
Chambers, T. V., Huggins, K. S., Locke, L. A., & Fowler, R. M. (2014). Between a "ROC" and a school place: The role of racial opportunity cost in the educational experiences of academically successful students of color. *Educational Studies*, 50(5), 464–497.
Cheng, A., Hitt, C., Kisida, B., & Mills, J. N. (2017). "No excuses" charter schools: A meta-analysis of the experimental evidence on student achievement. *Journal of School Choice*, 11(2), 209–238.
Chrobot-Mason, D., Gerbasi, A., & Cullen-Lester, K. L. (2016). Predicting leadership relationships: The importance of collective identity. *Leadership Quarterly*, 27(2), 298–311. http://doi.org/10.1016/j.leaqua.2016.02.003
Clayton, J. K. (2011). Changing diversity in U.S. schools: The impact on elementary student performance and achievement. *Education and Urban Society*, 43(6), 671–695.

Cohen, D. K., Spillane, J. P., & Peurach, D. J. (2018). The dilemmas of educational reform. *Educational Researcher, 47*(3), 204–212.

Conrad, D. L., & Hackmann, D. G. (2022). Implications of Illinois teacher evaluation reforms: insights from principals. *Leadership and Policy in Schools, 21*(3), 565–584.

Cook, D. A., & Dixson, A. D. (2013). Writing critical race theory and method: A composite counterstory on the experiences of Black teachers in New Orleans post-Katrina. *International Journal of Qualitative Studies in Education, 26*(10), 1238–1258.

Corbin, B., McNamara, O., & Williams, J. (2003). Numeracy coordinators: 'Brokering' change within and between communities of practice. *British Journal of Educational Studies 51*, 344–368.

Cornelius, J. (1983). "We slipped and learned to read": Slave accounts of the literacy process, 1830-1865. *Phylon, 44*(3), 171–186.

Cuban, L. (1990). A fundamental puzzle of school reform. In A. Lieberman (Ed.), *Schools as collaborative cultures: Creating the future now* (pp. 71–77). The Falmer Press.

Dancy, T. E., Edwards, K. T., & Earl Davis, J. (2018). Historically white universities and plantation politics: Anti-Blackness and higher education in the Black Lives Matter era. *Urban Education, 53*(2), 176–195.

Davis, C. (2016). *The panoptic plantation model: geographical analysis and landscape at Betty's Hope Plantation, Antigua, West Indies*.

Davis, B. W., Gooden, M. A., & Micheaux, D. J. (2015). Color-blind leadership: A critical race theory analysis of the ISLLC and ELCC standards. *Educational Administration Quarterly, 51*, 335–371.

Dee, T., & Jacob, B. (2010). Evaluating NCLB: Accountability has produced substantial gains in math skills but not in reading. *Education Next, 10*(3), 54–62.

Dei, G. (1996). *Anti-racism education: Theory and practice.* Fernwood Publishing.

Dei, G. J. S., & Calliste, A. (2000). Introduction. In G. J. S. Dei & A. Calliste (Eds.), *Power, knowledge and anti-racism education: A critical reader* (pp. 11–22). Fernwood Publishing.

Delle, J. A. (2002) Power and landscape: Spatial dynamics in early nineteenth-century Jamaica. In: M. O'Donovan (Ed.,) *The dynamics of power* (pp. 341–361). Center for Archaeological Investigations, Southern Illinois University.

Diem, S., Welton, A. D., Frankenberg, E., & Holme, J. J. (2016). Racial diversity in the suburbs: How race-neutral responses to demographic change perpetuate inequity in suburban school districts. *Race, Ethnicity and Education, 19*, 731–762.

Donnor, J. K. (2021). The last plantation: Toward a new understanding of the relationship between race, major college sports, and American higher education. In M. Lynn & A. Dixson (Eds.), *Handbook of critical race theory in education* (2nd ed.) (pp. 166–178). Routledge.

Dorn, E., Hancock, B., Sarakatsannis, J., & Viruleg, E. (2021). *COVID-19 and education: The lingering effects of unfinished learning.* McKinsey & Company.

Douglas. T. M. O., & Witherspoon Arnold, N., & Wilbon-White, T. (2015). Crises, critical incidents and community and educational leadership. In M. Khalifa, Witherspoon Arnold, N., A. Osanloo, & C. Grant (Eds.), *Handbook of urban educational leadership* (pp. 546–557). Lanham, MD: Rowman & Littlefield.

Dumas, M. J. (2014). 'Losing an arm': Schooling as a site of black suffering. *Race Ethnicity and Education, 17*(1), 1–29.

Easton-Brooks, D. (2019). *Ethnic matching: Academic success of students of color.* Rowman & Littlefield.

Easton-Brooks, D. (2021). Ethnic-matching in urban schools. In H. R. Milner IV & K. Lomotey (Eds.), *Handbook of urban education* (2nd ed., pp. 234–252). Routledge.

Edmonds, R. (1979). Effective schools for the urban poor. *Educational leadership*, 37(1), 15–24.

Education Commission of the States (ECS) *State education policy tracking*. Retrieved May 19 2023, from https://www.ecs.org/state-education-policy-tracking/

Edwards, T., & Tomlinson, S. (2002). *Selection isn't working: Diversity, standards and equality in secondary education*. Catalyst Publications.

Egalite, A. J., Kisida, B., & Winters, M. A. (2015). Representation in the classroom: The effect of own-race teachers on student achievement. *Economics of Education Review*, 45, 44–52.

English, F. W., & Steffy, B. E. (2001). Deep curriculum alignment: Creating a level playing field for all children on high-stakes tests of educational accountability. Scarecrow Press.

Epperson, T. W. (2000). Panoptic plantations: The garden sights of Thomas Jefferson and George Mason. In S. A. Mrozowski, J. A. Delle, & R. Paynter (Eds.), *Lines that divide: Historical archeologies of race, class and gender* (pp. 58–5). University of Tennessee Press.

Evans, R. (2021). Geomemory and genre friction: Infrastructural Violence and plantation afterlives in contemporary African American novels. *American Literature*, 93(3), 445–472.

Fanon, F. (1961). *The wretched of the earth*. Grove Press.

Farley, A. N., Leonardi, B., & Donnor, J. K. (2021). Perpetuating inequalities: The role of political distraction in education policy. *Educational Policy*, 35(2), 163–179.

Feagin, J. (2013). *Systemic racism: A theory of oppression*. Routledge.

Foucault, M. (1977). *Discipline and punish: The birth of the prison*. Vintage.

Frazier-Anderson, P. N. (2008). Public schooling in post–Hurricane Katrina New Orleans: Are charter schools the solution or part of the problem? *The Journal of African American History*, 93(3), 410–429.

Fusarelli, L. D., & Fusarelli, B. C. (2018). Instructional supervision in an era of high-stakes accountability. In S. J. Zepeda & J. A. Ponticell (Eds.), *The Wiley handbook of educational supervision* (pp. 131–156). John Wiley & Sons.

Gage, N. A., Whitford, D. K., Katsiyannis, A., Adams, S., & Jasper, A. (2019). National analysis of the disciplinary exclusion of black students with and without disabilities. *Journal of Child and Family Studies*, 28, 1754–1764.

Ganon-Shilon, S., Finkelstein, I., Sela-Shayovitz, R., & Schechter, C. (2022). Inclusive leadership in times of COVID-19 crisis: The role of district and school leaders in fostering school sense-making processes within a national inclusion and integration reform. *Leadership and Policy in Schools*, 1–21.

Garman, N. (2020). The dream of clinical supervision, critical perspectives on the state of supervision, and our long-lived accountability nightmare. *Journal of Educational Supervision*, 3(3), 7.

Garrett, M. T., Borders, L. D., Crutchfield, L. B., Torres-Rivera, E., Brotherton, D., & Curtis, R. (2001). Multicultural supervision: A paradigm of cultural responsiveness for supervisors. *Journal of Multicultural Counseling and Development*, 29(2), 147–158.

Gershenson, S., Holt, S. B., & Papageorge, N. W. (2016). Who believes in me? The effect of student–teacher demographic match on teacher expectations. *Economics of Education Review*, 52, 209–224.

Glanz, J. (1991). *Bureaucracy and professionalism: The evolution of public school supervision*. Fairleigh Dickinson University Press.

Glanz, J. (1998). Histories, antecedents, and legacies: Constructing a history of school supervision. In J. Firth & E. Pajak, (Eds.), *Handbook of research on school supervision* (pp. 39–79). Macmillan.

Glanz, J. (2018). Chronicling perspectives about the state of instructional supervision by eight prominent scholars of supervision. *Journal of Educational Supervision, 1*(1), 1.

Glanz, J., Shulman, V., & Sullivan, S. (2007, April). Impact of instructional supervision on student achievement: Can we make the connection? [paper presentation]. American Educational Research Association, Chicago, IL.

Glickman, C., & Mette, I. M. (2020). *The essential renewal of America's schools: A Leadership guide for democratizing schools from the inside out*. Teachers College Press.

Goldenberg, B. M. (2014). White teachers in urban classrooms: Embracing non-white students' cultural capital for better teaching and learning. *Urban Education, 49*(1), 111–144.

Gordon, S. P. (1997). Has the field of supervision evolved to a point that it should be called something else? In J. Glanz & R. F. Neville (Eds.), *Educational supervision: Perspectives, issues, and controversies* (pp. 114–123). Christopher-Gordon.

Gordon, S. P., & Espinoza, S. (2020). Instructional supervision for culturally responsive teaching. *Educational Considerations, 45*(3), 7.

Gordon, S. P., & McGhee, M. W. (2019). The power of formative evaluation of teaching. Differentiated teacher evaluation and professional learning: Policies and practices for promoting career growth. In M. L. Derrington & J. Brandon (Eds.), *Differentiated teacher evaluation and professional learning* (pp. 15–35). Springer.

Gorski, P. C. (2017). *Reaching and teaching students in poverty: Strategies for erasing the opportunity gap*. Teachers College Press.

Green, T. L. (2015). Leading for urban school reform and community development. *Educational Administration Quarterly, 51*(5), 679–711.

Green, T. L. (2017). Community-based equity audits: A practical approach for educational leaders to support equitable community-school improvements. *Educational Administration Quarterly, 53*(1), 3–39. https://doi.org/10.1177/0013161X16672513

Grissom, J. A., & Redding, C. (2016). Discretion and disproportionality: Explaining the underrepresentation of high-achieving students of color in gifted programs. *AERA Open, 2*(1), 1–25.

Gross, S. J. (1998). *Staying centered: Curriculum leadership in turbulent times*. Association for Supervision and Curriculum Development.

Guerra, P. L., Baker, A. M., & Cotman, A. M. (2022). Instructional supervision: Is it culturally responsive? A textbook analysis. *Journal of Educational Supervision, 5*(1), 1–26.

Hallett, T. (2010). The myth incarnate: Recoupling processes, turmoil, and inhabited institutions in an urban elementary school. *American Sociological Review, 75*(1), 52–74.

Hallinger, P., & Wang, W. C. (Eds.). (2015). *Assessing instructional leadership with the principal instructional management rating scale*. Springer.

Haraway, D. (2015). Anthropocene, capitalocene, plantationocene, chthulucene: Making kin. *Environmental Humanities, 6*(1), 159–165.

Haraway, D., Endy, D., & Lejeune, L. (2019). Tools for multispecies futures. *Journal of Design Science, 1*, 1–22.

Hassan, S., & Daniel, B. J. (2020). During a pandemic, the digital divide, racism and social class collide: The implications of COVID-19 for Black students in high schools. *Child & Youth Services, 41*(3), 253–255.

Hazi, H. M. (2020). On instructional improvement: A modest essay. *Journal of Educational Supervision, 3*(3), 90.

Henry, K. L., Jr. (2021). Zones of nonbeing: Abjection, white accumulation, and neoliberal school reform. *Teachers College Record, 123*(14), 129–149.

Henry, K. L., Jr., & Dixson, A. D. (2016). "Locking the door before we got the keys": Racial realities of the charter school authorization process in post-Katrina New Orleans. *Educational Policy, 30*(1), 218–240.

Hesse, B. (2007). Racialized modernity: An analytics of white mythologies. *Ethnic and Racial Studies, 30*(4), 643–663.

Hightower, A. M., Delgado, R. C., Lloyd, S. C., Wittenstein, R., Sellers, K., & Swanson, C. B. (2011). *Improving student learning by supporting quality teaching* Editorial Projects in Education. https://epe.brightspotcdn.com/96/bd/c7ea3e084ade93466ae02042ba7d/eperc-qualityteaching-12.11.pdf.

Holquist, S. E., & Walls, J. (2021). "Not present in our ranks": Exploring equitable representation in student voice efforts for policy change. *Teachers College Record, 123*(8), 3–30.

Hook, T. (2023). Schooling as plantation: Racial capitalism and plantation legacies in corporatized education reform in Liberia. *Comparative Education Review, 67*(S1), S89–S109.

Horsford, S. D., Cabral, L., Touloukian, C., Parks, S., Smith, P. A., McGhee, C., Qadir, F., Lester, D., & Jacobs, J. (2021). *Black education in the wake of COVID-19 and systemic racism*. Black Education Research Collective, Teachers College, Columbia University. https://www.tc.columbia.edu/black-education-research-collective/research/

Hull, R. D. (2013). *Principal perceptions of school capacity to meet requirements of No Child Left Behind* [Unpublished doctoral dissertation]. Texas A&M University.

Hung, M., Smith, W. A., Voss, M. W., Franklin, J. D., Gu, Y., & Bounsanga, J. (2020). Exploring student achievement gaps in school districts across the United States. *Education and Urban Society, 52*(2), 175–193.

Ingersoll, R. M., May, H., & Collins, G. (2019). Recruitment, employment, retention and the minority teacher shortage. *Education Policy Analysis Archives, 27*(37), 1–38. http://dx.doi.org/10.14507/epaa.27.3714

Irizarry, J. (2015). *Latinization of U.S. schools: Successful teaching and learning in shifting cultural contexts*. Routledge.

Irvine, J. J. (1988). An analysis of the problem of disappearing Black educators. *The Elementary School Journal, 88*(5), 503–513.

Ishimaru, A. M. (2020). *Just schools: Building equitable collaborations with families and communities*. Teachers College Press.

Jacobs, J., & Casciola, V. (2016). Supervision for social justice. In J. Glanz & S. J. Zepeda (Eds.), *Supervision: New perspectives for theory and practice* (pp. 221–240). Rowman & Littlefield.

Jefferson, N. R., & Smith-Peterson, M. (2021). The physics of power: Stories of panopticism at two levels of the school system. *Theory, Research, and Action in Urban Education, 6*(1), 27–37.

Jenlink, P. M., & Townes, F. H. (Eds.). (2009). *The struggle for identity in today's schools: Cultural recognition in a time of increasing diversity*. R&L Education.

Jennings, M. E., Noblit, G. W., Brayboy, B., & Cozart, S. (2007). Accountability and abdication: School reform and urban school districts in the era of accountability. *Educational Foundations, 21*, 27–38.

Kafka, J., & Wilson, A. (2023). Interest Convergence and market-based school reform: The promise and limits of using controlled choice to desegregate schools. *The Urban Review, 55*, 505–533.

Keegan, C. (2021). "Black workers matter": Black labor geographies and uneven redevelopment in post-Katrina New Orleans. *Urban Geography, 42*(3), 340–359.

Khalifa, M., Douglas, T. M. O., & Venzant-Chambers, T. (2016). White gazes of Black Detroit: Milliken v. Bradley, post-colonial theory, and why inequities persist. *Teachers College Record, 118*(3), 1–34.

Kozol, J. (2012). *Savage inequalities: Children in America's schools*. Crown.

Ladson-Billings, G. (2004). Landing on the wrong note: The price we paid for Brown. *Educational Researcher, 33*(7), 3–13.

Ladson-Billings, G. (2006). From the achievement gap to education debt: Understanding achievement in U.S. Schools. *Educational Researcher, 35*(7), 3–12.

Ladson-Billings, G. (2013). "Stakes is high": Educating new century students. *The Journal of Negro Education, 82*(2), 105–110.

Lance, T. (2021). Chasing down the educational debt by centering race in educational supervision. *Journal of Educational Supervision, 4*(1). https://doi.org/10.31045/jes.4.1.2

Lee, Y. A. (2011). Self-study of cross-cultural supervision of teacher candidates for social justice. *Studying Teacher Education, 7*(01), 3–18.

Levitt, J. I., & Whitaker, M. C. (2009). *Hurricane Katrina: America's unnatural disaster*. University of Nebraska Press.

Lindsay, C. A., & Hart, C. M. (2017). Exposure to same-race teachers and student disciplinary outcomes for Black students in North Carolina. *Educational Evaluation and Policy Analysis, 39*(3), 485–510.

Littlefield, D. C. (n.d.) The varieties of slave labor. *Freedom's Story*, TeacherServe©. National Humanities Center. https://nationalhumanitiescenter.org/tserve/freedom/1609-1865/essays/slavelabor.htm

Lipman, P. (2004). *High stakes education: Inequality, globalization, and urban school reform*. Routledge.

Lipman, P. (2021a). Austerity politics, coercive neoliberal urbanism and the challenge of counter-hegemonic education movements. In J. M. Paraskeva (Ed.), *Critical transformative educational leadership and policy studies-A reader: Discussions and solutions from the leading voices in education.* (pp. 91–106). Myers Press.

Lipman, P. (2021b). *Free city!: The fight for San Francisco's City College and education for all.* PM Press.

Lipman, P., & Haines, N. (2007). From accountability to privatization and African American exclusion: Chicago's "Renaissance 2010." *Educational Policy, 21*(3), 471–502.

Loewen, J. W. (2008). *Lies my teacher told me: Everything your American history textbook got wrong.* The New Press.

Lopez, A. E., & Jean-Marie, G. (2021). Challenging anti-Black racism in everyday teaching, learning, and leading: From theory to practice. *Journal of School Leadership, 31*(1-2), 50–65.

Louis, K. S., Leithwood, K., Wahlstrom, K. L., & Anderson, S. E. (2010). *Investigating the links to improved student learning.* The Wallace Foundation.

Lynch, M. E. (2018). The hidden nature of whiteness in education: Creating active allies in white teachers. *Journal of Educational Supervision, 1*(1), 18–31.

Mabokela, R. O., & Madsen, J. A. (2005). 'Color-blind' and 'color-conscious' leadership: A case study of desegregated suburban schools in the USA. *International Journal of Leadership in Education*, 8(3), 187–206.

Macpherson, R. J. (1998). Accountability in city schools: Theory and practice in urban educational administration. *Education and Urban Society*, 30(4), 443–458.

Marshall, S. L., & Khalifa, M. A. (2018). Humanizing school communities: Culturally responsive leadership in the shaping of curriculum and instruction. *Journal of Educational Administration*.

McGhee, M. W., & Stark, M. D. (2021). Empowering teachers through instructional supervision: Using solution focused strategies in a leadership preparation program. *Journal of Educational Supervision*, 4(1), 43.

McKittrick, K. (2011). On plantations, prisons, and a black sense of place. *Social & Cultural Geography*, 12(8), 947–963.

McKittrick, K. (2013). Plantation futures. *Small Axe: A Caribbean Journal of Criticism*, 17(3 (42)), 1–15.

Mette, I. (2020). Reflections on supervision in the time of COVID-19. *Journal of Educational Supervision*, 3(3). https://doi.org/10.31045/jes.3.3.1

Mette, I. M., Cormier, D. R., & Oliveras-Ortiz, Y. (2023). Culturally responsive instructional supervision: (Re)Envisioning feedback for equitable change. In A. Lavigne & M. L. Derrington (Eds.), *Actionable feedback for PK–12 teachers* (pp. 75–87). Rowman & Littlefield.

Mette, I. M., Nieuwenhuizen, L., & Hvidston, D. J. (2016). Teachers' perceptions of culturally responsive pedagogy and the impact on leadership preparation: Lessons for future reform efforts. International Journal of Educational Leadership Preparation, 11(1).

Mette, I. M., & Riegel, L. (2018). Supervision, systems thinking, and the impact of American school reform efforts on instructional leadership. Journal of Cases in Educational Leadership, 21(4), 34–51.

Mills, C. W. (2002). The racial contract as methodology (not hypothesis). Philosophia Africana, 5(1), 75–100.

Milner, H. R., IV. (2012). Beyond a test score: Explaining opportunity gaps in educational practice. Journal of Black Studies, 43(6), 693–718. https://doi-org.tc.idm.oclc.org/10.1177/0021934712442539

Mitman, G. (2021). *Empire of rubber: Firestone's scramble for land and power in Liberia*. New Press.

Mitra, D. (2018). Student voice in secondary schools: The possibility for deeper change. *Journal of Educational Administration*, 56(5), 473–487.

Morgan, P. D. (2017). Task and gang systems: the organization of labor on New World plantations. In D. A. Pargas & F. Roşu (Eds.), *Critical readings on global slavery* (pp. 1263–1293). Brill.

Murphy, M. W., & Schroering, C. (2020). Refiguring the plantationocene: Racial capitalism, world-systems analysis, and global socioecological transformation. *Journal of World-Systems Research*, 26(2), 400–415.

Newton, M. (2021). Wise feedback. *Instructional Modules for Professional learning Responding to Opportunities and Valuing Educators (IMPROVE)*, 31. https://digitalcommons.gardner-webb.edu/improve/31/

Nielsen, C. R. (2011). Resistance is not futile: Frederick Douglass on panoptic plantations and the un-making of docile bodies and enslaved souls. *Philosophy and Literature*, 35(2), 251–268.

Nordentoft, H. M., Thomsen, R., & Wichmann-Hansen, G. (2013). Collective academic supervision: A model for participation and learning in higher education. *Higher Education, 65*(5), 581–593. https://doi.org/10.1007/s10734-012-9564-x

No Child Left Behind Act of 2001 (2002). P.L. 107–110.

Oakes, J., Maier, A., & Daniel, J. (2017). Community Schools: An Evidence-Based Strategy for Equitable School Improvement. National Education Policy Center. Retrieved May 13, 2023 from http://nepc.colorado.edu/publication/equitable-community-schools

Omi, M., & Winant, H. (2014). *Racial formation in the United States.* Routledge.

Orfield, G., & Eaton, S. E. (1996). *Dismantling desegregation. The quiet reversal of* Brown v. Board of Education. The New Press.

Page, T. G. (2019). Beyond attribution: Building new measures to explain the reputation threat posed by crisis. *Public Relations Review, 45*(1), 138–152.

Patton, L. D., & Davis, S. (2014). Expanding transition theory: African American students' multiple transitions following Hurricane Katrina. *Journal of College Admission, 22,* 6–15.

Payne, C. M. (2008). *So much reform, so little change: The persistence of failure in urban schools.* Harvard Education Press.

Pierre, J. (2020). The racial vernaculars of development: A view from West Africa. *American Anthropologist, 122*(1), 86–98.

Purifoy, D. M. (2021). The plantation town: Race, resources, and the making of place. In M. Himley, E. Havice, & G. Valdiva (Eds.), *The Routledge handbook of critical resource geography* (pp. 114–125). Routledge.

Roegman, R. (2020). Central office foci and principal data use: A comparative study of equity-focused practice in six districts. *Education Policy Analysis Archives, 28*(181), n181.

Ross, D. J., & Cozzens, J. A. (2016). The principalship: Essential core competencies for instructional leadership and its impact on school climate. *Journal of Education and Training Studies, 4*(9), 162–176.

Russell, B., & Slater, G. (2011). Factors that encourage student engagement: Insights from a case study of 'first time' students in a New Zealand university. *Journal of University Teaching & Learning Practice, 8*(1), 1–15. http://ro.uow.edu.au/jutlp/vol8/iss1/7/

Sandy, L. (2012). Supervisors of Small Worlds: The role of overseers on colonial South Carolina slave plantations. *Journal of Early American History, 2*(2), 178–210.

Saultz, A., Schneider, J., & McGovern, K. (2019). Why ESSA has been reform without repair. *Phi Delta Kappan, 101*(2), 18–21.

Schaeffer, K. (2021. December 10). *America's public school teachers are far less racially and ethnically diverse than their students.* PEW Research Center. https://www.pewresearch.org/short-reads/2021/12/10/americas-public-school-teachers-are-far-less-racially-and-ethnically-diverse-than-their-students/

Schwartz, Sarah. (2022, July 20). Which states have passed 'science of reading' laws? What's in them? *Education Week.* https://www.edweek.org/teaching-learning/which-states-have-passed-science-of-reading-laws-whats-in-them/2022/07

Sharpe, C. E. (2016). *In the wake: On blackness and being.* Duke University Press.

Simpson, R. L., Lacava, P. G., & Sampson Graner, P. (2004). The no child left behind act: Challenges and implications for educators. *Intervention in School and Clinic, 40*(2), 67–75.

Skerritt, C. (2020). School autonomy and the surveillance of teachers. *International Journal of Leadership in Education*, 1–28.

Sleeter, C. E., & Banks, J. A. (2007). *Facing accountability in education: Democracy and equity at risk*. Teachers College Press.

Smyth, W. J. (Ed.). (1984). *Case studies in clinical supervision*. UNSW Press.

Spiegelman, M. (2020). *Race and ethnicity of public school teachers and their students* [Data point, NCES 2020–103]. National Center for Education Statistics.

Spring, J. (2011). *The politics of American education*. Routledge.

Sofia, M. K. (Host). (2020, June 5). Coronavirus and racism are dual public health emergencies [Audio podcast episode]. In *Shortwave*. NPR. https://www.npr.org/2020/06/04/870025677/coronavirus-and-racism-are-dual-public-healthemergencies

Squire, D., Williams, B. C., & Tuitt, F. (2018). Plantation politics and neoliberal racism in higher education: A framework for reconstructing anti-racist institutions. *Teachers College Record*, *120*(14), 1–20.

Sriprakash, A., Nally, D., Myers, K., & Pinto, P. R. (2020). *Learning with the past: Racism, education, and reparative futures*. UNESCO.

Sun, M. (2018). Black teachers' retention and transfer patterns in North Carolina: How do patterns vary by teacher effectiveness, subject, and school conditions? *AERA Open*, *4*(3), 1–23.

Swalwell, K. (2011). *Why our students need "equity literacy."* Teaching Tolerance. http://www.tolerance.org/blog/why-our-students-need-equity-literacy

Taie, S., & Lewis, L. (2022). *Characteristics of 2020–21 public and private K–12 school teachers in the United States: Results from the National Teacher and Principal Survey*. National Center for Education Statistics. U. S. Department of Education.

Tesfaw, T. A., & Hofman, R. H. (2014). Relationship between instructional supervision and professional development. *International Education Journal: Comparative Perspectives*, *13*(1), 82–99.

Theoharis, G., & Haddix, M. (2011). Undermining racism and a whiteness ideology: White principals living a commitment to equitable and excellent schools. *Urban Education*, *46*(6), 1332–1351.

Tomich, D. (2011). Rethinking the plantation: Concepts and histories. *Review Fernand Braudel Center*, *34*(1/2), 15–39.

Townsend, T., Acker-Hocevar, M., Ballenger, J., & Place, A. W. (2013). Voices from the field: What have we learned about instructional leadership? *Leadership and Policy in Schools*, *12*(1), 12–40.

Trujillo, T. (2013). The reincarnation of the effective schools research: Rethinking the literature on district effectiveness. *Journal of Educational Administration*, *51*(4), 426–452.

Turner, C. S. V., Myers, S. L., Jr., & Creswell, J. W. (1999). Exploring underrepresentation: The case of faculty of color in the Midwest. *The Journal of Higher Education*, *70*(1), 27–59.

Turner, D. (2020). Globalisation and neo-liberal higher education reforms. In J. Zajda (Ed.), *Globalisation, ideology and neo-liberal higher education reforms* (pp. 141–149). Springer.

Villegas, A. M., & Lucas, T. F. (2004). Diversifying the teacher workforce: A retrospective and prospective analysis. *Teachers College Record*, *106*(13), 70–104.

Vintimilla, C. D., & Pacini-Ketchabaw, V. (2020). Weaving pedagogy in early childhood education: On openings and their foreclosure. *European Early Childhood Education Research Journal*, *28*(5), 628–641.

Waite, D. (1997). Power and teacher-administrator discourse. In R. Wodak & D. Corson (Eds.), *Encyclopedia of language and education: Language policy and political issues in education* (pp. 43–52). Springer.

Welton, A. D., & Freelon, R. (2018). Community organizing as educational leadership: Lessons from Chicago on the politics of racial justice. *Journal of Research on Leadership Education, 13*(1), 79–104.

Williams, T. M. (2018). When will we listen and heed?: Learning from black teachers to understand the urgent need for change. *Western Journal of Black Studies, 42*(1), 3–17.

Wisevoter. (2023). *States that have banned critical race theory*. Retrieved December 1, 2023, from https://wisevoter.com/state-rankings/states-that-have-banned-critical-race-theory/

Witherspoon, N. (2010, February). *Leading after the Levees: Perspectives on disaster, crisis, and educational leadership*. College of Education Research Roundtable, Louisiana State University.

Witherspoon Arnold, N. (2014). *Ordinary theologies: Religio-spirituality and the leadership of Black female principals*. Peter Lang.

Witherspoon Arnold, N., Douglas. T. M. O., & Wilbon-White, T. (2015). Crises, critical incidents and community and educational leadership. In M. Khalifa, N. Witherspoon Arnold, A. F. Osanloo, & C. M. Grant, *Handbook of urban educational leadership* (pp. 546–557). Rowman & Littlefield.

Witherspoon, N., & Taylor, D. L. (2010). Spiritual weapons: Black female principals and religio-spirituality. *Journal of Educational Administration and History, 42*(2), 133–158.

Wolford, W. (2021). The Plantationocene: A Lusotropical contribution to the theory. *Annals of the American Association of Geographers, 111*(6), 1622–1639.

Woods, C. (2017). *Development drowned and reborn: The blues and bourbon restorations in post-Katrina New Orleans*. University of Georgia Press.

World Population Review. (2023). *Critical race theory ban states 2024*. Retrieved December 15, 2023, from https://worldpopulationreview.com/state-rankings/critical-race-theory-ban-states

Wynter, S. (1971). Novel and history, plot and plantation. *Savacou, 5*(1), 95–102.

Yeager, D. S., Purdie-Vaughns, V., Garcia, J., Apfel, N., Brzustoski, P., Master, A., Hesert, W. T., Williams, M. E., & Cohen, G. L. (2014). Breaking the cycle of mistrust: Wise interventions to provide critical feedback across the racial divide. *Journal of Experimental Psychology: General, 143*(2), 804.

Ylimaki, R. M. (2007). Instructional leadership in challenging US schools. *International Studies in Educational Administration (Commonwealth Council for Educational Administration & Management (CCEAM)), 35*(3), 11–19.

Zepeda, S. J. (2014). *Job-embedded professional development: Support, collaboration, and learning in schools*. Routledge.

Zepeda, S. J., & Ponticell, J. A. (2018). Introduction. In S. J. Zepeda & J. A. Ponticell (Eds.), *The Wiley handbook of educational supervision* (pp. 1–14). Wiley.

CHAPTER 4

Toward a Praxis Orientation for Teacher Candidate Supervision

Megan Lynch and Rebecca West Burns

It would not be hyperbole to declare that public education in the United States is in an extremely volatile state. And perhaps this has been the case since its inception. There is a real danger in looking backward and expecting to find an unblemished, faultless version of the public education system to reproduce today. That simply does not exist. Both historically and today, schools "structurally produce and perpetuate inequity, poverty, and cultures of apathy while pretending to be designed to do the opposite" (Milner, 2010, p. 27). Structures such as instructional supervision—a developmental process, or function, aimed at supporting teacher learning to improve student learning (Glickman et al., 2018; Nolan & Hoover, 2011; Sergiovanni & Starratt, 2007)—are intended to address such inequities, yet they have fallen short of that goal.

For those responsible for instructional supervision and invested in improving PK–12 public education, our efforts would be better served examining the current material conditions of schooling in the United States, identifying the "ideal" (i.e., a more just system), and asking ourselves what we can do to enact concrete substantial change. This requires instructional supervision and teacher candidate supervision, a developmental process aimed at supporting preservice teachers' learning (Burns et al., 2016), to develop a social justice lens (Jacobs & Casciola, 2016) to not only foster "greater equity and justice for ALL students in the classroom" (p. 221) but also recognize that teacher candidate supervision is influenced/shaped by the political, historical, sociocultural, and economic systems that shape and are shaped by PK–12 schools and institutions of higher education and therefore can be a space for transformational *praxis* (Freire, 2005) for liberating and humanizing ways of being.

Teacher candidate supervision is well-positioned to undertake this responsibility, as it is "the act of supporting teacher candidates' growth and development in becoming equity-minded and equity-driven in their practice while they are learning to teach in their clinical experiences" (Jacobs & Burns, 2021, p. 314). It is "the missing link between calls for social justice and actualizing changes for students in schools" (Jacobs & Casciola, 2016, p. 234).

Students in PK–12 U.S. schools are owed an educational debt (Ladson-Billings, 2006) due to a long-standing opportunity gap (Milner, 2012) in how students of color and students living in poverty are treated. Indeed, Irvine (2010) highlights gaps in education that have amassed such an overwhelming educational debt, gaps in teacher quality and professional learning, high-quality curriculum, school funding, wealth, housing, employment, healthcare and nutrition, and more. Indeed, with these gaps, "Disadvantage, like privilege, comes from a complex network of mutually reinforcing economic and educational mechanisms that only can be dealt with through a multifaceted economic and educational policy response" (Powell, 2013, p. 13). At the same time, at a more micro-level, teachers and teacher candidates can teach students in ways that are validating and affirming, inclusive, multidimensional, empowering, transformative, emancipatory, humanistic, and ethical (Gay, 2018), yet teachers must learn how to skillfully enact these humanizing, culturally pedagogies.

For teacher candidate supervision to have such an impact on PK–12 students and schooling, it must be disentangled from its current conceptualization as a workflow detached from the world outside of the classroom, and as a stepwise cyclical process of observation and feedback. Thus, in this chapter, we intend to bring the literature on teacher candidate supervision into the conversation with a praxis orientation that values the dialectical unity of practice and theory, to bring about changes in the social conditions of schooling.

SITUATING SUPERVISION WITHIN THE STRUCTURES OF INSTITUTIONS OF HIGHER EDUCATION

Preparing teachers should include increased clinical experiences, and, thus, be a joint endeavor between schools and universities, where both entities have vested interest and input (American Association of Colleges for Teacher Education [AACTE], 2018; National Association for Professional Development Schools [NAPDS] 2021; National Council for the Accreditation of Teacher Education [NCATE], 2010). Thus, clinical experiences need to be "well-supervised" since clinical aspects are the "holy grail" of teacher preparation (Darling-Hammond, 2014). Teacher candidate supervision, then, stands to be the keystone to preparing the next generation of teachers who can be equity-centered in their approach to teaching (Burns & Lynch, forthcoming; Jacobs & Burns, 2021). And while teacher candidate supervision should be a boundary-spanning endeavor with shared decision-making and input among both PK–12 schools and universities, it currently resides primarily within institutions of higher education (IHEs). By that we mean IHEs serve as the governing body for supervision and assume responsibility for the accreditation of their teacher preparation programs, which require some aspect of teacher candidate supervision. Therefore, teacher candidate supervision is impacted by and at the mercy of the larger systems and structures that supervision is a part of, including IHEs, state departments of education, state and local government, and national accreditation bodies for higher education and educator preparation.

For example, in the state of Florida, Florida Statute section 1004.04 (5)(a) (2022) requires university supervisors to have the following: "specialized training in clinical supervision; at least 3 years of successful, relevant PK–12 teaching, student services, or school administration experience; and an annual demonstration of experience in a relevant PK–12 school setting as defined by State Board of Education rule." This statute goes back as far as 2013 when there were multiple options for meeting state requirements to serve as a university supervisor. Interestingly, language embedded in the policies, like those requiring "three years of successful, relevant PK-12 teaching" can be traced as far back as a 1968 position paper titled *The College Supervisor: Standards for Selection and Function* published by the Association for Student Teaching's Commission on Standards for Supervising Teachers and College Supervisors, which is now known as the Association of Teacher Educators. One of the 12 qualifications listed in the position paper was that the university supervisor "presents evidence of having had at least three years of successful teaching experience at the level he [sic] is to supervise" (p. 7). The example in Florida is a manifestation of the ways in which IHEs are influenced by the political systems and other governing organizations that IHEs are a part of.

In the United States, the dominant political system is a neoliberal capitalist system. Neoliberalism (see Block, 2018; Harvey, 2020) has shaped our social world in "class-based, class-organized, and class-functional" ways (Ratner, 2015, p. 66). Neoliberal policies promote limitless growth and the accumulation of wealth and capital by any means necessary. These policies also promote the idea that "human well-being can best be advanced by liberating individual entrepreneurial freedoms and skills" (Harvey, 2005, p. 2). Neoliberalism has had powerful influence at both the macro level of structures and processes in IHEs and at the micro level of the individuals and practices within IHEs. Neoliberal ideologies have shifted the notion from the belief that education is for the public good and a healthy democracy, to one of education as a business. As such, schools and IHEs must do more with less to maximize profits, thus cutting costs while simultaneously increasing growth through recruitment and enrollment. This has also led to an isolated, siloed workforce akin to the oppressive factory assembly line model of work. In the sections that follow, we show the ways in which neoliberal ideologies have led to teacher candidate supervision being an under-resourced, undervalued, deskilled, and marginalized profession.

THE MARGINALIZED STATUS OF SUPERVISION AND OF INDIVIDUALS WHO SUPERVISE IN TEACHER PREPARATION

Teacher candidate supervision suffers from the oppressive positioning of what Nolan (2022) termed "nested marginalization," meaning that the layers of bias against supervision run deep and are systemic. IHEs themselves are part of interconnected webs of state and local policies, accreditation requirements, and university governance. So while there are state guidelines on what qualifications supervisors should have, IHEs have their own guidelines and policies, processes, and practices they subscribe to for who in the IHE is hired to enact teacher candidate supervision. Individuals who supervise may be in various formalized roles in teacher preparation programs. The best-known role has been that of university supervisor, but with the turn toward clinically based teacher education, the roles of those who supervise, and the nature of what teacher candidate supervision looks and sounds like, are changing (Burns et al., 2016). In a meta synthesis of the empirical literature, Burns and Baker (2016) found 14 different terms for individuals in roles that performed the function of supervision, such as clinical educator, clinical faculty, boundary spanner, hybrid teacher educator, liaison, professor-in-residence, and reassigned teacher. Teacher candidate supervision is also becoming more expansive, to include partnering with schools to ensure they are places where teachers can learn to teach (Burns et al., 2016). And, even though the literature is clear that clinical experiences are the most important aspect of teacher preparation (Cuenca, 2012; Darling-Hammond, 2014; Wideen et al., 1998; Wilson et al., 2001), teacher candidate supervision and those individuals who supervise remain marginalized, undervalued, under-resourced, and underutilized aspects of teacher preparation.

IHEs have historically marginalized supervision (Beck & Kosnik, 2002; Capello, 2022; Feiman-Nemser, 2001; The Holmes Group, 1986; Hoover et al., 1988; Nolan, 2022; Soder & Sirotnik, 1990). They have institutional barriers that perpetuate what scholars refer to as "the marginalization of supervision cycle" (Butler et al., 2023). This cycle begins with the fact that there is less consideration of supervision practice and scholarship in IHEs, which leads to a general lack of support, structures, and resources for supervision. This deficit of support creates malpractices in supervision, which perpetuates the status quo and, therefore, contributes to less consideration of supervision, while the cycle continues. This cycle is perpetuated because many faculty and educational leaders are unfamiliar with supervision conceptually, perceiving it as merely a technical activity (Butler et al., 2023) rather than as a robust scholarly field with a significant, extensive, and longitudinal knowledge base dating back hundreds of years (McIntyre & McIntyre, 2020). One reason for this ignorance could be that much of the work of those who supervise is invisible (Cuenca et al., 2011; Niemi & Bozack, 2022) and, therefore, "considered an aside to campus-based teacher education" (Cuenca et al., 2011, p. 1069). Another reason is connected to gender, given that many who supervise are (cis)women (Niemi & Bozack, 2022; Nolan, 2022). When invisibility is coupled with gendered cultural expectations of the professions, which is especially prevalent in education, supervision is viewed, many times unconsciously, as women's work (Capello, 2022), not nearly as important as other disciplines or activities on campus (Cuenca et al., 2011). As Niemi and Bozack (2022) state, "Supervisors are women with deep experience crossing the boundaries of higher education and public school: needed in both, fully wanted in neither."

Such misperceptions perpetuate the marginalization of supervision because those in positions of power give the practice and scholarship of supervision less consideration than other disciplines in colleges of education (Butler et al., 2023; Cuenca et al., 2011). This disrespect leads to a lack of support, inadequate structures, and minimal resources for supervision, which become visible through several malpractices of supervision in IHEs. One malpractice is relying predominantly on transient populations like doctoral students (Zeichner & Paige, 2008) or on others who are "outsourced labor" (Capello, 2022), like adjunct faculty (NCATE, 2010; Slick, 1998; Zeichner, 2005) because they cost significantly less than tenured or tenure-track faculty. Such individuals have little if any job security and are grossly underpaid (Niemi & Bozack, 2022). As a result, these individuals may be "minimally invested" in the programs (Zeichner, 2005).

Another malpractice lies in neglecting professional learning for those who are supervising. This has been a prevailing issue in teacher education dating back more than a quarter century (Burns et al., 2016; McIntyre & Byrd, 1998). Other malpractices include assigning impossibly high numbers of teacher candidates to one individual and discouraging tenure-earning faculty from supervising teacher candidates and working in and with schools (Butler et al., 2023). Thus, faculty invested in supervision must make a choice between earning tenure (Yendol-Hoppey et al., 2013; Yendol-Hoppey & Hoppey, 2018) or doing "service work" (Capello, 2022, p. 4). These malpractices reinforce the idea that supervision is an undervalued activity (Capello, 2022).

The Deskilled Nature of Teacher Candidate Supervision

Inseparable from the devaluing and marginalization of those who supervise teacher candidates is the deskilling and de-professionalization of the function of supervising teacher candidates. This is in large part because, in a neoliberal society, labor is constructed in relation to the value it produces. Organizations/businesses, IHEs included, calculate the concrete and abstract labor value of each employee to maximize commodity and capital profits. Thus, IHEs must balance—in the labor cost of teacher candidate supervision so that the quantity and quality of labor asked of supervisors cannot cost more to the IHE than the IHE deems it to be worth. This has resulted in an exploitation of supervisors' labor and teacher candidate supervision being forced to operate with the fewest resources possible and the least amount of labor required. When this occurs, teacher candidate supervision has a "preoccupation with *techniques, control* and with means-end criteria of *efficiency* and *effectiveness*" (Van Manen, 1977, as cited in Smyth, 1985, italics in original).

Teacher candidate supervisors are often required to execute compliance-oriented tasks—submitting forms and documentation of evidence of teacher candidate learning in checklist fashion. Largely because state evaluation and credentialing requirements are so extensive, they dominate supervisors' practices, leaving them little time or opportunity to engage in practices that actually support teacher candidate learning (Cuenca et al., 2022). State evaluation systems for teachers are often adapted for teacher candidates, which supervisors and mentor teachers are required to complete via a checklist or rubric with mostly quantitative data. Supervisors engage in variations of coaching cycles and the submission of documentation of a pre-conference discussion, observation notes, and post-observation feedback on university-created templates. The tasks supervisors are asked to engage in and methods for evaluating teacher candidates are often determined by the university and are usually an amalgamation of various interpretations of what national accreditation bodies require. In this way, the scope and skill set required for supervision becomes increasingly narrow. In Kolman's (2018) study of supervisory practices, he found that supervisors rarely went beyond the task of providing feedback on teacher candidates' lesson plans, and when supervisors mentioned providing more meaningful and varied support to teacher candidates, this information was not readily documented and "rarely described within the written feedback unless required by the template of the teacher preparation program" (Kolman, 2018, p. 283).

While teacher candidate supervisors are said to hold roles such as liaisons who represent the district, schools, and universities, coaches, mentors, and instructors (Soslau & Alexander, 2021), the role of the evaluator frequently takes prominence and conflates supervision and evaluation. Teacher candidate supervision does involve the formative assessment of teaching to determine the extent to which teacher candidates' practice is developing and supporting student learning (McIntyre et al., 2023). Yet teacher candidate supervision is distinct from teacher candidate evaluation, which is defined as "the process of making a summative determination about a teacher candidate's competence." That definition says that it encompasses "the teacher candidate's ability to handle all the roles and responsibilities of being a professional teacher" (Jacobs & Burns, 2021).

Understanding the distinctions between teacher candidate supervision and evaluation is imperative because when they are conflated in practice, the outcomes for teacher candidates are not good. Nolan and Hoover (2011) were the first to identify seven dimensions that distinguish teacher candidate supervision from evaluation. And while both evaluation and supervision are necessary, "when tasked with only producing evaluations, and positioned primarily as an evaluator, supervisors will likely continue the status quo, focusing on how teacher candidates are currently performing in areas they see as being within their locus of control (e.g., lesson planning)" (Kolman, 2018, p. 284). Without change, unjust systems will continue to operate as normal.

COUNTERNARRATIVES OF DESKILLED TEACHER CANDIDATE SUPERVISION

Contemporary scholars of teacher candidate supervision (see Cuenca, 2012; Buchanan, 2020; Burns et al., 2016; 2020; Capello, 2020, 2022; Diacopoulos &

Butler, 2020; Haberlin, 2020; Jacobs, 2014; Kolman, 2018; Lynch, 2021; Schroeder & Currin, 2019; Snow et al., 2020, Soslau & Alexander, 2021; Willey & Magee, 2018; Yeigh, 2020) represent a new wave of advocacy for the value and significance of supervision and its purpose in creating more equitable schooling conditions for all students. In response to what they recognize as the deskilling of teacher candidate supervision, through theory and practice, scholars have demonstrated what Sergiovanni (1982) described not as a "technique that mechanically specifies a series of steps through which supervisor and teacher must travel" but instead "a process, a way of life, a cultural structure within which one works with teachers," to produce more equitable and just outcomes (p. 69).

In this wave of scholarship, teacher candidate supervision holds a more significant purpose than providing targeted assistance and actionable feedback to students. In a meta-synthesis of the literature on teacher candidate supervision from 2001–2017, Burns et al. (2020) extracted the core practices of supervisors of teacher candidates and synthesized them into a framework that includes two supervisory tasks (collaboration & community and curricular & instructional support), eight high-leverage practices (four for each task), and 84 pedagogical routines of supervisory practice. Their framework achieves a balance of the historical, sociocultural, and political dimensions of the clinical context. In naming and categorizing the practices within teacher candidate supervision, Burns et al. (2016, 2020) counter the invisibility of clinical education for teacher education (Niemi & Bozack, 2022) and the nested marginalization of supervision (Nolan, 2022). Burns et al.'s (2020) framework emphasizes that teacher candidate supervision is a highly skilled profession that has a legitimate knowledge base and the potential for a powerful impact on educational systems.

For example, in one of Burns et al.'s (2020) high-leverage practices, *developing interpersonal familiarity*, a supervisor has to understand how people in a specific organization communicate in meetings, how humans socialize in meetings/conversation, how people develop relationships with one another, or how people determine the norms of communication. A pedagogical routine of practice for developing interpersonal familiarity is to begin meetings with community-building activities that foster social conversation. Thus, tsupervisors must be able to draw upon concepts/theories that help them select appropriate activities, facilitate the activity, and so on. The routines and practices the teacher candidate supervisor must enact and have the skill and knowledge to enact well highlight the depth and nuance of teacher candidate supervision.

Similarly, Burns and Lynch (in press) and Burns and Yendol-Hoppey (2016) articulate how supervision in professional development schools (PDS) and other school–university partnerships must extend beyond compliance and evaluation. Burns and Lynch (in press) highlight how an inquiry stance in teacher candidate supervision can be a keystone in creating and sustaining school–university partnerships. Burns and Yendol-Hoppey (2016) note five guiding principles in PDS supervision: (1) PDS supervision requires recognizing, respecting, and developing a complex set of knowledge and skills as well as a personal theory that include a lens of social justice; (2) unification is essential to PDS supervision; (3) PDS supervision is differentiated; (4) PDS supervision is enacted through community professional learning tasks; and (5) supervision in the PDS targets simultaneous renewal through shared professional learning and enhanced P–12 student learning. The guiding principles highlight not the individualized teaching and supervision of teacher candidates, but the larger impact of supervision on the school community and collective professional learning for P–12 learning.

In addition to naming and legitimizing the invisible and devalued "service work" of teacher candidate supervision, contemporary scholars have ushered in a wave of equity and justice dispositions into the field. In 2021, Jacobs and Burns expanded the definition of teacher candidate supervision beyond enacting particular practices, to defining it as "the function, or act, of supporting teacher candidates' growth and development in becoming equity-minded and equity-driven while they are learning to teach in their clinical experiences" (Jacobs & Burns, 2021). This was the result of an explicit turn toward equity that has highlighted specific supervisory practices that develop and support teacher candidates' beliefs and practices of culturally responsive, socially just, equity-oriented teaching (Lynch, 2021; Price-Dennis & Colmenares, 2021) and the role of supervision in developing social justice in teacher candidates (Jacobs & Casciola, 2016; Lynch, 2021). Focusing on equity has also highlighted supervisors' professional learning, to better support teacher candidates' asset orientations and advocacy skills in clinical settings that promote deficit orientations (Yeigh, 2020), and the interrogation of supervisors' own biases and identity (Lynch, 2018; Willey & Magee, 2018).

This wave of scholarship has also demonstrated how, when supervisors and faculty take collective action, structural changes to the nature of teacher candidate supervision is possible. Cuenca et al. 2011, for instance, contend that their creation of a third space for supervisors to remain connected to the teacher preparation program in light of university budget cuts, alienation, and additional constraints, demonstrated how these individuals were "not powerless to respond to broader political and financial challenges that threaten to undercut efforts to prepare highly qualified teachers" (p. 1076). In the constant "doing" of teacher candidate supervision, busyness has distracted supervisors from being able to address the neoliberal, efficiency demands in institutions of higher education. Neoliberal efficiency demands target supervisory load, enrollment figures, "outsourcing labor" to adjunct faculty, and constant recruitment initiatives.

Thus far we have described what teacher candidate supervision is, not what it *can* be. In the next section we ask the reader to consider how teacher candidate supervision, when put in the frame of the praxis (Freire, 2005; Marx 1845), can reciprocally lead to equitable outcomes for PK–12 students and dismantle the neoliberal structures that inhibit teacher candidate supervision from being a humanizing practice (Bartolomé, 1994; Salazar, 2013).

TEACHER CANDIDATE SUPERVISION AS PRAXIS

The counternarratives in contemporary research on teacher candidate supervision highlight a major contention raised for many decades in the larger field of instructional supervision, which is "whether supervision should be construed as a force for the preservation and maintenance of the status quo, or whether it should be an active force towards reform and change" (Smyth, 1985, p. 6). Further, Smyth (1985) reminds us that "[i]t has been convenient to label the *form* as having failed or as being unworkable, rather than looking in a critical fashion at the frustrating conditions and the nature of oppressive institutional arrangements" (p. 2, italics in original).

Questions that we might pose in taking a critical look to examine the contentious ways in which power, oppression, and hegemonic forces impact teacher candidate supervision may include:

- Who makes decisions about what teacher candidate supervision is/is not?
- How are supervisors positioned within hierarchical systems?
- What social, political, historical, and economic forces are impacting supervision?
- In what ways are PK–12 students impacted by teacher candidate supervision?
- What responsibility do those who engage in the function of teacher candidate supervision have to each other, the institutions they are partnering with, the students (PK–16) they teach and serve, and the greater communities and societies they are a part of?
- In what ways does teacher candidate supervision preserve and maintain the status quo? In what ways does it lead to reform and change?

These questions extend beyond supervising teacher candidates such that they develop dispositions of social justice, learn socially just pedagogies, and/or teach teacher candidates in culturally responsive ways. Moreover, teacher candidate supervision should not be limited only to learning within specific classrooms or school sites; it must extend beyond the classroom walls and lead to both lasting change and more equitable and just opportunities more broadly. As emphasized in this chapter and elsewhere (Burns & Lynch, forthcoming; Jacobs & Casciola, 2016), teacher candidate supervision can be conceptualized in ways that align with the critical theory construct of *praxis* (Freire, 2005), which recognizes the dialectical unity of theory and practice that changes both the actor/subject internally and the material conditions of the social world externally. To enact *praxis* is to enact revolutionary change as a "revolutionary transformation of society [. . .] necessary to change the material conditions (production, standard of living, economic opportunities), social relations, educational opportunities, and cognitive and other psychological capabilities" (Vygotsky, 1994). Indeed, praxis is in "the service of emancipatory efforts that uproot the tendency for schooling to reproduce bourgeois society and its class structure" (Roth, 2012, p.7).

When applied to teacher candidate supervision, *praxis,* a humanizing pedagogy, can be seen as a revolutionary approach to teacher candidate supervision that— through a process of *becoming*—engages teachers, teacher candidates, and students as active participants of the co-construction of knowledge through problem-posing education with the goal of developing a critical consciousness (Bartolomé, 1994; Freire, 2005). Problem-posing and a process of becoming is made possible through the dialectical relationship of reflection and action, theory and practice. Coupled with the concept of critical consciousness, or conscientização, as the ability to "learn to perceive social, political and economic contradictions, and taking action against the oppressive elements of reality" (Freire, 2005, p. 35), it is possible to see that supervisors of teacher candidates are able to make a significant transformation to the schooling systems they constitute and are constituted by.

Cochran-Smith and Lytle's (1999) concept, *inquiry as stance,* puts the idea of *praxis* in a conversation with teacher education and professional learning. They describe *inquiry as stance* as the embodiment and orientation of educators to continuously "investigate their own assumptions; [which] begins with identifying and critiquing one's own experiences, assumptions, and beliefs" (Cochran-Smith & Lytle, 1999, p. 279). Burns and Lynch (in press) argue that "to develop *inquiry as stance* is to develop an orientation and a position of knowledge-*of*-practice that grounds ourselves within the complex, political, social, and historical act of teaching in order to begin to pose questions and challenge normative practices within schooling."

What Is Needed to Enact Praxis-Oriented Teacher Candidate Supervision

The neoliberal systems and structures that shape clinical practice and are actively de-professionalizing and deskilling university supervisors can be shaped themselves. Through a dialectical approach to the relationship between the macro and micro, the collective and the individual, university supervisors have the opportunity to re-constitute the systems that are constraining them by de-professionalizing and alienating the field, as described in this chapter. Smyth writes, "For those of us involved in clinical supervision, the crucial question that needs to be addressed relates to what it means to be engaged in the process of clinical supervision and of the circumstances that permit and constrain it" (1985, p. 12).

To enact teacher candidate supervision as *praxis*, supervisors must:

(1) have a vision and ideal for the work of transforming unjust systems, schools, and institutions into more equitable ones,
(2) have access to professional learning through a knowledge-*of*-practice approach, and
(3) develop an *inquiry stance* that draws from critical pedagogies to enact systems level change.

A Vision for Transformation

To overcome the neoliberalized nature of teacher candidate supervision in its current state, supervisors must recognize the neoliberal ideologies that they are being constrained by, yet also simultaneously maintaining. This requires unlearning the harmful practices, and beliefs, and dispositions that are made to appear "natural." Practices that privilege competition, individual attainment, and hierarchical positioning (which all have a basis in neoliberal and Eurocentric ideologies) are commonplace in the classroom and without our being able to see how these neoliberal values are obfuscated as everyday common expectations, transformation will not be realized. Lynch (2021) shows how during a post-observation conference between a supervisor and a teacher candidate, the teacher candidate shifted in her understanding of a schoolwide practice that reflected competition, exploitation of workers, and class privilege. Lynch (2021) shows how with support from her supervisor, the teacher candidate was able to "recognize acts of injustice embedded in the underlying policies of schooling, link current school practices to the neoliberal political economy, examine who has power and privilege in what spaces, and imagine alternatives" (p. 96). While this was only an initial shift in thinking over a very short period of time, the teacher candidate's ability to critically reflect on a commonplace practice may not have been possible without the supervisor already having some understanding of obfuscated neoliberal ideologies and how they are manifested in the classroom.

In place of neoliberal ideologies, teacher candidate supervision should transform educational spaces to center liberation and humanity. Salazar (2013) shares five tenets that are fundamental in enacting a humanizing pedagogy: (1) the full development of the person is essential, (2) denying someone else's humanization is denying one's own, (3) humanization is an individual and collective act toward critical consciousness, (4) critical reflection and action can transform structures to facilitate liberation, and (5) educators are responsible for promoting a more fully human world through their principles and practices. In Lynch's (2021) analysis of her teacher candidate "imagining alternatives" to the neoliberal schoolwide practice, the teacher candidate suggested "an attendance policy that valued community over the individual in favor of community health being the goal and a rejection of reinforcing and rewarding unearned privilege" (p. 95). Community, care, and "being safe" were the teacher candidate's new ideal and placed at the center of their practice related to the schoolwide practice.

Professional Learning Through Knowledge-of-Practice

Developing the ability to recognize, unpack, and unlearn ideologies reflective of a neoliberal, capitalist political economic system requires a skill set and knowledge base that takes time to develop. Some ways in which supervisors of teacher candidates can develop this capacity are to engage in critical reflection, ask questions about their identity as a supervisor, participate in critical dialogue, and study critical frameworks and concepts (Jacobs & Casciola, 2016). As Jacobs and Casciola (2016) point out, this work must be incorporated into the supervisor's worldview and dispositions toward supervision and participation in greater society. Supervisors cannot be resistant to taking on a "social justice lens" (Jacobs & Casciola, 2016, p. 226).

Additionally, teacher candidate supervision can engage in knowledge-*of*-practice, which is the knowledge "generated when teachers treat their own classrooms and schools as sites for intentional investigation at the same time that they treat the knowledge and theory produced by others as generative material for interrogation and interpretation" (Cochran-Smith & Lytle, 1999, p. 250). Supervisors who embrace knowledge-*of*-practice are not only making a local impact on their own practice and the teacher candidates they work with, but a broader impact by disseminating their work with that of others (see Alexander, 2019; Cuenca et al., 2011; Diacopoulos & Butler, 2020; Haberlin, 2020; Lynch, 2021; Schroeder & Currin, 2019; Soslau, 2015). Engaging in self-study methodology (Butler, 2019; Loughran, 2007) and practitioner inquiry (Dana & Yendol-Hoppey, 2020) are two methods that teacher candidate supervisors can use to make intentional the theorizing and reflecting that they are already doing.

A knowledge-*of*-practice approach to professional learning provides the conduit for teacher candidate supervisors to link their theory and practice to the larger socio, political, historical, and economic policies that shape and are shaped by their work. Professional learning is a necessity for teacher candidate supervisors to develop the skills and dispositions needed to lead to transformation of not only supervision as a field, but also the inequitable structures, policies, and practices within PK–16 educational systems. (Kolman, 2018; Willey & Magee, 2018; Yeigh, 2020). In doing so, teacher candidate supervisors can help enact practices that allow teachers *and* students to discover more humanizing and liberatory ways of being and interacting with one another.

An Inquiry Stance to Enact Systems Level Change

As described above, an inquiry stance is an orientation towards dialectical reflection and action on one's own position, dispositions, and practices in the aim of broader transformation of schools and communities toward more egalitarian, democratic, and communal spaces. Teacher candidate supervisors must be able to "speculate about the possibilities for change" and "actively follow through this commitment to change" (Smyth, 1985, p. 12).

Supervisors of teacher candidates who have an inquiry stance continuously engage in problem-posing, challenging "everyday" and "natural" practices within their work and in schools. Having an inquiry stance requires "understanding, articulating, and ultimately altering practice and social relationships in order to bring about fundamental change in classrooms, schools, districts, programs, and professional organizations" (Cochran-Smith & Lytle, 1999, p. 279). The self is also actively involved in *praxis,* as we are all reifying the neoliberal ideologies that are creating inequitable schooling conditions and oppressing those who identify as being from minoritized groups. As such, an inquiry stance means that one assumes their knowledge, beliefs, and dispositions are problematizable (Cochran-Smith & Lytle, 1999) and they have a "preparedness to reflect upon one's own history and practice" (Smyth, 1985, p. 12).

Mobilizing, organizing, and partnering are all features of an inquiry stance and are required for systems' level change. When teacher candidate supervisors have *inquiry as stance*, they have agency. They ask questions that matter, and they form inquiry communities of teachers, teacher candidates, and other supervisors to investigate, research, and problematize their practices as well as institutionalized practices. *Inquiry as stance* takes the everyday theory-and-practice linkage that teacher candidate supervisors in clinical practice are expected to make for their teacher candidates and extends it beyond the every day to larger social and political issues, to policy, in an effort to form a more just society.

CONCLUSION

This chapter builds on Smyth's (1985) argument that supervision can and should be "an emancipatory or liberating process through which teachers assist each other to gain control over their own professional lives and destinies" (p. 12) and Jacobs and Casciola's (2016) argument that by incorporating a social justice lens into supervision, supervision can "move beyond just uncovering injustices within schools toward taking action or *praxis*" (p. 231). Teacher candidate supervisors are in unique positions to support school and university partners in developing a critical *praxis* that can overcome and transform institutional and societal inequalities to create the best possible learning opportunities for all students. This requires, however, disrupting the "divisions that keep teachers 'in their place'—the separation of practitioners from researchers, doers from thinkers, actors from analysts, and actions from ideas" (Cochran-Smith & Lytle, 1999, p. 289). As such, there is a great need to further develop how teacher candidate supervision framed as praxis and a critical pedagogy might be conceptualized and implemented to help transform the U.S. education system, which in turn will help create a more just and equitable U.S. society.

REFERENCES

Alexander, M. (2019). Pedagogy, practice, and mentorship: Core elements of connecting theory to practice in teacher educator preparation programs. *Journal of Educational Supervision, 2*(2), https://doi.org/10.31045/jes.2.2.6

American Association of Colleges of Teacher Education. (2018). *A pivot toward clinical practice, its lexicon, and the renewal of educator preparation: A report of the AACTE Clinical Practice Commission*. AACTE. https://aacte.org/2018/01/aacte-commission-issues-proclamations-for-effective-clinicaleducator-preparation/

Association for Student Teaching. (1968). *The college supervisor: Standards for selection and function*. Association for Student Teaching: Commission on Standards for Supervising Teachers and College Supervisors of the Association for Student Teaching.

Bartolomé, L. (1994). Beyond the methods fetish: Toward a humanizing pedagogy. *Harvard Educational Review, 64*(2), 173–195. https://www.doi.org/10.17763/haer.64.2.58q5m5744t325730

Beck, C., & Kosnik, C. (2002). Components of a good practicum placement: Pre-service teacher perceptions. *Teacher Education Quarterly, 29*, 81–98. http://www.teqjournal.org/backvols/2002/29_2/sp02beck_kosnick.pdf

Block, D. (2018). *Political economy and sociolinguistics: Neoliberalism, inequality, and social class*. Bloomsbury Academic.

Buchanan, R. (2020). An ecological framework for supervision in teacher education. *Journal of Educational Supervision, 3*(1), 76–94. https://doi.org/10.31045/jes.3.1.6

Burns, R. W., & Baker, W. (2016). The boundary spanner in professional development schools: In search of common nomenclature. *School-University Partnerships, 9*(2), 28–39.

Burns, R. W., & Lynch, M. E. (forthcoming). Teacher candidate supervision as praxis: The keystone to creating school-university partnerships for educational renewal. In J. Dresden, J. Ferrara, J. Neapolitan, & D. Yendol-Hoppey (Eds.) *Handbook on school-university partnerships*. Cambridge University Press.

Burns, R. W., Jacobs, J., & Yendol-Hoppey, D. (2016). The changing nature of the role of the university supervisor and the function of preservice teacher supervision in an era of increased school-university collaboration. *Action in Teacher Education, 38*(4), 410–425. https://doi.org/10.1080/01626620.2016.1226203

Burns, R. W., Jacobs, J., & Yendol-Hoppey, D. (2020). A framework for naming the scope and nature of teacher candidate supervision in clinically-based teacher preparation: Tasks, high-leverage practices, and pedagogical routines of practice. *The Teacher Educator, 55*(2), 214–238. https://doi.org/10.1080/08878730.2019.1682091

Butler, B. M. (2019). Self-study and preparing the next generation of teacher educators. In D. Yendol-Hoppey, D. T. Hoppey, & N. F. Dana (Eds.), *Preparing the next generation of teacher educators for clinical practice* (pp. 227–247). Information Age Publishing.

Butler, B. M., Burns, R. W., & Willey, C. (2023). Toward a renewal of supervisory scholarship and practice in teacher education: A collaborative self-study. *Journal of Educational Supervision, 6*(3), 47–68. https://doi.org/10.31045/jes.6.3.3

Capello, S. (2020). Tensions in the preparation of university supervisors: Dual perspectives from supervisors and administrators. *Journal of Educational Supervision, 3*(1), 18–35.

Capello, S. (2022). "I wanted to give back to the profession:" Preservice teacher supervision as service work. *Action in Teacher Education, 44*(1), 4–20. https://doi.org/10.1080/01626620.2021.1935362

Cochran-Smith, M. & Lytle, S. (1999). Relationships of knowledge and practice: Teacher learning in communities. *Review of Research in Education, 24*, 249–305. http://www.jstor.org/stable/1167272

Cuenca, A. (2012). *Supervising student teachers: Issues, perspectives and future directions*. Sense Publishers.

Cuenca, A., Zaker, J., & Dupell, M. (2022). High-stakes performance assessments and supervising student teachers: The increasingly complex roles of university supervisors. In R. W. Burns, L. Baecher, & J. McCorvey (Eds.), *Advancing supervision in clinically based teacher education: Advances, opportunities, and explorations*, (pp. 67–86). Information Age Publishing.

Cuenca, A., Schmeichel, M., Butler, B. M., Dinkelman, T., & Nichols Jr., J. R. (2011). Creating a "third space" in student teaching: Implications for the university supervisor's status as outsider. *Teaching and Teacher Education, 27*, 1068–1077. https://www.doi.org/10.1016/j.tate.2011.05.003

Dana, N. F., & Yendol-Hoppey, D. (2020). *The reflective educator's guide to classroom research: Learning to teach and teaching to learn through practitioner inquiry* (4th ed.). Corwin.

Darling-Hammond, L. (2014). Strengthening clinical preparation: The holy grail of teacher education. *Peabody Journal of Education, 89*, 547–561. https://doi.org/10.1080/0161956X.2014.939009

Diacopoulos, M. M., & Butler, B. M. (2020). What do we supervise for? A self-study of learning teacher candidate supervision. *Studying Teacher Education, 16*(1), 66–83. https://doi.org/10.1080/17425964.2019.1690985

Feiman-Nemser, S. (2001). Helping novices learn to teach: Lessons from an exemplary support teacher. *Journal of Teacher Education, 52*(1), 17–30. https://doi.org/10.1177/002248710105200100

Fla. Stat. § 1004.04 (5)(a) (2022). http://www.leg.state.fl.us/Statutes/index.cfm?App_mode=Display_Statute&Search_String=&URL=1000-1099/1004/Sections/1004.04.html

Freire, P. (2005). *Pedagogy of the oppressed*. (3rd ed.) The Continuum International Publishing Group.

Gay, G. (2018). *Culturally responsive teaching: Theory, research, and practice*. Teachers College Press.

Glickman, C. D., Gordon, S. P., & Ross-Gordon, J. M. (2018). *SuperVision and instructional leadership: A developmental approach*. Pearson.

Haberlin, S. (2020). Mindfulness-based supervision: Awakening to new possibilities. *Journal of Educational Supervision, 3*(3), 75–89. https://doi.org/10.31045/jes.3.3.6

Harvey, D. (2005). *A brief history of neoliberalism*. Oxford University Press.

Harvey, D. (2020). *The anti-capitalist chronicles*. Pluto Press.

The Holmes Group. (1986). *Tomorrow's teachers: A report of the Holmes Group*. The Holmes Group.

Hoover, N. L., O'Shea, L. J., & Carroll, R. G. (1988). The supervisor–intern relationship and effective interpersonal communication skills. *Journal of Teacher Education, 39*(2), 22–27.

Irvine, J. J. (2010). Foreword. In H. R. Milner (Ed.), *Culture, curriculum, and identity in education* (pp. xi–xvi). Palgrave Macmillan.

Jacobs, J. (2014). Fostering equitable school contexts: Bringing a social justice lens to field supervision. *Florida Association of Teacher Educators Journal, 1*(14), 1–16. http://www.fate1.org/journals/2014/Jacobs.pdf

Jacobs, J., & Burns, R. W. (2021). *(Re)Designing programs: A vision for equity-centered, clinically based teacher preparation*. Information Age Publishing.

Jacobs, J., & Casciola, V. (2016). Supervision for social justice. In J. Glanz & S. J. Zepeda (Eds.), *Supervision: New perspectives for theory and practice* (221–240). Rowman & Littlefield.

Kolman, J. S. (2018). Clinical supervision in teacher preparation: exploring the practices of university-affiliated supervisors. *Action in Teacher Education, 40*(3), 272–287. https://doi.org/10.1080/01626620.2018.1486748

Ladson-Billings, G. (2006). From the achievement gap to the education debt: Understanding achievement in U.S. schools. *Educational Researcher, 35*(7), 3–12. http://www.jstor.org/stable/3876731

Loughran, J. (2007). Research teacher education practices: Responding to the challenges, demands, and expectations of self-study. *Journal of Teacher Education, 58*(1), 12–20. https://www.doi.org/10.1177/0022487106296217

Lynch, M. E. (2018). The hidden nature of whiteness in education: Creating active allies in white teachers. *Journal of Educational Supervision, 1*(1), 18–31. https://doi.org.10.31045/jes.1.1.2

Lynch, M. E. (2021). Supervision to deepen teacher candidates' understanding of social justice: The role of responsive mediation in professional development schools. *Journal of Educational Supervision, 4*(2), 80–100. https://doi.org/10.31045/jes.4.2.5

Marx, K. (1845). *Theses On Feuerbach*. https://www.marxists.org/archive/marx/works/1845/theses/theses.htm

McIntyre, D. J., & Byrd, D. M. (1998). Supervision in teacher education. In G. R. Firth & E. F. Pajak (Eds.), *Handbook of research on school supervision* (pp. 409–427). Macmillan.

McIntyre, D. J., Byrd, D. M., & Burns, R. W. (2023). *Standards for clinical experiences: Promoting excellence in teacher preparation* (3rd ed.). Association of Teacher Educators.

McIntyre, D., & McIntyre, C. (2020). The evolution of clinical practice and supervision in the United States. *Journal of Educational Supervision, 3*(1), 5–17. https://doi.org/10.31045/jes.3.1.2

Milner, H. R., IV. (2010). *Start where you are, but don't stay there: Understanding diversity, opportunity gaps, and teaching in today's classrooms*. Harvard Education Press.

Milner, H. R., IV. (2012). Beyond a test score: Explaining opportunity gaps in educational practice. *Journal of Black Studies, 43*(6). 693–718. https:///www.doi.org/10.1177/0021934712442539

National Association for Professional Development Schools. (2021). *What it means to be a professional development school: The nine essentials* (2nd ed.) [Policy statement]. Author.

National Council for Accreditation of Teacher Education. (2010). *Transforming teacher education through clinical practice: A national strategy to prepare effective teachers*. Retrieved from http://caepnet.org/~/media/Files/caep/accreditation-resources/blue-ribbon-panel.pdf

Niemi, N. S. & Bozack, A. R. (2022). (In)Visibility, value, and the clinical educator. In R. W. Burns, L. Baecher, & J. K. McCorvey (Eds.), *Advancing supervision in clinically based teacher education: Advances, opportunities, and explorations* (pp. 19–46). Information Age Publishing.

Nolan, J. F., Jr., & Hoover, L. A. (2011). *Teacher supervision and evaluation: Theory into practice*. Wiley.

Nolan, J. F., Jr. (2022) Foreword. In R. W. Burns, L. Baecher, & J. K. McCorvey (Eds.), *Advancing supervision in clinically based teacher education: Advances, opportunities, and explorations* (pp. xi-xviii). Information Age Publishing.

Powell, J. A. (2013). Deepening our understanding of structural marginalization. *Poverty & Race 22*(5), 3–4, 13. Retrieved from https://belonging.berkeley.edu/sites/default/files/Sept-Oct%202013%20PRRAC%20Disparities%20Article.pdf

Price-Dennis, D., & Colmenares, E. (2021). Exploring the impact of field-based supervision practices in teaching for social justice. *Journal of Educational Supervision, 4*(2), 1–22. https://doi.org/10.31045/jes.4.2.1

Ratner, C. (2015). Classic and revisionist sociocultural theory, and their analyses of expressive language: An empirical and theoretical assessment. *Language and Sociocultural Theory, 2*(1), 51–83. Doi:10.1558/lst.v2i1.26988

Roth, W. (2012). Societal mediation of mathematical cognition and learning. *Orbis Scholae, 6*(2), 7–22. https://www.doi.org/10.14712/23363177.2015.37

Salazar, M. (2013). A humanizing pedagogy: Reinventing the principles and practice of education as a journal toward liberation, *Review of Research in Education, 37,* 121–148. https://www.doi.org/10/3102/00091732X12464032

Schroeder, S., & Currin, E. (2019). Syncing our cycles: An inquiry-based coaching model for distant supervision. *Journal of Practitioner Research, 4*(1), p. 1–19. https://doi.org/10.5038/2379-9951.4.1.1098

Sergiovanni, T. (1982). Toward a theory of supervisory practice: Integrating scientific, clinical, and artistic views. In Sergiovanni, T. (Ed.), *Supervision of teaching* (pp. 67–78). Association for Supervision and Curriculum Development.

Sergiovanni, T. J., & Starratt, R. J. (2007). *Supervision: A redefinition* (8th ed.) McGrawHill.

Slick, S. K. (1998). A university supervisor negotiates territory and status. *Journal of Teacher Education, 49*(4). https://doi.org/10.1177/0022487198049004008

Smyth, J. (1985). Developing a critical practice of clinical supervision. *Journal of Curriculum Studies, 17*(1), 1–15.

Snow, J., Carter, H., Dismuke, S. A., Larson, A., & Shebley, S. (2020). Scaffolding development of clinical supervisors: Learning to be a liaison. *Journal of Educational Supervision, 3*(1), 36–54. https://doi.org/10.31045/jes.3.1.4

Soder, R., & Sirotnik, K. A. (1990). Beyond reinventing the past: The politics of teacher education. In J. I. Goodlad, R. Soder, & K. A. Sirotnik (Eds.), *Places where teachers are taught* (pp. 385–411). Jossey-Bass.

Soslau, E. (2015). Development of a post-lesson observation conferencing protocol: Situated in theory, research, and practice. *Teaching and Teacher Education, 49,* 22–35. Doi:10.1016/j.tate.2015.02.012

Soslau, E., & Alexander, M. (2021). *The comprehensive guide to working with student teachers: Tools and templates to support reflective professional growth.* Teachers College Press.

Vygotsky, L. S. (2004). *Thought and language.* MIT Press. (Original work published 1986)

Wideen, M., Mayer-Smith, J., & Moon, B. (1998). A critical analysis of the research on learning to teach: Making the case for an ecological perspective on inquiry. *Review of Educational Research, 68*(2), 130–178. https://doi.org/10.3102/00346543068002130

Willey, C., & Magee, P. A. (2018). Whiteness as a barrier to becoming a culturally relevant teacher: Clinical experiences and the role of supervision. *Journal of Educational Supervision, 1*(2), 33–51. https://doi.org/10.31045/jes.1.2.3

Wilson, S. M., Floden, R. E., & Ferrini-Mundy, J. (2001). *Teacher preparation research: Current knowledge, gaps, and recommendations.* Center for the Study of Teaching and Policy.

Yeigh, M. J. (2020). Disrupting the deficit gaze: Equity work with university supervisors. *Journal of Educational Supervision, 3*(3). 43–58. https://doi.org/10.31045/jes.3.3.4

Yendol-Hoppey, D., Hoppey, D., Morewood, A., Hayes, S. B., & Graham, M. S. (2013). Micropolitical and identity challenges influencing new faculty participation in teacher education reform: When will we learn? *Teachers College Record, 115*(7), 1–31. https://doi.org/10.1177/01614681131150070

Yendol-Hoppey, D., & Hoppey, D. T. (2018). *Outcomes of high-quality clinical practice in teacher education*. Information Age Publishing.

Zeichner, K. (2005). Becoming a teacher educator: A personal perspective. *Teaching and Teacher Education, 21*, 117–124. https://www.doi.org/10.1016/j.tate.2004.12.001

Zeichner, K., & Paige, L. (2008). The current status and possible future for 'traditional' college and university-based teacher education programs in the United States. In T. Good (Ed.), *21st century education: A reference handbook, Vol. 2* (pp. 33–42). Sage.

CHAPTER 5

Rethinking Teacher Evaluation as Professional Development for Culturally Responsive Pedagogy

Helen M. Hazi

As today's schools in the United States face continuing cultural and political tensions in communities, a climate of fear of "the other" has resulted in community attempts to control an unprecedented number and variety of educational policies and practices that hearken back to the end of the Civil War. Books have been banned, parents want topics such as race and gender censored from the curriculum, and U.S. society increasingly expresses its distrust of teachers and schools (PDK, 2022). While such challenges to and controversies about the curriculum appear episodically, they are becoming embedded in various state laws due to the rise in federalism, and there is a fear they may soon be discussed at the national level in Congress (Mahnken, 2022).

The consequences of these Imposed state restrictions are real (Najarro, 2022). Teachers have been suspended or have lost their jobs, schools have been threatened with losing accreditation, and educators are deeply conflicted about discussing race, privilege, and discrimination perpetuated by U.S. society more broadly. Girls, Black students, and LGBTQA+ students have been targeted with dress code violations, and students have seen their parents notified every time they've checked out a book. From these forms of educational surveillance, educators are self-censoring topics to avoid punishment, and at the same time, schools are re-segregating (Walsh, 2022).

By the end of the 2022–2023 school year, 1,477 books had been banned in 32 states, concentrated in the states of Florida, Missouri, South Carolina, Texas, and Utah. Political conservatives, far-right Christian advocates and racist groups have backed school board candidates and filed complaints against public schools claiming, that they are usurping parental rights or promoting an evil agenda. Florida, the epicenter of much activity, has specifically restricted the teaching of topics in Black History and AP African American Studies about various resistance figures such as Frederick Douglass, Black Lives Matter, and reparations for the injustices of slavery. The state has also prohibited culturally responsive teaching among its practices that could result in what some of the U.S. public fears is "indoctrination" (e.g., Pendharkar, 2023). The U.S. Department's Office for Civil Rights, PEN America and other free speech advocacy groups have begun to challenge some of these laws, claiming First Amendment rights, discrimination, and hostile climate.

Republican lawmakers and former President Donald Trump, who made it acceptable to express hate, fueled a growing fear of race, gender orientation, and promoted the concept that there are privileged sociocultural identities that much of the U.S. public either does not understand or does not want to accept. Yet, despite (or because of) this climate, we are challenged to promote culturally responsive pedagogy that uses "the cultural knowledge, prior experiences, frames of reference, and performance styles of ethnically diverse students to make learning encounters more relevant to and effective for them" (Gay, 2018, p. 36). Such pedagogy teaches "the whole child," addresses cultural differences as assets, and differentiates different forms of instruction.

How should educators promote culturally responsive teaching? Not by mandate or coercion, but by rethinking teacher evaluation as a tool for teacher professional development. Teachers should be able to define culturally responsive teaching, co-create knowledge with their students, and self-evaluate their behavior with evidence to transform their teaching practice. Such a goal is by its nature participatory, collaborative, and democratic—yet it is also ambitious.

In this chapter I take the position that the existing structure of most teacher evaluation systems in the United States oppresses teachers in its definitions and decontextualizing of "good teaching," to objectify teachers and students and emphasize performativity through feedback to manage and control teachers. While changing teacher evaluation is problematic for many reasons, one can only hope to supplement—not supplant—it.

This is, indeed, ambitious and requires groundwork to be laid drawing from many discourses. To reveal the limitations of teacher evaluation, I draw from the discourses of evaluation, teacher evaluation, and feedback. To identify the conditions that can help foster culturally responsive pedagogy, I draw upon the discourses of culturally responsive pedagogy, teacher learning, teacher data use, and clinical supervision.

THE LIMITATIONS OF TEACHER EVALUATION IN THE UNITED STATES

After 2 decades of state activity and billions of dollars invested in complex and rigorous evaluation systems in the United States, a recent study shows that teacher evaluation had no discernible effect on student achievement in PK–12 schools (Bleiberg et al., 2021). Still, advocates for teacher quality remain hopeful that "teacher evaluation [reform], when well-implemented . . . is . . . possible" (Will, 2021, para 31) with more teacher buy-in and time to address the challenges of implementation. Such a belief is unwarranted, as teacher evaluation in the United States is far too flawed a practice to use in culturally responsive instructional supervision (CRIS); clearly, both the evaluation instruments and processes have grave limitations. These arguments are presented here in brief but explicated in greater depth elsewhere (e.g., Hazi, 2019, 2022). Broadly speaking, teacher evaluation is an annual, dysfunctional ritual that often results in fault-finding. It is a time-consuming chore for the principal and rarely helps a teacher improve.

The Instrument

Teacher evaluation instruments tend to be generic, contain definable items more suitable for skill-based subjects, promote a certain model of teaching, and omit items that have cultural and contextual relevance. Their developers view students who diverge from the model student as deficit-based, and in need of fixing. These limitations, related to instrument design, tend to exclude culturally responsive pedagogy from both the teacher's and observer's eyes.

As such, teacher evaluation instruments tend to be based on generic teaching behaviors (e.g., teacher praise, criticism, questioning, wait time, direction practices, and the use of advanced organizers). Originating in teacher effectiveness research, and consequently promoted in the school effectiveness movement, researchers traditionally wanted to identify those behaviors that correlate with increased student achievement. In doing so, these researchers simplified teaching, ignored the critical features of its context, and streamlined their research (e.g., no randomization of students) to identify general principles of instruction (Shulman, 1987). Then, in the 1980s, generic items were used in teacher evaluation instruments so that principals, who lacked content expertise, could have credibility when evaluating teachers and providing feedback about what constitutes "good" teaching (Ellett, 1987).

Due to this approach, teacher evaluation instruments tend to contain items from research at the elementary grades to teach skills such as reading and math. While they may be called an observation tool, most teacher evaluation instruments contain a limited number of in-classroom behaviors of teacher and students that are observable. Classroom management tends to be one example. The remaining items of these instruments (e.g., planning, collaboration with other teachers, and professional development) require knowledge of out-of-classroom behavior. Policymakers, who promoted statewide evaluation instruments, traditionally accepted process-product research findings as sufficient to define teaching standards, "while the researchers understood them to be simplified and incomplete" (Shulman, 1987, p. 6). In addition, those who designed instruments or select standards (e.g., Danielson) used their interpretation of effective teaching research and what they valued most in teaching. Herein lies the notion that positionality (race, gender, socioeconomic status, etc.) influence how identities shape perceptions and biases about the power applied through teacher evaluation models.

Given these realities, teacher evaluation instruments often promote a model of teaching that may differ from the teacher's own sociocultural identities. For example, Danielson's Framework for Teaching, a popular and widely used instrument, promotes a constructivist model of teaching. She contrasts it with the "traditional approach" with an example of teaching the mathematical concept of *pi*. Danielson portrays the traditional as superficial and outdated, while presenting the constructivist teacher as "innovative, current, producing high-achieving 'minds-on' students" because she presents deep, higher-level, and more powerful learning (Hazi, 2014, p. 6). To be rated "Distinguished," the highest rating, teachers must use constructivism, usually involving time-intensive group work, whether it is or is not appropriate for all lessons, subjects, students, families, and schooling contexts.

Additionally, teacher evaluation instruments may omit those items most relevant to culturally responsive teaching. Because a model of teaching is the organizing principle for many instruments, developers tend to focus on those elements for whole group instruction and ignore individual students and their cultural influences. Observers tend to be busy trying to understand a large group's behavior, then notice and judge anything different to be aberrant, without discerning why or caring to understand nuance. For example, some student behavior may be judged to be off-task, when a student, not behaving as directed, is imagining a different lesson product while talking aloud to a friend.

In CRIS, principals notice individual students and their unique backgrounds, their interactions with the teacher and other students, and cultural and contextual information about the lesson, grade, student ability, and subject that influence behaviors. Such evidence is important to understand if and how teachers differentiate instruction, so that it meets the needs of each student, pays attention to various sociocultural identities and lived experiences and takes care to avoid deficit-based perspectives. Teachers will need to learn to collect data about their students in a way that highlights how culturally responsive practices lead to greater achievement outcomes for children and are tied to rigorous instruction as suggested by Gay (2018).

The Process

The current teacher evaluation process in the United States tends to emphasize training the principal to be accurate in rating and to focus on delivering feedback that is rarely considered useful to teachers. These limitations, related to the design of the process, tend to make the teacher the object of evaluation rather than a participant. While training varies greatly from state to state, principals tend to have 3–4 days of training on how to use the instrument and deliver feedback—not on effective teaching. Further compounding the issue, teachers tend to receive only a few hours of orientation regarding the use of the instrument.

In the United States, the observer—almost always the principal—is trained to rate behaviors with a rubric, according to levels that may range from "Distinguished," as the highest, to "Developing" or "Unsatisfactory" as the lowest. Principals may have to achieve a level of accuracy, or inter-rater reliability, to be correlated with a system-trained coder to demonstrate expertise (Hazi, 2019).

Because of this training and assurances of accuracy, the observer's feedback is presumed to be both accurate and what the teacher needs. Worse yet, evidence is rarely collected and seldom is a principal's judgment challenged.

As such, it is assumed that principals have the will, skill, and time to deliver the feedback teachers need. In their review of research, Hallinger et al. (2014) found little change in the amount of time principals spend on teacher evaluation when there is an increased emphasis on instructional leadership. Even with increased training, time, and support, principals struggle to provide teachers with high-quality feedback (Goldring et al., 2020). Furthermore, Hallinger et al. (2014, p. 21) concluded that "the 'policy logic' supporting and driving teacher evaluation remains considerably stronger than the empirical evidence of positive results." Ironically, a process that's supposed to improve teaching rarely does. Adams et al. (2018) observed that we are limited in our understanding of how to change principal behavior to promote pedagogical leadership (Hazi, 2022), at least within the current system, which tends to reinforce the formal authority of a principal over teachers.

Due to this reality, teachers rarely find principal feedback useful in improving their teaching. Teachers tend not to trust principals because they are rarely in classrooms, are unaware of what happens on a daily basis, give generic suggestions (Oliveras-Ortiz, 2017), and lack content expertise (Lochmiller, 2019). While there has been much emphasis on research and initiatives to help principals, "[w]e still know very little about how to improve the quality of feedback administrators provide" (Kraft & Christian, 2021, p. 2). Furthermore, teachers are rarely given feedback they are receptive to (Glasman & Paulin, 1982), and an evaluator's corrective or "negative feedback is very likely to be misperceived and not accepted" (Ilgen et al., 1979, p. 367).

Therefore, both instrument and process tend to oversimplify teaching so that its behaviors can be easily quantified and measured, then correlated with benchmarks and student test scores, and ultimately norm-referenced and compared with the practices of other teachers. These instruments become the metrics by which teachers are judged to be excellent and come to judge themselves, including those new to the profession who may resist such metrics during their first years of teaching (Holloway & Brass, 2018). Ball (2003) calls this the culture of performativity, where, according to Holloway and Brass (2018),

> [c]ollegiality is replaced with competition, and autonomy is replaced with bounded (and calculable) expectations, providing the means through which teachers (and their supervisors) can know their ranks relative to their peers. This process not only changes the teacher's behavior, but it also changes the teacher. (p. 363)

The "terrors of performativity" can result in ethical dilemmas, personal struggles, and concerns about teachers' professional identity, even their mental health within the profession. The "good teacher" is "one who responds to external performance targets, subjects oneself to constant surveillance and who seeks continuous self-improvement... to be more competitive and more excellent" (Holloway, 2021, p. 35). This also narrows the curriculum and encourages teachers to teach to the test. These criteria prompt teachers to change for the worse by focusing on deficit-oriented perspectives about themselves and thus the children in their classroom, and rarely, if ever, leads to asset-based instruction that values the sociocultural identities of all children.

AN APPROACH THAT CAN FOSTER CULTURALLY RESPONSIVE TEACHING

The simplest approach would be for evaluators to collect relevant evidence, give teachers feedback, and then assume they will find it useful. However, such an approach continues a culture of performativity, and keeps the principal in power, controlling definitions and models of "good teaching." Administrators cannot coerce their way to culturally responsive teaching.

Given the many flaws of teacher evaluation, what approach is desirable? CRIS must be voluntary, supplemental, and experienced by other teachers, and it must focus on the professional development of teachers as learners. As such, teachers should define and evaluate their culturally responsive teaching with peer assistance. In turn, principals should provide support, helping teachers learn and be more in control of their practice. The purposes of this section are to explain each and describe the responsibilities of administrators and teachers as related to rethinking teacher evaluation as professional development for culturally responsive teaching.

System Prerequisites for Developing Culturally Responsive Instruction

To be more culturally responsive, participation should be voluntary and supplemental to each teacher's annual rating. The annual rating process of teachers is coercive to begin with, especially when trust is absent, and tensions exist between teachers and their supervisors. Teachers may choose—but not be required—to use some of the information they collect about their culturally responsive teaching for their annual evaluation.

As such, a district should attach both importance and privilege to participation in culturally responsive pedagogy and supervision, where teachers can feel safe in self-evaluating and voluntarily disclosing information and evidence that are potentially threatening. "The teacher, not the supervisor, controls supervision. It is the teacher who permits or refuses access to self, and it is the supervisor who needs to obtain an invitation..." (Blumberg & Jonas, 1987, p. 59). Teachers should be in control of their learning.

To support this type of growth, teachers should learn about culturally responsive teaching in a reflective and inclusive community of learners (Gay, 2018; Shulman & Shulman, 2004). Such teaching's goals are to acquire knowledge and skill so that teacher words, plans, and actions support Gay's (2018) eight qualities of culturally responsive pedagogy. Teachers should first assess their cultural competence with tools that focus on what they do, rather than what they know (e.g., Cormier, 2020) to direct their learning and goals. Teachers in such a community should be willing to teach, reflect on, and learn from their experiences and those of others in their community. Their learning should be "communal, reciprocal, [and] interdependent" so that they are "held accountable for one another's learning as well as their own" (Gay, 2018, p. 38). Thus, teachers should experience what Gay and others hope teachers will create for their own students.

In fact, other teachers can model thinking that helps teachers see evidence with new eyes. Teachers in situations such as coaching, mentoring, and professional learning communities can use other teachers to help make sense of the evidence they encounter that has the potential to disrupt and shake their confidence (Coburn & Turner, 2011). This community of peers can share knowledge, thinking, and resources and encourage experimentation in a safe space. In addition, there is "power of stating out loud, and intention to practice [a new skill or routine that] makes it more productive and . . . creates an intentional learning environment" (Buckley et al., 2015, p. 380), where a teacher is also accountable to the community. Thus, after initial professional development, each teacher engages in continuous cycles of goal setting, classroom experimentation, and public reflection on learnings, where the community challenges teachers to take the next steps of even more experiential learning and subsequent growth.

To rethink teacher evaluation as professional development, culturally responsive pedagogy should be learner-centered and "content-conscious" (Shulman & Gamoran Sherin, 2004). If done well, culturally responsive teaching makes great demands on teachers to design and adapt curricula that attend to cultural diversity, manage multiple approaches to learning, and choose assessments that advance student learning and success and attend to students' cultural assets. Since teacher skills will develop over time, it may require both the veteran and novice to have an incremental—rather than a grand—plan for implementing culturally responsive practices. This plan includes critical reflection that is both public and protected in the community. Since change may be slow to occur, any and all progress should be celebrated, whether it be a change in thinking or change in behavior. Because prior beliefs and experiences may support or hinder learning (Coburn & Turner, 2011), time is needed to publicly examine, affirm, or replace practices.

Administrator Responsibilities

Hiring teachers with experience in what Sherfinski with Hayes (2023) called critical place-based learning is preferable. Experienced teacher educators can help pre-service teachers "pop the bubble" of their ingrained deficit thinking, which prevents them from questioning their white privilege and the privileges afforded to them by other identities that affect how they interact with children who are minoritized, marginalized, and otherized in U.S. public school systems. Since this is not always possible, principals and other administrators must seek out teacher educators with this expertise. Both are needed as partners to deliver a system of critical place-based learning for teachers.

In addition, principals should promote professional development that is ongoing and job-embedded. This includes: identifying teaching that may be culturally distracting or damaging for referral; providing the routines, time, incentives, and safe space needed; and placing evaluation in the hands of teachers (Khalifa et al., 2016). All of these structures will help teachers who have the will, but also need the knowledge and skills to develop a new way of teaching that is asset-based and honors the various sociocultural identities students bring to the classroom. Professional development should include readings and experiences in culturally responsive pedagogy and explorations of privilege via critical self-reflection. It should also address data literacy so that teachers can learn how to use data to understand and transform their practice. To have the most impact, professional development should actively engage teachers in classroom-based problem-solving and help them see their own classrooms differently. Teachers can plan lessons and review results, as well as experience them as if they were their students, so they can learn mistakes that students will likely make with the curriculum (Kennedy, 2019).

If a principal or teacher leader observes or hears of an incident that could be construed as culturally distracting or damaging (see e.g., Cormier, 2020*)*, they should bring it to the teacher's attention and refer the incident anonymously to the teacher-learning community for further consideration. Incidents should focus on teacher behavior rather than intent and on the need to be more aware of culturally responsive practices moving forward.

A distracting incident may be one that has the potential to stereotype an individual or group. For example, if a student is grooming themself during the lesson, the teacher may refer to a student's weave or baggy pants to publicly correct off-task behavior. An example of a culturally damaging incident is Jane Elliott's role play where she required blue-eyed students to be slaves and those with brown eyes to be their masters to understand the nature of discrimination ("The Eye of the Storm," 2023). While these examples may seem extremes on a continuum (Cormier, 2020), if, and when they come to the community's attention, teachers with administrator assistance should discuss them and generate school policy to address them.

An initiative has the potential to be successful when teachers choose to participate. Therefore, the principal or administrator must provide incentives and safe space for teachers to disclose weaknesses, express doubts, and be vulnerable in the name of learning. If teachers must learn to trust their administrators, then they should be selectively invited to attend some meetings. For example, principals could be invited, with teacher knowledge, when teachers are scheduled to share their progress and improvement in using culturally responsive pedagogy in their learning community.

Teacher Responsibilities

Standards and standardized testing can keep teachers in what Krakowski (2022) called a *normative stance* that focuses on student deficits. Krakowski (2022) insisted that teachers not abandon standards during this age of accountability but find a way to balance the normative (i.e., what ought to happen) with the narrative pedagogy (i.e., what is happening in the classroom with the students), by "allowing their ideas, interests, stories, and experiences to shape the direction of the curriculum" (p. 10).

To do this, teachers need to build bridges between standards and students' lived experiences, identities, and prior learnings for the curriculum. Teachers need to learn about their students and help them discover localized funds of knowledge, cultural pride, and personal efficacy in their community (Gay, 2018). Teachers should then build lessons that scaffold students' prior knowledge, experience, and information about their community, cultural background, and ethnic identities. This helps reduce the strangeness of new knowledge and emphasizes strengths rather than weaknesses. The curriculum should reflect Gay's (2018) eight distinguishing traits of culturally responsive teaching, namely that instruction be: validating, comprehensive and inclusive, multidimensional, empowering, transformative, emancipatory, humanistic, and normative and ethical.

Cultural responsiveness cannot be addressed by curriculum content alone, however. Such a focus has led educators to think of culture as add-ons, e.g., Taco Tuesdays and Native American Day, instead of content integration and more inclusive teaching strategies. Many of Gay's (2018) instructional strategies and programs reflect the following principles:

- *Relationships:* Teachers need to promote a caring classroom where teacher–student and student–student relationships build community. Caring does not just happen but must be deliberately built, one communication at a time. Attitude and action must communicate respect for the student as an individual as well as a person. This, in turn, can lead to engagement.
- *Flexible grouping:* Grouping of students in teams and small groups is appropriate as long as students are not segregated into permanent ability groups. Cooperative learning is especially desirable since it results in increased engagement, relationships, and achievement (Gay, 2018). Students should be accountable for their own learning as well as that of other group members to help establish relationships and a sense of community.
- *Choice:* Students should be able to choose topics of interest as well as products or processes that best demonstrate their learning (e.g., portfolios, project-based learning, storytelling, performance) in a variety of ways. This is especially important since educators emphasize academic performance that is exclusively measured in quantifiable and statistically comparable ways, discounting rich local cultural knowledge that defies

quantification. Student success can be judged by looking at their change in thinking and behavior as well as their progress made over time, just as administrators would judge teacher change.

THE VALUE OF SELF-EVALUATION TO PROMOTE CULTURAL RESPONSIVENESS

Since teacher evaluation *should* (and can) *not* address cultural responsiveness, teacher self-evaluation might. Self-evaluation that is peer supported requires an evaluative mindset and data literacy.

To empower educators to drive their own learning, teachers should engage in self-evaluation, "a process in which teachers make judgments about the adequacy and effectiveness of their own knowledge, performance, beliefs, and effects for the purpose of self-improvement" (Airasian & Gullickson, 2006, p. 186). Self-evaluation has "historically . . . been considered to be of little value. Most dismiss it as a strategy of self-improvement that is fraught with problems" (Barber, 1991, p. 216). However, self-evaluation has begun to receive some recent interest for professional development (Stronge & Tucker, 2003), especially when the teacher frames the criteria and then uses those measures to collect, interpret, and judge his/her practice and its effects on students (Airasian & Gullickson, 2006). Self-evaluation is in addition to a teacher evaluation system, not a replacement for it. While it may involve inquiry and reflection, self-evaluation differs in that it is both assisted by and publicly shared with other teachers in their chosen learning community.

Self–evaluation requires an evaluative mindset. Buckley et al. (2015) defined an evaluative mindset as an attitude as well as a process of seeking evidence about one's impact. It involves "asking questions of substance, determining what data are required to answer specific questions, collecting data using appropriate strategies, analyzing collected data . . . and using the findings" (Baker & Bruner, 2012, p.1). An evaluative mindset makes sure that data collected is both useful and used, ensures teacher engagement and participation in the process, and prevents "evaluation being 'done to them'" (Clinton & Dawson, 2018, p. 318). The concept can be taught, modeled, cultivated, and acquired (see Buckley et al., 2015). Furthermore, when developed incrementally, it can help mitigate against blind spots and confirmation bias (Buckley et al., 2015), which may exist within a diverse classroom.

Self-evaluation also requires data literacy. The literature on teacher data use helps fill a gap in our understanding of the problems with feedback. We can no longer assume that teachers (or students) know how to use feedback. In fact, it requires both will and skill.

Data literacy requires teachers to learn to collect and use evidence to study their teaching. Sun et al. (2016) found that U.S. teachers tend to be limited in these skills, particularly when data has been "weaponized" against them (Henig, 2021). When they do have access, they tend to use data to reteach or refer students for support services, rather than to further adjust their teaching. Barriers to data use include: anxiety, resistance, data overload, lack of resources, and capacity.

To help attain this goal, teachers should define culturally responsive pedagogy for their own classrooms and then share in small trusted peer groups. These definitions should come from their readings, discussions with other teachers, and classroom observations of other teachers. These definitions will be used to identify data to be collected in each cycle to judge the lesson's impact on selected students. Definitions of culturally responsive pedagogy will vary depending on the lesson, the type of instruction (i.e., direct teaching, small group work, differentiated instruction, project-based, etc.), type of diversity in the classroom, and student needs. These definitions should evolve over time in complexity, as teachers experiment in and learn from their classrooms. They should also evolve as teachers learn how others define culturally responsive pedagogy in their learning communities.

Data literacy can begin with simple data collection forms such as seating charts and room diagrams that help teachers see students in their classrooms. For data to be useful, it must be "accessed, collected, and analyzed to be turned into information, and must be combined with understanding and expertise to become meaningful and useful for actions" (Ebbeler et al., 2017, p. 84–85). A stable database or record of what occurred in the classroom then helps guard against premature judgment and helps acquire a common language to discuss practice (Cogan, 1973; Garman, 1986).

As their definitions of culturally responsive pedagogy become more complex, teacher-made forms can be designed to reflect data that teachers can collect on individuals and groups of students. Of course, administrators need to establish an affirming data culture (Mandinach & Gummer, 2015) where data is valued and not used against teachers.

CREATING A NEW ENVIRONMENT AROUND DATA COLLECTION AND VALUE

In summary, advocacy for equity and culturally responsive pedagogy comes at a time of extreme challenges to and distrust of teachers and the schools. Some even question whether culturally responsive teaching is possible because some have tried to link it to critical race theory (e.g., Najarro, 2022). However, culturally responsive pedagogy is an asset-based strategy that involves "us[ing] students' customs, characteristics, experiences, and perspectives as tools for better classroom instruction" (Najarro, 2022, para 2). Teachers should rightly claim they *differentiate instruction* based on their students' various sociocultural identities, of which they will share similarities and differences.

This pedagogy requires a different way of thinking about one's students and one's teaching. As previously stated, administrators cannot coerce their way to culturally responsive pedagogy. They must treat teachers as they expect teachers to treat their students. They must take teachers with the will and provide them the knowledge and skill through long term, job-embedded professional development, creating an environment where culturally responsive teaching is valued. As teachers grow in knowledge, they engage in cycles of self-evaluation. After they learn more about their students, they identify an aspect of culturally responsive pedagogy that they'd like to try out in their classroom, collect data on it by themselves and with other teachers, and publicly share what they did and learned in their community of teachers.

Shifting how we conceptualize teacher evaluation will require administrators to think about teachers as learners and to develop a school culture that is a safe space for teachers to learn, experiment with new strategies, and sometimes fail. This should occur vis-à-vis the professional development system. Teachers may voluntarily choose—but not be required—to use evidence of their experiences with culturally responsive teaching in their annual evaluations. Administrators need to provide professional development in curriculum content, pedagogical strategies, and data literacy, providing the incentives and space for teachers to learn a complex pedagogy over time that takes them from being teacher-centered to student-centered. Furthermore, administrators and teachers may have to identify teaching that is potentially culturally distracting or damaging in a nonthreatening way, then help teachers develop policy to address and prevent such behavior.

Only those who are willing can be expected to become culturally responsive teachers over time as they grow into their knowledge and skill. However, principals can play their part by supporting, promoting, and protecting a safe space for teachers to reflect upon their privileged sociocultural identities and then learn more deeply how to meet the needs of their students based on the latters' identities and lived experiences. In turn, teachers will need to develop an evaluative mindset, define culturally responsive pedagogy, collect evidence (co-create knowledge) related to their evolving definitions, interpret the evidence (sense making), self-evaluate, and then set goals (transform evidence into usable knowledge) for new cycles of reflection and action. Culturally responsive pedagogy occurs one lesson at a time.

While there are a variety of factors that contribute to inequity, and disparity varies widely from state to state, schools appear to be re-segregating (Walsh, 2022). Desegregation of the late 1960s, which eventually began as an enforcement of *Brown v. Board of Education*, resulted in benefits that included increased high school and college attendance and graduation rates, increased wages as adults, decreased incarceration rates, and improved health for Black and Brown students (Reardon et al., 2022). These benefits did not last and schools remain highly segregated by race and income, requiring states to spend billions of dollars to address spending gaps (Lieberman, 2022). In the meantime, students cannot wait. There is an old adage in education that states, "We measure what we value." If we value inclusion and belonging, and we want to ensure more equitable outcomes for all students, we need to continue to find ways to measure these outcomes and support teachers through appropriate professional development that helps increase culturally responsive practices. As such, educators are morally obligated to provide a more inclusive and representative school system that welcomes all children through culturally responsive pedagogy.

REFERENCES

Adams, P., Mombourquette, C., Brandon, J., Hunter, D., Friesen, S., Kok, K., Parsons, D., & Stelmach, B. (2018). A study of teacher growth, supervision, and evaluation in Alberta: policy and perception. *Journal of Educational Supervision, 1*(2), 1–16. https://digitalcommons.library.umaine.edu/jes/vol1/iss2/1/

Airasian, P., & Gullickson, A. (2006). Teacher self-evaluation. In J. Stronge (Ed.), *Evaluating teaching: A guide to current thinking and best practice* (2nd ed.) (pp.186–211). Corwin Press.

Baker, A., & Brunner, B. (2012). *Integrating evaluative capacity into organizational practice*. The Bruner Foundation. http://www.evaluativethinking.org/docs/Integ_Eval_Capacity_Final.pdf

Ball, S. (2003). The teacher's soul and the terror of performativity. *Journal of Education Policy, 18*(2), 215–228. https://doi.org/10.1080/0268093022000043065

Barber, L. (1991). Self-assessment. In L. Darling-Hammond & J. Millman (Eds.). *Handbook of teacher evaluation* (pp. 216–228). Sage.

Bleiberg, J., Brunner, E., Harbatkin, E., Kraft, M., & Springer, M. (2021, December). The effect of teacher evaluation on achievement and attainment: Evidence from statewide reforms. (EdWorkingPaper: 21–496) Annenberg Institute. https://www.edworkingpapers.com/ai21–496

Blumberg, A., & Jonas, R. (1987). Permitting access: The teacher's control over supervision. *Educational Leadership, 44*(8), 58–62. https://eric.ed.gov/?id=EJ353887

Buckley, J., Archibald, T., Hargraves, M., & Trochim, W. (2015). Defining and teaching evaluative thinking: Insights from research on critical thinking. *American Journal of Evaluation, 36*(3), 375–388. https://doi.org/10.1177/1098214015581706

Clinton, J., & Dawson G. (2018). Enfranchising the profession through evaluation: A story from Australia. *Teachers and Teaching: Theory and Practice, 24*(3), 312–327. https://doi.org/10.1080/13540602.2017.1421162

Coburn, C., & Turner, E. O. (2011). Research on data use: a framework and analysis. *Measurement: Interdisciplinary Research and Practice, 9*(4), 173–206. https://doi.org/10.1080/15366367.2011.626729

Cogan, M. (1973). *Clinical supervision*. Houghton Mifflin Company.

Cormier, D. R. (2020). Assessing preservice teachers' cultural competence with the cultural proficiency continuum q-sort. *Educational Researcher, 50*(10), 17–29. https://doi.org/10.3102/0013189X20936670

Ebbeler, J., Poortman, C., Schildkamp, K., & Pieters, J. (2017). The effects of a data use intervention on educators' satisfaction and data literacy. *Educational Assessment, Evaluation Accountability, 29*, 83–105. https://doi.org/10.1007/s11092-016-9251-z

Ellett, C. (1987). Emerging teacher performance assessment practices: Implications for the instructional supervision role of school principals. In W. Greenfield's (Ed.) *Instructional leadership: Concepts, issues, and controversies* (pp. 302–327). Allyn and Bacon, Inc.

The Eye of the Storm. (2023, May 29). Wikipedia. https://en.wikipedia.org/wiki/The_Eye_of_the_Storm_(1970_film)

Garman, N. B. (1986). Clinical supervision: Quackery or remedy for professional practice. *Journal of Curriculum and Supervision, 1*(2), 148–157.

Gay, G. (2018). *Culturally responsive teaching: Theory, research, and practice*. Teachers College Press.

Glasman, N. S., & Paulin, P. J. (1982). Possible determinants of teacher receptivity to evaluation. *Journal of Educational Administration, 20*(2), 148–171. https://doi.org/10.1108/eb009859

Goldring, E., Clark, M., Rubin, M. Rogers, L., Grissom, J., Gill, B., Kautz, T., McCullough, M., Neel, M., & Burnett, A. (2020, July). *Changing the principal supervisor role to better support principals: Evidence from the principal supervisor initiative*. Mathematica/Vanderbilt University. https://www.wallacefoundation.org/knowledge-center/Documents/Changing-the-Principal-Supervisor-Role.pdf

Hallinger, P., Heck, R., & Murphy, J. (2014). Teacher evaluation and school improvement: An analysis of the evidence. *Educational Assessment, Evaluation and Accountability, 26*(1), 5–28. https://doi.org/10.1007/s11092-013-9179-5

Hazi, H. M. (2014). The marketing of teacher evaluation: The seductive claims of instruments. *The WERA Educational Journal, 6*(1), 2–9. http://www.wera-web.org/wp-content/uploads/2014/04/TheWERAEd32014.pdf

Hazi, H. M. (2019). Coming to understand the wicked problem of teacher evaluation. In S. J. Zepeda and J. Ponticell (Eds.), *Handbook of educational supervision* (pp. 183–208). Wiley Blackwell Publishing.

Hazi, H. M. (2022). Rethinking the dual purposes of teacher evaluation. *Teachers and Teaching: Theory and Practice*. https://doi.org/10.1080/13540602.2022.2103533

Henig, J. (2021, February 9). 'Data' has become a dirty word to public education advocates. It doesn't have to be. *Education Week*. https://www.edweek.org/policy-politics/opinion-data-has-become-a-dirty-word-to-public-education-advocates-it-doesnt-have-to-be/2021/02

Holloway, J. (2021). *Metrics, standards, and alignment in teacher policy: Critiquing fundamentalism and imagining pluralism*. Springer.

Holloway, J., & Brass, J. (2018). Making accountable teachers: The terrors and pleasures of performativity. *Journal of Education Policy, 33*(3), 361–382. https://doi.org/10.1080/02680939.2017.1372636

Ilgen, D., Fisher, C., & Taylor, M. S. (1979). Consequences of individual feedback on behaviors in organizations. *Journal of Applied Psychology, 64*(4), 349- 371. https://psycnet.apa.org/doiLanding?doi=10.1037%2F0021-9010.64.4.349

Kennedy, M. (2019). How we learn about teacher learning. *Review of Research in Education, 43*, 138–162. https://doi.org/10.3102/0091732X19838970

Khalifa, M. A., Gooden, M. A., & Davis, J. E. (2016). Culturally responsive school leadership: A synthesis of the literature. *Review of Educational Research, 86*(4), 1272–1311. https://doi.org/10.3102/0034654316630383

Kraft M., & Christian, A. (2021, June). Can teacher evaluation systems produce high-quality feedback? An administrator training field experiment (EdWorkingPaper No. 19–62). Annenberg Institute at Brown University. https://www.edworkingpapers.com/sites/default/files/ai19-62_2.pdf

Krakowski, P. (2022). *Entering a child's world: Narrative pedagogy in early childhood art education*. Learning Moments Press.

Lieberman, M. (2022, December 8). How much states need to pony up to make school spending equitable. *Education Week*. https://www.edweek.org/policy-politics/how-much-states-need-to-pony-up-to-make-school-spending-equitable/2022/12

Lochmiller, C. R. (2019). Credibility in instructional supervision: Catalyst for differentiation. In M. L. Derrington & J. Brandon (Eds.), *Differentiated teacher evaluation and professional learning: Policies and practices for promoting career growth* (pp. 83–105). Palgrave Macmillan.

Mahnken, K. (2022, April 20). Change from the bottom up: Political science research suggests that more CRT bills could come to Washington new year. *The 74.* https://www.the74million.org/change-from-the-bottom-up-political-science-research-suggests-that-more-crt-bills-could-come-to-washington-next-year/

Mandinach, E., & Gummer, E. (2015). Data-driven decision making: Components of the enculturation of data use in education. *Teachers College Record, 117*(4), 1–8. DOI:10.1177/016146811511700402

Najarro, I. (2022, April 21). How laws on race, sexuality could clash with culturally responsive teaching. *Education Week.* https://www.edweek.org/policy-politics/how-laws-on-race-sexuality-could-clash-with-culturally-responsive-teaching/2022/04

Oliveras-Ortiz, Y. (2017). School administrators as instructional coaches: Teachers' trust and perceptions of administrators' capacity. *School Leadership Review, 12*(1), 39–46. https://scholarworks.sfasu.edu/slr/vol12/iss1/6/

Pendharkar, E. (2023, May 19). State laws are behind many book bans, even indirectly, report finds. *Education Week.* https://www.edweek.org/teaching-learning/state-laws-are-behind-many-book-bans-even-indirectly-report-finds/2023/05

Phi Delta Kappan (PDK). (2022). The 54th Annual PDK Poll: Local public school ratings rise, even as the teaching profession loses ground. https://pdkpoll.org/2022-pdk-poll-results/

Reardon, S., Fahle, E., Jang, H., & Weathers, E. (2022). Why school desegregation still matters. *Educational Leadership, 80*(4). https://www.ascd.org/el/articles/why-school-desegregation-still-matters-a-lot

Sherfinski, M. (2023). *Rooted in belonging: Critical place-based learning in early childhood and elementary teacher education.* Teachers College Press.

Shulman, L. S. (1987). Knowledge and teaching: Foundations of the new reform. *Harvard Educational Review, 57*(1), 1–22. http://hepg.org/her-home/issues/harvard-educational-review-volume-57,-issue-1/herarticle/foundations-of-the-new-reform_461

Shulman, L., & Gamoran Sherin, M. (2004). Fostering communities of teachers as learners: disciplinary perspectives. *Journal of Curriculum Studies, 36*(2), 135–140. https://doi.org/10.1080/0022027032000135049

Shulman, L., & Shulman, J. (2004). How and what teachers learn: A shifting perspective. *Journal of Curriculum Studies, 36*(2), 257–271. https://ed.stanford.edu/sites/default/files/step/page/shulman_and_shulman_how_and_what_teachers_learn.pdf

Stronge, J., & Tucker, P. (2003). *Handbook on teacher evaluation: Assessing and improving performance.* Eye on Education.

Sun, J., Przybylski, R., & Johnson, B. (2016). A review of research on teachers' use of student data from the perspective of school leadership. *Educational Assessment, Evaluation and Accountability, 28*(1), 5–33. https://doi.org/10.1007/s11092-016-9238-9

Walsh, M. (2022). Schools are resegregating. There's a push for the supreme court to consider that. *Education Week.* https://www.edweek.org/leadership/schools-are-resegregating-theres-a-push-for-the-supreme-court-to-consider-that/2022/11

Will, M. (2021, November) Efforts to toughen teacher evaluations show no positive impact on students. *Education Week.* https://www.edweek.org/teaching-learning/efforts-to-toughen-teacher-evaluations-show-no-positive-impact-on-students/2021/11

CHAPTER 6

Using Cultural Knowledge to Develop Structures and Systems That Lead to Equitable and Emancipatory Outcomes

Ian M. Mette, Dwayne Ray Cormier, and Yanira Oliveras

Across the United States, those with privileged sociocultural identities often fail to acknowledge how inequities are reified through various social systems. This has been magnified with recent Supreme Court decisions, namely the overturning of race-conscious admission policies, the erosion of LGBTQIA+ protections, (Liptak & Murray, 2023), and the overturning of *Roe v. Wade* that had provided constitutional rights to women and their reproductive rights (Totenberg & McCammon, 2022). The U.S. PK–12 education system continues to protect privileged sociocultural identities, specifically "those who identify as White, cis gender, heterosexual, male, middle-to-upper class, able-bodied, and of Western European decent" (Mette et al., 2023). As such, there is a significant need to develop structures and systems that can enact culturally responsive instructional supervision (CRIS).

To develop critically conscious supervisors who are able to understand and/or acknowledge the lived experiences of students who are minoritized, marginalized, and otherized, school leaders need to leverage the cultural knowledge of high-functioning teachers within education systems and not assume that the sole perspective of an administrator will be enough to provide CRIS. Doing so will allow groups of supervisors, comprised of teacher leaders throughout a building, to better attend to the needs of students based on various sociocultural identities, including race, ethnicity, class, sex, orientation/identity, geography, and other lived experiences (Fisher-Ari et al., 2020). By flattening the hierarchy of feedback provided in the schoolhouse and shifting toward practices that incorporate various sociocultural perspectives from teacher leaders about what culturally responsive instruction looks like, schools can create representative supervision teams that not only are more democratic, but are also more likely to close sociocultural gaps by providing equity-based instruction that meets the needs of all students.

As such, we believe CRIS requires educators to work collaboratively and collectively to continually deepen their cultural competence as a group. Given that 80% of all educators in the United States are racialized as White (NCES, 2017), we know that teachers and administrators within the U.S. education system must work diligently to develop a deeper understanding of inequities based on racial identities. However, we also know that U.S. society discriminates in a variety of ways, which is why it is important to be aware of, discuss, and address how education reinforces the power afforded to privileged sociocultural identities. By developing structures and systems that acknowledge various identities and lived experiences, it is significantly more likely that a school system will be able to support the development of teachers who are able to provide instruction that is inclusive—and perhaps most importantly—are able to consider how instruction is provided as well as how it is perceived.

In developing a framework for CRIS, one of our main arguments is that education systems in the United States cannot close sociocultural gaps if feedback remains hierarchical (Mette et al., 2023). This requires us to shift away from plantation practices—specifically abandon the failed accountability movement that has enacted damaging, deficit-based ideologies—that seek to maintain serving privileged sociocultural identities. As such, to successfully apply and implement CRIS, educators need to develop individually, collaboratively in small groups, and as a collective building of teachers, to acknowledge how their various identities influence the way feedback is provided regarding the instruction that is observed in a classroom. It is the unpacking of these various sociocultural identities that is pivotal to providing an educational experience that is equitable and inclusive for all students. With this approach, feedback from a variety of structures and systems can help reduce the likelihood that sociocultural opportunity gaps are exacerbated, with the eventual outcome being that they begin to be closed or are eliminated.

In contributing to the development of a CRIS framework, in this chapter we offer a review of what we have developed previously in our *Making a Difference: Instructional Leadership that Drives Self-Reflection and Values the Expertise of Teachers* (Mette et al., 2023), specifically what we see as the negative effects of summative feedback in U.S. schools, how schools can develop structures that help create data collection systems that support formative growth, and systems that can be used to support ongoing development at the individual level, with critical colleagues, and through peer-led classroom observations (see Mette et al., 2023). From this developing framework, we offer insights into how scholars and practitioners can create more equitable forms of feedback for inclusive instructional practices. It is from these reflections that we hope to see instruction changed within the schoolhouse—instruction that is capable of addressing the history of violence and oppression in the United States enacted on a wide range of identities and people.

THE LONGSTANDING PROBLEM WITH SUMMATIVE FEEDBACK IN U.S. SCHOOLS

In U.S. society, and more specifically U.S. education systems, educators must be able to engage in a radical reimagination of moral obligations (Laymon, 2018) that empowers both teachers and students to deeply reflect upon the ways in which societal systems enact discrimination. This requires coalitions of educators from various sociocultural backgrounds to work together, to deprivatize instruction within the schoolhouse, and to ensure education does not reinforce instruction that is apolitical or ahistorical. It is through the reimagination of feedback—formative structures that allow people to grow in real time and to develop cultural competence through repeated feedback that is structured to support culturally responsive instruction—that educators can address historical inequities based on race, gender, ethnicity, socioeconomic status, and other forms of biases.

Flattening the Feedback Cycle

An important aspect of implementing CRIS is the notion that feedback should be more democratic and truly representative if instructional practices are to help contribute to a more equitable society. Currently, as a result of the high-stakes accountability movement, most feedback given to teachers is summative in nature, fails to be ongoing and provide feedback on a weekly basis, and overvalues the use of test scores to determine the "effectiveness" of a teacher (Mette et al., 2020). As such, principals, the educators who have the most responsibility to serve as equity-based instructional leaders, must learn to enact distributive leadership to create a system of formative feedback that is constructive and empowers teachers to engage in reflection about their instruction which considers various sociocultural identities.

This requires a shift of mind about the purpose of schools—namely, that schools should exist to support the development of individual communities to contribute to the development of a democratic society. As such, educators must learn to be critical of the high-stakes summative evaluation policies that have flourished since the inception of *No Child Left Behind* (NCLB, 2001), specifically how education benefits privileged sociocultural identities such as race, socioeconomic status, and language, among other identities. It is through more critical, formative, and ongoing feedback cycles that educators can raise their awareness of social power and privilege within the U.S. society and begin to close sociocultural opportunity gaps.

To accomplish this shift, the CRIS framework should focus on empowering teachers to reflect on their instruction and cocreate knowledge about what is culturally responsive based on the needs of students who have historically been minoritized, marginalized, and otherized. It also requires creating safe spaces for teachers to engage in vulnerable reflections about shifting away from deficit-oriented perspectives to asset-based mindsets to honor the strengths students bring

Using Cultural Knowledge to Develop Structures and Systems 115

with them to the classroom every day. This can happen, but it must be through the intentional creation of structures and systems that values learning at the individual level, learning with critical colleagues, and learning as a large group of faculty members.

Calling Out the Corporate Nature of Teacher Evaluation Systems

One of the main issues within the U.S. education system is how feedback about instruction is provided through prepackaged teacher evaluation systems. These evaluation systems are not only aligned with high-stakes assessments, but they also reinforce the interests of corporations who believe education exists only to support workforce development. Perhaps most damning, these systems reinforce a deficit-oriented perspective that suggests few teachers should ever be ranked at the highest level, which is directly counter-intuitive to adult learning theory (Mezirow, 2009).

Prepackaged evaluation systems also reify techno-rational feedback structures (Cheng, 2015) that fail to question sociocultural identities of the supervisor or the teacher, center the perspective of the supervisor, and are designed to educate in a manner that benefits the system and reinforces deficit-beliefs about learning. Conversely, CRIS requires supervisors to deeply question their sociocultural identities (Milner, 2017); center the voice of the minoritized, marginalized, and otherized; and educate in a manner that benefits the development of students based on assets and strengths. As such, CRIS asks educators to move away from techno-rational improvement efforts that are standardized and corporate-based, and instead shift toward more humanizing forms of instructional improvement efforts.

The CRIS framework is important in that it creates ongoing reflection in a way that prepackaged evaluations systems cannot and do not. Prepacked evaluation systems are summative and are used for human resource decisions, which certainly serves a purpose if a teacher is culturally damaging or destructive. However, these prepackaged evaluation systems do not function in the way that the CRIS framework does. CRIS is intentionally designed to support ongoing discussions about what inclusive instruction looks like in the classroom, to use observable data to help drive these conversations and to use structured time to unpack these data; from these conversations educators can begin to change beliefs about culturally responsive instructional practices at the conscious and subconscious level. It is through the CRIS framework that educators can begin to increase their cultural competence (Cormier, 2022) and ultimately ensure instruction is aligned to the identities of all children.

Creating a Structure to Close Sociocultural Gaps

If the U.S. education system is to ever help address and close the sociocultural gaps that exist in our society, it will need to come from a community of instructors who are able to reflect upon their own biases and the prevalence of sociocultural gaps in their own classrooms. Through the creation of a community of culturally responsive instructors (CCRI), groups of educators can learn to gather and analyze data from their own classrooms that lead to more equitable instructional practices. Perhaps most importantly, a CCRI can learn collectively—and by proxy as individuals—to let go of destructive and harmful instructional practices that reinforce deficit narratives about various sociocultural identities and the role of education more broadly.

Different from a traditional professional learning community (PLC), a CCRI leverages teacher autonomy to empower educators to come together based on equity-oriented interests (Cooper et al., 2018). This bottom-up approach not only helps flatten the hierarchy of a feedback system, but it also can help support school reform efforts that focus on liberation and emancipation from oppressive educational practices (Love, 2019). From this approach, educators are encouraged to grow at the individual level, with critical colleagues in their CCRI, and eventually as a schoolwide faculty group.

Perhaps most importantly, a CCRI supports the efforts of educators unmooring themselves from the failed accountability movement that started in the early 2000s. By focusing on ways to promote teacher reflection and learning at the individual and small group level, schools can engage in instruction that is inclusive, liberating, and equity oriented. In doing so, school leaders can enact a CRIS framework that deeply questions instructional systemic inequities from various perspectives and in a democratic fashion—and in a way that is not solely from the perspective of a few administrators.

REIMAGINING SUPERVISION TO BE CULTURALLY RESPONSIVE

Supervision—which is the formative feedback that has historically been used to drive instructional improvement efforts and the development of reflective stances (Dana & Yendol-Hoppey, 2020; Goldhammer, 1969)—by and large has been replaced by top-down teacher evaluation systems that focus on summative feedback. Due to this transition in how feedback has been conceptualized, there has been a dramatic shift in how principals and instructional coaches have engaged in instructional leadership (Mette et al., 2017). To provide CRIS, educators need to reimagine how feedback can be provided from a group of teacher leaders, how walkthrough data can drive reflection on culturally responsive practices, and how to develop a plan to determine what supports are needed when instruction is observed and is culturally damaging or destructive.

The Importance of Supervision Teams

Feedback about culturally responsive pedagogy is more effective when supervision is provided from a variety of people who have various sociocultural identities and lived experiences (Gay, 2020). When feedback is provided by only one sociocultural identity—for example, from principals, 80% of whom are racialized as White—education systems will struggle to close sociocultural gaps and implement more inclusive instruction. This requires school leaders to think drastically differently about how feedback is provided, and to attempt to create a representative supervision team that intentionally takes into account race, birth sex, ethnicity, socioeconomic status, spatiality, orientation/identity, ability, and other lived experiences (Mette et al., 2023). While they might not always be possible to create intentionally representative supervision teams in homogenous communities, schools will benefit from creating these teams that value understanding the lived experiences of the students they serve.

Mills (1997) writes about the racial contract, which highlights the social construct of whiteness and the power and privileges afforded to people who are racialized as White. The U.S. education system reifies the racial contract, placing value in the culture of whiteness, reinforcing Eurocentric ideologies, and valuing English as the only spoken language in schools. This is institutionalized through a variety of anti-CRT bills that make it illegal for teachers to discuss the violent and racialized history of the United States (Schwartz, 2021). Conversely, Pateman (1998) writes about the sexual contract, which describes the ways in which society devalues people who are born female at birth and places restrictions and controls on their bodies. These societal contracts reinforce the view of women as property, restrict reproductive rights, and uphold patriarchal ideologies. As such, both race and sex should be considered when creating a representative supervision team.

A variety of other sociocultural identities should also be taken into account in the creation of supervision teams. Ensuring there are a variety of ethnic identities will help challenge White, European, Christian-based, and English-speaking paradigms. Taking into account socioeconomic status will help educators consider how education either continues to marginalize people or how they can move away from deficit-oriented perspectives about students who experience poverty. Understanding the role space and geography play on various lived experiences will allow educators to question paradigms about the deficit-oriented beliefs of both urban and rural students. Attempting to include LGBTQIA+ identities will help challenge heteronormative perspectives that currently dominate the U.S. education system. Including individuals who come from the disability community can counter ablism and ableist language within the schoolhouse.

In creating representative supervision teams, it is important to ensure instructional leaders reflect deeply on their privileged sociocultural identities. In acknowledging these identities, educators must then work together—as a team—to engage in ongoing development of cultural consciousness. In working together, a representative supervision team can challenge each other and learn from each other to ensure inclusive instruction is provided that helps close deeply engrained sociocultural gaps.

The Power of Collecting Observable Data About Culturally Responsive Practices

Contemporary teacher evaluation systems lack structures that allow for ongoing and constant formative feedback about observed instructional practices. For the most part, teacher evaluation systems are high stakes, are summative in nature, and do little to help teachers reflect on their cultural competence. Conversely, the CRIS framework is designed to value ongoing data collection based on quick observations by the representative supervision team. Using these walkthrough data, instructional leaders can empower building-wide faculty members to analyze the degree to which they provide culturally responsive pedagogy, how much equity is centered within their instructional practices, and the degree to which students are encouraged to address societal injustices through their learning, among other areas of focus.

Using the eight principles of culturally responsive teaching (Gay, 2018), we suggest the representative supervision team develop measurable and observable outcomes they look for when conducting their walkthroughs. One area of focus could be the rigor of pedagogical principles used in the classroom to determine the level of critical thinking to address societal inequities. A second area of focus could target the creation of a reflective and inclusive community of learner that values student voices and validates cultural identities and lived experiences. A third area of focus could determine the level to which instruction is emancipatory and liberating, including the degree to which sociocultural identities are reflected upon and how students are empowered to enact change.

From these data, departments, teams of teachers, and building-wide faculty could analyze formative data about culturally responsive pedagogical practices. From these data sets, goals could be established, instruction could change and be measured over time, and professional development could occur to help close sociocultural gaps. From this process, too, teachers could see their efforts lead to change and begin to shift the needle in how CRIS can be applied to support teachers and their cultural competence.

What to Do When Instruction is Culturally Damaging

From the process of ongoing and constant data collection of classroom observations collected by the representative supervision team, teachers can engage in CRIS by raising their critical consciousness about instruction that is equitable and inclusive. When culturally damaging or culturally destructive instruction is observed, instructional leaders must have tools to disrupt and remediate instruction that is considered deficit-oriented, fails to consider student voice or identities, or reinforces harmful practices that center on the privileged. As such, a central function of CRIS is to develop structures and systems that not only help large groups of educators reflect on instructional practices at the building level, but also focus on small-group development as well as at the individual level. This is especially important when a small group of teachers, or an individual teacher, exhibits instruction that is not culturally responsive and needs more intensive support efforts.

Through individualized efforts led by one or more members of the representative supervision team, instructional leaders can help model instruction and set goals to help teachers move forward on the cultural proficiency continuum (Lindsey et al., 2009). Using the notion of developmental supervision (Glickman et al., 2018), supervisors can determine how to apply directive control, directive informational, collaborative, or non-directive supervision to help develop and/or extend cultural competence development. Using various types of support structures can fulfill the hope and intent that instructional leaders will apply the CRIS framework to help teachers increase their awareness of the sociopolitical realities of the United States (Ladson-Billings, 1999).

Through CRIS, educational leaders can support the development of critical consciousness within teachers. Through a deepened understanding of how various U.S. social systems—including but not limited to the U.S. education system—contributes to how groups of students are minoritized, marginalized, and otherized, educators can provide liberatory instruction to address social inequities. And it is through this development that CRIS can support the growth of educators individually, in small groups, and at the building level to deliver equitable instruction.

STRUCTURES TO SUPPORT GROWTH AT MULTIPLE LEVELS

In developing a CRIS framework, we have been adamant about the need for educators to use formative feedback—not summative teacher evaluation—to grow at the individual level, with small groups of critical colleagues, and in large groups at the building level. We believe this structure is important because ultimately growth must be driven at the individual level if teachers are to deeply question their own privileged sociocultural identities as well as develop a critical consciousness. However, we also believe that this can be expedited when working in small groups of colleagues who have similar interests and develop a level of trust to help one another grow in their application of culturally responsive instructional practices. Most importantly, this then must translate across the building so that no matter the classroom, students have an educational experience that provides them equitable and inclusive instruction throughout the schoolhouse.

Supporting Growth at the Individual Level

Many teachers in the United States can acknowledge there are sociocultural gaps among various identities, but very few know how to address and close these gaps (Milner, 2020). Using the CRIS framework, individual teachers can focus on deepening their own personal understanding of how to provide a rigorous pedagogy that is also culturally responsive and aligned to sociocultural identities and lived experiences (Gay, 2018). As such, CRIS requires teachers to drive their own equity-minded instructional improvement efforts which are asset-based and leverage the developmental and content expertise.

By acknowledging that each student learns differently, teachers can drive their own development to implement culturally responsive practices. At the heart of this growth is the belief that teachers have autonomy and agency to develop a critical consciousness about how they can deliver culturally responsive instruction, and that in doing so they can contribute to the development of a move inclusive and democratic schoolhouse. To accomplish this shift, teachers must be willing to constantly ask themselves how students who are minoritized, marginalized, and otherized internalize the instruction provided in a classroom (Muhammad, 2022).

To eliminate instructional inequities, individuals can examine the inequitable outcomes that are replicated within their own classrooms. Once those have been identified, individual teachers can develop and implement plans to reduce the opportunity gaps within their classrooms. Over a period of time, individual teachers can then assess if the efforts to increase culturally responsive instruction have worked, and then continue the self-study cycle. It is through the accountability of individual teachers that inequitable education systems can change over time and transform the schoolhouse into a more inclusive instructional space.

Growing With Critical Colleagues

While it is critical for individual teachers to drive their own growth within the CRIS framework, it is also necessary for educators to work in small groups to engage in vulnerable reflection and discussion. Through the development of small critical colleague groups, teachers can deconstruct how schools marginalize, minoritize, and otherize different groups of students (Cevik et al., 2020). In these settings, educators can continue to engage in deep reflection about their own sociocultural identities and push each other in their thinking about to transform education to provide strengths-based opportunities in their classrooms.

Contrary to traditional professional learning groups (PLCs), learning in these small groups should be driven by interests and experiences to increase the application of culturally responsive instructional practices. From these groups of critical colleagues, educators can engage in vulnerable acts of learning and growth that cannot be accomplished in isolation. It is from these learning groups that educators can learn to identify, address, and close sociocultural gaps.

At the core of this work is the deprivatization of teaching that needs to occur across the schoolhouse. The science and art of both receiving and providing feedback about instructional practices that lead to more equitable outcomes for all students is critical to the development of a more inclusive U.S. education system. As such, learning in small groups with trusted colleagues helps educators move beyond their comfort zone and develop asset-based approaches that contribute to a more democratic society.

Empowering Faculty-Level Reflections to Drive Equity-Oriented Instruction

Engaging in peer-based observations is yet another structure and system that can help drive building-wide discussions about the equity-oriented instruction that is occurring throughout the schoolhouse. By leveraging individual reflections and growth about culturally responsive practices, as well as critical colleague groups, teachers can engage in peer-based observations that disseminate sociocultural understanding and cultural proficiency on a wide-scale basis. By developing these types of formative feedback structures, teams of teachers and departments based on content can capitalize on educator expertise to improve instruction so that it is more inclusive for all students.

Central to this structure is the idea of transitioning formative feedback structures from the intentionally representative supervision team to the teachers at the team or department level. Using a train-the-trainer model, teams/departments can set goals, conduct peer-based observations, and analyze observation data for formative feedback purposes. From these smaller conversations, goals can be set at the building level to help ensure equitable instruction is delivered across the entire building and not just at the team or departmental level—which is another way to deprivatize instruction and ensure equitable instruction is at the center of all classrooms.

From these faculty-level reflections, educators can engage in a CRIS framework by reimagining how planning time is used. Through face-to-face discussions, schools can deconstruct practices that lack cultural responsiveness and shift towards practices that honor the assets and strengths that students bring to the classroom. From these structures and systems, teachers can drive improvement efforts that help schools function as systems of opportunities.

CONCLUSION

In this chapter we reviewed the burgeoning development of a CRIS framework from our previous work (Mette et al., 2023). The development of CRIS, broadly speaking, helps continue the process of decentering whiteness and other privileged identities in the formative feedback cycle that can help improve equitable instructional applications and outcomes. In order to make the schoolhouse a place that addresses the inequities of the U.S. society, it is imperative that school leaders and instructional leaders embody strength-based approaches to instruction that honor the sociocultural identities and lived experiences of the students a school serves.

REFERENCES

Çevik, S., Yıldırım, S., & Zepeda, S. J. (2020). Leadership for socially-just supervision in K-12 schools in the context of the United States. *Multicultural Education Review, 12*(4), 306–322.

Cheng, L. C. (2015). From subjectivity to objective evaluation: A techno-rationalist approach of assessment design for art and design education. In O. Hassan, S. Abidin, R. Legino, R. Anwar, & M. Kamaruzaman (Eds.), *International Colloquium of Art and Design Education Research (i-CADER 2014)*. Springer. https://doi.org/10.1007/978-981-287-332-3_44

Cheng, L. C. (2015). From subjectivity to objective evaluation: A techno-rationalist approach of assessment design for art and design education. *International Colloquium of Art and Design Education Research*, 421–430. http://dx.doi.org/10.1007/978-981-287-332-3_44

Cooper, K. S., Stanulis, R. N., Brondyk, S. K., Hamilton, E. R., Mascaluso, M., & Meier, J. A. (2018). The teacher leadership process: Attempting change within embedded systems. *Journal of Educational Change, 17*, 85–113.

Cormier, D. R. (2022). Prototyping the Cultural Proficiency Continuum Dialogic Protocol with professional development school teacher interns. *Urban Education*. https://doi.org/10.1177/00420859221140405

Dana, N. F., & Yendol-Hoppey, D. (2020). *The reflective educator's guide to classroom research: Learning to teach and teaching to learn through practitioner inquiry* (4th ed.). Corwin.

Fisher-Ari, T. R., Speights, R., Veazie, M., Haile, H., Tennies, E., & Ngo, H. (2020). Organizational cultural competence in PDS networks and teacher certification programs. In J. Ferrara, J. L. Nath, & R. S. Beebe (Eds.), *Exploring cultural competence in professional development schools* (pp. 1–25). Information Age Publishing.

Gay, G. (2018). *Culturally responsive teaching: Theory, research, and practice* (2nd ed.). Teachers College Press.

Glickman, C. D., Gordon, S. P., & Ross-Gordon, J. M. (2018). *Supervision and instructional leadership: A developmental approach* (10th ed.). Pearson.

Goldhammer, R. (1969). *Clinical supervision: Special methods for the supervision of teachers*. Holt, Rinehart and Winston.

Ladson–Billings, G. (1999). Preparing teachers for diverse student populations: A critical race theory perspective. *Review of Research in Education, 24*, 211–247.

Laymon, K. (2018). *Heavy: An American memoir*. Scribner.

Lindsey, R. B., Robins, K. N., & Terrell, R. D. (2009). *Cultural proficiency: A manual for school leaders*. Corwin.

Liptak, A., & Murray, E. (2023). The major Supreme Court decisions in 2023. *The New York Times*. https://www.nytimes.com/interactive/2023/06/07/us/major-supreme-court-cases-2023.html

Love, B. L. (2019). *We want to do more than survive: Abolitionist teaching and the pursuit of educational reform*. Beacon Press.

Mette, I. M., Aguilar, I., & Wieczorek, D. (2020). A thirty state analysis of teacher supervision and evaluation systems in the ESSA era. *Journal of Educational Supervision, 3*(2), 105–135.

Mette, I. M., Cormier, D. R., & Oliveras, Y. (2023). *Making a difference: Instructional leadership that drives self-reflection and values the expertise of teachers*. Rowman & Littlefield.

Mette, I. M., Range, B. G., Anderson, J., Hvidston, D. J., Nieuwenhuizen, L., & Doty, J. (2017). The wicked problem of the intersection between supervision and evaluation. *International Electronic Journal of Elementary Education, 9*(3), 709–724.

Mezirow, J. (2009). Transformative learning theory. In J. Mezirow, & E. W. Taylor (Eds.), *Transformative learning in practice: Insights from community, workplace, and higher education* (pp. 18–32). Jossey-Bass.

Mills, C. W. (1997). *The racial contract*. Cornell University Press.

Milner, H. R., IV. (2017). Where's the race in culturally relevant pedagogy? *Teachers College Record, 119*, 1–32.

Milner, H. R., IV. (2020). *Start where you are, but don't stay there: Understanding diversity, opportunity gaps, and teaching in today's classrooms* (2nd ed.). Harvard Education Press.

Muhammad, G. (2022). On identity. *Voices From the Middle, 30*(1), 14–16.

National Center for Education Statistics (NCES). (2017). *2017 digest of education statistics*. https://nces.ed.gov/programs/digest/d16/tables/dt16_236.10.asp?current=yes

NCLB (2001). No Child Left Behind Act of 2001, P.L. 107–110, 20 U.S.C. § 6319.

Pateman, C. (1998). *The sexual contract*. Stanford University Press.

Schwartz, S. (2021). 8 states debate bills to restrict how teachers discuss racism, sexism. *Education Week*. https://www.edweek.org/policy-politics/8-states-debate-bills-to-restricthow-teachers-discuss-racism-sexism/2021/04

Totenberg, N., & McCammon, S. (2022, June 24). *Supreme Court overturns* Roe v. Wade, *ending right to abortion upheld for decades*. NPR. https://www.npr.org/2022/06/24/1102305878/supreme-court-abortion-roe-v-wade-decision-overturn

CHAPTER 7

The Role of Equity Audits in Culturally Responsive School Leadership

Bodunrin O. Banwo, Kashmeel D. McKoena, Coy Carter Jr., and Muhammad Khalifa

Since the earliest days of organizational theory in education, few transformative frameworks and approaches have spoken to how actors (educators) within organizations (schools) design structures that inform and determine our interactions and experiences. Louis (2015) perceived this as a result of the emphasis on how sociological perspectives handle certain odious ideologies of our society entering the formal organizational structure. Critical scholars, like Sexton, have recognized how harmful and complicated social reproduction practices are embedded inside our formal systems tasked with shaping and molding our society's most vulnerable members. Additionally, Sexton (2011) troubled Black social experiences as a dialectic of Black humanity by asking fundamental questions about the nature and form of being considered human by our social systems of control, which he sees as creating a sort of "psychic force" or, for the purposes of this chapter, organizational systematic shared and social practices of anti-Blackness, passed down through the ages. Sexton, theorizing, asks:

> What is the nature of a human being whose human being is put into question radically and by definition, a human being whose being human raises the question of being human at all? Or, rather, whose being is the generative force, historic occasion, and essential byproduct of the question of human being in general? (p.6)

Sexton, here, sees the question of anti-Blackness as an independent force that human beings have imbued with power. We want readers to understand that this negative meaning-making of Blackness is how we regard racism and white supremacy as the force that socially privileges whiteness through rewards and access to power.

SCHOOLS AND WHITENESS

Let's look at our schools from a panoramic view and consider Sexton's comments through our current and historical data. We see Sexton raising issues as to whether minoritized people can participate in formal systems, as actors in a healthy way. Indeed, we can push this notion further and wonder how minoritized students are experiencing mainstream educational institutions rooted in Western societies with traditions devaluing Blackness. Moreover, we raise questions about how minoritized students are being socialized, and whether that process is occurring healthily or productively.

Through scholars like Banwo (2022), we can see how formal systems have been used as tools to sometimes intentionally and unintentionally forward practices and arrangements of oppression. We can also appreciate how leadership has neglected to find frameworks and disruptive practices informed by critical data collection that challenge the historical echoes of oppression. Moreover, we can also see how these leadership failures color and define the social-cultural arrangements, activities, and organizational practices which Sexton and Banwo speak about. Indeed, Sexton's concern about the humanity of people with dark skin leads to our questioning what and how practices like culturally responsive leadership look like since George Floyd's murder and in the wake of the unchecked rage that swept across the United States. Some of these questions include:

> *What does it mean to be anti-racist? What does it mean to challenge the social construct of "whiteness" and its default position of ordinary? And importantly, what does it mean to face the challenge and pushback from organizational members with power protecting their privileged position?*

As a team of educators and researchers who use equity data to bring forward the stories and experiences of minoritized people (i.e., those who don't fit the social construct of whiteness), we believe that fore-fronting the humanity of racialized persons is the first step for any organization seeking to improve. However, as you read this chapter, we would like you to keep at the front of your mind a question serving as the through-line idea of our work: **How will educational leaders and thinkers use this moment to challenge harmful practices and the tools of white supremacy within organizational cultures?** Are you ready for the challenge? And more importantly, are you prepared to challenge the embedded power structures in your institution that are supported and maintained by the practices of whiteness?

LEADERSHIP AND EQUITY

Equity leadership in school buildings informs classroom practices, which govern how teachers within classrooms approach and think of educational practice and curriculum choices. In a larger sense, we view these social-cultural arrangements as part of a much larger socialization scheme that desperately needs to be made anew through examination and organizational intervention (i.e., equity audits).

Organizations are made of interrelated parts of rules and regulations that produce cooperation in meeting a common goal; however, for educational organizations, these parts also serve as the tools our society uses to socialize our most valuable population (children) into adult members. Indeed, with care and intention, these systems can serve as a powerful engine for disrupting social inequities and fulfilling the promise of equal opportunity for all. At the same time, these systems can also be seen as captured by dominant social members intent on reproducing the harm and history of past injustices, i.e., whiteness (Asante, 2020; Monteiro-Ferreira, 2014).

The questions we raise when thinking about "schools as social tools" are: What type of adults are we producing when a significant portion of our children are experiencing our social tools in a harmful manner? And what does it mean for a child not racialized as white to be socialized in a system that favors and privileges their white peers?

When entering a district, we often find people focused on macro issues, such as school discipline, which involve policies that target and negatively affect Black and Brown students. Other times, we see this focus shifted towards a much larger policy or gap issue. While it is always important to tailor our work towards the goals and policies on the local level, we believe that when districts take a holistic approach to equity improvement (via curriculum, personnel, procedures, routines, and practice), we can produce more significant and profound systematic changes.

The following chapter will explore issues of equity, racism, and data collection to improve marginalized children's schooling and life experiences. This chapter intends to guide leaders and classroom practitioners in using data gathered through district data and equity audits. Although the presented case study focuses on a district-level equity leader, we want Jessica's story to serve as an example of how (1) districtwide personnel can work with building-base staff to shift equity strategies in a way that encourages a strong culture of diversity and inclusion; and (2) how classroom teachers can also use district data to move classroom instruction toward equitable practices. The chapter is in three sections. Section 1, titled "Setting the Stage for Improvement," explores the concepts and definitions of an equity audit. This section will explain the reasoning and rationale behind doing what we term "mini-audits" designed for department and classroom equity improvement. Section 2 is a case study of an equity leader, Jessica Williams, who serves as her district equity representative. The role requires the district to navigate the tricky role of being a student advocate and being tasked with training and improving equity. Jessica's case is where we gather the information to design the mini-audit process. Finally, Section 3 discusses how we encourage teachers and leaders to take a holistic approach to equity improvement through curriculum, personnel, policies, and practice as it relates to Jessica's story—and how it can be a transformational process for healthy student socialization.

SETTING THE STAGE FOR IMPROVEMENT

Skrla at al. (2012) described the overall equity audit process as a systematic way for school leaders (e.g., principals, superintendents, curriculum directors, and teachers) to assess the degree of equity or inequity present in their schools or districts. Indeed, an equity audit (Hanover Research, 2020) can occur through three approaches: (a) The Insight Approach, which seeks to understand how and in what areas the organization is succeeding or failing (Skrla, 2012); (b) The Community-based Audit, which is viewed as helping leaders reconsider underserved communities from resilient and asset-based perspectives (Green, 2017); or (c) Khalifa's Culturally Responsive School Leadership Model, which focuses on how oppressive and inequitable structures and practices in schools inform marginalized students, parents, and a community's organizational experiences.

Politics, Social Tools and Schooling

When preparing leaders for an equity audit, the first key to moving a classroom or school building forward is the explicit understanding that schools are political, with members who dominate and members who are dominated. Moreover, this understanding requires us to recognize that in mainstream or traditional public schools, education system are the socialization tools of society and are the agents that reproduce white supremacy as such they serve an ideology that often is obscured as normal or just the ways we *do business here*. Since each participant in mainstream schools tacitly accepts the ideological rules, leaders can claim whiteness as normal, and thus blunt true cultural responsiveness aims and outcomes (Banwo, 2022). For example, many West African traditions emphasize "community and cooperation" over competition. However, you find many mainstream American institutions in communities with traditions of cooperation unable to incorporate customs of collaboration. This occurs even when customs and practices of cooperation are found locally in African American communities that emphasize Black communal cohesion over capitalist notions of individualism (Anwisye, 2017; Karenga, 1995).

Viewing the positions of schools as social institutions of society provides a lens to explore the theory behind the legal and organizational realities we are asking children to participate in. Handel (2006) observes these systems as agents of socialization, a kind of orientation mechanism used by societies to "shape the behaviors and values of the less powerful members of our society." (p. 400). Additionally, Handel views this process as the basis for the social construction of its cultural identity, theorizing that these institutions (e.g. church, family, and schools) are responsible for transmitting traditions and values that the broader society deems necessary and essential. However, this process of socialization does not happen in a vacuum. Societal attitudes and cultural traditions define which cultural norms are essential and, thus, which norms will be institutionalized in organizational cultures and attitudes.

Organizational scholars like March (1991) see these formalized systems, particularly the organizational method of "best practices," as a way for organizations to learn, remember and hold on to cultural cues that can inform future members of the organization. In other words, organizations can become "learning organizations," which permits them to build cultures and maintain norms through multiple cycles of participants and decades of operations (Groysberg et al., 2018). Bearing these organizational and social notions in mind raises the issue of minoritized students' participation and socialization in mainstream educational institutions rooted in Western societies with traditions devaluing Blackness. Moreover, it raises questions about how minoritized students are being socialized and whether that process is occurring healthily and productively.

Cultural Liaisons and School Equity Personnel

Districts are creating culturally responsive and inclusive spaces for marginalized students, and tapping into their communities, by hiring cultural liaisons (Howland et al., 2006). Cultural liaisons provide a community/cultural-centric epistemology that has long been excluded from inside the school walls. They help bridge the gap for schools to confront the historical oppressions and language barriers that impact students' learning and outcomes (Colombo et al., 2006; Villa et al., 1996). The literature identifies the role of cultural liaisons as cultural brokers (Weiss & Cambone, 1994) or buffers who can serve as a "translator and a transmitter" (Smiley, Howland, & Anderson, 2008, p. 342). As the role of the cultural liaison is relatively new in schools, particularly in the United States, there is no clarity or universality regarding the expectations or job description involved. A cultural liaison can be a parent, teacher's aide, community member (Howland et al., 2006; Martinez-Cosio & Iannacone, 2007), or someone who is specifically hired to be a liaison.

Though Martinez-Cosio and Iannacone (2007) discuss the advantages of a parent liaison who can learn and navigate unwritten and inaccessible rules to access adequate resources and make other demands to help their student, it would seem as though this would apply to any cultural liaison. Cultural liaisons are advocates for marginalized students. The literature addressing cultural liaisons' roles, expectations, and even location (e.g., school level, district, contractor) is limited. However, what we have found within the literature is that cultural liaisons must be placed in a leadership role—formal or informal—to enact notable change (House & Hayes, 2002; Nolan & Palazzolo, 2011). Indeed, when entering a district, equity professionals placed in decision-making and policymaking roles has been essential to identify whether leaders were committed to change. Merely having or hiring a cultural liaison is very different from placing these individuals in a position of power or influential organizational location to contribute to the change desired.

Access to hidden processes and procedures that traditionally benefit well-served students historically, and sharing those "rules" with marginalized families, allows a cultural liaison to advocate for those students and families within the school. Last, there is a unique, shared cultural community connection that a cultural liaison provides that a teacher or administrator cannot. Lane (2017), discusses this through the example of a teacher's aide providing insights to visualizing and verbalizing hidden procedures and practices for marginalized students and their families that the teacher might not be able to do. Cultural liaisons can serve as a conduit of clarity for marginalized communities (Martinez-Cosio, & Iannacone, 2007).

Practicing Culturally Responsive School Leadership (CRSL)

Culturally Responsive Leadership emphasizes practitioners' deep reflection and self-awareness as a force or engine of change. We also regard its prioritization of anti-oppressive and culturally responsive education, what we see as systematic and behavior change, as a required element of equity improvement. According to Khalifa (2018), practitioners and leaders must develop schools that embrace the identities of minoritized youth, implement and promote culturally responsive pedagogy, and establish culturally responsive relationships with parents and community members. Indeed, one of the most significant objectives of culturally responsive practitioners is the humanization of minoritized youth in and out of school.

Khalifa's framework places significance on a leader's ability to do critical self-reflection. This requires leaders to recognize and reckon with the histories of marginalization of oppressed groups and the role organization's cultures, leadership failure, and practitioner practices played in reproducing: (1) anti-Blackness, (2) elevating the normality (i.e., supremacy) of whiteness, and (3) failing to contest oppressive contexts. Moreover, we believe that leaders and practitioners are responsible for explicitly articulating how a school's organization will center students' concerns, particularly regarding cultural productions like inclusion and acceptance of minority students (Asante, 1991). Four specific behaviors provide opportunities to drive cultural responsiveness within a school:

I. **Critical Self-Awareness**: focuses on the need to interrogate ways that leaders personally (along with their organizations) contribute to, reproduce, or contest oppressive practices in schools (Gooden, 2005; McKenzie et al., 2008).
II. **Culturally Responsive Curricula and Teacher Development**: requires responsive leaders to support new curricula and instruction modes that improve the learning and humanization of minoritized students (Khalifa, 2018). This includes accessing community assets and experiential knowledge and ensuring they are included.
III. **Culturally Responsive and Inclusive School Environments**: addresses school climate and spaces and how they influence disparities in educational outcomes. Environments that affirm students' identity are critical, as is a school leader's ability to leverage resources that foster

embedded cultural affirmation (DeMatthews & Mawhinney, 2014; Riehl, 2000).

IV. **Engaging Students and Parents in Community Contexts:** incorporates adults outside the school as bearers of culturally appropriate knowledge. Thus, leaders establish routines for learning from the community and advocating for community knowledge, self-determination, and goals, which leads to a more culturally responsive education (Ishimaru, 2018). This component highlights the place-based focus of CRSL.

When we work in school districts struggling with being culturally responsive, we often find leaders and practitioners failing to grapple with how their community's harmful ideologies of racial and cultural expropriation enter their formal systems. Most critically, they grapple with how these cultural practices inform how their vulnerable students experience their organizational culture and social productions (Apple, 2004; Watkins, 2001; Wilderson, 2014). The latter are among the many scholars who regard the concealment and underestimation of ideology as indicative of our society failing to see or care about how notions like Berger and Luckmann's social constructionism[1] are operationalized as an apparatus to control weaker members of our community. Moreover, particularly for Watkins, this concealment serves as the machinery by which dominant members of our society reproduce the *social scripts*—"A series of behaviors, actions, and consequences that are expected in a particular situation or environment (Mead, 1934; Linton, 1936)"—and *inequality regimes*—involving "interrelated practices, processes, actions, and meanings that result in and maintain class, gender, and racial inequalities within particular organizations" (Acker, 2006, p. 443). These are factors that critical educational scholars find so troubling.

At the heart of our equity-audit theoretical framework is the unpacking and examination of school-building practices and ideologies centered around a series of "why," "how," and "for whom" ideas that function as jumping-off points for practitioners and leaders interested in organizational change:

a. How does society reproduce?
b. Why does society reproduce?
c. Most importantly, for school leaders: for whose benefit is this occurring?

These questions of "why," "how," and "for whose" are equally picked up and advanced by leaders and practitioners of organizations that have taken a critical perspective of society, principally how harmful cultural practices and attitudes are privileged and constructed to harm and determine the life outcomes of marginalized peoples. Suppose we know from Berger and Luckmann's research that cultural patterns and ideas are replicated, defined, and passed down to future generations. In that case, we also know from researchers like Cyert and March (1963) that normalizing social learning and memory can survive through time, and through organizational behavior, which makes organizational learning possible. Cyert and March (1992) described organizational learning as an organization's adaptive behavior over time. However, let us take their notion from another viewpoint. It can also be seen as a school's capacity to historicize saved actions and behaviors into practices, traditions, and ideas as systematic memories. The approach that many see as normal is actually a social construction that can, if desired, be unconstructed.

Equity Audits and Uncovering Inequalities

Culturally relevant pedagogy (CRP) is a theoretical model that focuses on multiple aspects of student achievement and supports students in upholding their cultural identities. However, CRP also encourages students to develop critical perspectives that challenge social norms and assumptions. Ladson-Billings (2014), for example, proposed three main components of culturally relevant pedagogy: (1) a focus on student learning and academic success; (2) the advancement of students' cultural competence to assist them in developing positive ethnic and social identities; and (3) support for students' critical consciousness and their ability to recognize and critique societal inequalities. Although many across the educational field have taken Ladson-Billings's notion of CRP and applied it to many areas of leadership and education, Khalifa (2018) argues that a leader's critical self-reflection recognizes both the history of marginalization of oppressed groups and the role leaders play in reproducing or contesting oppressive contexts.

In many mainstream (traditional) public school systems, as stated earlier, there is a lack of political clarity driving the *purpose and reasoning* of why we, as a society, invest in and appreciate our tradition of K–12 education (Ilies et al., 2007; Murphy & Louis, 2018). Indeed, when we first begin our work with a district, the questions we ask our district leaders and teachers to consider are informed by our understanding of, Khalifa's CRSL framework and the hidden quality of organizational politics through systems control and protection of resources:

I. *Critical Self-Awareness:* Why are you educating children? What is your reason for being in the classroom or school building?
II. *Culturally Responsive Curricula and Teacher Development:* Why are we teaching specific themes, literature, and educational materials? What other learnings and teaching materials are available, and why did "I or We" select what we did?
III. *Culturally Responsive and Inclusive School Environments:* How are my minoritized children receiving my building culture, teaching practice, and curriculum?
IV. *Engaging Students and Parents in Community Contexts:* How many minoritized families come to parent-teacher conferences? Do we ask community members for input? Or suggestions about learning and teaching material? How engaged are our minoritized students?

The purpose of these starting questions, for us, is to shift the systematic thinking of teachers and leaders from that of whiteness, which we regard as property and as intangible resources used to reproduce the system we view as harmful, into that of responsiveness which considers minoritized students and their families. Moreover, we regard this as a political process that protects the resources and power of dominant members of the organization. When thinking about the social frameworks and ideas raised by Khalifa and Ladson-Billings, we see the organization and its actors as participants in a process awash in ideologies of harm. In other words, racism, bigotry, and harm within an organizational culture are not just the results of someone bringing in racist attitudes. It is actual participation in a process that serves to advance the agenda of the powerful. Our equity-audit work serves to uncover, expose, and bring this agenda into the light, so that school actors can resist replicating racialized harm

CASE STUDY EQUITY AUDIT IN ACTION

20 years in, and I am still kicking butt!

The role of the cultural liaison in the district of Jessica Dawson, a 20-year leader in the Dakota Public Schools (a pseudonym), has evolved from a classroom helper to a professionalized position tasked with enacting effective cultural change that impacts the school and its community. The role is distinct from other equity positions in surrounding districts. Jessica's district's cultural liaison model intentionally builds a direct pipeline to the minoritized communities identified for intervention (Weiss & Cambone, 1994). Moreover, through its liaison program, her district understands that the positionality of traditionally marginalized persons provides the district with insights and capacities to engage with students in ways other surrounding communities may not have the ability to replicate. For example, Jessica views her position as infusing cultural responsiveness into the organizational structure of her district, which she regards as transforming the people (actors) in her district and their understanding of inclusion and cultural differences. She believes her work is about "seeing and acting on these discourses she believes could harm or help her district's organizational culture, which she believes reveal themselves through the actions and behaviors of her schools' organizational citizens" (Carter et al., 2021, p. 15). Jessica made intentional and authentic inroads into the communities and lived experiences of the district's Black and Brown students. She is the head of the DPS Office of Equity and Inclusion (OEI), where she implements equity reform through a cultural liaison system that creates a space for minoritized students and their families to be heard institutionally.

During one of our interviews with Jessica, she described an ongoing discrimination concern with some of her district's white female teachers. Jessica began hearing reports of teachers targeting Somali male students for exclusionary discipline practices because of a pervasive belief that Muslim men did not fully respect women. These students were exposed to the harm of a whiteness-centered social construction of education, which described them as incapable of developing foundational critical thinking skills—thus making them incompatible with their school's definition of academic success or promise. Coupled with the grim realities of xenophobia, Islamophobia, and anti-Blackness, these young men were further marginalized in a setting that should have been their haven from the oppressive structures of whiteness in society. Their plight and Jessica's response of advocacy at a district level—which led educators through a data-instructed process of unlearning implicit biases toward equitable pedagogical paradigms—present a striking example of the impact of an equity audit developed over decades of practiced culturally responsive school leadership.

Valuing Minoritized Communities

Cultural liaisons invite community values and experiences to the formal academic space, where such concerns are rarely welcomed (Howland et al., 2006). These are roles where community members who mirror the identities of a school district's students bridge the cultural gaps between a school administration and its students by hearing concerns about inequity from the youth and their families, bringing them urgently to the agentic leaders of the institution for consideration and intervention. Essentially, these concerns create the site for meaningful equity audits. This elevation of community voices and values requires humility in recognizing the inherently different cultural lens that is being translated by liaisons, along with intentionality in welcoming what would otherwise be ignored or perceived as threatening to established organizational culture.

Jessica expanded the cultural liaison program in DPS—which predated her leadership role—to develop a team of eight culturally diverse and institutionally adept liaisons. This team was tasked with creating safe spaces for families and students within the school system. Their role also doubled as an indispensable data collection tool for equity audits conducted by Jessica's office. For example, it was a Somali-identifying member of this team that first heard the equity issue raised by the Somali male students.

While this process of listening and responding seems less than revolutionary, we argue that it is essential in engaging diverse school communities in equity-minded solution-building. There is inherent risk involved whenever youths of marginalized backgrounds—especially potential noncitizens—speak up against an institution that needs improvement. In this case, the risk was compounded by their grievance against white female teachers, those with institutional power over them. These educators—who, in Dakota and elsewhere around the nation, make up the majority of the teaching force (Bristol & Martin-Fernandez, 2019)—were entrenched in a normative whiteness-centering liberal ethos of how education worked. They deemed their Black Muslim male students culturally incongruous with their academic structure, centered on a belief that their religion and culture did not value or respect the knowledge production and leadership of women. Thus, it was implied that they characteristically could not learn from their white female teachers. Furthermore, not only were they stereotyped, but they also were disproportionately targeted by exclusionary discipline and denied opportunities for authentic engagement in the school community. They were treated as hostile to school culture. How, then, could they expect to find someone who heard them at the administrative level of the same institution that fiercely excluded them?

Listening and Seeing the Signs

The understanding and critically responsive space they found with a cultural liaison was a direct result of the groundwork laid by Jessica, who herself expressed frustration with the complacency of the district. She shared with us that school leadership teams often stopped trying to break down the justifiable reluctance of hesitant marginalized families, despite the longevity of their equity initiatives in the district. However, this was an initiative near to her own heart. As such, her passion led her to key characteristics that made any equity auditing meaningful: intentionality and empathy. Without these, a team of dedicated community representatives would not be able to penetrate the cultural barriers between the district and its student communities. We implore practitioners to consider these characteristics in their work.

Jessica leads with full transparency around her own racialized experiences as a lighter-skinned Black woman, teased for her freckles and put into a box of whiteness that she has not benefited from (Carter et al., 2021). In her approach, built from lived experiences and community involvement, she led from a place of close observation, training her team in the same skillset. They are trained to identify nonverbal "social signals" as deeper indicators of well-being, concern, or warnings. She understood what one may dismiss as a parent playing with a tissue during a meeting as a silent sign of displeasure over her son's school experiences: "the tissue represented a Klan member's hood," she told us. Her deeper relationships with the community, established by investing in family visits and meetings, helped her to notice and intervene: "every time she threw that tissue on the table . . . I swipe it off" (Carter et al., 2021). Her interventions are not from a place of dominance or invalidation, but are about seeing and wanting more for her families than what they are experiencing as inequitable. This is how she stays real and relatable with her students and their families. On one occasion, she describes bantering with a parent, making sure she put on a coat before heading to a meeting. Her method of establishing a community presence, observing and intervening in small, meaningful ways consistently over time created an environment of trust, whereupon families and students of minoritized backgrounds felt safe opening up to her, knowing that her interventions were different from the oppressive dictates of the school district institutionally.

This approach to her equity audit led her to see and understand the inequitable realities of her Somali male students in their grievance over treatment by white female teachers. She immediately understood a form of essentialism not unlike what she experienced in her youth. But instead of relying on her own lived experiences exclusively, she strategically engaged with a Somali cultural liaison to invite important considerations of cultural background to the conversation. This conversation included the more arduous task of unearthing and explaining the anti-Muslim essentialism behind these interactions—so the young men could remain on guard, with their integrity and authenticity intact, while she and her team worked on dismantling these pervasive attitudes within the district. This also included Jessica using her position, along with the data collected by her and her liaison, to address a senior district administrator in pursuit of meaningful change. The takeaway from Jessica's role in this intervention was a careful balance of personal authenticity and reflexivity met with humbling cultural awareness and decentralizing of self.

Digging Deeper into Organizational Practice

In the DPS, cultural liaisons are tasked with advocating for all students. However, the very existence of the cultural liaison of Somali heritage is an example of the district recognizing and solving an organizational problem (that of Somali student cultural and social integration). Though this individual's role is to advocate for all students, through intentional hiring and retention practices, the role represents the student community as a mirror for authentic and meaningful advocacy. If we look closely at Jessica's story, we see the Somali students' first point of contact was their cultural liaison, who, in this example, was their first line of defense against the teachers' essentialist attitudes. DPS's organizational structure, on the other hand, demonstrated the importance of data collection and community engagement. The positioning of the Somali cultural liaison—who first investigated, advocated, and took the initial steps—allowed the issue to reach Jessica, a senior district administrator.

A second important point of this story identifies how the teachers' unchallenged view at first of students by adults in the building initiated an organizational crisis. The teachers had intentionally constructed a harmful social reality through organizational behavior that would have continued unabated if not for Jessica and her team's strong relationships with minoritized families through a cultural liaison's equity assessment. Indeed, the teacher's behavior was undoubtedly damaging to the Black and Muslim students in the schools; however, the damage was more acute when we consider this case from an organizational sense. The teacher not only denied the students their rightful access to education, but denied them an opportunity to be a part of the broader community as their authentic cultural selves.

From our point of view, the actors involved in the story had two paths to follow: On the first path were the unchanging beliefs that initiated and drove an organizational crisis. On this path alone, the Somali youth and their teachers both hardened their social positions. Conversely, the other accessible path was through an organizational leader, ombudsman, or broker who could lead the system out of an organizational crisis to growth. Jessica, using her 20 years in DPS, showed how a "strong and trusted leadership" can bridge the cultural gaps, in this case between families and school district officials. This audit also exposed blind spots in instructional equity that would have been a missed opportunity for practitioners working with marginalized student groups. Jessica's ability to effectively build trust and organizational capacity is a critical juncture that helps DPS move past its racialized roadblocks and internal concerns. Interestingly, although Jessica had spent 20 years doing equity work in DPS, issues around race and differences still arose and required her to mediate organizational citizens' past racism. This underscores the necessity of continuous reflective equity audits for leaders, as they must continue to be vigilant and not assume that racism is ever fully eradicated in their institution.

"Good Teaching, but Awful Experiences for Students"

A significant component of equity audits aims to elevate students' voices by focusing on their experiences and lived realities. Jessica believed that sharing how the students understood racialized events in the district was paramount. Moreover, she also saw the process of equity audits as an opportunity for teachers to unpack, reflect and improve their classroom instruction. We had the chance to interview Jessica nine months after DPS returned from the COVID-19 pandemic. Our goal for re-visiting DPS was to, of course, see how Jessica's passion and championing of culturally responsive leadership and education had progressed over the COVID-19 emergency. However, it was also an opportunity for us to learn how the educational experiences of the young Somali men, from before the pandemic, had changed.

"*We are five years past that story, and I would say not just their classroom experiences, but a lot of Black boys' experiences have changed quite a bit.*" For Jessica, the biggest and most pressing matter that improved for the students was allowing them to participate equally in the educational setting (classroom). What initially made Jessica's office first take notice of this problem was the report of parents whose children were left outside the classroom and not involved in learning. These exclusionary practices on paper appeared unusual because the teachers featured in this case were seen as "good" teachers (determined by high ratings and high student test scores). This performance of "good" teaching" was actually creating awful experiences for their minoritized students. Jessica reflected on the outcomes of their cultural liaison's audit and where those classrooms went from there: "*What we saw with those teachers and students was first an improvement in their classroom participation. We saw the teachers use self-reflection as an opportunity to see how their bias[es] were arriving in the classroom instruction.*" Jessica continued by highlighting that these teachers were professionals who loved teaching, but failed to see that what Jessica described as their misguided "*attention to gendered equity through their intentional actions and teaching*" was producing harm. Thus, this case study reveals the necessity of critical self-reflection supported by an audit response process that allows professional development around implicit bias and improvements to instructional practice.

How does a district develop the infrastructure for this type of work? Jessica believes that productive OEI intervention must begin with a process of mutual understanding among the school, teachers, students and mostly minoritized communities. Teachers, through simple engagement, begin to better understand their minoritized and "newcomer" communities and how parents and students prefer to be engaged. Moreover, this process allows these teachers to see how their biases directly affect student learning. So, 5 years after Jessica's office's intervention, this intervention, she said, disrupted three key factors that directly affected student classroom experiences.

1. **Equitable use of data:** Through processes like equity audits, Jessica's office was able to see data identifying who was being excluded from learning. Access to classroom data pointed to previously unidentified realities and allowed Jessica and the teachers to ask "why?" Moreover, when investigating parental concerns and teachers' negative assumptions about students, OEI needed to present hard data as a starting point for engagement and improvement.
2. **Moving toward diversifying the curriculum and classroom dynamism:** Five years following this OEI intervention, Jessica has found these teachers to still be striving to unlearn biases in what Jessica describes as what "*appears to be a continuous practice.*" Before this intervention, the teachers were, in reality, using the curriculum to interject a form of politics into the learning environment and curriculum. This interjection of politics took up space as barriers in both the physical classroom and curriculum—which also prevented other topics, practices, and goals from being realized. Jessica found that once this political agenda was disrupted and redirected, the classroom became more open to culturally responsive learning. The teachers began to view all their students's cultures as something that needed to be understood, engaged, and seen in pedagogy.
3. **Avoiding assumptions about students' backgrounds:** Finally, through ongoing training, Jessica believed teachers began to see the problematic nature of their cultural beliefs and assumptions. For Jessica, negative assumptions took up space and time, which led to educators teaching *at* students with a political agenda. Teachers began to explore how to include students. By disrupting the teachers' negative beliefs, their need to use the classroom as a form of political education was transformed. It turned out that the students didn't need to learn about how to treat women correctly—the teachers instead needed to learn and examine why they believed their cultural ideas and practice were superior to that of the

students'. In other words, these teachers were enacting a form of white supremacy by degrading another culture through assumptions. Once this was interrupted, equitable learning practices could bring everyone into the classroom justly.

THINKING DEEPER ABOUT AUDITS

If we recall from earlier in this chapter, Khalifa regards equity improvements as depending on the interrogation of: (1) oppressive and inequitable structures; and (2) improvement in organizational learning and instructional experiences. This equity improvement is accessed and measured in four focal areas:

A. Equity trends (acceptance of a data-driven process);
B. Survey data, targeted toward majority and minority organizational participants (equity culture, healthy and diversity climates, engagement with complex equity issues)
C. Policy analysis (examining how disparities can become embedded in policy and organizational culture); and finally,
D. Developing Culturally Responsive Curriculums and Pedagogical Practice (an examination of instructional & leadership practices through an equity lens)

When we enter a district, we center this equity process around educators' interest in creating systems of healthy socialization. Indeed, during the early stages of the audit process, we request leaders to be self-reflective equity agents, interested and engaged in tricky questions encountered in systems of white supremacy. Additionally, we require leaders to be anti-racist practitioners who first look inward and take stock of what they know to be accurate and, most importantly, what they know to be fabricated. This effort takes patience, reflection, and commitment, along with the will to confront the pushback from the beneficiaries of white supremacy's historical and ingrained system.

Equity Audits on the District Level

Although this chapter uses a case study of small-scale audits used to change school building or classroom equity processes, audits typically also take place on a district level. We believe that the more data and understanding of the district that school leaders have, the better they can respond to racial incidents, crises, conflicts, and injustices. In our district-level work, we encourage a focus on relationships and questioning about how leaders cultivate culturally responsive pathways with students and families. A significant component of equity audits is to elevate students' voices by focusing on their experiences and lived realities. As evident in Jessica's case study, she believed it was paramount to understand and bring forward how her students understood racialized events in the district. She also saw the process of equity audits in her district from earlier years as opportunities for leadership to understand how a lack of inclusion and responsiveness harmed their students. For her, the equity audit became the data and tool needed to finally get the district out of denial and into a state primed for equity change.

Using Jessica's initial audit as an example, we found marginalized students in her district voicing how organizational culture prohibited them from showing up authentically in their schools and classrooms. Additionally, students reported bullying, harm, and exclusion from classes by their white peers when expressing their traditional and cultural practices. In another district we examined, we found that teachers and administrators responded to their marginalized students experiencing racialized harm by telling them to "ignore it," or by claiming that "it isn't that bad." This was in response to racialized slurs and inappropriate touching by other students. Due to teachers' and administrators' aversion to legitimate student concerns, minoritized students were forced to learn in an environment where some white students would get away with (and sometimes were tacitly given permission for) continued racist behavior. Consider Jessica's story about the Somali male students and ask yourself: Do you think the other students in the classroom could pick up on the dislike of Black male students excluded from the behavior of their teachers—meaning the classroom leaders and supposedly morally upstanding adults in the classroom who were paid a wage to set an example of scholarly decorum? Further, do you not think their actions and dislike had reverberations in how students interacted with them, or responded to them?

Indeed, when we first entered Jessica's school system, it was of course, in a strong position for change. But we found that students and adults used colorblind language to shift from conversations about race to those of gender and sexuality. Indeed, we found this obfuscation had ripple effects in the classroom and served as a silencing tool for students facing genuine racial harm and danger within the school building and larger district.

In the first section, we presented questions that Khalifa raised in districts when beginning the data gathering and organizational change process:

I. *Critical Self-Awareness:* Why are you educating children? What is your reason for being in the classroom or school building?
II. *Culturally Responsive Curricula and Teacher Development:* Why are we teaching specific themes, literature, and educational materials? What other learnings and teaching materials are available, and why did "I or We" select what we did?
III. *Culturally Responsive and Inclusive School Environments:* How are my minoritized children receiving my building culture, teaching practice, and curriculum?

IV. *Engaging Students and Parents in Community Contexts:* How many minoritized families come to parent–teacher conferences? Do we ask community members for input? Or suggestions about learning and teaching material? How engaged are our minoritized students?

When we first presented these overarching questions, we found a district primed for change but struggling to challenge entrenched power sources protecting their pet programs and projects. When we first spoke with Jessica and her staff in the Office of Equity and Inclusion, we found a group of professionals who worked on two levels: (1) OEI staff who cultivated a reputation with students and families as an honest and fair team where those families could find a caring adult and a place that had the best interest of children as its primary focus; and (2) Jessica, as part of the leadership cabinet, who could bring those experiences into more significant "whole" system discussions.

Politics of School Change

Earlier, we discussed the structural questions leaders ask themselves when examining their school culture to root out injury and danger for minoritized students. Their process must first be understood as an intentional choice about which practices, techniques, and cultural signifiers will be embraced and incorporated into the broader school or classroom culture. The key to understanding the change equity leaders seek is acknowledging the politics of the larger organization. Jessica's district's embrace of CRSL as an equity strategy framework highlighted how higher-level leaders could help school building staff focus on equity through small but essential areas of practice and organizational improvement, which are (1) cultural competency education; (2) community engagement; and (3) parent, teacher, and student conflict management. In our pre-COVID interview, we saw Jessica as an example of someone developing close and authentic relationships between caring adults and students to build healthy communication pathways that could uncover and improve upon negative organizational experiences. Indeed, our leaders did use this strategy to collect data and information about how students and families were experiencing their school district (for example the data about Somali male students).

Jessica regards student voices as a critical and culturally responsive tool that must be continuously examined by developing healthy, culturally responsive relationships with students and their home communities. Throughout Jessica's tenure, she has cultivated her district's equity approach through her team's care and responsiveness to marginalized voices. Her 20 years of equity leadership has helped develop healthy communication pathways between leadership and the broader organization, which still serves as Jessica's motivating leadership goal. Indeed, during an interview which took place 3 years after we first met her, she emphasized healthy communication as *"creating a mechanism through which marginalized parents and students could express concerns for needed changes."* For her, this two-way communication pathway broke down barriers to understanding and alerted the OEI staff to problems and concerns bubbling under the surface.

We bring attention to Jessica's story because it demonstrates how valuable this work is to organizational culture, but also because it shows how student voices can be used to transform how the district approaches equity issues, particularly those around instruction. Although Jessica's district had been doing equity training for 25 years by the time of our interview, we found that work at the building level with small groups of building staff helped the leaders shift equity work to the systematic without much pushback. We believe districts can mirror this response with relationship building done in years prior to incidents, as done by Jessica performed over her tenure. Jessica's office did not approach the teachers as adversaries. In fact, through their investigation of their Somali cultural liaison, they felt dual action needed to be taken: involving, first, cultural training for the larger Somali community about the racialized reality their students were now being socialized in; and, second, additional training for the teachers, to ensure that they felt empowered by culturally competent education. It was this strategy that Jessica felt had the most significant breakthrough. Teachers, over time, came to see OEI as partners and resources; as Jessica stated, *"[They] began to see us more than just people who translated papers and made calls to families. They started understanding how much further they could get when they fully embraced the families and the cultures they come from."*

Data and the Classroom

As an action step for practitioners responding to this chapter, we have created a framework by which teachers and school leaders can conduct equity assessments that will achieve two goals: (1) priming the process we described throughout the chapter as "deep internal reflection" and (2) generating data that can be used to justify equity changes at the instructional level. Again, when we enter a district, we encourage our leaders to think about what is at the center of their organizational goals. At the heart of our equity audit theoretical framework is the unpacking and examining of school-building practices and ideologies centered on a series of "why," "how," and "for whose" questions. These function as jumping-off points for practitioners and leaders interested in organizational change.

   a. How does society reproduce?
   b. Why does society reproduce?
   c. For whose benefit is this occurring?

Like district leaders, instructional supervisors must be able to engage with classroom teachers and ask these questions; most importantly, they must utilize

Table 7.1. Culturally Responsive Self-Reflective Questions Framework

I.	Critical Self-Awareness	Why am I educating children? What is my reason for being in the classroom or school building?
II.	Culturally Responsive Curricula and Teacher Development	Why am I teaching specific themes, literature, and educational materials? What other learnings and teaching materials are available, and why did I (or we) select what was chosen from these options?
III.	Culturally Responsive and Inclusive School Environments	How are my minoritized children receiving my building culture, teaching practice, and curriculum?
IV.	Engaging Students and Parents in Community Contexts	How many minoritized families come to my parent-teacher conferences? Do we ask community members for input or suggestions about learning and teaching material? How engaged are our minoritized students?

this self-reflection as a tool to transform spaces of white supremacy into places of liberation. Often when we work with teachers, there is a desire to have a clear-cut, white-and-black process that instructs practitioners on "how to do." Indeed, from our experience, the equity audit process is messy and often requires flexibility and intentionality of goals and purpose.

Like school districts, school buildings and classrooms are also formal organizations with (1) a common purpose, (2) a coordinated effort, (3) a division of labor, and (4) a hierarchy of authority (Schein, 2010). As such, as seen in Table 7.1, instructional supervisors must be able to engage with teachers in developing a reflective stance about their instructional practices, particularly by addressing their roles as classroom leader.

PRACTICES OF CHALLENGE

As we conclude this chapter, we will apply the above equity audit framework to Jessica's district; we want this section, too, of course, to serve as a concrete example of implementing transformative approaches to organizational culture but also an opportunity for you to begin to imagine yourself performing an audit in your school. Through the answers unpacked in this framework, districts can begin the deeply reflective work of uprooting harmful reproductions of whiteness in our schools and identify clear individual roles in the change process. While the equity audit in her case study was triggered by data collection from a dedicated cultural liaison, we will focus on Jessica's role as a leader overseeing this initiative.

Critical Self-Awareness

Positing Jessica's role in her district to consider the tenet of Critical Self-Awareness (i.e., answering the questions, "Why am I educating children? What is my reason for being in the classroom or school building?"), it is evident that her personal experiences as a marginalized and misidentified youth motivated her involvement in education at the district level. Positionality is invaluable at this first level of culturally responsive leadership, change, as is data collection. Thus, Jessica identifying her own entanglement with the privileges, assumptions, and burdens of racializing young people informs her investment in the situation that emerged with not only the Black Somali youth at the core of this situation, but with other students struggling to find a place in the Dakota Public Schools.

Being misrepresented for her proximity to whiteness—while simultaneously being denied its privileges—gave Jessica a primary sensitivity to how assumptions of character based on racial or cultural signifiers can impact a young person's sense of belonging in schools. This no doubt allowed her—and the team of cultural liaisons trained by her—to see the harm that might have otherwise gone unnoticed because the Somali youth in her district's schools were easily "othered" by their teachers. Revisiting one's own experiences of being "othered" and stereotyped is an emotionally risky step, but is necessary to unpack why one chooses to return to schools that may have been the site of suffering as a youth. This affords educators the ability to be introspective and empathetic to youth, which leads to the second tenet of this framework. In effect, when a leader is critically self-aware (and creates infrastructure for critical self-awareness across a district or school), that scenario provides opportunities for classroom practitioners to be made more critically self-aware to that which they would not otherwise recognize.

Culturally Responsive Curricula and Teacher Development

Unpacking the second tenet of Culturally Responsive Curricula and Teacher Development (i.e., questioning the selection of learning materials), Jessica's situation would no doubt require the white female educators of these students to examine precisely where and how cultural assumptions implicit in curricular materials would impact instruction. While these educators may not navigate the first tenet of critical self-awareness on their own with the same experiences as Jessica, a Black woman, has, they may be able to identify where other assumptions have impacted their curricular acuity. For example, asking questions about the origins of curricular focuses in white and Western practices—and how responsibly this can be applied to the education of students from Eastern, African, and Muslim cultures as well as students with disabilities—can help educators be more thoughtful in their selection of curricular materials, even if they share none of the background or experiences of their students. This is why we implore practitioners to apply all four tenets rigorously in the equity audit process. If the roots of inequitable reproductions of society are not unmasked at one level, they will be exposed at another.

Culturally Responsive and Inclusive School Environments

The third tenet steps away from the educator and the curriculum to ask how students receive their school's culture and their teachers' instruction. A culturally responsive educator or administrator knows that the most reflective educators with the most responsive materials cannot teach effectively if they do not first understand how their students sit in the school's organizational culture. Exposing incongruities such as that discussed in this case study requires the voice of youth to inform and ultimately correct the decisions made in the reproduction of societal harms. This is why Jessica's team of cultural liaisons provides safe spaces to prioritize those youth experiences as a way to ensure that our teacher development, school culture, and curricular decisions are aligned with their needs.

We cannot assume students' feedback; we need their transparent responses. Thus it is paramount to create safe spaces where their honest reflections can be shared with minimal consequences, ideally to adults who can facilitate the change they need and elevate their voices without chastising them or creating discomfort from their authority over them. Their own teachers did not create safe spaces for them to share this harmful experience. However, cultural liaisons whose roles respond intentionally to the reflected identities of the district's marginalized students can create these spaces where empowered representation otherwise does not exist. We must create and support roles outside of classrooms within schools and districts that can capture these experiences.

Engaging Students and Parents in Community Contexts

The fourth tenet speaks to the importance of Engaging Students and Parents in Community Contexts. The most authentic way to create a safe space to understand how students receive building culture is to richly contextualize them in the safety of their own culture and community. This empowers students by giving them confidence in sharing from their home context and allows school personnel to understand a student's experiences from the perspective of their authentic selves and communities of origin.

Jessica demonstrated a commitment to reaching beyond the school walls on behalf of students in her home visits over 20 years of work in her district. This allows the students facing injustice to recontextualize the situation from a home base that affirms them. In Jessica's district, this would have been facilitated by the Somali cultural liaison opening the door to their community's context as an interruption of the whiteness-centered educational experiences wherein the students were being harmed.

Developing relationships with families allows a culturally responsive leader to understand, identify with, and support the dreams and hopes of the student's families—even at the expense of the institutional agenda, as Jessica practiced in-home visits and resulting interventions on behalf of parents and families. This corrects the harmful mistakes made by the teachers of these students, who assumed their values in education and equity were more important and present than what their students walked into class with every day. Walking alongside one's students—by understanding their homes, families, and communities—informs culturally responsive decision-making in schools.

CONCLUSION

Equity audits serve to empower marginalized students with the safety of knowing that their adverse experiences will be heard and responded to seriously and intentionally. The result of this confidence in a culturally reflexive and attentive school environment is the development of student agency in their education, as they and their communities are responded to with equity, value, and collaborative justice. Instruction improves when the educator considers all students' perspectives, cultural identities, and needs. Moreover, being willing to grow and meet young people where they are demonstrates a strengths-based lens that directly correlates with achievement. Educators who can be trained to see the best in their students will work with them and their communities to produce the best in their classrooms.

As school leaders, it is imperative that we be critically self-reflective and open to growth, change, and action in response to the needs of our students. Cutting through the intensely politicized nature of schools and districts, we believe that the equity audit process is a dynamic and invaluable tool to begin the inquiry process in our systems in an effort to root out all forms of white supremacy culture, especially at the level of educator biases. We encourage practitioners to adopt this practice in full, by considering the application of Jessica's work, even as we continue to hold ourselves and our school systems accountable to the equitable and healthy development of our most marginalized students.

As we close this chapter, we want to encourage you to humanize school organizations. Think about the people inside your school and remember that formal systems have been used to sometimes intentionally and unintentionally forward practices and arrangements of oppression. Jessica's connection to the Somali community of her district allowed her to see the blind spots missed by most and use her authentic human connection and knowledge of Somali culture and norms to say, *"That's not right, what is going on here?"* These questions and this mindset goes to what Khalifa (2018) describes as Humanizing School Community or practice.

NOTE

1. Social constructionism is the idea that people and groups interact in a social system, which creates, over time, concepts or mental representations of each other's actions,

and that these concepts eventually become habituated into reciprocal roles played by the actors in relation to each other (Berger & Luckmann, 1967).

REFERENCES

Acker, J. (2006). Inequality regimes gender, class, and race in organizations. *Gender and Society, 20*(4), pp. 441–464.

Anwisye, F. S. (2017). *African education: Engine for our liberation*. Blessings Not Curses Publications.

Apple, M. W. (2004). *Ideology and curriculum*. Routledge.

Asante, M. K. (1991). The Afrocentric idea in education. *The Journal of Negro Education, 60*(2), 170–180. https://doi.org/10.2307/2295608

Asante, M. K. (2020). From critical pedagogy to revolutionary pedagogy: Toward transformative practice. In K. G. Shockley & K. Lomotey (Eds.), *African-centered education: Theory and practice* (pp. 65–83). Myers Education Press.

Banwo, B. (2022). A community within a community: Collectivism, social cohesion and building a healthy black childhood. *Anthropology & Education Quarterly, 54*(2), 122–154.

Berger, P. L., & Luckmann, T. (1967). *The social construction of reality: A treatise in the sociology of knowledge*. Anchor Books.

Bristol, T. J., & Martin-Fernandez, J. (2019). The added value of Latinx and Black teachers for Latinx and Black students: Implications for policy. *Policy Insights from the Behavioral and Brain Sciences, 6*(2), 147–153. https://doi.org/10.1177/2372732219862573

Carter, C., Yousuf, E., Banwo, B. O., & Khalifa, M. A. (2021). Leadership with a purpose: Responding to crises through culturally responsive district leadership. *Journal of Family Diversity in Education, 4*(2), 115–129.

Colombo, M. G., Grilli, L., & Piva, E. (2006). In search of complementary assets: The determinants of alliance formation of high-tech start-ups. *Research Policy 35I*(8), 1166–1199.

Cyert, R. M., & March, J. G. (1963). *A behavioral theory of the firm*. Prentice Hall/Pearson Education.

Cyert, R. M., & March, J. G. (1992). *Behavioral theory of the firm* (2nd ed.). Wiley-Blackwell Publishing.

DeMatthews, D., & Mawhinney, H. (2014). Social justice leadership and inclusion. *Educational Administration Quarterly, 50*, 844–881.

Gooden, M. A. (2005). The role of an African American principal in an urban information technology high school. *Educational Administration Quarterly, 41*(4), 630–650.

Green, T. L. (2017). Community-based equity audits: A practical approach for educational leaders to support equitable community-school improvements. *Educational Administration Quarterly, 53*(1), 3–39.

Groysberg, B., Lee, J., Price, J., & Cheng, J. -J. (2018, January–February). The Leader's guide to corporate culture. *Harvard Business Review*. https://hbr.org/2018/01/the-leaders-guide-to-corporate-culture

Handel, G. (2006). *Childhood socialization, social problems and social issues*. Transaction Publishers.

Hanover Research (2020). Research brief: Conducting an equity audit.
House, R. M., & Hayes, R. L. (2002). School counselors: Becoming key players in school reform. *Professional School Counseling*, 5(4), 249–256.
Howland, A., Anderson, J. A., Smiley, A. D., & Abbott, D. J. (2006). School liaisons: Bridging the gap between home and school. *School Community Journal*, 16(2), 47–68.
Ilies, R., Nahrgang, J. D., & Morgeson, F. P. (2007). Leader-member exchange and citizenship behaviors: A meta-analysis. *Journal of Applied Psychology*, 92(1), 269–277.
Ishimaru, A. M. (2018). Re-imagining turnaround: families and communities leading educational justice. *Journal of Educational Administration*, 56(5), 546–561. https://doi.org/10.1108/JEA-01-2018-0013
Karenga, M. (1995). Afrocentricity and multicultural education: Concept, challenge, and contribution. In B. P. Bowser, T. Jones, & G. A. Young (Eds.), *Toward the multicultural university* (pp. 41–61). Praeger Publishers.
Khalifa, M. (2018). *Culturally responsive school leadership*. Harvard Education Press.
Ladson-Billings, G. (2014). Culturally relevant pedagogy 2.0: A.k.a. the remix. *Harvard Educational Review*, 81(1), 74–84.
Lane, K. L. (2017). Building strong partnerships: Responsible inquiry to learn and grow together: TECBD–CCBD keynote address. *Education and Treatment of Children*, 40(4), 597–618.
Linton, R. (1936). *The study of man: An introduction*. D. Appleton-Century.
Louis, K. S. (2015). Linking leadership to learning: state, district and local effects. *Nordic Journal of Studies in Educational Policy*, 2015(3). https://doi.org/10.3402/nstep.v1.30321
March, J. G. (January 1991). Exploration and exploitation in organizational learning. *Organization Science*, 2(1), 71–87.
Martinez-Cosio, M., & Iannacone, R. M. (2007). The tenuous role of institutional agents: Parent Liaisons as cultural brokers. *Education and Urban Society*, 39(3), 349–369.
McKenzie, K. B., Christman, D. E., Hernandez, F., Fierro, E., Capper, C. A., Dantley, M., González, M. L., Cambron-McCabe, N., & Scheurich, J. J. (2008). From the field: A proposal for educating leaders for social justice. *Educational Administration Quarterly*, 44(1), 111–138. https://doi.org/10.1177/0013161X07309470
Mead, G. H. (1934). *Mind, self, and society from the standpoint of a social behaviorist*. University of Chicago Press.
Monteiro-Ferreira, A. (2014). *The demise of the inhuman: Afrocentricity, modernism, and postmodernism*. SUNY Press.
Murphy, J. F., & Louis, K. S. (2018). *Positive school leadership: Building capacity and strengthening relationships*. Teachers College Press.
Nolan, B., & Palazzolo, L. (2011). New teacher perceptions of the "Teacher Leader" Movement. *NASSP Bulletin*, 95(4), 302–318.
Riehl, C. J. (2000). The principal's role in creating inclusive schools for diverse students: A review of normative, empirical, and critical literature on the practice of educational administration. *Review of Educational Research*, 70(1), 55–81.
Schein, E. H. (2010). *Organizational culture and leadership* (4th ed.). Jossey-Bass.
Sexton, J. (2011). The social life of social death: On Afro-pessimism and Black optimism. *InTensions Journal*. 2011(5). Retrieved from https://www.yorku.ca/intent/issue5/articles/pdfs/jaredsextonarticle.pdf

Skrla, L., McKenzie, K. B., & Scheurich, J. J. (2012). *Using equity audits to create equitable and excellent schools.* Corwin Press.

Smiley, A. D., Howland, A. A., & Anderson, J. A. (2008). Cultural brokering as a core practice of a special education parent liaison program in a large urban school district. *Journal of Urban Learning, Teaching, and Research, 4,* 86–95.

Villa, R. A., Thousand, J. S., Meyers, H., & Nevin, A. (1996). Teacher and administrator perceptions of heterogeneous education. *Exceptional Children, 63(1),* 29–45. https://doi.org/10.1177/001440299606300103

Watkins, W. H. (2001). *The White architects of Black education: Ideology and power in America, 1865–1954.* Teachers College Press.

Weiss, C. H., & Cambone, J. (1994). Principals, shared decision making, and school reform. *Educational Evaluation and Policy Analysis, 16(3),* 287–301.

Wilderson, F. B., III. (2014, 10). "We're trying to destroy the world" Anti-Blackness & Police Violence After Ferguson (J. Ball, T. S. Burroughs, & D. Hate, Interviewers). Retrieved from https://illwilleditions.noblogs.org/files/2015/09/Wilderson-We-Are-Trying-to-Destroy-the-World-READ.pdf

CHAPTER 8

Culturally Responsive Instructional Supervision and Mindfulness
A Somatic, Embodied Practice

Steve Haberlin

After a half-century of work, several major legislative initiatives, and hundreds of billions of taxpayer dollars, closing racial achievement or opportunity gaps in U.S. public schools remains elusive (Khalifa et al., 2016; Khalifa, 2020; Payne, 2008). While culture, racialized and gendered identities, and lived experiences have been recognized as playing a major role in influencing educators' and other educational stakeholders' thinking, behavior, and teaching practices, historically oppressed groups remain marginalized (Khalifa et al., 2016). For example, despite various efforts and reforms, disparities between the academic achievement of the highest and lowest socioeconomic groups have shown minor improvement. When looking specifically at closing the achievement gap between White and Black students, there is "little change over the last two decades" (Hanushek et al., 2019; pp. 4–5). Furthermore, schools are expected to grow even more culturally and racially diverse as the United States progresses into the 21st century (Prescott & Bransberger, 2008), requiring teachers, 80% of whom are White, to engage in teaching pedagogies that help close sociocultural and opportunity gaps.

Given our history as a country, it can be argued that the United States, including its historical, economic, social, political, legal, and educational structures, has been designed and systematically maintained for the betterment of people racialized as White (Mills, 1997). Currently, ideologies that are considered culturally destructive are being codified into policy and law, as political movements have pushed to ban or limit discussion on topics such as race (Critical Race Theory), sexual orientation, and gender identity (the "Don't Say Gay" bill in Florida) from public classrooms (Hernandez, 2022; Morgan, 2022).

One of the most direct approaches for PK–12 educational leaders to support and enhance culturally responsive, nonoppressive practices is through culturally responsive instructional supervision (CRIS) (Mette et al., 2020). Traditionally defined as formative structures that involve reflection conversations overseen by a supervisor, a principal or a university field supervisor (Glickman et al., 2018), supervision has traditionally failed to center its work to address issues of social justice to help educators move past inequitable and exclusive practices (Cormier, 2018; Mette, 2020). For example, if a principal wants to be more inclusive as while observing and coaching teachers at a public school, how do they move beyond reading about changing their approach to equitable school leadership? How might this educational leader delve deeper, past surface-level discussions, to facilitate real change at the level of consciousness, which in turn will lead to changes in actions and outcomes to ensure education is equitable for all students? The answer seems to be to change how they think of themselves and be more mindful of the lived experiences of groups who are marginalized.

Since school leaders hold power over policy, curriculum, and other aspects of implementation in the classroom, for real change to occur, those working with historically marginalized student populations must have an awareness of self, of their beliefs, values, and dispositions as well as possess what has been called *critical consciousness* (Brown, 2004; Dantley, 2005a; Gay & Kirkland, 2003; McKenzie et al., 2008). Of course, this does not imply, as noted by Waite (2021), that educational leaders bear the entire burden of transforming schools into culturally responsive environments, but rather to pursue a complete overhaul of the education system if needed. As Waite (2021) notes, "Oppression is interwoven into the fabric of education and requires a critical lens to examine the myriad of ways it manifests" (p. 76).

This requires that school leaders engage in *critical self-reflection* (Khalifa, 2018) about who they are as leaders, specifically, who they are as instructional leaders. Culturally responsive school leaders must be willing to authentically turn inward, meditate and rid themselves of their own bias and their systems of any oppressive school structures that have been normalized and become invisible. Additionally, they must find ways to critically examine their values, beliefs, and life experiences, coming from a lens of power and privilege (Khalifa, 2018). Without this type of self-reflection and self-awareness, school leaders assume a neutral position that simply reinforces and sustains oppressive instructional practices (Cormier & Pandey, 2021).

Thus, the transformation needed for schools and the education system comes down to how or if those in leadership positions are able and willing to change at the *individual level*. For instructional leaders to engage in critical self-reflection, it is necessary to unpack how educators—specifically instructional supervisors—can be more aware of discrimination and bias aimed toward minoritized and marginalized identities in order to have a better understanding of how this impacts the way educators might think about instructional improvement efforts.

DISCRIMINATORY AND MARGINALIZED EXPERIENCES ON THE BODY

Racism, as well as various other forms of other discrimination, involves beliefs, attitudes, interpersonal acts, and institutional arrangements that malign a person or group of people based on their race, ethnicity, culture, or other lived experience

(Clark et al., 1999). Experiencing racism and discrimination carries transgenerational consequences, specifically the physiological and psychological toll on the health of those who are racially minoritized, marginalized, and otherized in U.S. society. Rather than adjusting normally from stressful situations, body systems remain in a constant state of chronic stress, leaving the marginalized more vulnerable to illness and negative factors that reduce life expectancy. When living and working in a colonial culture informed by racism, patriotism, and capitalism, Blackwell (2023) writes the more a person of color deviates from the most valued body (e.g., White, upper middle class, landowning), the more they must contort their own body to survive by adjusting. This contortion has a price, ranging from anxiety, to depression, to fear.

According to the Biopsychosocial Model of Racism, the stress related to racial discrimination contributes to substantial health disparities in African Americans due to the physiological responses to chronic stress caused by racist experiences perpetuated in the racialized U.S. society (Clark et al., 1999; Goosby & Heidbrink, 2013). Black males are most vulnerable to racially related stress. For example, college-educated black men accumulate stress through regular encounters with seemingly subtle and ambiguous forms of racial discrimination or microaggressions, which can intensely impact their psychological and physiological functioning in negative ways (Watson, 2019). In addition, the body possesses a form of knowledge that is different from that of our cognitive brains. Eastern traditions, such as Buddhism, have long taught that the body has its own form of wisdom which can be tapped through being in tune with the senses. Neuroscience has caught up with this notion, acknowledging a mind-body system, where the two are intimately related (Baker, 2022). This knowledge can be felt as a sense of constriction or expansion, pain or comfort, and energy or depletion. Our bodies experience fight, flight, or freeze responses, and advances in neuroscience show that our deepest emotions, such as love, anger, fear, sorrow, disgust, and hope, activate various bodily structures. While our experiences might seem completely psychologically based, stress and trauma are also housed in the physical body. Intergenerational transmission, or "soul wounds," occur when trauma experienced from racism is passed down through family abuse or mistreatment, unsafe or abusive systems, structures, and institutions, or our genes and DNA expression (Menakem, 2021). We create our sense of self through the body. As Owens (2020) notes, the physical body "is an anchor for how our identities are created and expressed" (p. 126).

Thus, while racism might be considered a purely psychological experience, various scholars of color have asserted that racism lives in the physical body (Blackwell, 2019; Owens, 2020). As Blackwell (2019) explains:

> Racism is about bodies. It's a reality that can be tasted, seen, felt. The restrictions to access to nutritious food and adequate healthcare; the over-policing of low-income neighborhoods and profiling of Black and Brown bodies; the insecurity of being excluded from voting booths, good schools, good jobs, 'good' hair, property ownership, business loans, media portrayals of success, and more all land, as author Ta-Nehisi

Coates has named, as physical and psychological blows to the body. When we are witness to these actions, a pain is felt in the body. (p. 11)

Racism, in its various facets, is also carried in the body of White people, or as Menakem (2021) asserts, "a different but equally real form of trauma lives in the bodies of most white Americans" (p. 9). While racism may not surface as cognitive beliefs, attitudes, ideas, or philosophies, such as with white supremacist groups like the KKK or Aryan Nations, it is experienced in the body as nonverbal sensations along with fear, hate, or constriction. Studies have shown that when White people simply view photos or have inter-racial interactions, they can experience a form of racial anxiety, which can manifest as sweating, increased heart rates, twitching, or avoiding eye contact (Godsil & Richardson, 2016). These examples of how racialized experiences impact the mind and body necessitate the need for educational leaders to be even more intentional in their practices, creating inclusive, supportive schools that minimize marginalization, microaggression, and other situations that perpetuate the intergenerational transmission of racial trauma.

IMPLICIT BIAS AND THE BODY

While it's difficult to admit, we all have implicit bias—unconscious stereotypes and judgments about groups of people that impact our daily interactions, work lives, and communities (Blackwell, 2019). The reality is people do see race and it is not possible to perceive people without observing their socially constructed racialized identities (Goldin & Rouse, 2000; Valian, 2005). Psychologists teach that our brains create mental shortcuts, or "schemas," to help us make sense of the world by placing people, places, and things into categories (Fiske & Taylor, 1991).

However, schemas can be extremely harmful in society when we start assigning them to groups of people based on race, ethnicity, gender, class, and other differences. Left unchecked, implicit bias can trigger our fight, flight, or freeze stress response by hijacking the brain's prefrontal cortex, activating the amygdala, and overriding our ability to rationalize. Just reading words such as *Homeless. Terrorist. Undocumented. Handicapped:* All can cause a churning in the stomach, a tenseness in the chest, a constricted feeling in the throat, or an increased heartbeat, for those who have these labels applied to their lived experiences (Blackwell, 2019).

These unconscious, deep-seated reactions occur until we bring our implicit bias to light and learn to disrupt the conditioned fear of the "other" at the level of embodiment, understanding the language of the body in its relationship to bias. Thus, if racism lives in the body, working the "somatic muscle" is essential for social justice work (see Blackwell, 2019). As Menakem (2021) writes, when addressing racism and bias, "few skills are more essential than the ability to settle your body" (p. 151).

As forms of critical self-reflection, settling the body and recognizing implicit bias at the physical level requires courageously and intentionally placing ourselves in situations that might make us uncomfortable, or at least imagining them, to provoke and unearth negative stress responses regarding race, ethnicity, and other "differences." Blackwell (2019) provides the following recommendations:

- *Recognize the Implicit Bias.* Do an honest assessment of possible implicit bias in yourself. Reflect on past and present experiences. What people, situations, and environments make you uncomfortable or make you have physical reactions?
- *Feel What Happens in Your Body.* When you come across a bias, how does your body feel? Sit with the feeling. Experience it. Do you experience tension in a certain area of the body (e.g., tightness in the chest or stomach, tension in the arms, hands, or feet, strain in the neck or shoulders)? What happens to your breathing when you think about the bias? Does it become shallow or elevated?
- *Intentionally Place Yourself in Situations; Face What Happens in the Body When Tension Arises.* Have experiences that provoke bodily sensations and reactions. Join groups or clubs or attend events with people of different sociocultural backgrounds and identities (such as race, ethnicity, gender, orientation/identity, class, etc.) to increase awareness of your bodily response. Blackwell explains that intentionally placing ourselves in a relationship with those from communities outside our own helps to dissipate conscious and unconscious judgments that produce fear and anxiety, specifically that which is felt in our bodies. The more exposure we have to meeting others in the context of shared humanity, the more chances we have to disrupt our implicit biases and conditioning. However, along with this added exposure, educational leaders will need specific tools they can use to help them sit with these experiences and reflect upon them.

EMBODIED MINDFULNESS (AS A MEANS OF SOMATIC CRITICAL SELF-REFLECTION)

While these steps are helpful places to begin facing bias, having additional tools and a vehicle for embodiment can further assist in the form of *somatic critical self-reflection*. Scholars, including Scholars of Color (Magee, 2019; Owens, 2020) have turned to the ancient, Buddhist practice of *mindfulness* to help settle the body and investigate how we marginalize, minoritize, and otherize people at a physiological level. These scholars view mindfulness practices as a method to not only deeply examine one's own unconscious, deeply rooted bias and prejudices, but also help engage in often uncomfortable, tense situations with more presence and compassion. Mindfulness is "the awareness that emerges through paying attention on purpose, in the present moment, and non-judgmentally to the unfolding of experience moment by moment" (Kabat-Zinn, 1994, p. 4).

Originating in India some 2,500 years ago, mindfulness methods were introduced and developed by the Buddha. However, the concept of mindfulness and various secularized techniques can be found in nearly every aspect of Western society, including medicine, counseling, psychology, business, sports, and education. Mindfulness methods have been proposed as a framework to enhance instructional supervision as well (Haberlin, 2020), and mindfulness practices can serve as an ideal vehicle to help educators settle the sensations experienced within the body and be in tune with nonverbal sensations. This attunement can assist with the fight–flight response associated with being racially minoritized, marginalized, and otherized, but also aid educational leaders to gain clarity into deeply rooted bias perpetuated throughout the U.S. society. As Duran (2004) states, "Through intense meditation practice . . . I came to uncover how I internalized negative racist and sexist opinions and also came to see more clearly the truth of those experiences in my social and professional interactions" (p. 166).

The Buddha laid out a framework for cultivating mindfulness called the Four Foundations or Four Applications of Mindfulness. As Neale (2017) explains, "the aim of this meditative pedagogy is to systematically strengthen one's attention by applying it to four discrete domains of experience to refine the mind's natural capacity for insight (wisdom) and behavior change (ethics)" (p. 20). Another way to think of the foundations is this way: Imagine someone is trying to become more physically fit. They might walk or run to work their cardiovascular system but also engage in stretching or yoga and strength training with weights. As occurs with this example, practicing the foundations enables one to hone mindfulness from various aspects or angles. This mindfulness framework is particularly relevant to the somatic work needed to confront and disrupt implicit bias and subsequent discriminatory responses and behaviors based on race, ethnicity, class, sexuality/orientation, and other identities. The four foundations of mindfulness are: (1) body, (2) sensations, (3) mind, and (4) phenomena. These can be used by educators to reflect upon applying aspects of CRIS.

The First Foundation (Body)

When practicing this foundation, one learns to calm the mind, develop concentrative powers, and elicit a relaxation response by narrowing the focus of attention to a specific focal point or stimulus, commonly the breath. Even within the breath, the focal point can be further narrowed to the point where the breath enters and leaves the nostrils, leading to the rising and falling of the abdomen. A calm, centered mind can serve as an ideal platform to practice critical self-reflection, which will involve confronting or leaning into uncomfortable experiences regarding the marginalizing, minoritizing, or otherizing of a group or groups of people.

The Second Foundation (Sensations)

As one's concentration develops, the idea is to expand the scope of mindfulness to paying attention to the physical sensations that arise in the body, "specifically noting if the experience is pleasant, unpleasant, or neutral . . . one learns to override habitual reactive tendencies of clinging to the pleasant, avoiding the unpleasant, and becoming disinterested in the neutral" (Neale, 2017, p. 21). The possible benefit of somatic critical reflection for school leaders becomes apparent with this application. For instance, fine-tuning one's ability to pick up bodily sensations, including those that feel unpleasant, in the context of culturally responsive work, and bringing them into conscious awareness can be of tremendous value.

The Third Foundation (Mind)

During this application of mindfulness, one focuses awareness on the nature of the mind itself, noticing and observing mental states as they arise (e.g., agitation, overstimulation, focused, afflicted). As Neale (2017) explains, "One learns to observe the states and qualities of awareness without being compelled by them or needing to suppress them on the other" (p. 21). In much the same way one practices overriding habitual reactions to physical sensations (clinging or avoiding), the third foundation trains an individual to avoid compulsive reactions to what are known as mental hindrances: restlessness, lethargy, greed, hostility, and doubt. Again, there is much value in school leaders learning to attune to their mental states. For instance, school leaders can learn to become more aware of unconscious thoughts and mental states that might arise in connection with culturally responsive issues, for example, noticing a narrowing of the mind when it comes to discussing or acting on various policies or practices at one's school.

The Fourth Foundation (Phenomenon)

While this application is mentioned along with the others, the four foundations of mindfulness involve memorizing and internalizing a list of psychological phenomena, elements, or realities, and observing these realities as they surface during mediation; these may not be suitable for school leaders in their critical self-reflection of oppressive educational practices. One general application might be for educational leaders to simply and objectively attempt to observe the experiences occurring in their schools and then reflect on whether they are culturally responsive and empowering, or exclusive and oppressive.

Embodied mindfulness involves practicing awareness of the body, bringing the quality of mindful awareness to the present again and again (Brown et al.,

2016). As Owens (2020) explains, embodied mindfulness is the work of returning home to the body and remembering the body in the present moment and context. As outlined in the Four Foundations, embodied mindfulness requires working with the breath, feelings and sensations, impulses, and what is known as a felt sense, or physical sensations that normally go under the mental radar. In regards to educational leaders, how many are continually reinforced to ignore the sensations of inequities they experience daily in school systems that focus on deficit-based mindsets about students and the parents the school is intended to serve?

This skill of embodied mindfulness has been brought to the tensions and challenges of social justice and the systemic inequities that are perpetuated through U.S. PK–12 school systems. Mindfulness can assist us in sitting with difficult thoughts and emotions and engaging in the kind of authentic conversations around bias and oppression in our schools. Mindfulness cultivates awareness of ourselves and makes us more cognizant of our experiences, which allows a person "to see more clearly and with compassion the institutional and individual racism and privilege" and provide more space and grace when addressing issues of racial justice (Duran, 2004, p. 168). This skill, of more deeply and compassionately perceiving inequities within a school that is contributing to the sociocultural gaps in U.S. society, is of tremendous value for a school principal or a district leader and connects directly to the cultivation of critical consciousness.

Mindfulness practice provides the *gap* needed to break the unconscious, negative cycles that reinforce separateness bias. Magee (2019) describes it this way: "We can slow down the reactive habit long enough to see what there is to see about our habits, our conditionings, our patterns of emotional. And we can choose a better way to respond" (p. 36).

Engaging in mindfulness as a somatic practice to critically reflect on our own implicit bias and to be aware of how we unconsciously allow for the marginalization of others provides a much-needed methodology to do the work we might naturally avoid: *facing what is uncomfortable and settling the body*. This ancient technology can give school leaders, for example, a contemplative support structure to do the kind of work that Khalifa (2018) believes is needed to truly transform schools into culturally responsive and equitable places. Deep, authentic, unabashed, critical reflection—meditating on our own stories about marginalized sociocultural identities and the trauma, hurt, prejudices, and bias surrounding that—is what Magee (2019) calls *the inner work of racial justice*. She writes, "Mindfulness is about seeing ourselves, our biases, our wounds, and the gifts that come from our relationships along the road we've traveled all more clearly" (p. 152). Magee's work includes a concept she calls *body-based color insight*: being present in one's own body, down-regulating reactivity when feelings are triggered, and engaging in mindfulness as a form of body-based racial awareness. Such an approach shows promise in assisting school leaders in engaging in critical self-reflection on cultural responsiveness.

THE INNER WORK OF CULTURALLY RESPONSIVE INSTRUCTIONAL SUPERVISION

While considerable research, discussion, and writing has been given to the technical aspects of supervision (e.g, the practical knowledge and skills needed to be a supervisor, working with school partnerships, providing feedback and support to teachers, conferencing, etc.), the inner work of supervision—increasing our self-awareness about our sociocultural identities and the privileges these afford us—has been largely ignored. As suggested by Haberlin (2020), the concept of mindfulness has received relatively little attention in the field of supervision. However, it is this dimension of school leadership that might be the missing catalyst to facilitate organizational and individual transformation regarding the execution of CRIS.

Educational leaders, whether they are superintendents, principals, teacher leaders, or university-based supervisors, would benefit greatly by looking at methods for meditating deeply, to become acutely aware of their bodies' sensations, impulses, and reactions, to become aware of unconscious reactions and fight-flight-freeze responses related to questioning, and to acknowledge privileged identities to engage in the inner work of CRIS. To unearth and shine a light on oppressive educational practices and make them visible, school leaders must arrive at the physiological level of the problem: *Their bodies*. Our bodies tell us there is a problem and to be aware of the issue—namely, how education systems often employ oppressive practices that approach students with a deficit mindset. Then, from this personal level of transformation, school leaders can enter more compassionate, open conversations about practices at the group level (e.g., departments, school-building-wide, district-wide).

SPECIFIC EMBODIED MINDFULNESS PRACTICES FOR EDUCATIONAL LEADERS

There are specific methods and practices for school leaders to use to gain familiarity with the body, including sensations and feelings connected to reactivity, as well as practices to help settle the body when marginalization is observed or experienced. The advice is to begin with a method that resonates, practice it, then try another method to determine what best "clicks." These practices can be done individually or in a group. Below are some examples of these practices.

Body Scan

This activity can serve as a foundation and introduction to mindful somatic practices. An ideal starting point for embodied mindfulness practice is using a method known as body scanning. The technique takes about 10 minutes and can be practiced lying down or sitting in a chair. The body scan involves systematically sweeping through the body with openness and care to various regions (Kabat-Zinn, 2005). Practicing this method enables one to become more in-tune and familiar with bodily sensations, both pleasant and unpleasant, and become more attuned to how one holds and experiences stress, and how the body reacts or responds to experiences and situations.

Begin by bringing gentle awareness to the top of the head, and observing any sensations. Gradually move your attention down to the forehead, sensing into the region. Continue moving the attention down through the eyes, nose, and mouth, to the jaw, allowing it to relax. Bring your awareness down to the shoulders, then down the arms through the triceps, biceps, and forearms, settling into the hands, and sensing into the muscle tissue. Then, scan back up through the arms to the chest area, feeling any sensations in the heart area. Move down to the abdomen, then bring the awareness to the hips and buttocks, then the thighs. Finally, bring the awareness down through the calves, ankles, and feet. After systematically scanning various parts of the body, the meditation can be concluded by experiencing the body as a whole, allowing the mind to pick up any sensations (e.g., pain, aches, tingling, tension, relaxation, lightness, heaviness) that arise. When ready, slowly open your eyes.

Mindfulness of Intentions Around Racial Justice Work

In this meditation based on Magee's (2019) teachings, the practitioner utilizes mindfulness to see more clearly any pain caused by racism and possibly any bias caused as a result. The notion of self-compassion is brought to bear on one's race story, or as Magee describes, "an experience of race in American life" (p. 16). Begin by taking a comfortable sitting position and become aware of your breath as it enters and leaves the nostrils. Bring up the idea of racial justice and just allow whatever comes to mind; feel in the body what happens. Next, ask yourself: *Where am I seeing marginalization up close? How am I living notions tied to my own "race"?*

Don't force any answers, just pose questions from an open space of awareness, paying attention to what happens in the body. Then, ask yourself "*What racial slurs am I using or hearing in my interactions with others?*" "*What stereotypes am I noticing about various identities? Black women or men? Asians? Latinos? Mexicans? Filipinos? Puerto Ricans?*

Go further by contemplating ideas you might have picked up about race from your family or neighborhood. *How do these ideas shade or influence information I pick up now from media?* Again, continue to experience bodily sensations. Pay attention to any tension, tightness, or pleasant or uncomfortable feelings in the body.

Further investigate by inquiring, *how might my notions of race, including those I picked up from my family and my upbringing, be influencing, shaping, or affecting my work as a school leader? How are these unconscious beliefs and ideas driving or influencing my decisions on school policy, use of resources, school discipline, teacher recruitment, and other factors?*

Culturally Responsive Instructional Supervision and Mindfulness

After these series of questions, simply sit with this experience. "This is perhaps, the most important aspect of the practice: See if you can just be present to any pain or distress that remains" in your body (Magee, 2019, p. 101).

Mindfulness of Community Exercise

Adapted from the work of Magee (2019), this mindfulness exercise can help school leaders become more consciously aware of the nuances of their community. This meditation focuses on how notions of separateness and being apart might have been reinforced by the places we lived and in the communities where we were raised.

Begin by taking a comfortable sitting position. Close your eyes and take a few deep breaths. Then, simply observe the breath flowing in its natural rhythm. Feel any tension or strain in the body, just briefly scanning from toes to head.

- Visualize the neighborhood or community surrounding one of your earliest homes. *Whom do you picture?*
- *Who were the people there? Was there a mix of people, or was there one race that represented a larger portion of the community? Was race often correlated with job opportunities? If so, in what way? Who were the leaders?*
- *What did it feel like to be in that community? Did you feel like you belonged? Did you feel like an outsider?* Allow yourself time to feel the reactions or sensations in the physical body.
- Now consider: *How were the boundaries of the community formed (legal, social, cultural, or otherwise)—that determined who was accepted and who was not? What do you know about that? How does it feel to reflect on this aspect of the community?*
- Again, just allow any thoughts, feelings, or physical sensations to arise, and sit with them. After you have sat with them long enough to feel them in your body, slowly allow them to dissolve.
- As the meditation comes to an end, reflect on *how others suffered from feeling apart, excluded, or marginalized* and vow to incorporate compassion into action as an educational leader.

Imagining Yourself in Marginalized Situations

In this meditation, adapted from ideas presented by Menakem (2021), one purposely utilizes the imagination to place oneself in situations that might cause stress responses or reactivity, to more deeply explore and unearth potential bias.

Begin by sitting comfortably and taking a few, deep breaths. Gently become aware of the natural flow of the breath, as it goes in and out. Briefly scan the body, feeling any tension. Next, imagine yourself in a situation that involves race, gender, or other sociocultural identities. For example, imagine as a principal that you are observing or completing an evaluation for a new teacher at your school. Picture yourself sitting in the back of the classroom, writing notes as you observe a Black female teaching the students. *What comes up in the body? What do you feel?* Sit with those feelings and sensations without judgment. Now, allow that image to dissipate and then imagine yourself sitting in the same classroom observing White female teaching. *What sensations do you experience? Are the feelings more comfortable, or less comfortable? Do you feel more or less tightness in the chest, the stomach? Does the feeling change when you imagine a man? A man of color? Someone who is an immigrant? A person who identifies as part of the LGBTQ+ community?* Contemplate any differences, as subtle as they may be, in your bodily responses. Let yourself be aware of what society has reinforced within you. What do you feel? How might this connect to how you were raised, the messages that were reinforced within your family, your schooling, and what you experienced through various forms of media?

Drop the visualizations and let yourself sit with this experience. Just allow any thoughts, insights, or questions to come. *What has this mental simulation taught you about yourself and your practices as an instructional leader?* In the following section, ideas for how these mindfulness practices can move educational leaders from consciousness to action, from the world of thought and emotion to specific actions in their workplace.

MOVING TOWARD A MORE CULTURALLY RESPONSIVE INSTRUCTIONAL SUPERVISION FROM THE INSIDE-OUT

As Khalifa (2018) argues, addressing oppressive educational practices begins with the school leader. The first step in moving toward a more culturally responsive model of instructional supervision starts with school leaders taking a courageous, hard look within themselves and examining their privileges and beliefs. With care, compassion, and nonjudgment, they must take an honest assessment of their identities, their upbringings, and their current educational practices. From this space, critical reflections, and ideally transformation can occur. Embodied mindfulness lends a tool to this challenging process. Grounding within the body, seeing the body as a place where bias, racism, and other forms of marginalization reside, and using mindfulness practices to unearth and expose these deep-seated notions can be extremely valuable to the field of supervision. But how does engaging in mindfulness meditations and tuning into the body, as exercises provided in this chapter suggest, actually translate to more positive, inclusive, equitable educational outcomes?

For real transformation to happen, school leaders must first transform or change their consciousness to that of a critical one, remaining aware of themselves but also the needs of students and teachers. From that raised consciousness, ideally, new thinking, behaviors, and responses will naturally arise. As Magee (2019) asserts, "Moving from color blindness to Color Insight, requires the will to see things differently, to act differently as a result, and to stay committed to doing so for the rest of our lives" (p. 310). Einstein believed that problems could not be solved from the same level of consciousness in which they were created. A new awareness is needed if school leaders are to operate in new, more inclusive ways.

Embodied mindfulness practices can serve as the technology to raise the consciousness of school leaders. However, how exactly school leaders will act and what changes will occur from this new level of consciousness can only be theorized, since this is a highly individualized process. For example, school leaders who come from various backgrounds will have varying degrees of implicit bias, varying amounts of knowledge and training in culturally responsive pedagogy, and different levels of resistance to critical self-reflective practices. Nevertheless, raising consciousness by itself is not enough. For real change to occur, a change in behaviors and changes to structures, in this case, ones that are inequitable and perhaps oppressive, must also follow. Like hooks (1996) articulated, "There must exist a paradigm, a practical model for social change that includes an understanding of ways to transform consciousness that are linked to efforts to transform structures" (p. 118). On those grounds, several "glimpses of culturally responsive leadership" (Khalifa et al., 2016, p. 21) ideally sparked from meditative critical self-reflection, will be shared here. The term "glimpses" is used in this chapter, since the truth is, no one can predict exactly how a change in consciousness will translate to a change in action in the physical world. Individuals have their unique compositions of past experiences, beliefs, worldviews, and levels of consciousness. For example, one principal or teacher leader engaging in mindfulness meditation practices may begin to become more aware of their direct interactions with teachers, and thus, begin to respond in more inclusive, supportive ways. Meanwhile, another school leader engaging in the same practices may begin to focus more on culturally diverse students and call for more faculty training in the form of shared readings, workshops, and so forth.

Glimpse #1: Mindful Social Connection and Compassionate Dialogue

By practicing methods such as those outlined in this chapter, school leaders gain more ability to facilitate open, heard-felt, supported dialogue at their schools about topics that can be difficult or uncomfortable for some to discuss. Engaging in deep reflection, such as body awareness exercises coupled with Mindfulness of Community, for example, leaders learn to sit with what may at first feel very uncomfortable and ideally to listen to others with more compassion and openness. Principals, university supervisors, and teacher leaders, through such mindfulness practices, might grow more aware of their language, both verbal and body language, subtle aggressions, and unconscious upholding of colonial culture, which may be causing stress and physical and psychological harm to educators and students of color as well as those from other diverse backgrounds. From this place, leaders can encourage discussions at their school about race, culture, and other identities and related topics such as how marginalized students and families might be viewed or treated and what needs to be transformed. Leaders can also share these mindfulness tools with others—teachers, fellow administrators, counselors, and parents—to foster interconnectedness and create a foundation for further discussion.

Glimpse #2: Culturally Responsive Teacher Preparation and Curriculum

Mentoring and coaching teachers for cultural responsiveness as part of regular, ongoing professional development falls within the purview of school leadership activities (Khalifa et al., 2016). Khalifa (2011) provided an example of a principal who regularly coached a teacher who was exclusionary toward low-income, minoritized students. However, for these types of situations to transpire, school leaders must first engage in critical reflection. A principal, for example, engaging in the type of meditations explained in this chapter might become more self-aware of their disposition and potential bias toward minoritized students at their school, realizing that more should be done or that additional resources or professional development is needed in the area of cultural responsiveness. On a more specific level, a principal or university supervisor conducting classroom observations as part of a district-required evaluation process, after deeply examining their own bias and bodily reactions, might begin to also notice the tendencies of their teachers when instructing students.

For example, they might develop a heightened sensitivity toward the type of language a teacher uses with students who are marginalized based on race or SES, a lack of attention toward some students with less visible forms of sociocultural othering, or a disproportionate use of discipline toward students who are minoritized in other ways. The principal must also come to realize that the curriculum for a particular lesson lacks cultural diversity—perhaps students cannot see themselves in the textbook being used or relate to the historical narrative being discussed. From this place, the principal, more mindful of their sensations and reactions within, could facilitate a conversation with the teacher that provokes new questions and new perspectives about instruction provided to certain students. The school leader might even share some of these mindfulness-based practices, either helping the teacher individually or holding a schoolwide workshop, to encourage educators to become more aware of their stress responses concerning the reflection of their own internalized biases.

Glimpse #3: Creating Culturally Responsive, Inclusive School Communities

School leaders who engage in critical self-reflection and embodied mindfulness might operate from a space that better advocates for traditionally marginalized children and families and establish a welcoming school environment for all students and parents. After becoming more acutely aware of one's own implicit bias, and the body's reaction to certain situations, such as pigeonholing a group of parents who may be discounted as having poor involvement due to culture and different expectations and beliefs, leaders could recognize, accept, investigate, and transform these perceptions into more positive, nourishing ones. With new views, a principal, for example, might be more willing to experiment with innovative or more constructive ways to get parents from minoritized, marginalized, and otherized groups involved with school activities. Rather than reproducing "racism and other systemic oppressions in their schools" (Khalifa, Gooden, & Davis, 2016, p. 18), CRIS can be more aware of their internal responses and model cultural responsiveness, and "transform attitudes and convince teachers to embrace new teaching approaches that were inclusive and empowering to students, especially to students of color" (Madhlangobe, 2009, p. 236), specifically around issues of inclusive and equitable instruction.

SEEING THROUGH THE FOG

Of course, these glimpses should be further explored by school leaders and the instructional supervision community. Principals practicing the mindfulness-based methods in this chapter should journal their experiences, complete autoethnographies, and/or work with researchers in higher education to capture direct links between embodied critical self-reflection and positive outcomes regarding CRIS. At a minimum, we should be encouraging instructional leaders to get in touch with their bodies, their stress reactions, and their associated implicit bias with pedagogical approaches, to increase equitable outcomes for all students. Such practices encourage turning inward, seeing where problems first manifest in our psyche, our consciousness—expressed and held in the body—and operating from an awareness where leaders can change their actions, and thus, outcomes in schools and classrooms.

Those in the field of instructional supervision must encourage school leaders to take time to reflect on how established systems and educational structures can unfairly marginalize and limit the potential of students and see "through the fog of our everyday lives" to consider what measures can be taken to remedy these situations. Through embodied mindfulness practices, leaders can get in touch more deeply with themselves to break through old paradigms. As Magee (2019) articulates, "We need to see reality through lenses not shaped by the soul-crushing dictates of systems that got us here. The first step to seeing clearly is breathing again, coming home to the body" (p. 327).

REFERENCES

Baker, W. B. (2022, August 18). *Embodiment*. Mind & Life Institute. https://www.mindandlife.org/insight/embodiment/

Blackwell, K. (2019). Race and the body: Why somatic practices are essential for racial justice. *The Arrow, 6*(1), 10–23.

Blackwell, K. (2023). *Decolonizing the body: Healing, body-centered practices for women of color to reclaim confidence, dignity, and self-worth.* New Harbinger Publications.

Brown, K. M. (2004). Leadership for social justice and equity: Weaving a transformative framework and pedagogy. *Educational Administration Quarterly, 40,* 77–108.

Brown, R. C., Simone, G., & Worley, L. (2016). Embodied presence: Contemplative teacher education. In *Handbook of mindfulness in education* (pp. 207–219). Springer.

Clark, R., Anderson, N. B., Clark, V. R., & Williams, D. R. (1999). Racism as a stressor for African Americans: A biopsychosocial model. *American Psychologist, 54*(10), 805.

Cormier, D. R. (2018). *Culturally responsive supervision: An appropriate epistemology for attending to the demographic transformation within US PK–12 public schools.* Paper presented at the annual meeting of the Council of Professors of Instructional Supervision, Orono, ME.

Cormier, D. R., & Pandey, T. (2021). Semiotic analysis of a foundational textbook used widely across educational supervision. *Journal of Educational Supervision, 4*(2), https://doi.org/10.31045/jes.4.2.6

Dantley, M. E. (2005). African American spirituality and Cornel West's notions of prophetic pragmatism: Restructuring educational leadership in American urban schools. *Educational Administration Quarterly, 41,* 651–674. doi:10.1177/0013161X04274274

Duran, B. (2004). Race, racism, and the dharma. In H. G. Baldoquin (Ed.), *Dharma, color, and culture: New voices in western Buddhism* (pp. 135–140). Parallax Press.

Fiske, S. T., & Taylor, S. E. (1991). *Social cognition* (2nd ed.). McGraw-Hill

Gay, G., & Kirkland, K. (2003). Developing cultural critical consciousness and self-reflection in preservice teacher education. *Theory Into Practice, 42,* 181–187. doi:10.1207/s15430421tip4203_3

Glickman, C. D., Gordon, S. P., & Ross-Gordon, J. M. (2018). *SuperVision and instructional leadership: A developmental approach* (10th ed.). Pearson.

Godsil, R. D., & Richardson, L. S. (2016). Racial anxiety. *Iowa Law Review, 102,* 2235.

Goldin, C., & Rouse, C. (2000). Orchestrating impartiality: The impact of blind auditions on female musicians. *American Economic Review, 90*(4), 715–741.

Goosby, B. J., & Heidbrink, C. (2013). The transgenerational consequences of discrimination on African-American health outcomes. *Sociology Compass, 7*(8), 630–664.

Haberlin, S. (2020). Mindfulness-based supervision: Awakening to new possibilities. *Journal of Educational Supervision, 3*(3), 75.

Hanushek, E. A., Peterson, P. E., Talpey, L. M., & Woessmann, L. (2019). The achievement gap fails to close. *Education Next, 19*(3), 8–17.

Hernandez, J. (2022, February 24). Florida House passes controversial measure dubbed the 'Don't Say Gay' bill by critics. *National Public Radio.* https://www.npr.org/2022/02/24/1082969036/florida-house-passes-controversial-measure-dubbed-the-dont-say-gay-bill-by-criti

hooks, b. (1996). Teaching to transgress: Education as the practice of freedom. *Journal of Leisure Research, 28*(4), 316.

Kabat-Zinn, J. (2005). *Coming to our senses: Healing ourselves and the world through mindfulness.* Hachette UK.

Kabat-Zinn, J. (1994). *Wherever you go, there you are.* Hyperion.

Khalifa, M. (2018). *Culturally responsive school leadership.* Harvard Education Press.

Khalifa, M. (2011). Principal expectations and principal behavior: Responding to teacher acquiescence. *The Urban Review, 43*(5), 702–727.

Khalifa, M. A., Gooden, M. A., & Davis, J. E. (2016). Culturally responsive school leadership: A synthesis of the literature. *Review of Educational Research, 86*(4), 1272–1311.

Madhlangobe, L. (2009). *Culturally responsive leadership in a culturally and linguistically diverse school: A case study of the practices of a high school leader* (UMI No. 3470470) [Doctoral dissertation, Texas State University-San Marcos]. Available from ProQuest Dissertations and Theses database.

Magee, R. V. (2019). *The inner work of racial justice: Healing ourselves and transforming our communities through mindfulness*. Tarcher Perigee.

McKenzie, K. B., Christman, D. E., Hernandez, F., Fierro, E., Capper, C. A., Dantley, M., . . . Scheurich, J. J. (2008). From the field: A proposal for educating leaders for social justice. *Educational Administration Quarterly, 44*, 111–138. doi:10.1177/00 13161X07309470

Menakem, R. (2021). *My grandmother's hands: Racialized trauma and the pathway to mending our hearts and bodies*. Penguin UK.

Mette, I. M. (2020). Reflections on supervision in the time of COVID-19. *Journal of Educational Supervision, 3*(3), 1–6. https://doi.org/10.31045/jes.3.3.1

Mette, I. M., Aguilar, I., & Wieczorek, D. (2020, April). *A fifty state review of teacher supervision and evaluation systems: The influence of ESSA and implications for policy and practice*. Paper session at the Annual Meeting of the American Educational Research Association, San Francisco, CA.

Mills, C. W. (1997). *The racial contract*. Cornell University Press.

Morgan, H. (2022). Resisting the movement to ban critical race theory from schools. *The Clearing House: A Journal of Educational Strategies, Issues and Ideas, 95*(1), 35–41.

Neale, M. (2017) in Loizzo, J. E., Neale, M. E., & Wolf, E. J. (2017). *Advances in contemplative psychotherapy: Accelerating healing and transformation*. Routledge/Taylor & Francis Group.

Owens, L. R. (2020). *Love and rage: The path of liberation through anger*. North Atlantic Books.

Payne, C. M. (2008). *So much reform, so little change: The persistence of failure in urban schools*. Cambridge, MA: Harvard Education Press.

Prescott, B. T., & Bransberger, P. (2008). *Knocking at the college door: Projections of high school graduates by state and race/ethnicity, 1992–2022*. Western Interstate Commission for Higher Education. Retrieved from http://wiche.edu/info/publications/knocking_complete_book.pdf

Valian, V. (2005). Beyond gender schemas: Improving the advancement of women in academia. *Hypatia, 20*(3), 198–213.

Waite, S. R. (2021). Towards a theory of critical consciousness: A new direction for the development of instructional and supervisory leaders. *Journal of Educational Supervision, 4*(2). https://doi.org/10.31045/jes.4.2.4

Watson, K. T. (2019). *Revealing and uprooting cellular violence: Black men and the biopsychosocial impact of racial microaggressions* (ProQuest ID: Watson_ucla_0031D_18094) [Doctoral dissertation, University of California Los Angeles] eScholarship. https://escholarship.org/uc/item/7sq9t3pw

CHAPTER 9

Using Classroom Observation and Schoolwide Supervision Data to Facilitate Culturally Responsive Conversations About Diversity, Equity, Inclusion, and Belonging

Sally J. Zepeda, Sevda Yildirim, and Salih Cevik

Research illustrates that highly effective teachers do not typically teach in Title I or under-resourced schools (García & Weiss, 2019; Sutcher et al., 2019). Moreover, the U.S. student population as of 2016 has transformed into a majority-minority student population. This transformation denotes that the U.S. student population is composed of more than half of students of color (e.g., Black, Hispanic, Latino/a, Asian). Demographic trends illustrate that between 2001 and 2023, White student enrollment will decrease from 60% to 45% (Maxwell, 2014; National Center for Education Statistics, 2019). Conversely, the teaching force does not represent the majority-minority U.S. student population. In fact, the U.S. Department of Education School and Staffing Survey (SASS) has reported that 82% of the teaching population identifies as White, with the majority being middle-class, female, and monolingual (Tanase, 2022).

Trends in the racial and ethnic makeup of prospective teachers indicate most preparation programs are preparing predominantly White cohorts of future educators, and that in most preparation programs teachers are inadequately prepared to teach racially and ethnically diverse students through a course or two on multicultural education (Sleeter, 2017). However, there is little connection between the acknowledgment of preservice teachers' sociocultural constructions and privileged identities and how these factors compete with the aims of culturally responsive practices. These teachers enter classrooms filled with students from diverse racial and ethnic backgrounds. Adding complexity, in 2017–2018, approximately 78% of public-school principals were White, 11% were Black, and 9% were Latinx (National Center for Education Statistics, 2021).

The reality is two-fold. First, the majority of students within PK–12 schools are not taught by teachers who look like them or share a common racial or ethnic identity. Second, principals and other building-level leaders who supervise and support teachers' instructional practices do not reflect the racially and ethnically diverse student populations in the schools they lead. Compounding this reality, instructional leaders often lack the training (e.g., cultural competence) to acknowledge how their privileged identities influence their leadership to ensure effective teaching and success for all students (Horsford et al., 2011; Johnson, 2014; Khalifa, 2018).

This chapter begins with an examination of asset-based practices and then moves to exploring culturally responsive teaching. Next, the leadership needed to champion cultural responsiveness lays the foundation for an in-depth exploration about culturally responsive instructional supervision (CRIS). Exploring the touchpoints between culturally responsive leadership and instructional supervision, a culturally responsive framework for classroom observations is offered, reimagining the components of the clinical model of instructional supervision. The uses of data from such efforts are examined and conclusions about CRIS are drawn from the focus of this chapter.

ASSET-BASED APPROACHES

Students bring a wide array of educational experiences, cultural practices, and individual identities to the classroom. However, traditional classrooms often ignore the cultural wealth of students even though several research projects argue that the effective teaching of historically marginalized students begins with an asset-based approach to students' cultural and personal experiences (Gay, 2013; Ladson-Billings, 1995; López, 2017; Paris & Alim, 2014, Yosso, 2005). An asset-based approach "emphasizes strengths over weaknesses, resilience over risk, and assets over deficits" (Rose, 2006, p. 236).

Asset-based learning approaches reject traditional deficit-based educational practices by focusing on the funds of cultural knowledge and assets students bring with them to school. Whereas deficit thinking focuses on what students cannot do, an asset-based approach focuses on what students can do, including their strengths, talents, interests, and competencies (Rose, 2006). In other words, an asset-based approach focuses on the value of "assets" that students bring to the class, such as their experience, knowledge, skills, and attitudes. These approaches value "strength, resilience, and assets" (Morrison, 2017, p. 191).

An asset-based pedagogy aims to identify and explore how student knowledge, strengths, assets, and lived experiences can contribute to that knowledge construction. By understanding the broad range of assets that students bring to the classroom, an asset-based learning approach asks how those assets can be used as learning resources (Milner, 2017). The key to asset-based pedagogy is the openness and willingness of teachers to reshape education by providing opportunities for students to express their identities through choice (López, 2017).

Although developing an awareness of the social and cultural assets students possess is essential for teachers in the learning process, it is also important for students to recognize the contribution of their assets and experiences to their academic success (Morrison, 2017). As Milner (2017) states, asset-based pedagogy provides an "explanatory construct" so "students develop a critical consciousness and move beyond spaces where they simply or solely consume knowledge without critically examining it" (p. 9). Therefore, educators must encourage students to reflect their prior knowledge and skills to develop an awareness of their assets at the learning process.

Couched within the framework of asset-based pedagogy are various approaches to theorize and conceptualize teaching practices that are centered around student culture in the classroom. Several major approaches have been developed to counteract deficit-thinking and traditional deficit-based educational practices. Three approaches are culturally relevant pedagogy (Ladson-Billings, 1995), culturally responsive teaching (Gay, 2000, 2018), and culturally sustaining pedagogy (Paris & Alim, 2014). Although each approach is distinct, they build on and complement each other (Warren, 2018). With this chapter's focus on CRIS, the literature on culturally responsive teaching and leadership practices is examined.

CULTURALLY RESPONSIVE TEACHING

Culturally responsive practices evolved through the framework of multicultural education theorized by Banks (1994) as a set of knowledge, attitudes, and skills that students must develop to interact positively with people from diverse backgrounds (Banks et al., 2001). Culturally responsive educators believe that all students, regardless of their racial and cultural backgrounds, can be educated. However, Gay (2013) argued that this disposition is fundamentally different from the way that educational programs and practices have historically been designed for students of color.

In 2000, Gay conceptualized culturally responsive teaching as "an approach that emphasizes using the cultural knowledge, prior experiences, frames of reference, and performance styles of ethnically diverse students to make learning encounters more relevant to and effective for them" (p. 31). Gay (2018) described several dimensions of different learning styles of students to which culturally relevant teachers attend to the "procedural," "communicative," "substantive," "environmental," "perceptual," "relational," and "organizational" ways in which they interact with students (pp. 207–208). She argued that for teachers to effectively teach students, they must be aware of the individual differences and variations in each of these areas.

Gay (2013) noted how "[c]ulturally responsive teaching requires replacing pathological and deficient perceptions of students and communities of color with more positive ones" (p. 54). Table 9.1 identifies the five essential components and the eight dimensions of culturally responsive teaching developed by Gay (2002, 2018).

These components and dimensions of culturally responsive teaching point to valuing and validating the cultural capital that students bring with them to their classrooms. It is important to support their development and develop a clearer understanding of what the culturally responsive practices are, what are the characteristics of culturally responsive educators, and how teachers develop such practices. Teachers must look inwardly to unearth their biases and beliefs about children.

Leaders that engage teachers in developing their instructional practices cannot do so without knowledge and understanding of the components and dimensions of culturally responsive teaching, as elaborated in Table 9.1. The components and dimensions of culturally responsive teaching serve as the foundation for leaders as they conduct their efforts to supervise teachers in their classrooms. Later in this chapter, the Culturally Responsive Framework for Classroom Observations is offered (see Figure 9.1). The Culturally Responsive Framework for Classroom Observations embeds the components and dimensions of culturally responsive teaching. Without such knowledge and understanding, classroom observations can hardly support teachers to engage in ways that value the diversity of students.

Leaders must lead the work involved in culturally responsive supervision. High-leverage leadership skills focus on the work around improving instructional practice through the efforts of both teachers and leaders focused on one non-negotiable—all schools need highly qualified and effective teachers in every classroom. Developing culturally responsive teaching practices is dependent, in part, on the culture and climate of the school (Zepeda et al., 2023), the willingness of teachers to recognize that students bring cultural wealth and experiences to the schoolhouse (Alim & Paris, 2017), and the culturally responsive practices of leaders that champion such efforts (Khalifa, 2018).

LEADERSHIP TO CHAMPION CULTURAL RESPONSIVENESS

The work of the principal has shifted to focus on the instructional side of the house—its programs, the development of personnel, and the creation of an environment that is inclusive. Culturally responsive leadership follows the trail of teaching to support culturally responsive classroom practices and the anti-deficit treatment of students in ways that honor their cultural capital. Culturally responsive leadership has been envisioned as the ways in which leaders recognize and understand cultural differences and the focal point of their work supporting

Table 9.1. Essential Components and Dimensions of Culturally Responsive Teaching

Essential Components of Culturally Responsive Teaching (Gay, 2002)	Dimensions of Culturally Responsive Teaching (Gay, 2018)
Developing a cultural diversity knowledge base	Culturally Responsive Teaching Is Empowering
Designing culturally relevant curricula	Culturally Responsive Teaching Is Multidimensional
Demonstrating cultural caring and building a learning community	Culturally Responsive Teaching Is Validating
Implementing effective cross-cultural communication	Culturally Responsive Teaching Is Comprehensive and Inclusive
Facilitating cultural congruity in classroom instruction	Culturally Responsive Teaching Is Transformative
	Culturally Responsive Teaching Is Emancipatory
	Culturally Responsive Teaching Is Humanistic
	Culturally Responsive Teaching Is Normative and Ethical

Source: Gay (2002, 2018).

learners—both children and the adults entrusted to their care (Horsford et al., 2011; Johnson, 2014; Johnson & Fuller, 2014; Khalifa, 2018; Khalifa et al., 2016; Ladson-Billings, 2022).

Perhaps the most developed framework is offered by Khalifa (2018) and Khalifa et al. (2016). The *Culturally Responsive School Leadership Framework* is built on four pillars in which the leader engages in continuous processes to:

- Critically self-reflect on leadership behaviors;
- Develop culturally responsive teachers;
- Promote a culturally responsive/inclusive school environment; and,
- Engage students and parents in their community contexts.

These processes promote active engagement in creating a culture where teachers and leaders can learn and engage in the work of cultural responsiveness.

Khalifa (2018) is persuasive, clarifying that culturally responsive school leadership "is a process that cannot be completed. Rather it is a dynamic, fluid set of behaviors that regularly (re)develop the individual and the organization based on a steady stream of data from the school and community" (p. 60).

Culturally responsive leaders who fulfill supervisory practices guard against inequities by

- promoting access by eliminating barriers to equitable and socially just practices (Bogotch & Shields, 2014; Theoharis & Scanlan, 2015);
- acknowledging their own beliefs and biases by engaging in a process using inside-out approaches to reflect deeply and to articulate these beliefs both in private and public spaces (Cormier, 2021; Khalifa et al., 2016; Lopez, 2016; Russell, 2020);
- creating a culture of care, concern, and empathy to direct efforts toward ensuring a sense of belonging as the core value (Bogotch & Shields, 2014; Theoharis & Scanlan, 2015; Zepeda et al., 2023); and
- disrupting systems that perpetuate bias, inequities, and inequalities (Bogotch & Shields, 2014) related to the bloated distribution of special student populations (Theoharis, 2010; Theoharis et al., 2020); inclusion in gifted and talented programs for *all* minority students (DeMatthews et al., 2021; Shields & Hesbol, 2020); and the elimination of disproportionate discipline practices (Hines et al., 2022; Little & Welsh, 2022).

Leaders will encounter overt and covert push-back as they "seek to dismantle oppression and reveal privilege and entitlement within their respective organizations" (Horsford et al., 2011, p. 598).

Culturally responsive school leaders, regardless of circumstance or context, "constantly seek, find, and challenge the oppressive treatment of students and communities, and push their staffs to do so as well" (Khalifa, 2018, p. 61). The proverbial "push" is examined next with a culturally responsive focus on instructional supervision. As such, we believe that CRIS can serve as a mediator between culturally responsive teaching and culturally responsive school leadership.

SITUATING CULTURALLY RESPONSIVE INSTRUCTIONAL SUPERVISION

Adding to our understanding of CRIS, Gay (2005) wrote the first set of codified standards to address cultural competence for the field of instructional supervision. Gay (2005) believed that culturally responsive supervisory efforts needed to be more inclusive. Culturally responsive supervisory practices follow the literature and frameworks of Gay (2002) and Khalifa (2018), as presented in Table 9.2.

Supervision and Supervisors Are Visible

As supervisors, leaders must be a visible presence in teachers' classrooms. They engage in observing teachers in their classroom environments, and they engage in conversations about teaching and learning. CRIS is about developing capacity for: (1) an instructional program built on the foundations of culturally responsive pedagogy and culturally responsive teaching practices; and (2) for developing the capacity of teachers. Building these types of capacity will yield more inclusive learning environments for students and teachers; however, questions abound:

Table 9.2. Situating Culturally Responsive Instructional Supervision

Culturally Responsive Teaching (Gay, 2002)	Culturally Responsive Leadership (Khalifa, 2018)	Culturally Responsive Instructional Supervision (Gay, 2005)
Developing a cultural diversity knowledge base	Being critically self-reflective	Creating opportunities to reflect on cultural competence and responsiveness
		Helping teachers and students determine and continually improve the quality of their teaching and learning about ethnic and cultural diversity with respect to relevance, accuracy, and significance
		Encouraging classroom teachers and others to develop a deep knowledge and critical consciousness of how cultural diversity influences the educational opportunities, programs, practices, and outcomes for students from different ethnic groups
Designing culturally relevant curricula	Developing and sustaining culturally responsive teachers and curricula	Determining if multiple ethnic, cultural, social, and experiential perspectives are used in analyzing challenges and providing opportunities for learning about and responding to diversity
		Monitoring teaching and learning activities for and about cultural diversity
		Providing systematic assessment and constructive feedback to teachers and students
		Making necessary resources available and facilitates their use
Demonstrating cultural caring and building a learning community	Promoting inclusive, anti-oppressive school contexts	Promoting a sense of belonging and inclusiveness for teachers
Implementing effective cross-cultural communication	Engaging students' Indigenous (or local neighborhood) community contexts	Using data from formal and informal classroom observations, professional learning, and other sources to move learning for teachers and their students
		Assisting teachers to systematize their decision making, problem solving, implementation actions, and progress monitoring for making all aspects of the educational enterprise more inclusive of and responsive to ethnic, racial, cultural, social, and linguistic diversity
Facilitating cultural congruity in classroom instruction		Ensuring clarity and congruence of the mission and vision, both pointing to the urgency for teachers to use culturally responsive teaching approaches that match the needs of students

- How do supervisors see the culture of the classroom?
- What implications do the observed practices have for teaching and learning?
- How do instructional supervisors frame what they have observed when discussing the events of the classroom? And then,
- What types of data, including artifacts and evidence, would be included to illustrate culturally responsive teaching practices?

These questions and perhaps more assist in identifying and addressing the negative stereotypes, and culturally insensitive notions about students and the communities that the school serves.

Instructional Supervisors Unpack Beliefs and Bias

Creating engaging and inclusive school environments for students requires leadership that understands the issues that get in the way of valuing and seeing all students and the cultural capital they bring to the school and their classrooms. Effective school leaders acknowledge their own beliefs and biases by engaging in a process using inside-out approaches to reflect deeply and articulate these beliefs both in private and public spaces (Khalifa et al., 2016; Russell, 2020). Introspection is needed to reflect deeply about the community served, and student and teacher demographics—key data surrounding program enrollment (special education, gifted and talented, etc.)—and discipline data, noting discernable patterns.

As practice, supervisors would engage with members of the leadership team and teachers in unpacking the biases they hold and how these biases unfold in classrooms, policies concerning counting late assignments, grade distribution, and so forth. Supervisors and teachers would be able to discern the differences in beliefs each holds related to students, classroom practices, and school policies, by engaging in conversations to address the meanings associated with each belief structure.

To create a culturally responsive school whose teachers value diversity, supervisors must model and display values, behaviors, and attitudes that are congruent with the principles of equity by holding high expectations for students. Moreover, supervisors would be able to communicate what high expectations for students would look like in practice as espoused by Gay (2002, 2018) in Table 9.1, *Essential Components and Dimensions of Culturally Responsive Teaching*.

The Intents of Instructional Supervision Align With Cultural Responsiveness

The intents of instructional supervision are formative, focusing "efforts with teachers to promote growth, development, interaction, fault-free problem solving, and a commitment to build capacity" (Zepeda, 2017, p. 24). Two very important constructs align with the principles of culturally competent and responsive practices—differentiated supervision (Glatthorn, 1997) and developmental supervision

(Glickman, 1981). Differentiated supervision allows teachers to exert agency over the types and frequency of classroom observations and supports they engage.

Glickman (1981) brought forward that "the goal of instructional supervision is to help teachers learn how to increase their own capacity to achieve professional learning goals *for their students*" (p. 3, emphasis added). Developmental supervision is reliant on the supervisor and teacher being able to discern where the teacher falls—developmentally as an early career teacher, mid-career teacher, a seasoned veteran teacher, and then professional able to apply a supervisory approach that matches this level. Both developmental and differentiated supervisory practices give latitude and discretion to the types of classroom observations performed, their frequency, and the focus for each observation.

FRAMING CULTURALLY RESPONSIVE CLASSROOM OBSERVATIONS

Significant attention to culturally responsive instruction and frameworks has grounded the discussion about instructional supervision. Extending this discussion is the consideration of classroom observations. Leaders apply a culturally responsive supervisory lens while observing teachers, giving feedback, and engaging in conversations that aspire to transform instructional practices that are responsive to the needs of students (Zepeda, 2017). Figure 9.1 offers a Culturally Responsive Framework for Classroom Observations.

The Culturally Responsive Framework for Classroom Observations is built across three processes: the pre-observation conference, the classroom observation, and the post-observation conference. This framework follows the cyclical model of supervision embedded with the processes, serving as a foundation for examining culturally responsive practices before, during, and after classroom observations. However, cultural responsiveness cannot be compartmentalized as a series of discrete activities sprinkled across processes. The components and dimensions of culturally responsive teaching undergird supervisory efforts as presented through Gay's work presented in Table 9.1. Figure 9.1 illustrates the intersection of CRIS and classroom observations.

The Culturally Responsive Framework for Classroom Observations emphasizes the interconnected nature of clinical supervision by ensuring that culturally responsive practices are not viewed as isolated components. Rather, cultural responsiveness is an embedded foundation throughout the entire observation process, promoting a holistic approach to teaching and learning. The Culturally Responsive Framework for Classroom Observations starts with the pre-observation conference.

The Pre-observation Conference

Conversations about teaching and learning and the students in the classroom matter—a lot. Conversations open windows of opportunity for teachers and

Using Classroom Observation and Schoolwide Supervision Data   175

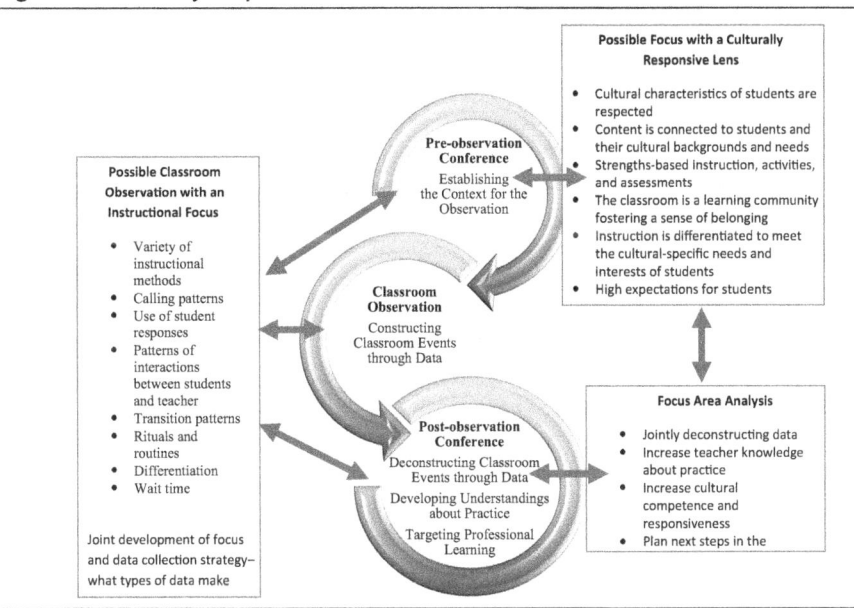

Figure 9.1. Culturally Responsive Framework for Classroom Observations

Possible Focus with a Culturally Responsive Lens
- Cultural characteristics of students are respected
- Content is connected to students and their cultural backgrounds and needs
- Strengths-based instruction, activities, and assessments
- The classroom is a learning community fostering a sense of belonging
- Instruction is differentiated to meet the cultural-specific needs and interests of students
- High expectations for students

Pre-observation Conference
Establishing the Context for the Observation

Possible Classroom Observation with an Instructional Focus
- Variety of instructional methods
- Calling patterns
- Use of student responses
- Patterns of interactions between students and teacher
- Transition patterns
- Rituals and routines
- Differentiation
- Wait time

Joint development of focus and data collection strategy—what types of data make

Classroom Observation
Constructing Classroom Events through Data

Post-observation Conference
Deconstructing Classroom Events through Data
Developing Understandings about Practice
Targeting Professional Learning

Focus Area Analysis
- Jointly deconstructing data
- Increase teacher knowledge about practice
- Increase cultural competence and responsiveness
- Plan next steps in the

leaders to think and reflect about classroom practices and students. The pre-observation conference opens the discussion and provides the opportunity to identify instructional goals, ultimately establishing a focus for the observation (Zepeda, 2017). The pre-observation conference should serve two purposes. The first purpose is to examine a classroom practice such as wait time or the ways in which instruction is differentiated. The second purpose is to examine culturally responsive practices and the ways in which teachers create a learning environment that is inclusive of students and the assets they bring to the classroom.

As illustrated in Figure 9.1, the pre-observation conference establishes the context for the observation, and it is an important first step for planning a classroom observation. During the pre-observation conference, the supervisor and teacher jointly develop a focus on a specific instructional area, and in tandem, possible aspects of culturally responsive teaching that are embedded within the instructional focus. By agreeing on a focus for the classroom observation, the supervisor and the teacher are clear about what types of observation data would be collected to shed light on areas of interest.

By embedding a culturally responsive lens to start the process during the pre-observation conference, the teacher and supervisor can engage in critical self-reflection to unearth their personal biases, assumptions, and values, which originate from their own personal, professional. or cultural backgrounds. These types of conversations help to unearth discrepancies related to prior experiences with students who may not share the same backgrounds played out in the classroom.

Moreover, critical self-reflection may help teachers leverage students' assets. With a purposeful approach, such areas of discussion could center broadly on overall practices including, for example:

- Respect and student identity;
- Validation of student efforts;
- Strength-based instruction, assessment, and activities; and
- Scaffolding based on students' cultural needs and interests.

Again, these types of conversations work in tandem regardless of the focus on an instructional or classroom practice.

Based on the concerns of the teacher, the supervisor works with the teacher to determine what kinds of data to gather and what tools can be used to gather that data during the classroom observation. The effectiveness of a culturally responsive pre-observation conference relies on the quality of the communication between the principal and teacher, the ability to target an area to focus attention during the observation, the best way to collect data that are stable, and the ability to infuse cultural relevance in the process. The rule of thumb is, the stronger the data collected during the classroom observation, the more that data will yield a stronger conversation in the post-observation conference, where the events of the classroom can be both deconstructed to construct new, more informed knowledge about instructional practices. The classroom observation is tied to the focus established in the pre-observation conference.

The Classroom Observation

Figure 9.1 illustrates that the classroom observation follows the pre-observation conference where a focus has been identified. Along with a few focus areas (e.g., wait time, calling patterns, etc.), Figure 9.1 also provides a broad overlay of culturally responsive areas to focus attention to during a classroom observation, including, for example:

- cultural characteristics of students are respected;
- content is connected to students and their cultural backgrounds and needs;
- strengths-based instruction, activities, and assessments are used;
- the classroom is a learning community fostering a sense of belonging;
- instruction is differentiated to meet the cultural-specific needs and interests of students; and
- high expectations for students are used regardless of the cultural differences.

Embedding a culturally responsive lens requires a more granular approach to collect and then analyze the data from the classroom observation. As a reminder, Gay (2018) stresses that culturally responsive teaching rests on cultural knowledge, prior experiences, frames of reference, and performance styles of ethnically diverse students to make learning encounters more relevant to and effective for them. It teaches to and through the strengths of these students. Culturally responsive teaching considers the behavioral expressions of knowledge, beliefs, and values that recognize the importance of racial and cultural diversity in learning. (p. 31)

To support culturally responsive classroom observations, supervisors must keep at the forefront key instructional and classroom practices that empower and validate students in a strengths-based environment.

Culturally responsive classroom observations present approaches to collect and analyze data in two complementary ways. First, a focus is presented to target a wide variety of instructional and other classroom practices. Second, the focus is presented to examine culturally responsive ways in which instructional and other classroom practices unfold. In other words, it's important to ask what is embedded in these practices that represents a culturally responsive approach to teaching, learning, and the classroom environment as students engage in learning?

There are a variety of classroom observation tools designed to collect data that reflect the ability to follow the events of the classroom. Perhaps the most comprehensive classroom observation tools and approaches for collecting classroom observation data are offered by Zepeda (2012, 2013, 2017). However, to conduct classroom observations with a focus on cultural responsiveness, the supervisor must refine and develop culturally responsive observation tools that are specifically designed to address the teacher's concerns (focus area), the overall context of the school, and the multiple populations in classrooms.

It is highly doubtful that one tool can serve all these purposes; therefore, supervisors must consider many variables about classrooms as learning environments and be ready to chronicle not only the events of the classroom but also examine these events from a culturally responsive lens.

For example, if the focus of the observation details matters of the curriculum (content), the supervisor may seek to discover the teacher's culturally diverse practices by focusing the observation on whether the teacher

- delivers instruction by matching learning objectives to the cultural and motivational styles of students;
- uses curriculum that reflects the cultures and experiences of a range of cultural groups in the classroom;
- uses instructional materials that reflect events from the perspectives of a range of cultural groups; and
- employs assessments that are culturally responsive.

Similarly, if the focus is broadly on interactions with students, the supervisor seeks data that illustrate whose voices are privileged in the classroom by chronicling what students are engaged in the discussion.

If the classroom focus was on calling patterns, the dual purpose would be first to chronicle data that identifies which students are asked to respond to the teacher's questions and then, with a culturally responsive lens, identify patterns such as the following:

- Gender: Are males and females called on equally? Are questions asked proportionately across students whose gender is nonmajority? Is one gender favored over another? Are students stereotyped in that males are asked to answer more complex questions (e.g., math and science)?
- Race: Are questions asked about race and/or ethnicity in a way that is proportionate and representative?
- Intersectionality: By considering the intersectionality of students' daily lives as the combination, or intersection, of important modes of social advantage and disadvantage, are questions asked proportionally across students by acknowledging their race, class, and gender, so that they can combine in ways that alter the meaning and effects of one another (i.e., Morris, 2007)?

Data could also illuminate whether the teacher favors one or two areas of the classroom (e.g., the front row) when calling on students to answer questions. Is attention paid to students in equitable and inclusive ways?

Digging deeper, a focus on calling patterns could also provide insights into the levels of questions that students are asked. Are higher-order questions asked evenly across all students? Or, possibly, what does the teacher do with student responses? That is, does the teacher use student responses to extend the lesson and if so, are these types of expansion offered to all students in the classroom? Does the teacher acknowledge all students' comments, responses, questions, and contributions? Does the teacher affirm and validate student responses—even if the response is not fully correct? Does the teacher probe students to share alternate points of view?

A culturally responsive lens can be applied to analyze data centering on, for example, how teachers reinforce students' contributions to classroom activities, the types and frequency of feedback given to students, the use of praise, and the patterns of questions that students ask. Observations that focus on cultural responsiveness go a long way in extending conversations to other aspects of the classroom learning environment.

Regardless of the focus, a supervisor who champions culturally responsive practices cues into other areas that shape the learning environment. An observer should be able to detail practices that promote a sense of belonging, where students are not afraid to take risks; they care for one another; and they are responsive to affirming messages offered by the teacher. The possibilities for examining a focus on cultural responsiveness in the classroom are endless. Regardless of approach, data collected during an observation must be shared in a post-observation conference.

The Post-Observation Conference

Figure 9.1 presents the cyclical nature of classroom observations: the pre-observation conference, the classroom observation, and the post-observation conference. Next in this discussion is attention to the post-observation conference. The post-observation conference should not signal an end to the process in that it focuses attention on:

1. the data collected during the observation: the data enables the teacher and supervisor to make sense of what was observed; and,
2. what comes next by identifying the types of professional learning that can support teachers and their growth. Often, teachers and supervisors discuss future instructional and classroom areas to focus attention as a result of the post-conference.

Data drives the post-observation conference. From the data, the teacher and supervisor examine patterns and trends pulled from the observation. These data points serve as the basis for the post-observation conference.

The post-observation conference is more than a reporting of what was observed. The teacher is not a mere spectator in the process. Rather, the post-observation conferences situates the teacher as an active learner engaged in analyzing data—the events of the classroom. The teacher would be the one extrapolating patterns and themes from the data with the supervisor working alongside the teacher or what Gall and Acheson (2010) referred to as holding a mirror to practice. With this image in mind and a focus on cultural responsiveness, the supervisor pulls patterns from the data that can extend the discussion about classroom practices, instructional methods, and student engagement.

Bellon and Bellon (1982) offered the technique of lesson reconstruction where the teacher and the supervisor examine data closely to reconstruct these events. Going further, an objective is to deconstruct the data looking for ways to apply a culturally responsive lens to the discussion. Perhaps data could lend itself to examining:

- The use of students; lived experiences as part of the curriculum;
- Higher-order questions and the engagement of students in extending their thinking to address an inequity in their world;
- Differentiation of instruction to ensure asset-based approaches to learning;
- Respect for diverse learners and the strengths they bring to the classroom; and
- Affirming cultural language and cultural knowledge.

The content for examining cultural responsiveness is dependent on what was observed.

These practices yield rich data not only for the teacher being observed but also for the school to focus on larger trends, both examined next.

USING DATA FROM CLASSROOM OBSERVATIONS

Ponticell (2016) made clear that data from supervisory processes are not the enemy. Data from classroom observations show patterns of interaction, word patterns, classroom procedures, and the rituals of learning between teachers and students. Data, if used to help teachers and leaders reconstruct the events of the classroom, can be a powerful tool in supporting teachers. The data should drive the conversations in which the teacher takes an active role in deconstructing classroom practices. From such an effort, the teacher can engage in more vested ways to develop new strategies and the knowledge to make appropriate changes to practice. And, the supervisor can more effectively work with the teacher on next steps, including, for example, more targeted professional learning opportunities.

Weighing in, Firestone (2014) established several conditions to support the use of classroom observation data and feedback:

1. The data must be "safe," in that teachers perceive that the information will not be used for reward or punishment.
2. Data and feedback must be provided quickly.
3. Feedback must be "fine grained enough to help teachers understand the learning challenges of their students." (p. 104)

There are two levels in which data from classroom observations can be leveraged to support teacher, leader, and school growth, as illustrated in Figure 9.2. Regardless of use, there must exist a transparency of data, unpacking the meaning of data and establishing how data can be leveraged to increase culturally responsive practices.

Level 1 of data use is focused on the individual, and Level 2 is for a larger collective of teachers as in a grade level, a subject area, and professional learning communities, for example. The first level of data use is situated in the post-observation conference. Recall that in the pre-observation conference, the teacher and supervisor set a focus for what will be observed in the classroom. From the data collected based on the focus, the teacher and supervisor then examine patterns and trends pulled from the data. These data points serve as the basis for the post-observation conference. At the end of the post-observation conference, the teacher and supervisor identify a target area to focus on, for professional learning. Subsequent observations will then focus on the target area(s) chosen, following the spiraling nature presented in the *Culturally Responsive Framework for Classroom Observations* (see Figure 9.1).

The second level of data that can inform practice involves pulling data from across individual classroom observations focusing on grade level, subject area, and so forth, and noting trends and patterns. The same would be true of other types of classroom observation data collected through informal classroom observations, walkthroughs, and learning walks. As a group effort, analyzing data from walkthroughs can also support the development of new practices. In Level 2, teachers within and across grade-levels, subject-area departments, professional learning communities, and other configurations can review data. In a group setting, teachers would

- engage in conversations about the meaning of data;
- focus conversations about instructional practices and classroom arrangements; and
- unpack and make sense of trends related to culturally responsive practices.

Figure 9.2. Levels of Data Use

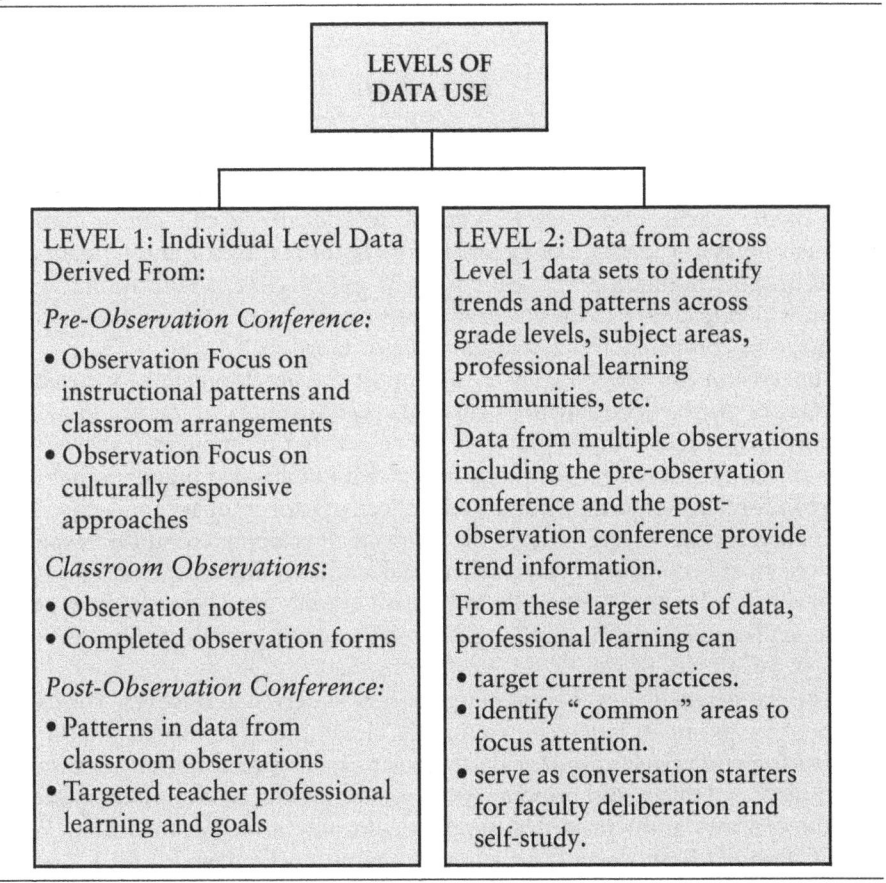

LEVELS OF DATA USE

LEVEL 1: Individual Level Data Derived From:

Pre-Observation Conference:
- Observation Focus on instructional patterns and classroom arrangements
- Observation Focus on culturally responsive approaches

Classroom Observations:
- Observation notes
- Completed observation forms

Post-Observation Conference:
- Patterns in data from classroom observations
- Targeted teacher professional learning and goals

LEVEL 2: Data from across Level 1 data sets to identify trends and patterns across grade levels, subject areas, professional learning communities, etc.

Data from multiple observations including the pre-observation conference and the post-observation conference provide trend information.

From these larger sets of data, professional learning can

- target current practices.
- identify "common" areas to focus attention.
- serve as conversation starters for faculty deliberation and self-study.

From these types of data, teachers and leaders can engage in conversations about practice, pinpoint the needs of teachers, and identify the types of professional learning and coaching that teachers can benefit from in their journey to grow into more culturally responsive teachers. Data from classroom observations are important in that the ". . . supervisor can connect the dots, so to speak, among teachers' instructional practices collectively and consider implications for professional development, learning communities, and the need for resources and/or central office support" (Ponticell et al., 2019, p. 255).

Level 1 and Level 2 data are important for leaders who supervise teachers. As practice, leaders can review trends in data over time, examining, for example, changes in student demographics and mobility rates, changes in teacher demographics, as in the number of new teachers to the building, and the types of professional learning teachers have engaged in. With a laser focus on culturally responsive teaching and an equally precise laser focus on the leader promoting these types of practices, data points will emerge—and these points can be leveraged to further the work of culturally responsive teaching.

DISCUSSION

Supervision unfolds in the context of the school that serves diverse student populations that have often been marginalized. Equally diverse are the developmental levels of the teachers who are responsible to educate *all* children in culturally responsive ways. The range of experience levels of teachers and the populations served in the schoolhouse ". . . calls for new approaches to educational leadership in which leaders exhibit culturally responsive organizational practices, behaviors, and competencies" (Madhlangobe & Gordon, 2012, p. 177).

Supervision can become a lever to support the development of instructional and classroom practices that hold cultural responsiveness as the foundation for the work that teachers do. Supervisory processes that promote inclusive environments do so by sustaining a learning culture with embedded practices that eliminate risks for teachers to take as they self-reflect, ask for feedback, and experiment with new techniques. Engaging in the work of developing culturally responsive practices must become for both teachers and leaders a fault-free endeavor with a long-term view because "culturally responsive schools are a work in progress and a never-ending work that is requiring to evolve as community's change" (Genano, 2021, p. 167).

The classroom observation is a large part of supervising teachers. The cyclical nature of the pre-observation conference, the classroom observation, and the post-observation conference can provide the means to engage teachers in examining their practices, beliefs, and bringing focus to instruction, classroom management, and the routines and rituals that support culturally responsive teaching. By using a Culturally Responsive Instructional Supervision Framework for Classroom

Observations approach to supervision, leaders and teachers can explore their own competence and responsiveness to the children in their classrooms.

The Culturally Responsive Instructional Supervision Framework for Classroom Observations is a model to focus both teachers and leaders on the classroom environment. No single framework or model is perfect and can always be improved. The improvement of the practices resides in the work that needs to be done to ensure that teachers and leaders are focusing their efforts on students in the classroom. For the Culturally Responsive Instructional Supervision Framework for Classroom Observations to work, supervisors will need to focus sustained attention on changing the often-heard narratives that are deficient about children and their learning.

The new narrative is rooted in equity, and based on the asset-based premises that all children can and will learn in a supportive classroom environment. The new narrative also includes teachers and leaders actively working together to unpack their beliefs and values and how these are manifested in instructional, assessment and classroom practices. Supervisors need to engage in the heavy lifting required to reflect upon their own beliefs and values if they are going to support teachers doing the same.

Like new narratives, the processes associated with classroom observations cannot be cut short, yielding incomplete or rushed processes that divert the intent of supervisors to be developmental and differentiated to the needs of teachers. The narrative "there is not enough time to supervise teachers" must be replaced with practices that are carried out with fidelity. Taking shortcuts and putting supervisory support on the back burner is akin to malpractice or what Zepeda and Ponticell (1998) have characterized as benign neglect. Today, supervisors must help teachers reimagine an education system that moves past deficit mindsets about children and empowers teachers to engage in culturally responsive teaching. The U.S. education system is at a crossroads where we must reconsider taken-for-granted pedagogical foundations and not repeat history and perpetuate the marginalization of students.

Like students, teachers need an inclusive environment where they feel that they belong in the larger community of the school, that their voices are heard, and that they can ask for and seek assistance as they face the often thorny and complex issues of teaching, working with families, and learning about how they can contribute to creating an inclusive community for their students. If supervisory relationships are built on a foundation of trust, teachers will look to their supervisors and colleagues as sources of new knowledge that can be co-created through conversations.

These conversations would include those before and after classroom observations, with the aspiration of more focused discussions as a norm of practice. The intent of these conversations is to be affirmative of teachers and their efforts. However, leaders must model cultural responsiveness through focused and courageous conversations with teachers about what is or perhaps not observed during classroom observations. The focus of these conversations must also include areas of practice and equity that address diversity.

CRIS is needed to ensure that the practices needed match the context of the site and the characteristics of both students and teachers (Zepeda, 2006). With the Efforts are needed to implement and sustain a Culturally Responsive Instructional Supervision Framework for Classroom Observations. As Cormier and Pandey (2021) assert, "supervision can and is beginning to play a central role in mitigating . . . the educational debt or unaddressed opportunities" (p. 126) too often found in schools.

REFERENCES

Alim, H. S., & Paris, D. (2017). What is culturally sustaining pedagogy and why does it matter? In D. Paris & H. S. Alim (Eds.), *Culturally sustaining pedagogies: Teaching and learning for justice in a changing world* (pp. 1–21). Teachers College Press.

Banks, J. A. (1994). *Multiethnic education: Theory and practice* (3rd ed.). Allyn and Bacon.

Banks, J. A., Cookson, P., Gay, G., Hawley, W. D., Irvine, J. J., Nieto, S., Schofield, J. W., & Stephan, W. G. (2001). Diversity within unity: Essential principles for teaching and learning in a multicultural society. *Phi Delta Kappan, 83*(3), 196–203. https://doi.org/10.1177/003172170108300309

Bellon, J. J., & Bellon, E. C. (1982). *Classroom supervision and instructional improvement: A synergetic process* (2nd ed.). Kendall/Hunt.

Bogotch, I., & Shields, C. (2014). Introduction: Do promises of social justice trump paradigms of educational leadership? In I. Bogotch & C. Shields (Eds.), *International handbook of educational leadership and social (in)justice*, Volume 1 (pp. 1–12). Springer.

Cormier, D. R. (2021). Assessing preservice teachers' cultural competence with the cultural proficiency continuum Q-sort. *Educational Researcher, 50*(1), 17–29. https://doi.org/10.3102/0013189X20936670

Cormier, D. R., & Pandey, T. (2021). Semiotic analysis of a foundational textbook used widely across educational supervision. *Journal of Educational Supervision, 4*(2), 101–132. https://doi.org/10.31045/jes.4.2.6

DeMatthews, D. E., Serafini, A., & Watson, T. N. (2021). Leading inclusive schools: Principal perceptions, practices, and challenges to meaningful change. *Educational Administration Quarterly, 57*(1), 3–48. https://doi.org/10.1177/0013161X20913897

Firestone, W. A. (2014). Teacher evaluation policy and conflicting theories of motivation. *Educational Researcher, 43*(2), 100–107. https://doi.org/10.3102/0013189X14521864

Gall, M. D., & Acheson, K. A. (2010). *Clinical supervision and teacher development: Preservice and inservice applications* (6th ed.). Longman.

García, E., & Weiss, E. (2019). *The teacher shortage is real, large and growing, and worse than we thought*. Economic Policy Institute. https://www.epi.org/files/pdf/163651.pdf

Gay, G. (2000). *Culturally responsive teaching: Theory, research, and practice*. Teachers College Press.

Gay, G. (2002). Preparing for culturally responsive teaching. *Journal of Teacher Education, 53*(2), 106–116. https://doi.org/10.1177/0022487102053002003

Gay, G. (2005). Standards of diversity. In S. P. Gordon (Ed.), *Standards for instructional supervision* (pp. 105–117). Routledge.

Gay, G. (2013). Teaching to and through cultural diversity. *Curriculum Inquiry, 43*(1), 48–70. https://doi.org/10.1111/curi.12002

Gay, G. (2018). *Culturally responsive teaching: Theory, research, and practice* (3rd ed.). Teachers College Press.

Glatthorn, A. A. (1997). *Differentiated supervision* (2nd ed.). Association for Supervision and Curriculum Development.

Glickman, C. D. (1981). *Developmental supervision: Alternative practices for helping teachers to improve instruction.* Association for Supervision and Curriculum Development.

Hines, E. M., Ford, D. Y., Fletcher, E. C., Jr., & Moore, J. L., III. (2022). All eyes on me: disproportionality, disciplined, and disregarded while Black. *Theory Into Practice, 61*(3), 288–299. https://doi.org/10.1080/00405841.2022.2096376

Horsford, S. D., Grosland, T., & Gunn, K. M. (2011). Pedagogy of the personal and professional: Toward a framework for culturally relevant leadership. *Journal of School Leadership, 21*(4), 582–606. http://dx.doi.org/10.1177/105268461102100404

Johnson, L. (2014). Culturally responsive leadership for community empowerment. *Multicultural Education Review, 6*(2), 145–170. https://doi.org/10.1080/2005615X.2014.11102915

Johnson, L., & Fuller, C. (2014). *Culturally responsive leadership.* Oxford University Press.

Khalifa, M. A. (2018). *Culturally responsive school leadership.* Harvard Education Press.

Khalifa, M. A., Gooden, M. A., & Davis, J. E. (2016). Culturally responsive school leadership. *Review of Educational Research, 86*(4), 1272–1311. https://doi.org/10.3102/0034654316630383

Ladson-Billings, G. (1995). Toward a theory of culturally relevant pedagogy. *American Educational Research Journal, 32*(3), 465–491. http://dx.doi.org/10.3102/00028312032003465

Ladson-Billings, G. (2022). *The dreamkeepers: Successful teachers for African American children* (3rd ed.). Jossey-Bass.

Little, S. J., & Welsh, R. O. (2022). Rac(e)ing to punishment? Applying theory to racial disparities in disciplinary outcomes. *Race Ethnicity and Education, 25*(4), 564–584. https://doi.org/10.1080/13613324.2019.1599344

Lopez, A. E. (2016). Toward a theory of culturally responsive and social justice leadership. In: *Culturally responsive and socially just leadership in diverse contexts,* (pp. 15–31). Springer.

López, F. A. (2017). Altering the trajectory of the self-fulfilling prophecy: Asset-based pedagogy and classroom dynamics. *Journal of Teacher Education, 68*(2), 193–212. https://doi.org/10.1177/0022487116685751

Madhlangobe, L., & Gordon, S. P. (2012). Culturally responsive leadership in a diverse school: A case study of a high school leader. *NASSP Bulletin, 96*(3), 177–202. https://doi.org/10.1177/0192636512450909

Maxwell, L. A. (2014). U.S. school enrollment hits majority-minority milestone. *Education Week, 34*(1), 14–15. https://www.edweek.org/ew/articles/2014/08/20/01demographics.h34.html

Milner, H. R., IV. (2017). Where's the race in culturally relevant pedagogy? *Teachers College Record, 119*(1), 1–32. https://doi.org/10.1177/016146811711900109

Morris, E. W. (2007). "Ladies" or "loudies"?: Perceptions and experiences of Black girls in classrooms. *Youth & Society, 38*(4), 490–515. https://doi.org/10.1177/0044118X06296778

Morrison, K. L. (2017). Informed asset-based pedagogy: Coming correct, counter-stories from an information literacy classroom. *Library Trends, 66*(2), 176–218. http://doi.org/10.1353/lib.2017.0034

National Center for Education Statistics. (2019). *Digest of education statistics: Enrollment in elementary, secondary, and degree-granting postsecondary institutions, by level and control of institution, enrollment level, and attendance status and sex of student: Selected years, fall 1990 through fall 2028* [Data file]. Author. National Center for Education Statistics. https://nces.ed.gov/programs/digest/d18/tables/dt18_105.20.asp

National Center for Education Statistics. (2021). Characteristics of public school principals. *Condition of Education*. U.S. Department of Education, Institute of Education Sciences. https://nces.ed.gov/programs/coe/indicator/cls

Paris, D., & Alim, H. S. (2014). What are we seeking to sustain through culturally sustaining pedagogy? A loving critique forward. *Harvard Educational Review*, 84(1), 85–100. https://doi.org/10.17763/haer.84.1.982l873k2ht16m77

Ponticell, J. A. (2016). A retrospective look at data embedded in instructional supervision: Data are not the enemy. In S. J. Zepeda & J. Glanz (Eds.), *Re-examining supervision: Theory and practice* (163–186). Rowman & Littlefield.

Ponticell, J. A., Zepeda, S. J., Lanoue, P. D., Haines, J. G., Jimenez, A. M., & Ata, A. (2019). Observation, feedback, and reflection. In S.J. Zepeda & J.A. Ponticell (Eds.). *The Wiley handbook of educational supervision* (pp. 251–279). West Sussex, UK: Blackwell/John Wiley & Sons.

Rose, H. A. (2006). Asset-based development for child and youth care. *Reclaiming Children and Youth*, 14(4), 236–240. https://reclaimingjournal.com

Russell, G. (2020). Reflecting on a way of being: Anchor principles of cultural competence. In J. Frawley, G. Russell, & J. Sherwood (Eds.), *Cultural Competence and the Higher Education Sector* (pp. 31–42). Springer.

Shields, C. M. (2010). Transformative leadership: Working for equity in diverse contexts. *Educational Administration Quarterly*, 46(4), 558–589.

Shields, C. M., & Hesbol, K. A. (2020). Transformative leadership approaches to inclusion, equity, and social justice. *Journal of School Leadership*, 30(1), 3–22. https://doi.org/10.1177/1052684619873343

Sleeter, C. E. (2017). Critical race theory and the Whiteness of teacher education. *Urban Education*, 52(2), 155–169. http://dx.doi.org/10.1177/0042085916668957

Sutcher, L., Darling-Hammond, L., & Carver-Thomas, D. (2019). Understanding teacher shortages: An analysis of teacher supply and demand in the United States. *Education Policy Analysis Archives*, 27(35). http://dx.doi.org/10.14507/epaa.27.3696

Tanase, M. F. (2022). Culturally responsive teaching in urban secondary schools. *Education and Urban Society*, 54(4), 363–388. http://dx.doi.org/10.1177/00131245211026689

Theoharis, G. (2010). Disrupting injustice: Principals narrate the strategies they use to improve their schools and advance social justice. *Teachers College Record, 112*(1), 331–373. https://doi.org/10.1177/016146811011200105

Theoharis, G., Causton, J., Woodfield, C., & Scribner, S. (2020). Inclusive leadership and disability. In *Leadership for increasingly diverse schools* (pp. 17–56). In G. Theoharis, & M. K. Scanlan (Eds.), *Leadership for increasingly diverse schools* (2nd Edition), (pp. 17–56). Routledge.

Theoharis, G., & Scanlan, M. K. (2015). *Leadership for increasingly diverse schools*. Routledge.

Warren, C. A. (2018). Empathy, teacher dispositions, and preparation for culturally responsive pedagogy. *Journal of Teacher Education*, 69(2), 169–183. https://doi.org/10.1177/0022487117712487

Yosso, T. J. (2005). Whose culture has capital? A critical race theory discussion of community cultural wealth. *Race Ethnicity and Education, 8*(1), 69–91. https://doi.org/10.1080/1361332052000341006

Zepeda, S. J. (2006). High stakes supervision: We must do more. *International Journal of Leadership in Education, 9*(1), 61–73. https://doi.org/10.1080/13603120500448154

Zepeda, S. J. (2012). *Informal classroom observations on the go: Feedback, discussion, and reflection* (3rd ed.). Routledge.

Zepeda, S. J. (2013). *The principal as instructional leader: A Practical Handbook* (3rd ed.). Routledge.

Zepeda, S. J. (2017). *Instructional supervision: Applying tools and concepts* (4th ed.). Routledge.

Zepeda, S. J., Lanoue, P. D., Rivera, G. M., & Shafer, D. R. (2023). *Leading school culture through teacher voice and agency*. Routledge.

Zepeda, S. J., & Ponticell, J. A. (1998). At cross-purposes: What do teachers need, want, and get from supervision? *Journal of Curriculum and Supervision, 14*(1), 68–87.

CHAPTER 10

Building Bridges for Change
Culturally Responsive Instructional Supervision for Indigenous Students

Hollie J. Mackey, Cailen M. O'Shea, and Sashay Schettler

Culturally Responsive Instructional Supervision (CRIS) is a concept that has garnered well-deserved attention in recent years. Though CRIS is an expansive concept, it is one that is embedded within the construct of Culturally Responsive School Leadership (CRSL). To begin the work of CRSL requires educational leaders to disrupt, affirm, sustain, and revitalize schools to authentically reflect the pluralistic communities in which they are situated (McCarty & Lee, 2014). Educational leaders working within a colonized system have to reflect on their own beliefs and axioms of what it means to be culturally responsive. This requires a high degree of reflection and introspection before they can enact practices to mediate the external pressures of any embedded colonized structures, in order to intentionally contest their reproduction (Khalifa et al., 2019). For many Indigenous school leaders, this work is particularly more demanding, as previously held beliefs of Native students and communities are continually colored by historically inaccurate representations and a lack of contemporary knowledge about their strengths and needs. These school leaders are often stifled by the very political paradigm their schools are confined within (Brayboy, 2005).

To begin to understand CRIS requires an understanding of CRSL as well as how instructional leadership itself has been operationalized. Instructional leadership has a long history in educational research, going back 50 years to the effective school movement. The genesis of the concept has tended to explain instructional leadership as a trait-based, heroic form of leadership (Elmore, 2000; Heck et al., 1990; Neumerski, 2013). More contemporary studies focus on the behaviors and actions of educational leaders, including how they develop a vision for learning, a schoolwide culture focused on enhancing the learning environment for students, and the provision of professional development opportunities for their staff (Neumerski, 2013; Urick, 2016). Despite ubiquitous expectations, there remains a gap between these expectations and practice (Hallinger et al., 2020; Shaked, 2018). This gap is due in part to how educational leaders conceptualize instructional leadership and how their own belief systems and mental maps influence their beliefs and, ultimately, their actions (Shaked, 2018).

This individual conceptualization is paramount in the conversation around the importance of instructional leadership. Research has shown that while indirect, principals' focus on teaching and learning has the greatest impact on student outcomes through multiple pathways (Leithwood et al., 2004; Mireles-Rios & Becchio, 2018; Robinson et al., 2008). Using these numerous pathways, educational leaders enact instructional leadership by playing a key role in building the instructional capacity of others to support school improvement (Neumerski, 2013; Wahlstrom & Louis, 2008). Despite the importance of instructional leadership, research suggests that principals spend little time directly engaged in the improvement of instruction (Grissom et al., 2013), much less CRIS. In this chapter, we look to elaborate on some of the work done specifically in the Indigenous context around CRIS. We push back on traditional colonized framing and offer narratives for educators interested in learning more about CRIS. In these narratives, we highlight the importance of cultivating curiosity and commitment through developing relationships, the process of learning to support CRIS for Indigenous students, and the importance of community and scholarly resources. We conclude this chapter with the model of CRIS we use to fuse deeper learning with Indigenous knowledges.

TROUBLING THE NOTION OF CULTURALLY RESPONSIVE INSTRUCTIONAL SUPERVISION

Our work pushes back on the notion that CRIS (and by default, Culturally Responsive Teaching, Culturally Responsive School Leadership, and Culturally Responsive Schooling) hold the answers for meaningful integration of Indigenous identity into everyday school practices. In part, this is largely based on the idea that we find it difficult to imagine school or district leaders who are not from a specified culture who have the ability to "disrupt, affirm, sustain, and revitalize" (McCarty & Lee, 2014) content from cultures to which they are not directly integrated into themselves. We think this is an important topic to broach because we have found, time and time again, that school leaders also express this challenge. Even among our author team, we see that our own lived experiences, two of which come directly from Tribal communities, do not give us the ability to broadly assume that we have all of the content knowledge and tools necessary to fully sustain or revitalize cultural content from one another's communities. We imagine this is true of all cultural demographics represented under the umbrella of CRIS and do not presume that this is a unique situation for Indigenous communities alone. However, for the purpose of this chapter, our focus is narrowly tailored to Indigenous community identity. Our goal is to situate what we know about CRIS and work with Indigenous communities toward a framework that provides instructional leaders at all levels a place from which to start this important work.

Several states have worked to develop educational resources that provide a foundation from which to begin CRIS work in schools (see Montana Office of Public Instruction, 2019; North Dakota Department of Public Instruction, n.d.). These are important for a number of reasons, primarily due to the fact that in a U.S. context, regardless of whether one uses the terms Indigenous, Native American, or American Indian, there is a complex federal relationship that situates these communities separately from other racial, ethnic, or cultural groups represented in American schools. It is essential that educators understand that there are currently 574 federally recognized tribes and approximately 60 state-recognized tribes across the nation. Each of these tribes has a distinct political, socio-cultural, and linguistic history and contemporary approaches to cultural sustainability and revitalization, making it crucial that educators understand there is no simplified pan-Indigenous identity across these communities (Mackey, 2017). CRIS, for all its good intent, falls short of recognizing distinct differences among Native communities and the political status of Tribal nations.

Considering these shortcomings, we pose the question, why does this matter? We often get this question when we begin working with educators, and we have found that most educators are not aware of the status of Tribal communities as nations within a nation, of the federal trust responsibility for educating Native students, or of the separate body of federal legislation that outlines the unique tri-lateral relationship among federal, tribal, and state governments. Reinhardt and Maday (2006) characterize this as a shared, tri-lateral responsibility. The foundation for this government-to-government relationship is what sets apart Indigenous communities as racial/ethnic/cultural groups and extends to us all the responsibility to recognize and respect the distinct political status American Indians possess, unlike that of other racial/ethnic/cultural groups in the United States. The full discussion of this is beyond the scope of this chapter; however, we encourage readers to learn more as they engage with CRIS (see Faircloth, 2015, 2019). Authentically engaging in CRIS as it relates to Tribal nations requires leaders to learn more about both the political status of Indigenous communities and the specific histories, contributions, and contemporary conditions of the students and families they serve.

CULTIVATING CURIOSITY AND COMMITMENT

We work from the simple premise that relationships between educators and the communities they serve form the foundation for authentic CRIS for Indigenous students. In fostering and strengthening these relationships, we employ a two-pronged approach intended to: (1) cultivate educators' curiosity about the rich cultural history, contributions, and contemporary issues affecting Indigenous communities; and (2) cultivate educators' commitment to ensuring these are meaningfully infused across the curriculum, and the everyday lived experiences of schooling. While the concept of relationships being at the core of CRIS is not

Building Bridges for Change

novel, we extend this notion to instructional leaders as *bridges* for fostering authentic relationships. In other words, instructional leaders create the conditions that foster both cultivating curiosity and commitment while providing educators the resources and professional development necessary for engaging with Indigenous curricular content responsibly. Similarly, when we engage in professional development with educators, we see ourselves as equally responsible for bridging the divide between community and schools. Culturally responsive instructional leaders must concomitantly tend to school- and community-based relationships and understand that CRIS is both a process and a continuously evolving product.

We draw on data collected from approximately 3 years of professional development with educators to best illustrate the ways in which reflection and introspection are key aspects to enacting effective CRIS as it relates to Indigenous students, their families, and their broader communities. Represented among these educators are classroom teachers, instructional coaches, cultural coordinators, special education teachers, and administrators, as well as Indigenous families and community professionals such as members of parental advisory committees and Tribal Education Department personnel. Regionally, our participants represent communities from the Great Plains, Mountain West, Pacific Northwest, and the Southwest areas as they are defined within the United States. This context is important for a number of reasons. We have learned time and time again that traditional notions of instructional leadership, even those related to CRIS, require nuanced, differentiated approaches when applied to Indigenous students' learning across a diverse range of histories, customs, and community expectations. In addition, we have learned that regardless of the community, different Indigenous families' expectations for how CRIS is operationalized within their children's schools are not all that different, nor are the barriers different that are expressed by educators asked to identify why they struggle to meet these expectations (Zuckerman & O'Shea, 2021). To better illustrate both the expectations and struggles, we will use composite narratives that represent collective themes from this data set. An example is described in the vignette below.

> *It's professional development day and it's focused on strategies and resources for infusing Indigenous curricular content into everyday classroom content. As happens in most PDs, some teachers and administrators have arrived early and have their laptops set up, ready to get started, while others quietly sip their coffee, looking around for familiar faces as they seek out the best location from which to engage with the day's activities and speakers. The tone is hushed despite the room being filled with people who have come together for a specific purpose and, for the most part, know one other. This quiet is disrupted by an infectious laugh the Indian Education Director lets out as she sees the presenters walk in from the back of the room, exclaiming, "I'm so glad you are here!" Seeing her at the front, the presenters similarly smile, laugh, and rush to greet her—their enthusiasm matching hers. After rounds of hugs, teasing, loud laughter, and queries of "How is your family?" they are all ready to begin setting up*

for the day. As they look around, they notice the teachers and administrators have been watching them engage in this warm welcome event, yet none have increased their volume or engaged in similar greetings with colleagues they know. One presenter turns to the group, still smiling, and says, "It's a great day to have a great day! Please, find your friends, reconnect, make new acquaintances!" And then they do, resulting in the entire room being filled with laughter and hugs, summer plan discussions, and a feeling of togetherness that was missing just 10 minutes earlier.

While the vignette above may, at first glance, seem like a relatively common scene at professional development meetings, the meaning is deeper. It provides a glimpse into the ways different groups of people have been socialized into two types of greeting processes. As we engage with educators about CRIS, we are intentionally mindful of the ways we model cultural differences and invite non-Native participants into the process of connecting with one another, as we do in Indigenous communities, which is as critically important as the PD content. We are mindful that our work is situated within a system designed around an individualistic community mindset, yet our goal is to open up the possibility that within that system lies fertile ground for honoring those whose worldview is informed by a collectivist mindset. CRIS requires us to make explicit each learning goal, even the greeting process, as we guide educators into shifting their perspective to center relationships before content. As a result, our participants shared:

Starting with relationships created a space where we felt comfortable sharing our hesitation to engage in work where we just don't know what we don't know, and mostly, we are not even sure where to begin. Now it seems easy; we can learn just like we learn anything else, but the task of incorporating American Indian content into our lessons used to feel overwhelming. Being in relationships with our students and their families makes sense; in relationships, you want to know more about the other person, so it's not just learning historical facts but also learning about what they care about and what they think is important to put into the curriculum. Thinking about it in terms of shifts rather than a complete overhaul makes it feel like something more attainable.

We center our work with the goal of building relational and knowledge bridges aligned with our premise that cultivating curiosity about the unfamiliar can lead to the commitment of enacting the work necessary to engage in CRIS for Indigenous students. Our participants have repeatedly demonstrated that when we center the work of CRIS on relationships, we assist educators with establishing their foundation about "why" the work matters. We then shift to helping them identify "how" they will do the work. We have identified three recurring themes related to individual learning, resources, and instructional strategies that act as barriers when dedicated educators begin to delve in to CRIS as it relates to the Native American content. We will discuss these themes below, supplemented by composite participants' narratives to provide concrete examples for reference.

YOU DON'T KNOW WHAT YOU DON'T KNOW

As highlighted in the narrative above, the most common theme we encounter in our CRIS PD work is "You don't know what you don't know." While we acknowledge the truth to this, we turn to Khalifa et al. (2019) and begin by encouraging educators and instructional leaders to reflect on the existence of embedded colonized structures and ask them to identify how these structures serve to reify the notion that Western knowledge is somehow superior to Indigenous knowledge (Whyte, 2018). We then ask them how they see that infusing Indigenous knowledge can serve to mediate the effects of colonized systems designed to render Indigenous knowledges invisible. These are big questions that require educators to step into contested knowledge spaces and grapple with not only what they do not know, but often, the inaccuracy of what they do know. For example, part of our work intentionally incorporates land- and water-based pedagogy where we encourage educators to think about the relationship between peoples and land as well as the relationship between land and knowledge. We then take educators to sites of historic importance to regional Indigenous communities and guide them through both what they may know and what, from an Indigenous lens, should also be included.

Our strategy begins with taking macro-historical events or people and then interrogating how these events might be alternatively interpreted. We are mindful that educators often misunderstand Native histories and tend to relegate the experiences of Indigenous people only to historic narratives that exclude contemporary lived experiences. Below we share an example of how we guide educators using a baseline historical figure, Abraham Lincoln, who many believe they know enough about to teach his role in history. Near Bismarck, North Dakota, is a historic fort named after Abraham Lincoln. Educators in the region where this fort is located tend to express their familiarity with the fort and share that they use the site as a field trip for their students. When asked about Fort Abraham Lincoln, participants shared:

> *We are lucky to have a living historical site so close so our students can see firsthand where history plays out. We highlight why it was named after Abraham Lincoln, teach about his presidency, the civil war, and the end of slavery and what it meant for the country. Students also get to see the Mandan Village Historic Site that is also on the property, so they get to learn about two cultures at the same time. Sometimes we go there for Native American Heritage month.*

Our CRIS strategy then examines what else the educators know about the fort. Occasionally we hear about General Custer being stationed there; other times we hear about events or activities, but rarely do we hear anything beyond a Western interpretation about the importance of this space. We ask participants guiding questions and provide historical context from an Indigenous lens to challenge their thinking:

> *You are familiar with the Battle of Little Bighorn, correct? Custer's Last Stand? Did you know that Fort Abraham Lincoln was General George Armstrong Custer's last duty station before he was killed in the battle? That he was strategically stationed here to kill Native Americans? Where do you think people from the Nueta (the name the Mandan use for themselves rather than the Western name assigned to them) Village went when the fort was established on the same land?*

Participants are often unfamiliar with this history and are curious about it. Through simple questions we have introduced the notion of colonial displacement and language erasure and set the stage to think critically about American heroes who were actually on the losing end of one of the most historic battles in U.S. history. We take the time necessary to establish the parallel version of events as seen through their Indigenous students' frames of reference and discuss displacement and language erasure in depth before pushing them a little harder:

> *So, we have established that there are two vastly different versions of General Custer, and either way, he was killed at the Battle of Little Bighorn. Let's talk a little bit about Fort Abraham Lincoln itself. Why do you think it was named for him? What are the defining characteristics about Abraham Lincoln you tend to teach to students? Would you be surprised to know that the president credited for abolishing slavery is also responsible for the largest mass hanging in U.S. history? Would you be even more surprised to know that he ordered the mass hanging of 38 Dakota tribal members in response to their resistance to being displaced from their homelands in Minnesota? And what would you think if I told you that all of this happened a full year AFTER Abraham Lincoln signed the Emancipation Proclamation? Given that school districts in this region often have a large number of Dakota students, how do you think we should address these facts in the curriculum about Abraham Lincoln?*

This method of questioning leads participants to think about the ways they might address perpetuating colonial education structures and develop the critical thinking skills we hope they will then model to students. However, our commitment to CRIS demands that it go farther than cultural responsiveness and extend to address the political status and contemporary lived experiences of Indigenous students. After lengthy discussion with participants where they share other aspects they may know about the space and giving them time to exhaust all of their questions up to this point, we press further:

> *Now that you've disrupted your own thinking about Fort Abraham Lincoln, have you wondered why it matters so much today? Why is it important that we discuss multiple viewpoints in history? We know that Indigenous students likely already know the history of the fort and the Dakota 38, just as we know most students are likely familiar with, to some level, Abraham Lincoln and General Custer, but in what ways might our students better understand one another if we made explicit the reasons*

why these are contested historical sites? Let's think about this in a contemporary socio-political context that most are familiar with. The Standing Rock protest over an oil pipeline just north of the Standing Rock reservation, just south of Fort Abraham Lincoln is an example. What is signaled to sovereign Indigenous nations when the general populous has long held up these two historical figures up as American exemplars? Would these sites be so contentious if both Native and non-Native students understood the real-world, contemporary consequences of colonial displacement and historical erasure that are right in their own backyards?

There are many examples where this method of CRIS works to disrupt the notion that schools are value free, and where dominant stories subsume the true historical facts that lead to contemporary conditions that threatening Tribal sovereignty and self-determination in education. We selected the Fort Abraham Lincoln example because we believe most readers will have some sort of baseline understanding of the Emancipation Proclamation, The Battle of Little Bighorn, and the 2016 pipeline protest at Standing Rock; however, the same throughline can be drawn from thousands of land- and water-based sites across the country. Engaging in CRIS for Indigenous students begins with learning what it is you do not know. In this example, all of the content is used to nudge participants away from thinking that this material was merely a Google search away. Participants responded by sharing:

I had no idea all of these events were connected and that 38 people were hanged; it really puts it into perspective why Native students get uncomfortable when we go into these lessons. The curriculum just says what it says; it never really digs into the history more, but if I were Native, I wouldn't want to learn about any of the history if my story was not included. I guess we take for granted that U.S. history as it's taught is the end of the story. There is always a lot left out of curriculum; now I know that I need to learn more to also reflect the lives of Indigenous students.

There are two key components to why this method of CRIS works with participants. First, we prioritize relationship before content. We are well aware that the participants need to feel safe with us prior to their being pushed into uncomfortable content that requires them to question not only their curriculum, but to reflect on their own worldviews and biases in order to deeply engage with the content. The second component is that we are able to physically take them to a contested space where they can physically see the land and water formations, identify the proximity of the fort to the Nueta village, and understand the topics both cognitively and from a sensory-level perception. We are able to cultivate participants' curiosity about the aspects they do not know while cultivating the commitment to better represent the lived experiences of their students in the curriculum. Participants are afforded the opportunity to work on lesson plans and get feedback about how to authentically integrate content from the CRIS PD into their curriculum regardless of their subject area.

TRADITIONAL ECOLOGICAL KNOWLEDGE (TEK) 4+1

One of the ways educational leaders can look to serve as culturally responsive instructional leaders is to identify commonalities between the value systems that exist within their settings. One such example of this is our work with TEK4+1. Traditional Ecological Knowledge (TEK) is combined with the four shifts model of McLeod and Shareski (2018). In this framing, we understand that TEK is fundamental to community-engaged educational research that reflects Indigenous funds of knowledge (Adams et al., 2014). A holistic understanding of our world is valued over siloed, disconnected information held just long enough to demonstrate proficiency on a standardized test. Concepts like connectedness, place-based understandings of context, and communication are at the core of TEK. To guide educators from a CRIS frame requires educational leaders to move beyond the historically held framing of teachers as the givers of knowledge. The "sage on the stage" mantra is replaced with an understanding that knowledge acquisition is a shared experience enhanced by the background, interests, experiences, and expertise of the students and the teachers.

For school leaders, the responsibility is heavy, as it requires them to serve as a bridge between the school and the community to develop stronger relationships. From our perspective, we have seen this to be very difficult for some educational leaders, as they do not know where to begin or are nervous that they will offend community members if they get something "wrong." In our professional developments and continued conversations with educators, we attempt to change the narrative from what "we are doing wrong" to "what can we do to value the knowledge our students bring to our schools in an authentic way?" In doing so, we see CRIS as the umbrella and the four shifts +1 as the lever.

McLeod and Shareski (2018) share the idea that schools do not need to reform education to be engaging and equitable, but rather that they need to shift the way they look at instruction. The four shifts include looking for ways to make the tasks done in the classroom ones that promote deeper-level learning, authentic work, student agency, and technology infusion. Deeper-level learning activities are those that ask educators to look for assignments that are more thought-provoking and rigorous. This requires activities that require students to think and analyze, as opposed to regurgitating information they've heard previously. It requires activities that promote student agency to include ones that are student-centered and allow the students to make the majority of the decisions about what, why, and how they demonstrate their learning. Teachers can still be responsible for the standards covered in a course, but the students are the ones who make the decisions about the best ways for them to learn the content. Authentic work answers the age-old adage of "Why do I need this stuff?" These are learning opportunities that provide students with real-world opportunities to engage with and contribute to the real world.

For example, if a student were interested in marketing, authentic work would allow that individual to work toward this goal in the classroom. Finance class could be tailored to help students understand contracts and LLC development, and tax breaks for small businesses. Technology infusion could help students engage with issues and concepts far beyond their local communities and provide them with experiences and opportunities for collaboration that simply were not possible in years past. A student in rural North Dakota who is interested in learning about underwater archaeology could use technology to follow the work of a researcher specializing in shipwrecks in the Great Lakes and even have conversations with that specialist about their findings and process.

We have added two components to this exemplary work. The first is how we frame the fourth shift as authentic technology infusion. While this may seem semantic, we believe the wording is pivotal, as the majority of educational technology use lies in the lower tier of the Substitution, Augmentation, Modification, and Redefinition (SAMR) model and mostly asks students to passively engage with technology (e.g., reading a website or watching a video) instead of using it to create new information (e.g., developing videos, podcasts, code) (McVeigh-Murphy, 2019). Authentic technology infusion asks educators to not only utilize technology to redefine learning practices but to ensure that students' interests and backgrounds are centered.

The second component is the +1. We know the authors McLeod and Shareski personally and know they believe this component to be essential, but in our time working with educators, we believe it essential to explicitly state the importance of relationships. There is no way to minimize the value of relationships as they pertain to CRIS. Relationships, as stated previously, are at the core of this entire construct. We believe that to be an effective educational leader, relationships must be centered in everything done in schools. Instructionally, relational leadership can come from implementing the same instructional round framework differently based on the different needs of different teachers (Zuckerman & O'Shea, 2021). In these relationships, teachers also gain trust that can foster support for the school's mission and vision (Versland & Erickson, 2017).

From these four shifts, and the framework of TEK, we have coalesced our ways of thinking about CRIS. We examined the ways in which schools have positioned themselves in the development of their "portraits of a graduate" and how these values map themselves onto the tenants of TEK4 + 1. For example, in multiple settings, school districts have identified collaboration, problem solving, and community as characteristics they wish their students to possess when they graduate from high school. Regarding the four shifts, it is clear that instructional practices that promote deeper-level thinking, authentic work, and agency, and utilize technology in authentic ways can help develop students with these traits.

From a TEK perspective, this work is no different. TEK centers the need for holistic thinking, collaboration, and care, among others. This is the cornerstone of our utilization of this framework. We believe that when working with Indigenous students and communities, the goals of educators are closely aligned with, if not the same, as the goals of the community members. Everyone involved wants students to be happy and able to pursue their goals. To do this requires 21st-century skills which, we argue, are actually skills that are thousands of years old. We want students to think creatively about how to solve a problem. What is more creative than figuring out how to develop a project that addresses specific standards in a class that can also help solve a problem facing your community? A final integrant of this work is the clear benefit it can have for non-Native students. Educational leaders already have identified areas in which they believe students need to be successful in their futures. Our work highlights the significant overlap between what is usually done in schools and what can be done. On top of this, we see how TEK4 + 1 allows non-Native students the opportunity to learn more about their classmates and community members by allowing students the agency to make decisions about their learning. In such settings, students can more authentically understand one another and their backgrounds. Considering the wealth of knowledge Native students have about the histories and cultures of their non-Native classmates, it seems neglectful not to provide non-Native students with similar opportunities to learn more about their classmates.

CONCLUSION

We conclude this chapter with a call to action. For educational leaders invested in CRIS we ask that you do not write off the power of relationships when it comes to this work. We ask that you value and foster educators' curiosity about their commitments to the rich cultural history, contributions, and contemporary issues affecting Indigenous communities. We ask that you work to cultivate educators' commitment to ensuring these are meaningfully infused across the curriculum, and across the everyday lived experiences of schooling. We ask because we understand and value the potential these requests have. Instructional leadership is a concept that requires capacity building (Xia & O'Shea, 2022), teacher agency for innovation (O'Shea, 2021), and care. CRIS requires all of this as well as laughter, reflection, action, and humility. We all value connection and knowledge. The ways in which we attain knowledge and connection might occasionally differ, but each and every way should be celebrated and supported.

REFERENCES

Adams, M. S., Carpenter, J., Housty, J. A., Neasloss, D., Paquet, P. C., Service, C., & Darimont, C. T. (2014). Toward increased engagement between academic and Indigenous community partners in ecological research. *Ecology and Society*, *19*(3), 5. http://dx.doi.org/10.5751/ES-06569-190305

Brayboy, B. M. J. (2005). Toward a tribal critical race theory in education. *The Urban Review*, *37*, 425–446.

Elmore, R. F. (2000). *Building a new structure for school leadership*. Albert Shanker Institute.

Faircloth, S. C. (2015). *National Indian Education Study 2015: Setting the context*. U.S. Department of Education.
Faircloth, S. C. (2019). National Indian Education Study Setting the Context 2015. U.S. Department of Education.
Grissom, J. A., Loeb, S., & Master, B. (2013). Effective instructional time use for school leaders: Longitudinal evidence from observations of principals. *Educational Researcher, 42*(8), 433–444.
Hallinger, P., Gümüş, S., & Bellibaş, M. Ş. (2020). "Are principals instructional leaders yet?" A science map of the knowledge base on instructional leadership, 1940–2018. *Scientometrics, 122*(3), 1629–1650.
Heck, R. H., Larsen, T. J., & Marcoulides, G. A. (1990). Instructional leadership and school achievement: Validation of a causal model. *Educational Administration Quarterly, 26*(2), 94–125.
Khalifa, M. A., Khalil, D., Marsh, T. E., & Halloran, C. (2019). Toward an indigenous, decolonizing school leadership: A literature review. *Educational Administration Quarterly, 55*(4), 571–614.
Leithwood, K., Louis, K. S., Anderson, S., & Wahlstrom, K. (2004). *Review of research: How leadership influences student learning*. The Wallace Foundation.
Mackey, H. J. (2017). The ESSA in Indian Country: Problematizing self-determination through the relationships between federal, state, and tribal governments. *Educational Administration Quarterly, 53*(5), 782–808.
McCarty, T., & Lee, T. (2014). Critical culturally sustaining/revitalizing pedagogy and Indigenous education sovereignty. *Harvard educational review, 84*(1), 101–124.
McLeod, S., & Shareski, D. (2018). *Different schools for a different world*. Solution Tree Press.
McVeigh-Murphy, A. (2019). *What teachers need to improve tech integration in the classroom*. Learning.com. https://equip.learning.com/improve-technology-integration-in-the-classroom
Mireles-Rios, R., & Becchio, J. A. (2018). The evaluation process, administrator feedback, and teacher self-efficacy. *Journal of School Leadership, 28*(4), 462–487.
Montana Office of Public Instruction. (2019). *Essential understandings regarding Montana Indians*. https://opi.mt.gov/Portals/182/Page%20Files/Indian%20Education/Indian%20Education%20101/essentialunderstandings.pdf
Neumerski, C. M. (2013). Rethinking instructional leadership, a review: What do we know about principal, teacher, and coach instructional leadership, and where should we go from here? *Educational Administration Quarterly, 49*(2), 310–347.
North Dakota Department of Public Instruction. (n.d.). *North Dakota Native American essential understandings*. https://www.nd.gov/dpi/education-programs/indian-education/north-dakota-native-american-essential-understandings
O'Shea, C. M. (2021). Distributed leadership and innovative teaching practices. *International Journal of Educational Research Open, 2*, 100088.
Reinhardt, M., & Maday, T. (2006). *Interdisciplinary manual for American Indian inclusion*. Educational Options.
Robinson, V., Lloyd, C., & Rowe, K. (2008). The impact of leadership on student outcomes: An analysis of the differential effects of leadership types. *Educational Administration Quarterly, 44*(5), 635–674.
Shaked, H. (2018). Why principals sidestep instructional leadership: The disregarded question of schools' primary objective. *Journal of School Leadership, 28*(4), 517–538.

Urick, A. (2016). Examining US principal perception of multiple leadership styles used to practice shared instructional leadership. *Journal of Educational Administration*, *54*(2), 152–172.

Versland, T. M., & Erickson, J. L. (2017). Leading by example: A case study of the influence of principal self-efficacy on collective efficacy. *Cogent Education*, *4*(1), 1–17.

Wahlstrom, K. L., & Louis, K. S. (2008). How teachers experience principal leadership: The roles of professional community, trust, efficacy, and shared responsibility. *Educational administration quarterly*, *44*(4), 458–495.

Whyte, K. (2018). Settler colonialism, ecology, and environmental injustice. *Environment and Society*, *9*(1), 125–144.

Xia, J., & O'Shea, C. M. (2022). To what extent does distributed leadership support principal instructional leadership? Evidence from TALIS 2013 data. *Leadership and Policy in Schools*, 1–27.

Zuckerman, S. J., & O'Shea, C. M. (2021). Principals' schema: Leadership philosophies and instructional leadership. *Journal of School Leadership*, *31*(4), 274–296.

CHAPTER 11

Applying the Supervisory Behavior Continuum to Determine a Plan of Action and Support When Teaching Isn't Culturally Responsive

Patricia Virella

"That is so unfair!" Darlene choked out with tears streaming from her eyes. I was a first-year principal giving feedback to a White woman teacher at the time. The data showed a need for more achievement and growth across her classes. I prepared for the feedback session using a carefully detailed plan of why I thought her instruction needed improvement. I am a Black-Afro-Rican woman who led a school of Black and Brown girls. My staff needed to reflect the demographics of my students, and my identity was a common source of pushback. At the time, my school had primarily White women teachers. From the beginning, I knew we needed more cultural awareness and conversations, so I ensured that we had honest conversations about race, gender, and identity. We had professional development about culturally relevant instructional delivery. However, what was missing was what I directly confronted that day—culturally relevant instructional supervision practices (CRISP).

I remember looking the teacher in the eyes and expressing how, "I would be remiss if I didn't look at your impact on achievement." In my mind, I was addressing the low performance despite the intense coaching and feedback she had received, but Darlene thought I was being unfair. Sue et al. (2009) explain that a typical response to difficult conversations about race by White faculty is crying. I continued to navigate this conversation, expressing how I would charter a course for her and her students' growth. I needed a culturally relevant supervision approach that provided a pathway for her to be successful and connect to the students while increasing academic outcomes. I also had to include accountability in a culturally relevant sense. Lisa Delpit (2006) argues that when teachers change their attitudes and actions in classrooms, they can alter what happens in urban schools and transform students' lives. Further, some teachers and leaders are afraid to discuss sensitive topics in the current political climate. This genuine fear realizes white fragility because there is a refusal to discuss the violent, oppressive, and historical systems that limit marginalized children's success. Upon reflection, what I was countering in my conversation with Darlene was the refusal to believe her expressions of pedagogy and declarations that the students "were just low." Instead, I pushed past her white fragility and persisted in educational excellence for the students.

Difficult conversations, particularly those rooted around race, can be just that, difficult. Personal beliefs are challenged, and teaching, which is quite personal, feels like it's being attacked. However, what is missing is the fundamental understanding that we all bring biases to our work and into our classroom. It is our collective responsibility as a field to monitor one other and stand up for what is right. It is also the responsibility of a supervisor to hold those under their supervision accountable for extending their viewpoints and changing the potentially dismal outcomes for students.

Culturally relevant pedagogy has been in teaching and learning for decades (Ladson-Billings, 2014; Ladson-Billings & Dixson, 2021). Yet there are still calls for understanding. For example, when I trained many of my teachers on the skills and instructional delivery techniques of culturally relevant pedagogy, some of my teachers didn't understand why this was necessary. Similar to deepening a teacher's toolkit around development readiness or language acquisition, becoming a culturally relevant pedagogue requires learning new skills but, most importantly, challenging your own biases that arise in your classroom. Despite several scholars finding empirical evidence that teachers enact racism and biases in their classrooms, some teachers operate from a colorblind lens, not understanding or not willing to understand that they are further harming their students. Thus, it is the supervisor's role to upend these categorizations and forage in a new way.

In this chapter, I present the culturally relevant instructional supervision practices or CRISP approach. Just as they learn the particular culturally relevant instruction, supervisors must learn culturally relevant pedagogy and its direct alignment to supervision. Supervisors need to learn and enact an interconnected approach to refute teachers like Darlene, who cannot see how they are interconnected. Thus, I present an integrated model that allows supervisors to learn and model the integrated approach of culturally relevant instruction through supervision practices. First, I briefly distinguish the differences between supervision and evaluation. Second, I describe how discourse can provide a method of understanding to navigate supervisory challenges such as discussions about race, gender, identity, or class. Next, I describe an overview of the supervisory behavior continuum tethered to relevant instruction supervision literature. I then discuss the CRISP approach and conclude with reflections.

THE IMPORTANT DISTINCTION BETWEEN SUPERVISION AND EVALUATION

Supervision and evaluation are two distinct aspects of instructional supervision. Supervision is the process of observing, monitoring, and providing feedback on the quality of instruction that is occurring in the classroom. The primary purpose of supervision is to ensure that instructional goals and standards are met and that the instructional process is being implemented correctly. Supervision is an ongoing process of monitoring and providing feedback that can be both positive and corrective. On the other hand, evaluation is the process of assessing the effectiveness of instruction and student learning. Evaluation is typically more formal and involves using specific assessment tools and techniques. It also involves making judgments about the quality of instruction, student learning, and the effectiveness of the instructional process. Evaluation is typically done at the end of a unit or program and is often used to make decisions about the effectiveness of instruction and how to improve it.

Unlike supervision, the evaluation typically provides a more formal assessment of the quality and effectiveness of instruction. It is important to note these differences because teachers frequently express that they feel they are evaluated instead of supervised, providing an ongoing improvement cycle. Evaluation is used to rank, assess, or rate you. At the same time, supervision provides a track to growth and development. However, scholars have found that these two concepts must be clarified when working with teachers (DiPaula & Wagner, 2018). Knowing the distinction is also critically important for infusing ideas of cultural relevance and confronting implicit bias or racism with teachers and their effects on their students. Supervision allows discourse to occur so teachers can incrementally and progressively change their attitudes.

TALK AS THE MODALITY OF MEANING-MAKING IN THE CRISP APPROACH

The central mechanism by which improving instructional practices and delivering the CRISP approach requires a heavy reliance on talk. Scholars explain that talk allows us to feel we are actively making progress (Lawrence, 2017; Thurlow & Helms Mills, 2009). It also allows us to hear ourselves and listen to others. This dialogic relationship is critical when understanding our thoughts and feelings, such as biases arising. Similarly, conversations about race allow us to improve communication and learning, increase racial literacy, and expand critical consciousness (Friere & Macedo, 2005; Sue et al., 2015, 2017). Also, mishandling conversations can lead to detrimental outcomes such as becoming defensive, sidetracking the conversation, or simply walking away (Sue et al., 2015). With Darlene, I mishandled attempts to discuss culturally relevant pedagogy and her impact, resulting in her becoming defensive. It is important to note that the CRISP approach requires planning and answering the question, "How will you say this?" This will allow leaders to prepare effectively.

OVERVIEW OF SUPERVISORY BEHAVIOR CONTINUUM

Glickman (1980) established a supervisory behavior continuum that provides four distinct options for supervisors to evaluate and support their teachers. These four are: (1) Supervisor-assigned plan; (2) Supervisor-suggested plan; (3) Mutually developed plan; and (4) Teacher self-plan. Each element is directly tethered to the level of or lack thereof of proficiency in instructional delivery. Figure 11.1 shows how this continuum operates. The continuum begins with levels of autonomy being loose. This means that teachers are invited into the supervisory plan and asked for their thoughts and how to improve the work. In contrast, at the other end of the continuum are behaviors leaders must take for low-preforming teachers who need more structure, reinforcement, and direction. The continuum, as designed by Glickman (1980), highlights how teachers develop and are supported differently. Thus, when supervisors overlay culturally responsive instruction, we note that the continuum of understanding our teachers must not be static but progressive.

CONNECTING THE SUPERVISORY BEHAVIOR CONTINUUM TO CULTURALLY RESPONSIVE SCHOOL LEADERSHIP

Culturally responsive school leadership prioritizes an anti-oppressive and culturally responsive education. Khalifa (2020) states that culturally responsive leaders express four domains that center on combatting particular identities' marginalization. These domains are: (1) critical self-reflection; (2) inclusive and responsive school environments; (3) instructional leadership; and (4) community engagement. When leaders orient themselves to culturally responsive school leadership, they humanize minoritized groups while strengthening pedagogical practices. The existing research (Wickham, 2021) reveals that barriers to CRSL enactment have highlighted a need for division-level support in recruiting and retaining effective staff responding to students in culturally responsive ways. Ladson-Billings and Dixson (2021) argue that culturally relevant educators challenge the construction of knowledge that rarely gives students access to knowledge and information about how we make decisions about what counts as valuable. Thus, leaders must supervise culturally relevant ways to cultivate this thinking and instructional delivery among faculty and staff.

Figure 11.1. Supervisory Behavior Continuum Adapted from Glickman (1980)

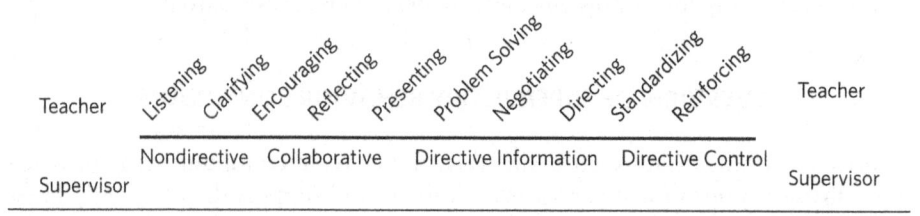

Teacher — Listening, Clarifying, Encouraging, Reflecting, Presenting, Problem Solving, Negotiating, Directing, Standardizing, Reinforcing — Teacher

Supervisor — Nondirective | Collaborative | Directive Information | Directive Control — Supervisor

OVERVIEW OF CULTURALLY RESPONSIVE INSTRUCTIONAL SUPERVISION PRACTICES (CRISP) APPROACH

The supervisor is responsible for tethering supervision and culturally responsive practices. This brings together the theoretical approach of culturally responsive teaching to practice. Part of understanding the importance of, and being effective in supervising in a culturally responsive way, is supervisors understanding their own implicit biases and reflecting on blind spots and expectations rooted in white supremacy. This is essential to ensuring that the culturally responsive supervisory lens is enacted in inequitable ways. Further, supervisors can evaluate how they view a professional teacher by reflecting on implicit biases. Culturally responsive teaching requires more than bringing materials to a curriculum where children from various backgrounds can see themselves. Instead, culturally responsive teaching requires supervisors to dismantle schooling systems and assumptions prioritizing whiteness and hegemonic ideologies (Emdin, 2016; Joseph-Salisbury & Connelly, 2018; Love, 2019; Tyack, 1974).

Additionally, a culturally responsive approach to supervision requires uncomfortable conversations about issues such as race, gender, identity, and class. If there is the ability to have these conversations, culturally responsive teaching will be sustained. When a supervisor reflects on their own biases, areas of growth, and topics of discomfort, they can enter the conversation with a clear understanding of their triggers, areas of improvement, and success. They can then guide their teachers by modeling their awareness. Finally, your work around culturally relevant instructional supervision must begin with you. As noted above, you must develop your own culturally relevant knowledge and approach and confront your implicit bias, or blind spots will be exacerbated, and this approach will be unsuccessful.

CRISP—SUPERVISORY BEHAVIOR CONTINUUM

Supervision requires various skills, such as learning how to coach adults, how to provide resources, and, most importantly, when to step in or step aside. Beginning this work in the current climate may seem daunting. Teachers are faced with an enormous amount of pressure, as are leaders. Yet, student learning marshals forward. To begin this work, I reflect on the processes needed in order to integrate the CRISP approach successfully. Culturally responsive pedagogy is synonymous with high-quality instruction coupled with relevant images, texts, experiences, and curricula. For many teachers, the notion of culturally responsive pedagogy is daunting. Thus, supervisors should start small with one practice or goal at a time. Learning a new pedagogical approach takes time. Moreover, confronting implicit bias and inequitable structures requires a mindset shift for many teachers. Thus, teachers need the opportunity to hone in on one practice they can identify and monitor toward success. These are the elements needed to consider prior to meeting with the teacher. Once determinations are made about the level of the teacher, and the supervisor has established a plan of action, they can meet with the teacher to discuss it. Below, I go into more detail about what each type of plan could look like tethered to culturally responsive action.

Courageous Conversations and Directive Control (Supervisor-Assigned Plan)

Supervisor-assigned plans are given to teachers in need of increased support. Supervisors give their teachers intensive support and limited opportunities in this continuum stage, assuming responsibility through restricted choice. For many teachers, the supervisor-assigned plan can feel as though their professional expertise and autonomy have been taken away, even with valid reasons. Thus, I encourage leaders who use this part of the continuum with their teachers to draw on elements of Singleton's (2014) Courageous Conversations (CC). Specifically, you want to use the norms for CCs to allow for a conversation structure. You then want to discuss the importance and reason why you will apply a more restrictive supervisory lens. Reflecting on my conversation with Darlene, who was on a supervisor-assigned plan, I missed an opportunity to provide her with norms and a rationale. In doing so, the conversation may have been emotional, but I would have had a structure to facilitate the dialogue.

You also want to discuss the importance of the CRISP approach because students of all ages, ethnicities, religions, races, and identities deserve an equitable and inclusive education that requires all of us to be culturally relevant. Certainly, being resistant to change, lacking awareness of a need to adapt, or not acknowledging a systemic oppressive system that functions on privilege and entitlement are all barriers to developing cultural responsiveness. Thus, providing concrete guidance for success is another strategy to deploy during your supervision. Develop a criterion for success for the teacher so they are not left with vague tasks such as "provide culturally relevant math problems." Instead, explain the frequency, look-for, and date you expect to see for implementation and fidelity. An example would be to "expect to see texts about Black women in three out of 10 lessons in a unit about Black History Month that are not commonly discussed (i.e., Shirley Chisholm) with matching DOK 4 levels of questioning for students. Teacher X will have until INSERT DATE to accomplish this." You then will want to provide resources to scaffold the learning of this teacher.

The critical aspect to remember is that teachers who require a supervisor-directed plan are functioning with a more of a lack of awareness, knowledge, or insight into a problem they need to solve. Moreover, action has to be urgently taken to correct the course. Thus, supervisors should prepare to provide as much support as possible, especially as it aligns with developing more culturally responsive teachers. Finally, supervisors should prepare for an off-boarding plan because a directed supervisory plan is intended only for a finite amount of time (See Table 11.1 at the end of this chapter).

Implicit Bias and Directive Informational (Supervisor-Suggested Plan)

Teachers who need a supervisor-suggested plan must be more experienced and understand highly effective and rigorous instruction. They often believe the supervisor is credible and possesses the knowledge to support them, demonstrating a foundational trusting relationship. Examining implicit biases arising in the teacher's instruction is necessary for these conversations.

A couple of years ago, I met with a principal struggling with a teacher and her instructional delivery. The principal went to observe and noticed that only boys were being called on to answer throughout the day. It was a rare occasion for girls to be asked to share their thoughts. The principal counted how many girls' hands went up to contribute and how that number dwindled throughout the day. The principal asked me how this could be. How could she not notice? And we discussed that implicit biases are sometimes right in our faces, but we are not tuned to them.

When supervisors observe teachers, it is imperative to assess the lesson's rigor, the curriculum's diversity, and attempts by the teacher to mitigate inequities. In this case, there was no attempt; thus, the conversation with the teacher had to illuminate these biases present in the classroom, and the supervisor-suggested plan had to echo these efforts. In a supervisor-suggested plan, the supervisor should present how these inequities or biases are expressed and be direct with the teacher to enable transformation. Like the supervisor-assigned plan, time is of the essence, so goals should be time bound and presented with a criterion for success. A teacher who may be resistant to infusing culturally responsive teaching might not understand how they benefit from privilege and may explain that they believe all children can learn while functioning from a colorblind position (Milner, 2012). These assertions serve as personal, professional, and organizational impediments limiting a socially just and equitable learning environment for children. Thus, supervisors must establish a culturally responsive approach while concretizing how this plan will be enacted.

A Culturally Responsive Collaboration (Mutually Developed Plan)

A mutually developed plan is created for teachers who are uneven in their practice. Sometimes, they hit a home run, and sometimes you walk into their classroom wondering if it is the same place you saw yesterday. The teacher who requires a mutually developed plan is performing at a moderate level which you can work at to develop a high-performing teacher.

Weaving in culturally responsive pedagogy for this teacher requires a systemic approach built on mutual respect. Teachers on this level can hold themselves accountable and want to be involved in making adjustments to their instruction. They are committed to solving the problem. The characteristics of this teacher are markedly different from one needing a supervisor-assigned or suggested plan. Thus, supervisors should be more willing to develop the plan by reflecting, problem-solving, and negotiating how improvements will be made. Typically, teachers who develop a mutual plan with their supervisors have the same level of expertise as their supervisor (Glickman, 1980). This is important to distinguish because when supervisors develop this plan, it can become a learning opportunity for the teacher and the supervisor.

Culturally responsive teaching requires centering students' cultures and lived experiences in such a way as to influence how they show up in the class and make sense of the world around them (Gay, 2018; Will & Najarro, 2022). "Culture" refers to more than just the child's race but also the customs, languages, values, beliefs, and achievements of a group of people. A student's culture becomes integral to who they are as learners. Thus, teachers and supervisors must develop cultural proficiency in various areas to support their students.

Supervisors designing a mutually developed plan with a teacher should be prepared with resources for the teacher. The goal should be mutually agreed upon and generated mainly by the teacher so they can take ownership of their practice. Additionally, the supervisor needs to describe what the teacher did well and how that can advance their culturally responsive pedagogy. For example, a teacher adding multiple perspectives of a historical event has previously demonstrated high-level questioning in their classroom. The supervisor can point this out and focus the goal around questioning multiple perspectives and asking critical-thinking questions to facilitate student thinking (Okolie et al., 2022). In this way, the supervisor creates a mutually developed plan, pointing out strengths to develop the teacher further. In contrast, the teacher takes on a new challenge of infusing culturally relevant pedagogical techniques.

Culturally Responsive Practices Through Nondirective Plans (Teacher Self-Plan)

A teacher-self plan is typically reserved for high-performing teachers who function at a high level. They possess a high knowledge and expertise while claiming full responsibility for their pedagogical actions. Moreover, they own what they do, do not know about culturally responsive practices, and seek development. A teacher who develops their plan should be given complete autonomy while a supervisor monitors their actions and implementation.

For example, a high-performing teacher may want to include more culturally responsive math problems and has prepared the problems for the supervisor to review. The supervisor is then tasked with reviewing these problems and assessing and thinking, being a thought partner with the teacher to go through the trajectory of the task given to students. Thus, supervisors should question and critique the teacher's plan to support their development. Additionally, because of the nature of this teacher's development, once the teacher's plan has concluded, the supervisor can use the teacher's process to demonstrate to other teachers within the school how to infuse culturally responsive practices. Moreover, a teacher who develops a self-plan should evaluate their own biases to determine other inequities worth exploring, to better facilitate their culturally responsive pedagogy.

DEVELOPMENT BEHAVIOR AND CULTURALLY RESPONSIVE CONTINUUM

At the heart of the supervisor-behavioral continuum are habits of mind developed alongside the plan to support the enactment of whatever plan is established. This is important to note because, many times, supervisors assume that all teachers develop in the same ways. Research has shown that adult developmentally appropriate feedback and interactions drastically improve how a teacher enacts a plan of support or improvement (Drago-Seversen & Blum-DeStefano, 2023). Similarly, Glickman (1980) informs us that there are a set of developmental behaviors tethered to a plan type. In Table 11.1, I merge the supervisory behavior continuum (Glickman, 1980) with the Cultural Proficiency Continuum (Lindsey et al., 2019) to illustrate how these elements are connected.

EMBEDDING CRISP FOR SUSTAINED PROGRESS

Since the George Floyd murder and following the Black Lives Matter protests, schools have spent over 20 million dollars on DEI initiatives. Schools were quick to ensure they had some training to tick a box. Culturally responsive instruction is often a topic of interest, and although several qualified consultants can support the initial induction of this work, administrators and school district leaders at some point are passed the baton to lead the work internally. To do so requires a commitment to introduce culturally responsive instructional, social, emotional, or other techniques to teachers and hold them accountable. Integrating the CRISP approach can further transform your school into a more equitable and socially just environment by layering how teachers are held accountable.

In these ways, supervisors promote continued growth and learning about culturally relevant instruction by tethering it to goals and outcomes. Leaders can infuse CRISP into their supervision strategies by, first, making it public. During the summer months, when teachers are often welcomed back, leaders should discuss how they are infusing this practice into supervision. Supporting teachers' understanding of cultural responsiveness requires concrete examples so they can formulate connections to what they are doing and what they are not doing.

Further, leaders should establish a common culturally responsive goal at the outset to develop a collective instructional and culturally progressive approach. In this way, the whole school or district can work together on one discrete goal. This allows teachers to observe one other and share resources while the leader develops their acumen in regards to developing their facility with the CRISP approach. This will also allow leaders to demonstrate the range of cultural competence practices which should exist in all school buildings. This focused approach deepens a leader's practice through consistent experiences within a range of abilities.

Another way leaders can implement the CRISP approach is with, again, a public acknowledgement of this new approach with a voluntary cadre of teachers. In this way, the leaders will be working with teachers who want to improve their cultural competence and pedagogy while learning how to apply the various dimensions of the framework. This allows leaders to mitigate one area of frustration within delivering feedback—recalcitrance. Issues of cultural competence are hard for some to discuss and receive feedback on. Starting with volunteers allows

Table 11.1. Alignment of Plan, Supervisory Behavioral, and Cultural Proficiency Continuum

Plan Type	Behavioral Continuum	Cultural Proficiency Continuum
Supervisor-assigned plan	Standardizing: the supervisor sets the expected criteria and time for implementing the decision.	Cultural Destructiveness—seeking to eliminate vestiges of others' cultures.
	Reinforcing: supervisor strengthens the directive and criteria by discussing positive and negative consequences.	Cultural Incapacity—seeking to make the culture of others appear to be wrong.
	Directing: the supervisor gives the participant choices or directions on how the participant will proceed.	
Supervisor-suggested plan	Directing: the supervisor gives the participant choices or directions on how the participant will proceed.	Cultural Blindness—unable or refusing to acknowledge the culture of others.
	Standardizing: the supervisor sets the expected criteria and time for implementing the decision.	Cultural Precompetence—knowing what one does not know about working in diverse settings. Initial levels of awareness, after which a person/organization can move in a positive, constructive direction or falter, stop and possibly regress.
Mutually developed plan	Reflecting: supervisor summarizes and paraphrases the speaker's message for accuracy	Cultural Competence—viewing one's personal and organizational work as an interactive arrangement in which the educator enters into diverse settings in a manner that is additive to cultures that are different from that of the educator.
	Presenting: the supervisor gives their ideas about the situation	
	Problem-solving: the supervisor generates a list of possible solutions	
	Negotiation: the supervisor uses the list of possible solutions to explore possible consequences	

(continued)

Applying the Supervisory Behavior Continuum 211

Table 11.1. (continued)

Teacher self-plan	Listening: looking at the speaker showing understanding of verbal and nonverbal utterances, to indicate listening Clarifying: questions and statements that shed light on the speaker's perspective Encouraging: supervisor responds in ways that help the speaker continue elaborating on their positions.	Cultural Proficiency—committing to life-long learning to be increasingly effective in serving cultural groups' educational needs, holding the vision of what can be, and committing to assessments that serve as benchmarks on the road to student success.

the leader to focus on a collaborative approach model and allows them to focus more deeply on the cultural competence portion of the CRISP framework.

The truth is that the CRISP approach should be used as the lens through which supervision is enacted, not only when a marginalized demographic is being targeted. This also lowers the connection that something "special" has to happen for "those kids" when, in fact, research shows that culturally relevant instruction improves outcomes for all students (Hammond, 2018; Safir, 2017). Thus, supervisors should embed the CRISP approach at the outset of the supervision cycle to spur sustainable and continuous improvement.

CONCLUSION

Hammond (2018, 2021) explains that culturally relevant pedagogy is the antidote to equity. It is a viable and empirically based pedagogical orientation that can lift achievement while improving teachers' instructional delivery and fostering inclusion. Thus, it is essential to note that culturally relevant pedagogy is not a fad or something to layer onto a teacher's practice, but it should be the way teachers *always* teach. Over the years, I have worked with several school leaders who wanted to include culturally relevant approaches but needed more time in their supervisory practices. One cannot happen without the other.

When you work with your supervisees through a culturally relevant lens, you must be prepared for and welcome questions and concerns. You should explicitly invite questions and concerns. Singleton (2014) states that one of the norms with Courageous Conversations, expecting to be uncomfortable—becomes more apparent when supervisors infuse another lens into their supervisory practices. When discussing this new approach, it is paramount that the supervisor inquire if their supervisee has any questions. As supervisor, you want to position yourself continuously, and this opportunity is a learning exercise to support students better and bolster student achievement. Therefore, in a high-stakes supervisory conversation, you can provide some questions that you think may or should be asked by the supervisee without fear.

REFERENCES

Delpit, L. (2006). Lessons from teachers. *Journal of teacher education*, 57(3), 220–231.

DiPaola, M., & Wagner, C. A. (2018). *Improving instruction through supervision, evaluation, and professional development* (2nd ed.). IAP.

Drago-Severson, E., & Blum-DeStefano, J. (2023). Developmental and Differentiated Feedback for Educators. In A. Lavigne & M. L. Derrington (Eds.), *Actionable feedback for PK–12 teachers* (pp. 35–48). Rowman & Littlefield.

Emdin, C. (2016). *For White folks who teach in the hood . . . and the rest of y'all too: Reality pedagogy and urban education*. Beacon Press.

Freire, P., & Macedo, D. (2005). *Literacy: Reading the word and the world*. Routledge.

Gay, G. (2018). *Culturally responsive teaching: Theory, research, and practice*. Teachers College Press.

Glickman, C. D. (1980). The Developmental Approach to Supervision. *Educational Leadership*, 38(2), 178–80.

Hammond, Z. (2018). Culturally Responsive Teaching Puts Rigor at the Center: Q&A with Zaretta Hammond. *Learning Professional*, 39(5), 40–43.

Hammond, Z. (2021). Liberatory education: Integrating the science of learning and culturally responsive practice. *American Educator*, 45(2), 4–11.

Joseph-Salisbury, R., & Connelly, L. (2018). 'If your hair is relaxed, white people are relaxed. If your hair is nappy, they're not happy': Black hair as a site of 'post-racial' social control in English schools. *Social Sciences*, 7(11), 219. https://doi.org/10.3390/socsci7110219

Khalifa, M. (2020). *Culturally responsive school leadership*. Harvard Education Press.

Ladson-Billings, G. (2014). Culturally relevant pedagogy 2.0: aka the remix. *Harvard educational review*, 84(1), 74–84.

Ladson-Billings, G., & Dixson, A. (2021). Put some respect on the theory: Confronting distortions of culturally relevant pedagogy. In *Whitewashed Critical Perspectives* (pp. 122–137). Routledge.

Lawrence, Paul. "Managerial coaching-a literature review." *International Journal of Evidence Based Coaching and Mentoring* 15, no. 2 (2017): 43

Lindsey, R. B., Robins, K. N., & Terrell, R. D. (2019). *Cultural proficiency: A manual for school leaders*. Corwin.

Love, B. L. (2019). *We want to do more than survive: Abolitionist teaching and the pursuit of educational freedom*. Beacon Press.

Milner H. R., IV. (2012). Losing the color-blind mind in the urban classroom. *Urban Education*, 47(5), 868–875.

Okolie, U. C., Igwe, P. A., Mong, I. K., Nwosu, H. E., Kanu, C., & Ojemuyide, C. C. (2022). Enhancing students' critical thinking skills through engagement with innovative pedagogical practices in the Global South. *Higher Education Research & Development*, 41(4), 1184–1198.

Safir, S. (2017). *The listening leader: Creating the conditions for equitable school transformation*. John Wiley & Sons.

Singleton, G. E. (2014). *Courageous conversations about race: A field guide for achieving equity in schools*. Corwin Press.

Sue, D. W. (2017). Microaggressions and "evidence": Empirical or experiential reality? *Perspectives on Psychological Science, 12*(1), 170–172. https://doi-org.tc.idm.oclc.org/10.1177/1745691616664437

Sue, D. W., Rasheed, M. N., & Rasheed, J. M. (2015). *Multicultural social work practice: A competency-based approach to diversity and social justice*. John Wiley & Sons.

Sue, D. W., Lin, A. I., Torino, G. C., Capodilupo, C. M., & Rivera, D. P. (2009). Racial microaggressions and difficult dialogues on race in the classroom. *Cultural diversity and ethnic minority psychology, 15*(2), 183.

Thurlow, A., & Helms Mills, J. (2009). Change, talk and sensemaking. *Journal of Organizational Change Management, 22*(5), 459–479.

Tyack, D. B. (1974). *The one best system: A history of American urban education* (Vol. 95). Harvard University Press.

Wickham, S. M. (2021). *How School Leaders Experience and Persist in Efforts of Diversity, Equity, and Inclusion Using Culturally Responsive Leadership* (Doctoral dissertation, William Woods University).

Will, M., & Najarro, I. (2022, April 18). What is culturally responsive teaching? *Education Week*. https://www.edweek.org/teachinglearning/culturally-responsive-teaching-culturally-responsivepedagogy/2022/04

CHAPTER 12

Developing Supervisors' Critical Consciousness

Shannon R. Waite

Across the United States, calls for Culturally Responsive Instructional Supervision (CRIS) can be heard far and wide; these calls have been heightened due to the effects of dueling pandemics. As the country attempts to rebound from COVID-19 and the tumultuous economic impact the pandemic has had around the globe, the field of education is in crisis. The global uprising against the murder of Black and Brown bodies triggered in 2020 by the high-profile, state-sanctioned murders of George Floyd and Breonna Taylor have amplified the call for CRIS (U.S. Department of Education, 2022). There is a significant need for educators and educational leaders that are equipped with a social justice–oriented disposition to assist students, families, and communities in districts around the United States with navigating this unprecedented time in history. In order to enable leaders to develop the skills need to provide CRIS, they must develop their own critical consciousness.

Within the field of education, the dueling pandemics have ushered in calls from states and districts around the country for increases in federal funding. States and districts have called for increases in federal resources to support social-emotional learning, trauma-informed pedagogical practices, culturally responsive teaching, and antiracist pedagogy (Lynch, 2021). Providing professional development (PD) to ensure that educators, school building administrators, and district leaders receive the training necessary to become versed with and develop the skills needed to employ culturally responsive, social-emotional, and trauma-informed pedagogical practices is essential.

While the call for districts to increase resources in response to the dueling pandemics is new, the concept that schools need culturally responsive educators is not. Both Ladson-Billings (1995) and Gay (2002) are foundational scholars who proffer insights into both the praxis as well as the practices associated with culturally responsive education. In 1995, Ladson-Billings theorized three propositions of culturally relevant pedagogy. She said that culturally relevant pedagogy requires that students experience academic success, develop and/or maintain cultural competence, and develop a critical consciousness that affords them the ability to challenge "the status quo of the current social order" (p. 160). Ultimately,

Ladson-Billings proffered that culturally responsive teaching *was* simply good teaching. Gay (2002) posited that there was, in fact, theory, research, and practice associated with the concept of culturally responsive teaching. She shared the following as the "essential elements of culturally responsive teaching" along with how the concept is defined:

> Developing a knowledge base about cultural diversity, including ethnic and cultural diversity content in the curriculum, demonstrating caring and building learning communities, communicating with ethnically diverse students, and responding to ethnic diversity in the delivery of instruction. Culturally responsive teaching is defined as using the cultural characteristics, experiences, and perspectives of ethnically diverse students as conduits for teaching them more effectively. (p. 106)

There is an established body of research supporting culturally responsive teaching and the positive impact of improving students' academic achievement by incorporating and embedding their [students'] cultural assets into their education (Byrd, 2016: Gay, 2018; Hammond, 2015; Ladson-Billings, 2014; Tanase, 2020). Conversely, the notion that culturally responsive teachers need to be supported by culturally responsive school leaders is a more recent discussion in the literature. Khalifa, Gooden, and Davis (2016) explored the research around culturally responsive school leadership in a comprehensive examination of the literature in their article *Culturally Responsive School Leadership: A Synthesis of the Literature*. The researchers found that "research suggests that unless promoted by the principal, implementation of cultural responsiveness can run the risk of being disjointed or short-lived in a school" (p. 1274). This reality heightens the need to ensure that leaders aspiring to provide CRIS are intentional about prioritizing the development of their own critical consciousness.

WHAT IS CRITICAL CONSCIOUSNESS?

The exiled Brazilian activist Paulo Freire conceptualized the term *critical consciousness*. Critical consciousness is translated into English from the word *conscientização*, which "refers to learning to perceive social, political, and economic contradictions, and to take action against the oppressive elements of reality" (Freire, 2011, p. 35). In 1970, Paulo Freire published *Pedagogy of the Oppressed*, in which he espoused his philosophy on liberation; specifically, he discussed *conscientização* as "the awakening of critical consciousnes," which he proffered could lead "to the expression of social discontents precisely because these discontents are real components of an oppressive situation" (p. 36) (Waite, 2021b). Freire believed that education—specifically, literacy—could liberate both the oppressor and the oppressed; he thought that it could do so by "the growth of an ethical consciousness in the learner that emerges through a pedagogy that respects the other" (Dussel, 2013, p. 10). The idea is that learners are the subjects of their own liberation, and it is only through struggling with the complexities, challenges, and cognitive dissonance of their lived experiences against dominant societal norms that one can be free, and he believed that true liberation can only be achieved by liberating oneself. Freire conceived this during his work with Brazilian peasants. He asserted that by "developing literacy skills while also raising their awareness of sociocultural and sociopolitical marginalization and oppression" these individuals learned to "read the word" while also "reading the world" (Diemer et al., 2016, p. 217). He hypothesized that engaging in this process would liberate the oppressed.

Freire is considered one of the foundational Latin American academics who questioned the epistemologies behind Western world perspectives (Cortina & Winter, 2021). He understood that examining the relationships among power, dominance, and hegemony in the development of consciousness is critical. This is relevant because in the United States, the field of education has "accepted" ontological and epistemological "truths" which are presented as objective. These "truths" are anchored in the beliefs of Western or European dominance and superiority, which is then taught as the accepted measure of truth in the United States (Tubbs, 2016). Freire (2011) believed that Latin Americans needed to challenge these ontological and epistemological "truths" and that through the process of challenging these "truths," the oppressed might "wage the struggle for their liberation . . . and perceive the reality of oppression not as a closed world from which there is no exit, but as a limiting situation which they can transform" (p. 49).

The struggle to free oneself and/or to navigate the reality in which one finds oneself as the oppressed or the oppressor requires that individuals develop their own critical consciousness. It is imperative that leaders who desire to practice CRIS engage in this work *as being the school leader can also situate one in the role of the oppressor in school communities*. And in cases in which the leader identifies as a member of a historical excluded group(s) and/or as a member of other oppressed class(es), the need for this work is even more significant. While Freire's text is discussed, and in some instances, studied in preparation programs the actual work associated with the aspiring and current leaders being supported to develop or extend their critical consciousness is missing (Waite, 2021a). This is why it is imperative that districts invest in leaders by providing professional development that supports the development of the critical consciousness for CRIS.

THE NECESSITY OF EMBEDDING CRITICAL THEORY INTO CRITICAL CONSCIOUSNESS

While Freire conceptualized *conscientização* and was exiled for proposing "a pedagogy of liberation capable of awakening the consciousness of teachers and learners to activate empowered human beings who identify their role in transforming an unjust world" (Cortina & Winter, 2021, p. 11), the critical consciousness Freire conceived did not and does not advocate for racial literacy. Though it might be assumed that the Brazilian peasants Freire discussed in his work *may* have experienced discrimination based on colorism, socio-economic, and sexual orientation, his work does not explicitly examine the role of race in oppression. The oppressed and oppressors shared a nationality, ethnicity, and culture. Freire's work heavily pushes individuals to *challenge their status related to class and the hegemonic structures binding them to said status*. While one might argue that the very Western epistemologies Freire challenged were undergirded by racism, his work is not situated in that context.

This is an important nuance to acknowledge because race is at the heart of inequity and poor educational outcomes in the United States. There are bodies of scholarship asserting that education in the United States is not only racist, but it is explicitly anti-Black (Caldera, 2020; Dumas, 2014; Lopez & Jean-Marie, 2021; Waite, 2021b). These realities make it necessary that any discourse about achieving racialized equity in educational outcomes within the United States (and possibly around the globe) through the development of critical consciousness be coupled with critical theory, specifically, Critical Race Theory (CRT). CRT emanated from Critical Legal Studies (CLS), which is used to examine "a practice of interrogating the role of race and racism in society that emerged in the legal academy and spread to other fields of scholarship" (Green, 2021). This is significant because "CLS was a significant departure from earlier conceptions of the law (and other fields of scholarship) as objective, neutral, principled, and dissociated from social or political considerations" (Green, 2021). Ladson-Billings and Tate (1995) cite Woodson and Du Bois as the thought leaders in academe that "used race as a theoretical lens for assessing social inequity" (p. 50). The authors go on to employ CRT in education in an "analogous" manner as when used in CLS (p. 47). Similarly, CRT scholars utilize CRT to interrogate the claims of neutrality and objectivity, and the claim that education is not political (Rembert, 1976). CRT provides an analytical tool to frame the lived experiences of communities of color, particularly the Black experience, in the United States (Waite, 2021a). Finally, these scholars share the following three tenets of CRT: race continuing to be significant in the United States, U.S. society being based on property rights rather than human rights, and the intersection of race and property creating an analytical tool for understanding inequity (p. 47).

In 2015, Capper offered the following as tenets in any study of CRT: permanence of racism [in American life], whiteness as property, counter storytelling and the recognition of dominant narratives as stories which may be interrogated rather than deemed as truth, interest convergence, a critique of liberalism, and intersectionality (p. 795). First, it is essential for educational leaders applying CRIS to understand that CRT can be used to disrupt the myth that educational outcomes are not influenced by race or racism, by utilizing the theory to examine how educational outcomes may be impacted by race. Additionally, CRT helps create the space needed for the critical reflection that is vital to developing critical consciousness. These are aspects that are necessary and vital in supporting the development of critical consciousness and why it should be embedded in PD.

CRITICAL-SELF REFLECTION AND PROFESSIONAL DEVELOPMENT

Darling-Hammond et al. (2017) identified seven essential characteristics of effective teacher PD in their research brief titled *Effective Teacher Professional Development*. Effective PD is (1) content focused; (2) incorporates active learning utilizing adult learning theory; (3) supports collaboration, typically in job-embedded contexts; (4) uses models and modeling of effective practice; (5) provides coaching and expert support; (6) offers opportunities for feedback and reflection; and (7) is sustainable. These characteristics have become the benchmarks for robust professional development, as these scholars are experts within the field of identifying research-based practices leading to improvements in teacher education and professional development. Shandomo (2010) offered a perspective of critical reflection which highlights how imperative the practice is to teacher education and PD:

> Critical reflection is the process by which adults identify the assumptions governing their actions, locate the historical and cultural origins of their assumptions, and develop alternative ways of acting (Cranton, 1996). Brookfield (1995, 2004) added that part of the critical reflective process is challenging the prevailing social, political, and cultural, or professional ways of acting. Through the process of critical reflection, adults come to interpret and create new knowledge and actions from their ordinary and sometimes extraordinary experiences. Critical reflection blends learning through experiences with theoretical and technical learning to form new knowledge constructions and new behaviors or insights. (Shandomo, 2010, p. 101)

Shandomo (2010) goes on to discuss the strategies and methods that should be used when teaching preservice teachers and highlights that there is a difference between reflection and critical reflection:

> When a teacher is involved in active and deliberate reflection and analysis regarding those events that may lead to formulating new strategies for changing behavior in the classroom (Regan et al., 2000), he or she is using reflection for professional growth. (Shandomo, 2010, p. 104)

It is important to note that there is a 7-year difference between the publication of these works and yet they both underscore the importance of reflection and/or critical reflection as *behaviors or actions*. These researchers do not describe reflection as passive; it is described as an action that must be taken, which is also consistent with research in the educational leadership space.

In their 2016 publication, Khalifa et al. proffer that the following four behaviors emerged from the literature on successful practices of culturally responsive school leaders: (1) critical self-reflection on leadership behaviors; (2) development of culturally responsive teachers; (3) promotion of culturally responsive/inclusive school environment; and (4) engagement with students, parents, and Indigenous contexts. The emphasis on critical self-reflection as a behavior is important, as Shandomo (2010) reminds us that "reflection itself is not, by definition, critical." Adding the context of criticality intimates that there will be some examination of power and hegemony. However, culturally responsive education and culturally responsive leadership require that teachers and leaders not only examine both power and hegemony but interrogate those constructs by analyzing the impact of each on the demographics of the student populations they serve. Additionally, they must analyze the historical context that has contributed to the condition and quality of education school communities experience today (Ladson-Billings, 1995; Royal & Gibson, 2017).

Shandomo's research emphasizes the importance of critical reflection in teacher education and PD. Darling-Hammond et al.'s (2017) research identifies the technical and practical components of effective PD. And Khalifa et al.'s (2016) research illuminates examples of the adaptive, theoretical, and actionable behaviors that have been identified in existing research on culturally responsive school leadership. Both the technical and adaptive perspectives are needed. However, there tends to be a hyperfocus on the technical components of this work as it relates to PD (Dobbs et al., 2016). Educators working in school communities and districts throughout the United States need real time, but practical tools can be implemented in schools to support students. Meanwhile, the continuing technical cycles of educational reform, district and school building turnover, and persistent ideological shifts that result in "churn" throughout the United States contribute to the ongoing conditions of PK–12 education (Knerl, 2021).

To develop cadres of educators who are equipped with the consciousness needed to effectively serve as CRIS PK–12 innovators, and institutions of higher education, must blend theory and praxis in preparation programs. This requires that the field of instructional leadership (supervision) spend time grappling with the deep-seated, vile, and uncomfortable reality that the field of education is founded on an ahistorical, white settler colonial, anti-Black, and racist ontology (Cormier & Pandey, 2021). Creating the ability and capacity for educators to engage in the adaptive work needed to make this shift requires that racialized discussions about critical consciousness be embedded in PD. PD must be continuous, must challenge deeply embedded paradigms, and must lead to changes, not just in thought but in practice, policies, and pedagogical practices.

WHY CRITICAL CONSCIOUSNESS IS ESSENTIAL FOR PROFESSIONAL DEVELOPMENT

PK–12 education needs to be completely overhauled to offer a more thorough, historically accurate, and unsanitized depiction of the factual, unabashed, and complex history of this country. And until that occurs, it is the responsibility of academia to do this work; unfortunately, ISLs (Instructional Supervisory Leaders) at both the school-building and district levels offer the last opportunity to disrupt the ideologies of white supremacy, racism, and otherness (Waite, 2021b, p. 73). Similarly, for PD to be effective, critical consciousness needs to be embedded, as "many professional development initiatives appear ineffective in supporting changes in teachers' practices and student learning" (Darling-Hammond et al., 2017, p. 1). Traditional PD needs to be reimagined and the research on best practices in androgyny, culturally responsive education/leadership, and critical theory should be embedded within it. Historical critiques of traditional professional development point out that traditional PD is conducted in a way that flies in the face of the science of teaching adults (Knowles, 1980). Contemporary critiques highlight a barrage of observations about traditional PD which run counter to the practices teachers are currently encouraged to exercise in their classrooms. For example, some criticisms of traditional PD allege that teachers are treated as passive learners and not valued as entities able to employ independent thinking skills; the result is that scripts must be prescribed for them to follow (Royal & Gibson, 2017). The nature of how PD is conducted prevents many potentially effective PDs progrmas from being substantive because there is limited time and a plethora of topics to cover. Additionally, PD tends to be standalone and does not offer follow-up support nor is it customized based on the needs of the teachers attending the PD. PD must be reimagined to offer space for both collaboration and reflection without forgoing a content-rich focus.

In *Critical Professional Development: Centering the Social Justice Needs of Teachers*, Kohli et al. (2015) shared an analysis of PD and offered a new perspective the authors titled critical professional development (CPD). Drawing on Freire's framework of dialogical action, or a process for social transformation, the researchers developed a concept they framed as antidialogical professional development (APD). Their study examines the gaps in PD articulated by teachers seeking PD from a social justice-oriented lens. The study centered on three teacher-led social justice-oriented organizations and highlighted that traditional PD is an antidialogical action, a process used for social control rather than social transformation (2015). "In both pedagogy and content, CPD develops teachers' critical consciousness by focusing their efforts towards liberatory teaching" (Kohli et al., 2015, p. 9). Ergo, liberatory pedagogical practices are an important outcome associated with CPD.

> Liberatory praxis accepts that teaching is a political act and rejects the position that it is politically neutral (Pitsoe & Mahlangu, 2014; Freire, 2000). Liberatory praxis centers the act of liberation requiring examination, interrogation, and exploration of the dynamics, constructs of power, and relationships in education broadly, and specifically, within schools. (Waite, 2021b, p. 69)

If PD does not involve interrogating the constructs of power upon which the dynamics of schooling and society at large are built, then it cannot support the development of CRIS. A central behavior of culturally responsive school leaders

(CRSL) is critical self-reflection on leadership behaviors. Examples of how this concept is manifested with classrooms can be seen in the research on integrating liberatory praxis with schools and in the professional development being utilized in schools (Hammond, 2021; Scharron-Del Rio, 2017; Todić & Christensen, 2022). This involves a number of practices that Khalifa et al. (2016) highlight in their analysis. A key behavior the authors emphasize is that CRSL challenges "Whiteness and hegemonic epistemologies in school (Theoharis & Haddix, 2011)" (Khalifa et al., 2016, p. 1284). The epistemologies are often centered, presumed to be shared by others, and represent a pretense of a shared, "traditional" or "American" experience which is accepted as the dominant norm in education.

Challenging dominant narratives about school and schooling within the field of education is complex. Historically, epistemological discussions in education have focused on the "relationships between epistemology and learning, cognition, academic success and how it fosters educational development" (Baxter Magolda, 1992; Hofer, 2001; Perry, 1970; Tubbs, 2016). Soleimani's (2020) empirical research found that significant relationships existed between participants' epistemological beliefs or "individual beliefs about knowledge and knowing" (Mason & Bromme, 2010, p. 1) and their teaching style (p. 10). Hofer (2001) contended that "epistemological thinking is related not only to school learning, but is a critical component of lifelong learning, in and out of school" (p. 354). Given that traditional PD is often antidialogical in nature, I concur with Kohli et al. (2015) and believe that CPD should be adopted as the benchmark for PD in order to authentically assist all educators with the development of their critical consciousness so that the goal of developing CRIS might be achieved.

According to Mizell's (2010) report by Learning Forward titled *Why Professional Development Matters*, "Professional development is the strategy schools and school districts use to ensure that educators continue to strengthen their practice throughout their career" (p. 1). If PD is a key strategy schools and districts leverage to support educators working collaboratively to problem-solve issues and ensure all students achieve success, then it is imperative educators be encouraged to interrogate their personal beliefs about the promise and potential of *all* students as they develop their critical consciousness.

The expectation that PD is supposed to remediate deficit mindsets and implicit bias without any explicit efforts to assist teachers with "the awakening of critical consciousness" is unrealistic (Freire, 2011, p. 36). Research indicates that our personal epistemologies, do, in fact, influence our professional praxis (Hofer, 2001; Mason & Bromme, 2010; Soleimani, 2020). Recognizing that our personal epistemologies are shaped by our lived experiences demands that developing one's critical consciousness be deeply embedded into PD. Without examining one's beliefs through a different lens, the antidialogical models that deposit training and development will persist. Additionally, ensuring that CRT is embedded in these dialogical discusses will address the white supremacist and anti-Black constructs that are deeply ingrained in the U.S. schooling context. Antidialogical models of

PD (APD) have been the benchmark for PD for years (Kohli et al., 2015). APD alone has not been proven to remedy the persistent inequities in education, such as opportunity gaps, disparate dropout rates, inadequate college readiness rates, and limited access to enrichment and gifted and talented programming. While there is a place for technical PD, the fact remains that APD has been marginally effective, at best, and it is time for increased intentionality about and openness to embedding critical consciousness anchored in racialized discourse as a standard best practice of PD.

CRITICAL CONSCIOUSNESS AND CULTURALLY RESPONSIVE INSTRUCTIONAL SUPERVISION

The current statistics on teachers and school building administrators heighten the urgency around ensuring that the field of education shifts its perspective on CRIS and on the necessity of developing critical consciousness in educational leaders (NCES, 2019). Communities across the United States are becoming increasingly diverse, and yet the statistics in the field are relatively flat. Nationally, the teaching force remains predominantly female (76.5%) and white (79.3%) (NCES, 2023b). According to the National Center of Education Statistics (2023a), there has been a steady decline in the number of male principals (46.3%) versus female principals (53.7%). However, the statistics on racial demographics for principals remain consistent, as 77.1% of principals are white (NCES, 2023a). Research indicates that "having a teacher of the same race/ethnicity can have positive impacts on a student's attitudes, motivation, and achievement and minority teachers may have more positive expectations for minority students' achievement than nonminority teachers" (NCES, 2019). The aforementioned statistics indicate that a chasm exists, and has for some time, between the growing diverse student population and the number of educators available who reflect the diversity of the students.

The dueling pandemics have irrevocably changed the landscape of education; leading in a "post" COVID-19 and global Black Lives Matter movement demands that leaders be both deliberate in their commitment and nuanced in their approach. Developing and leading school communities toward embracing the prospect of culturally responsive education requires that leaders commit to the development of their *own* critical consciousness. To lead classrooms, school communities, and/or districts toward adopting racial equity, *one must engage in their own racial equity journey. The development of critical consciousness is intrapersonal work* (Waite, 2021b). Critical self-awareness and a willingness to engage in the intrapersonal struggle to examine the ontological and epistemological beliefs one holds sacred are non-negotiable aspects of developing one's racialized critical consciousness. Interrogating the beliefs that contributed to the foundation of an individual's personal and professional identities, ethical beliefs, and educational philosophy is the type of work instructional leaders implementing CRIS must be willing to engage in personally to lead their school communities and districts effectively (Waite, 2021a).

TOWARD A CRITICAL THEORY OF PROFESSIONAL DEVELOPMENT

There are no catchall protocols, strategies, or continuous improvement PDSA cycles that can "instruct or teach" the *proper* approach to developing one's critical consciousness. *This work is internal, personal, and iterative.* Challenging deeply embedded principles that have formed the bedrock of what one believes and, moreover, that one has blindly accepted as objective truth is no small feat. And, yet this is exactly what one must do to interrogate the epistemologies that frame one's personal truths and beliefs because these are the very beliefs that shape, influence, and impact our professional praxis.

Countering the dominant narratives one has internalized and concertized as truth, requires criticality. Critical theory is "a complex theoretical perspective . . . that explores the historical, cultural, and ideological lines of authority that underlie social conditions" (Sensoy & DiAngelo, 2012). Again, it is necessary to embed a critical theory into racialized discussions on developing critical consciousness. Critical theories such as CRT, LatCrit, DisCrit, and Intersectionality can also be utilized to analyze data both qualitatively and quantitatively and explore disparate results. Assessing policies and practices through a critical lens affords expansion of perspective. In education,

> Criticality, specifically, CRT, offers a framework and lens through which we may all examine the world and interrogate both our role within education and the role we play in sustaining or interrupting the pathologies of white supremacy and racism in school districts across the country. (Waite, 2022, p. 13)

In addition to critical theory, critical pedagogies should be utilized to model how one may employ or utilize critical theories. Critical pedagogy should be embedded into PD as it supports one's ability to critically examine the world and "wage the struggle for liberation" (Freire, 2011, p. 49). Incorporating critical pedagogies into the training and development of CRIS is essential; critical pedagogies offer tools for leaders to examine the historical contexts of their schools, neighborhoods, and communities. Using critical pedagogies in education is a necessary function of providing a robust education. Criticality supports critical thinking skills. Critical thinking is considered a necessary component of adult learning (Darling-Hammond et al., 2017; Moore, 2010). PD designed to support the development of CRIS must counter the narratives found in the acritical and ahistorical narratives taught in education. PD must support CRIS leaders' ability to interrogate the assumptions that uphold any narratives which require the subjugation of PGM. Anchoring PD in critical pedagogy is not only needed, it is the linchpin which ignites or awakens consciousness.

SUPPORTING PRAXIS: A FRAMEWORK FOR DEVELOPING CRITICALLY CONSCIOUS CRIS

In *An Archaeology of Self for Our Times: Another Talk to Teachers*, Sealey-Ruiz (2022) reminds educators of the wisdom James Baldwin shared in his 1963 speech titled "A Talk with Teachers." In that speech, Baldwin discussed the impact of the social ills that were plaguing the field of education at that time: racism, educational inequality, disparate poverty, etc. In her article, Ruiz emphasizes that these same ills continue to plague society and underscores that these issues have been exacerbated by the dueling pandemics. She asserts that teachers must still answer the call of challenging systemic oppression in schools.

Sealey-Ruiz created *The Archaeology of Self,* which is a racial literacy development model to assist pre-service and current teachers with conducting "a deep excavation and exploration of beliefs, biases, and ideas that shape how we engage in our work" (Sealey-Ruiz, 2022, p. 22). In her model, she centers critical reflection and defines it as a process that requires one to "think through the various layers of our identities and how our privileged or marginalized status affect the work" (p. 22). Sealey-Ruiz proffers the following as the six components of the Archaeology of the Self: interruption, historical literacy, critical reflection, critical humility, critical love, and deep excavation and exploration. As an expert in teacher development, Sealey-Ruiz created the archaeology of the self for the purposes of supporting teacher practice and enriching student learning (Sealey-Ruiz, 2022). The research clearly indicates that critical self-reflection is a vital component to the development of one's critical consciousness (Freire, 2011; Gooden & O'Doherty, 2015; Khalifa et al., 2016; Lynch, 2021; Milner, 2008; Sealey-Ruiz, 2022; Waite, 2021b). As such, it seems imperative that practitioners aspiring to practice CRIS have access to a tool that explicitly supports their ability to engage in that work.

In a similar spirit, I would like to offer a framework CRIS leaders can use to help them commit to their own intrapersonal work so that they might be equipped to support their school community—students, families, teachers, and staff—with embracing the transition toward culturally responsive teaching (see Figure 12.1). In previous work, I have highlighted a conceptual framework and liberatory pedagogical tool I developed in which aspiring and current school building and district leaders continuously engage in cycles of Reflection, Interrogation, Self-examination, and Awareness (Waite, 2021a). RISA is an acronym I conceived based off the liberatory practices I utilized in my work with aspiring and current school building and district leaders as a faculty member.

> RISA is a conceptual framework; it is also an acronym for the aforementioned set of liberatory practices I use with students to center counternarratives and attempt to strategically disrupt any existing dysconscious racism. I also challenge the pathology of White supremacy and its role in the field of education. These practices are important to consider when teaching content about racialized people, engaging students in using frameworks, and exploring approaches to leadership as they all anchor the need to

Figure 12.1. RISA Framework for Leaders: Developing Critical Self-Awareness

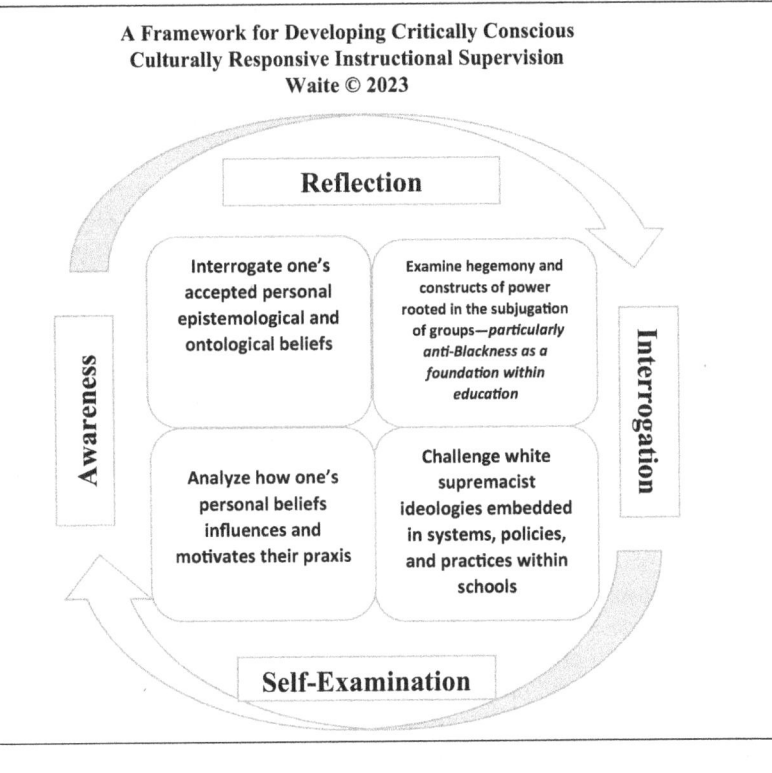

A Framework for Developing Critically Conscious
Culturally Responsive Instructional Supervision
Waite © 2023

Reflection

- Interrogate one's accepted personal epistemological and ontological beliefs
- Examine hegemony and constructs of power rooted in the subjugation of groups—*particularly anti-Blackness as a foundation within education*
- Analyze how one's personal beliefs influences and motivates their praxis
- Challenge white supremacist ideologies embedded in systems, policies, and practices within schools

Awareness — **Interrogation**

Self-Examination

center students' personal epistemological and ontological beliefs (Dumas & ross, 2016; Gooden & O'Doherty, 2015; Khalifa et al., 2016; King, 1991). (Waite, 2021a, p. 8)

RISA is both a conceptual framework and liberatory pedagogical tool designed from the perspective of a faculty member that worked with graduate-level students who were engaging with highly theoretical, conceptual, and critical texts. The premise of RISA was to push students toward the ongoing development of their racialized critical consciousness as they read, primarily, scholarly articles and texts. Students were challenged to think about how they made sense of the texts as both students and, perhaps more importantly, as practitioners. RISA was initially conceived as a tool faculty members could utilize to support the students they worked with in educational leadership-preparation programs and/or trainings, workshops, or PD series. I have extended RISA to support the work of CRIS seeking protocols or tools designed to help them as they engage in *intrapersonal interrogation as part of their own racial equity journey.*

The purpose of developing critical consciousness is grounded in the belief that developing this literacy—for critical scholars, a racialized literacy—will support one's ability to liberate oneself and others from oppression. Reflection plays an integral part in the process of liberation. Contemporary research on developing critical consciousness in youth through participatory action research (PAR) suggests that the following are key elements of what that process embodies: (1) critical reflection; (2) critical motivation (or, efficacy); and (3) critical action (Diemer et al., 2016, p. 216). These elements are suggested in the RISA framework; "the cycle of reflection, interrogation, self-examination, and awareness affords educators the ability to genuinely practice reflexivity and hold them accountable for doing the introspective work required for change to take place" (Waite, 2021a, p. 14). The theory of change is that the process of reflection pushes one to interrogate, which leads to self-examination and results in an awareness that inspires one to act. Ultimately, the purpose of developing critical consciousness in educational leaders is to push educators to do the internal work needed to change their praxis. While the impetus of a RISA cycle can be triggered by an act of self-examination, the practice of examining oneself requires reflection. Hence, reflection is at the heart of the RISA cycle. While reflection and critical self-reflection are deeply embedded in critical consciousness, the intention is not for the individual to remain stuck in practicing reflexivity (Gooden & Dantley, 2012). Reflection must, ultimately, lead to action, not talk and empty promises.

Our personal epistemologies influence and mold the beliefs we hold at the core of our beings (Avci, 2016; Soleimani, 2020). This framework is expanded to explicitly help push leaders that aspire to practice CRIS to embrace the struggle that comes with challenging narratives that one holds dear to their personal identity, core values, and ethics. Our beliefs shape how we see the world and as a result the default presumption is that others share your experiences and perspectives. I cannot overemphasize that this is intrapersonal work and that this work is necessary for those aspiring to practice CRIS. Critical self-awareness is imperative and allows one to commit to the interpersonal work needed to guide their school communities through the process.

A practitioner-oriented framework designed to support the development of critical consciousness in culturally responsive leaders can be useful. Originally informed by the literature on CRSLs (Khalifa et al., 2016), CRT (Ladson-Billings & Tate, 1995), Dysconscious Racism (King, 1991), and Critical Consciousness (Freire, 2011), I have expanded the RISA framework to include specific actions leaders must intentionally commit to in order to initiate, expand, and/or further the development of their critical self-awareness (Khalifa et al., 2016; Lopez & Jean-Marie, 2021; Lynch, 2018; Waite, 2021b). The RISA Framework for Leaders: Developing Critical Self-Awareness is an extension of the RISA Framework (2021) and can be utilized by an individual to analyze how their personal epistemologies impact and affect their professional praxis. Ideally, once a leader has begun this journey, they may use this framework within their schools and district communities to help their communities embrace the path toward culturally responsive instructional leadership and subsequently teaching.

RISA provides a pathway for individuals to critically reflect on their deeply held beliefs and challenges them to interrogate why they believe these things.

Cognitive dissonance is often an impact of this critical self-reflection or an exploratory excavation (Sealey-Ruiz, 2022). RISA, potentially, creates the conditions for one to experience varying levels of cognitive dissonance. The four interior tenets of this framework are grounded in critical race theory and push the leader to examine the pathologies of white supremacy and anti-Blackness as well as explore critiques of liberalism and capitalism commonly associated with education (Cappers, 2015; Delgado & Stefancic, 2017, Dumas & ross, 2016). Moreover, they are behaviors and actions identified in the literature that culturally responsive leaders utilize in their work. (Khalifa et al., 2016). The centering of these tenets is both metaphorical and practical; critical self-reflection is an internal and introspective process.

Leaders must center and interrogate *their* beliefs, examine the hierarchies and the social construction of power *they* sustain, and challenge *their* ideologies and the systems, policies, and practices that center whiteness that *they* subscribe to while they also perform "other" PGM actions. The tenets are centered in a cycle of reflection, interrogation, self-examination, and awareness. The cycle is fluid, may run in the inverse, or may be triggered by any of the four actions within the framework. However, it is my belief that if a person has had an experience that has triggered a new sense of awareness, they recognize this because they reflect on that experience, so ultimately it is reflection, critical self-reflection, that grounds the RISA cycle.

CONCLUSION

Critical reflection influences and expands one's capacity for critical efficacy (or motivation) and it is that motivation which pushes one toward critical action. The process of engaging in the struggle and intentionally resisting the discomfort associated with the process of awakening can lead to gaining a new lens of self. This new-found efficacy or motivation can assist in contextualizing the historical and sociopolitical context needed to support the development of one's understanding that they inherently have the right to demand relief from the injustices they experience. This applies to the case of CRIS specifically, and educators broadly, the obligation to dismantle the oppressive systems we maintain. CRIS leaders can model this process for school communities, demonstrate the commitment to the work of liberation, and walk their communities through this process if and only if they have engaged in this deeply personal work.

REFERENCES

Avci, O. (2016). Positionalities, personal epistemologies, and instruction: An analysis. *Journal of Education and Training Studies, 4*(6), 145–154 http://dx.doi.org/10.11114/jets.v4i6.1462

Byrd, C. M. (2016). Does culturally relevant teaching work? An examination from student perspectives. *SAGE Open, 6*(3). https://doi.org/10.1177/2158244016660744

Caldera, A. L. (2020). Eradicating anti-black racism in U.S. schools: A call-to-action for school leaders. *Diversity, Social Justice, and the Educational Leader, 4*(1), Article 3.

Capper, C. A. (2015). The 20th-year anniversary of critical race theory in education: Implications for leading to eliminate racism. *Educational Administration Quarterly, 51*(5), 731–833.

Cormier, D. R., & Pandey, T. (2021). Semiotic Analysis of a Foundational Textbook Used Widely Across Educational Supervision. *Journal of Educational Supervision, 4*(2). https://doi.org/10.31045/jes.4.2.6

Cortina, R., & Winter, M. (2021). Paulo Freire's pedagogy of liberation. *Current Issues in Comparative Education, 23*(2), 8–19. https://www.tc.columbia.edu/cice/issues/volume-23-issue-2-special-issue-2021/8577-Article-Text-19550-1-10-20211029.pdf

Darling-Hammond, L., Hyler, M. E., & Gardner, M. (2017). *Effective teacher professional development*. Learning Policy Institute.

Delgado, R., & Stefancic, J. (2017). *Critical Race Theory (Third Edition): An Introduction* (3rd ed., Vol. 20). NYU Press. https://doi.org/10.2307/j.ctt1ggjjn3

Diemer, M. A., Rapa, L. J., Voight, A. M., & McWhirter, E. H. (2016). Critical consciousness: A developmental approach to addressing marginalization and oppression. *Child Development Perspectives, 10*(4), 216–221. https://doi.org/10.1111/cdep.12193

Dobbs, C. L., Ippolito, J., & Charner-Laird, M. (2016). Scaling up professional learning: Technical expectations and adaptive challenges. *Professional Development in Education,43*(5), 729–748. https://doi.org/10.1080/19415257.2016.1238834

Dumas, M. J. (2014) 'Losing an arm': Schooling as a site of black suffering. Race Ethnicity and Education, 17:1, 1–29, DOI: 10.1080/13613324.2013.850412

Dumas, M. J., & ross, k. m. (2016). "Be real black for me": Imagining blackcrit in education. *Urban Education, 51*(4), 415–442. https://doi.org/10.1177/0042085916628611

Dussel, E. (2013). *Ethics of liberation: In the age of globalization and exclusion*. Duke University Press.

Freire, P. (2011). *Pedagogy of the oppressed* (30th anniv. ed.). Continuum International Publishing Group

Gay, G. (2018). *Culturally responsive teaching*. Teachers College Press.

Gay. G. (2002). Preparing for culturally responsive teaching. *Journal of Teacher Education, 53*(2), 106–116.

Green, J. (2021, January 11). *A lesson on critical race theory*. American Bar Association. Retrieved from: https://www.americanbar.org/groups/crsj/publications/human_rights_magazine_home/civil-rights-reimagining-policing/a-lesson-on-critical-race-theory/

Gooden, M. A., & Dantley, M. (2012). Centering race in a framework for leadership preparation. *Journal of Research on Leadership Education, 7*(2), 237–253.

Gooden, M. A., & O'Doherty, A. (2015). Do you see what i see? Fostering aspiring leaders' racial awareness. *Urban Education, 50*(2), 225–255. https://doi-org.tc.idm.oclc.org/10.1177/0042085914534273

Hammond, Z. L. (2015). *Culturally responsive teaching and the brain*. Corwin Press.

Hammond, Z. (2021). Liberatory education: Integrating the science of learning and culturally responsive practice. *American Educator Summer 2021*. American Federation of Teachers.

Hofer, B. (2001). Personal epistemology research: Implications for learning and teaching. *Journal of Educational Psychology Review, 13*(4), 353–383.

Khalifa, M. A., Gooden, M. A., & Davis, J. E. (2016). Culturally responsive school leadership: A synthesis of the literature. *Review of Educational Research*, *86*(4), 1272–1311.

King, J. E. (1991). Dysconscious racism: Ideology and the miseducation of teachers. *Journal of Negro Education*, *60*(2), 133–146.

Knerl, L. (2021, March, 22). Why professional development is key for meeting all students' needs. *The Columbus Dispatch*. Retrieved from: https://www.dispatch.com/story/sponsor-story/marburn-academy/2021/03/22/why-professional-development-key-meeting-all-students-needs/4753937001/

Knowles, M. S. (1980). *The modern practice of adult education: From pedagogy to andragogy*. Cambridge University Press.

Kohli, R., Picower, B., Martinez, A., & Ortiz, N. (2015). Critical professional development: Centering the social justice needs of teachers. *The International Journal of Critical Pedagogy*, *6*(2), 9–24.

Ladson-Billings, G. (1995). But that's just good teaching! The case for culturally relevant pedagogy. *Theory into practice*, *34*(3), 159–165. https://www.jstor.org/stable/1476635

Ladson-Billings, G., & Tate, W. (1995). Towards a critical race theory of education. *Teachers College Record*, *97*, 47–68.

Ladson-Billings, G. (2014). Culturally relevant pedagogy 2.0: A. K. A. the remix. *Harvard Educational Review*, *84*(1), 74–84. https://doi.org/10.17763/haer.84.1.p2rj1314854 84751

Lopez, A. E., & Jean-Marie, G. (2021). Challenging anti-black racism in everyday teaching, learning, and leading: From theory to practice. *Journal of School Leadership*, *31*(1–2), 50–65. https://doi.org/10.1177/1052684621993115

Lynch, M. E. (2021). Supervision to deepen teacher candidates' Understanding of social justice: The role of responsive mediation in professional development schools. *Journal of Educational Supervision*, *4*(2). https://doi.org/10.31045/jes.4.2.5

Lynch, M. E. (2018). The hidden nature of whiteness in education: Creating active allies in white teachers. *Journal of Educational Supervision*, *1*(1). https://doi.org/10.31045/jes.1.1.2

Milner, H. R., IV. (2008). Critical race theory and interest convergence as analytic tools in teacher education policies and practices. *Journal of Teacher Education*, *59*(4), 332–346.

Mizell, H. (2010). *Why professional development matters*. Learning Forward. https://learningforward.org/wp-content/uploads/2017/08/professional-development-matters.pdf

Moore, K. (2010). The three-part harmony of adult learning, critical thinking, and decision-making. *Journal of Adult Education*, *39*(1), 1–10. https://files.eric.ed.gov/fulltext/EJ917394.pdf

National Center for Education Statistics. (2019, February). *Status and trends in the education of racial and ethnic groups*. https://nces.ed.gov/programs/raceindicators/spotlight_a.asp#f1

National Center for Education Statistics. (2023a, January). *Status and trends in the education of racial and ethnic groups*. https://nces.ed.gov/programs/digest/d21/tables/dt21_212.08.asp

National Center for Education Statistics. (2023b, January). *Status and trends in the education of racial and ethnic groups*. https://nces.ed.gov/programs/digest/d20/tables/dt20_209.10.asp

Sensoy, Ö., & DiAngelo, R. (2012). *Is everyone really equal*. Teachers College Press

Rembert, A. (1976) Teaching about values: Remaining neutral vs. advocating one's own view, *Peabody Journal of Education, 53*(2), 71–75, https://doi.org/10.1080/0161956 7609538054

Royal, C., & Gibson, S. (2017). They schools: Culturally relevant pedagogy under siege. *Teachers College Record, 119*(1), 1–25. https://doi.org/10.1177/016146811711900108

Scharron-Del Rio, M. R. (2017). Teaching at the intersections: Liberatory and anti-oppressive pedagogical praxis in the multicultural counseling classroom as a queer Puerto Rican educator. *Feminist Teacher, 27*(2–3), 90–105. https://doi.org/10.5406/femteacher.27.2-3.0090

Sealey-Ruiz, Y. (2022). An archaeology of self for our times: Another talk to teachers. *English Journal, 111*(5), 21–26.

Sensoy, Ö., & DiAngelo, R. (2012). *Is everyone really equal?* Teachers College Press

Shandomo, H. M. (2010). The role of critical reflection in teacher education. *School-University Partnerships, 4*(1), 101–113.

Soleimani, N. (2020). ELT teachers' epistemological beliefs and dominant teaching style: a mixed method research. *Asian-Pacific Journal of Second and Foreign Language Education, 5*(12), https://doi.org/10.1186/s40862-020-00094-y

Tanase, M. (2020). Is good teaching culturally responsive? *Journal of Pedagogical Research, 4*(3), 187–202.

Todić, J., & Christensen, M. C. (2022). Integrating critical, engaged, and abolitionist pedagogies to advance antiracist social works education. *Advances in Social Work.* 22(2), 389–415. https://doi.org/10.18060/24972

Tubbs. N. (2016). Epistemology as education: Know thyself. Special Issue of *Education Sciences, 6*(4). https://doi.org/10.3390/educsci6040041

U.S. Department of Education. (2022). *Strategies for using American Rescue Plan funding to address the impact of lost instructional time.* https://www2.ed.gov/documents/coronavirus/lost-instructional-time.pdf

Waite, S. R. (2021a). Disrupting dysconsciousness: Confronting anti-blackness in educational leadership preparation programs. *Journal of School Leadership, 31*(1–2), 66–84.

Waite, S. R. (2021b). Towards a theory of critical consciousness: A new direction for the development of instructional and supervisory leaders. *Journal of Educational Supervision, 4*(2). https://doi.org/10.31045/jes.4.2.4

Waite, S. R. (2022). National leadership standards and the structured silence of white supremacy. In F. W. English (Ed.), *The Palgrave handbook of educational leadership and management discourse* (pp. 1757–1772). Palgrave Macmillan. https://doi.org/10.1007/978-3-030-39666-4_23-1

CHAPTER 13

Black Women as Instructional Leaders
Historical and Contemporary Perspectives

Terri N. Watson and Linda C. Tillman

It was in me to get an education and to teach my people.

—Frances (Fanny) Jackson Coppin

Our aim in this chapter is to highlight the efficacy of Black women in their roles as instructional leaders. We believe that the relationship between Black women and the schoolhouse is central to the academic success of Black students. We ground our conversation in Black Feminism (Combahee River Collective, 1977) and Black Feminist Theory (BFT; Collins, 1989, 2000), as both philosophies place Black women at the center of knowledge production. First, Black feminism is used as a lens to trouble traditional scholarship on instructional leadership. Then, we explore extant literature on historical and contemporary Black women school leaders. Next, we employ BFT's tenets of the use of dialogue and the ethic of care to hear and listen to the voices of two Black women principals as they share their experiences as instructional supervisors. Finally, based on this discussion and BFT's tenet of personal accountability, we proffer recommendations to inform the praxis of instructional leadership and to improve the academic success of Black students in particular.

INTRODUCTION

Black women are inherently valuable to society (Combahee River Collective, 1977). Extant literature extols the narratives of groundbreaking Black women who, despite their "continuous life-and-death struggle for survival and liberation" (Combahee River Collective, p. 293), propelled society forward. This cadre includes Phillis Wheatley, the first Black woman to publish a book of poetry; Sojourner Truth, a noted orator and abolitionist; and Harriet Tubman, a soldier in the Union Army and the "conductor" of an "Underground Railroad" that led scores of enslaved people to freedom. In addition to being skilled authors, orators, and abolitionists, many Black women were radical teachers and learners during the Antebellum period. Williams (2005) revealed how enslaved Black women learned to read and write by encouraging their young White charges to share their daily lessons with them. They would also entice White children, who were too young to understand anti-literacy laws, to "play school" (p. 20) with their own children.

Before the Civil War (1861–1865), more than a dozen states enacted anti-literacy laws to ensure Black subjugation. If Black people were caught learning to read or write, they faced severe consequences, which included lashings, mutilation, and even death (Williams, 2005). Black women routinely ignored these sanctions. They knew that literacy was essential to Black liberation and would improve their life chances. Watson and McClellan (2020) shared the lived experiences of foundational Black women school leaders, namely, Frances Jackson Coppin, Sarah J. Smith Tompkins Garnet, Mary Jane Patterson, and Anna Julia Cooper. All but one of these women, Tompkins Garnet, was born into bondage. Nevertheless, they were among the first Black women in the United States to earn college degrees, lead schools, and advocate for racially just schooling.

Black women are fundamental to the academic success of Black students. McCluskey (2014) shared the narratives of three pioneering Black women school leaders: Cornelia Bowen, Emma Wilson, and Elizabeth E. Wright. These women were all born one generation removed from slavery and established schools in the South after Reconstruction (1863–1877), when anti-Black racism was virulent. In addition to literacy, these schools provided Black students with the needed skills and workforce development to improve their economic standing. McCluskey (2014) described these trailblazers as, "an often-forgotten set of clubwomen whose response to the world of disadvantage and danger that African Americans inherited from enslavement was to place faith in God and themselves and bring about change by building institutions of learning" (p. 1). The deep commitment to Black education and forward-thinking pedagogical skills these Black women school leaders possessed are also omitted in extant literature on instructional leadership.

It is important to make clear that despite their substantial contributions to the academic success of Black students, often in the face of danger and at great personal cost, the lived experiences of the nation's earliest Black women school leaders are rarely examined in education research. This omission is problematic as the racial achievement gap persists, while the efficacy of Black women school leaders/principals[1] remains, by and large, untapped. This chapter contributes to the literature and is grounded in Black feminism (Combahee River Collective, 1977) and Black Feminist Theory (BFT; Collins, 1989, 2000), as both philosophies

---

1. The terms "school leader" and "principal" are used interchangeably throughout this chapter.

place Black women at the center of knowledge production. First, Black feminism is used as a lens to trouble traditional scholarship on instructional leadership. Then, we explore extant literature on historical and contemporary Black women school leaders. Next, we employ BFT's tenets of the use of dialogue and the ethic of care to hear and listen to the voices of two Black women principals as they share their experiences as instructional supervisors. Finally, based on this discussion and BFT's tenet of personal accountability, we proffer recommendations to inform the praxis of instructional leadership and to improve the academic success of Black students in particular.

BLACK FEMINISM AND BLACK FEMINIST THEORY

During the latter half of the 1970s a group of Black women, including Audre Lorde, Barbara Smith, and Beverly Smith, articulated the politics of Black feminism. They explained how the lived experiences of Black women were erased by the women's movement and further marginalized by Black Nationalist organizations. The resulting document, the Combahee River Collective Statement, provided an overview of the group's "herstory" and explains the origins of Black feminism. To be clear, Black feminism centers the lived experiences of Black women to challenge interlocking systems of oppression. The authors of the Statement position the liberation of Black women as a revolutionary and necessary response to injustice(s). We ground this work in Black feminism because as Black women and education researchers, we know that schools and the process of schooling is fundamentally a "white good" (Justice, 2023) and anti-Black (Dumas, 2014; Ladson-Billings, 2018).

Black feminism is an important lens to apply in education research because it recognizes Black women as creators of knowledge (Combahee River Collective, 1977). This paradigm shift is needed in the schoolhouse, as new and different ways of knowing are needed to address systemic and racialized inequities palpable in schools across the United States. Moreover, long-standing reports (see Coleman et al., 1966; Moynihan, 1965), along with deficit mental models of Black womanhood, position Black women as contrarian to the academic success and overall well-being of Black students. This is problematic because as mentioned, historically, Black women's distinct funds of knowledge and lived experiences were crucial to Black education and the praxis of instructional leadership (see Coppin, 1913; McCluskey, 2014; Watson & McClellan, 2020). Critical perspectives such as Black feminism are sorely needed in the schoolhouse to improve the academic success of students in general and Black students in particular.

Black feminism is grounded in Black womanhood and embodies love, care, and justice. Black feminist educationalists such as Angela Davis (1983), bell hooks (1984), and Audre Lorde (1984) demonstrate this praxis in their writings (Cox, 2022). Black Feminist Theory is an offset of Black Feminism. Sociologist Patricia Hill Collins (2000) crafted four tenets of Black feminist epistemology to contextualize the nuanced realities of Black womanhood. The resulting Black Feminist Theory (BFT) framework is comprised of the following tenets: (a) the lived experience—Black women's personal experience is valid and has value; (b) the use of dialogue to assess knowledge claims—the speaker and the listener are active participants in the exchange of knowledge; (c) the ethics of caring—in the knowledge validation process, personal expressiveness, emotions, and empathy are exchanged; and (d) the ethic of personal accountability—the knower is responsible for their knowledge claims (Collins, 2000, pp. 252–270).

In the next section we trouble traditional scholarship on instructional leadership.

TRADITIONAL SCHOLARSHIP ON INSTRUCTIONAL LEADERSHIP

While there are scores of definitions and models of instructional leadership, education researchers agree that the school leader is the primary instructional leader whose function is to support effective teaching and learning in the schoolhouse. Theories, frameworks, and discussions about school administration/leadership have usually focused on various administrative/leadership styles (Bolman & Deal, 1997; Leithwood & Duke, 1999), administrative/leadership functions (Farkas et al., 2003; Leithwood & Riehl, 2003), alternative perspectives of school leadership such as leadership for social justice (Dantley & Tillman, 2005), and diversity in educational administration/leadership (Tillman, 2003, 2020). Many of the theories and frameworks position the school leader as the instructional leader who performs numerous tasks in and outside of the schoolhouse, including using test data to monitor student progress; coordinating the curriculum in collaboration with teachers; providing various types of professional development to facilitate teacher competence; and establishing a school culture and climate that is conducive to student and teacher success.

Hallinger (2018) reviewed over five decades of research on instructional leadership and discussed the evolution of theory, practice, and research with respect to the principal's role as an instructional leader, as well as how these developments have implications for principal practice. He points to the Effective Schools Movement (Edmonds, 1979), which was focused primarily on urban schools, as an important school reform effort that prompted more research on instructional leadership. Hallinger defined instructional leadership as the process of "creating conditions in schools that support quality teaching and learning" (p. 505), and addressed four questions: (1) What is the relationship between school leadership and learning? (2) What is instructional leadership? (3) How can instructional leadership theory be applied in practice? (4) What are the most productive lines of inquiry in future research on instructional leadership? (p. 505).

According to Hallinger (2018), a great deal of the research on instructional leadership has been "conducted in so-called "Anglocentric' societies" (p. 520). He appears to suggest that for over five decades, theories, research, and frameworks about instructional leadership have paid scant attention to issues related to cultural context, race, and gender and have primarily presented a monolithic view of what instructional leadership is and how it is practiced. Indeed, instructional leadership has typically been defined from a majority (i.e., White male) perspective and has failed to capture the theory and instructional practices of Black principals, especially Black women principals (see Jang & Alexander, 2022). This is troubling, as Black women have significantly advanced an agenda for Black education and promoted Black student achievement pre- and post-*Brown v. Board of Education* (1954), the landmark school desegregation class action suit. Hallinger also notes that female principals tend to be more highly rated as instructional leaders. However, he fails to provide an analysis of "which females" and in what educational contexts they are more highly rated. Thus, Hallinger's analysis further marginalizes the instructional practices of Black women school leaders and the contexts in which they serve.

Brazer and Bauer (2013) define instructional leadership as "the effort to improve teaching and learning for PK–12 students by managing effectively, addressing the challenges of diversity, guiding teacher learning, and fostering organizational learning" (p. 650). Importantly, the researchers note that "aspiring leaders must be prepared to do more than manage schools and districts; they must also lead instruction" (p. 646). They proffered a model of instructional leadership which could be used to transform leadership preparation programs. In the Brazer and Bauer model, aspiring principals would learn about and practice instructional leadership through a problem-based learning pedagogy. While much of the Brazer and Bauer model is based on traditional, Eurocentric theories of instructional leadership, the pedagogical content knowledge component does, to some extent, address issues of race and culture in the schoolhouse.

Brazer and Bauer (2013) note that leadership preparation programs must address diversity among and within their principal candidates along two dimensions: (a) the candidates' own knowledge, skills, and dispositions with respect to diversity; and (b) the candidates' abilities to create culturally proficient schools (p. 660). They further note that because students come to school with a wide variety of cultural, socioeconomic, language, and learning backgrounds, recognizing who they are as learners is a complex task. According to the authors, "Understanding the diversity of student bodies and finding ways to make all students welcome in schools is made more urgent by the fact that the *typical prospective leader* [emphasis added] has little, or no direct knowledge of the roadblocks faced by underrepresented segments of the student population" (p. 660). Brazer and Bauer conclude that their model can be useful in the re-design of leadership preparation programs and how these programs prepare novice school administrators whose primary job is instructional leadership.

While the work of Hallinger, Brazer and Bauer, and others (see Bowers & White, 2014) is instructive, there is little discussion or analysis in their scholarship about gender, race, or the varied cultural contexts of the principalship. There is some mention of diversity in schools; however, there is a strict focus on Eurocentric norms and practices, and few specifics about the leadership of Black principals, their instructional leadership practices, and how their practices impact teacher practices, school culture, and student achievement. Thus, the framing of discussions about instructional leadership tends to be more general than specific, even while many of the most pressing challenges in education are in high poverty, under-served schools that are most often led by Black principals, and particularly Black women principals. Thus, there is a gap in the literature with respect to theory, research, models, and frameworks that include the lived experiences of Black women principals. In the following section we look back at select instructional leadership practices of historical and contemporary Black women principals.

BLACK WOMEN AS INSTRUCTIONAL LEADERS: A HISTORICAL PERSPECTIVE

Throughout history, Black women have been at the forefront of educating Black people: markedly in the pre-*Brown* era (Alston & Jones, 2002; Franklin, 1990; Perkins, 1987; Tillman, 2004a, 2004b). During the Reconstruction era, Black women who had the opportunity to be educated were instrumental in educating formerly enslaved Black people. Among them was Frances Jackson Coppin. Coppin was born into bondage in Washington, DC, in 1837, and is considered by many to be America's first Black woman school leader / instructional leader. She is credited for the success of more than 5,000 Black students with whom she worked during her long tenure at Philadelphia's Institute for Colored Youth (ICY). Many of her students became educators and taught in segregated schools throughout the nation. Coppin's deep love and care for Black students, along with her work ethic and commitment to racial uplift, embodied Black feminism and is clear evidence of "one of the earliest examples of the link between African American school leadership and African American student achievement" (Tillman, 2004a, p. 108).

Coppin's manuscript, aptly titled *Reminiscences of School Life and Hints on Teaching*, is the earliest model for culturally responsive instructional leadership. The narrative is filled with practical tools for *effective* instruction, while demonstrating how to *affectively* provide Black students with direction, support, and feedback. For example, in the chapter "Methods of Instruction," Coppin promotes the benefits of group instruction and corresponding feedback. She defined this practice as "co-operative correction" and explained:

> This correction by the teacher, coming immediately after the work is done, is very helpful to those being examined, and saves the teacher from carrying work home and having to go over it all by himself, and besides, the pupils get far more benefit from this co-operative correction as it may be called. (p. 46)

Published posthumously in 1913, Coppin's paradigm for instructional leadership was written with Black student achievement and racial uplift at its core and stands in stark contrast to traditional scholarship on instructional leadership and supervision.

Coppin was among scores of formerly enslaved Black women who worked diligently to prepare the next generation of thought leaders. These women served as teachers and school leaders, and some were employed as Jeanes Supervisors. The latter group worked in Southern rural schools and communities as instructional leaders from 1907 through 1967 (Alston & McClellan, 2011). Their duties included conducting what is now known as professional development for teachers and assisting the county superintendents of schools. In the North, Black people advocated for desegregated schooling (see *Roberts v. City of Boston*, 1850). Moreover, like their southern counterparts, scores of Black New Yorkers became teachers and school leaders to promote Black advancement and racial uplift. Sarah J. Smith Tompkins Garnet was a member of this cadre, and in 1863 she became New York's first Black woman principal.

Sarah J. Smith Tompkins Garnet was born in Brooklyn, NY, on July 31, 1831. Her parents were successful farmers, and she was the oldest of their 11 children. Her sister, Susan Smith McKinney Steward, was the first Black woman to earn a doctorate in medicine in New York (Watson & McClellan, 2020). Growing up, Garnet was a natural leader. At the age of 14 she began her career in the schoolhouse as a teaching assistant at the African Free School in Brooklyn. In 1854 she became a teacher, and in 1863, she was named principal of Colored School No. 7. This was one of seven segregated schools established in 1834 by the New York Manumission Society, a coalition of wealthy White men who endeavored to gradually abolish slavery in New York. Garnet retired in 1900. During her 55-year tenure in New York's public schools, Garnet is credited with educating thousands of Black children and adults. In addition, she advocated for equal pay for Black teachers, established a series of evening classes for adults, and co-founded the Equal Suffrage League of Brooklyn (Watson & McClellan, 2020).

Anna Julia Cooper was born into bondage in 1858 in Raleigh, NC. Like Frances Jackson Coppin, Cooper attended Oberlin College where she earned a Bachelor of Arts in 1884 and a Master of Arts in Mathematics in 1887. She went on to earn a Doctor of Philosophy degree from the University of Paris-Sorbonne in 1924, making her the fourth Black American to attain this terminal degree. In 1902, Cooper was hired to teach at the M Street School in Washington, DC, which was the city's only Black high school (Stewart, 2013). She crafted a rich curriculum and was known as an accomplished instructional leader. She also established and propagated a rigorous school culture that prepared M Street students to attend prestigious colleges and universities, including Harvard, Brown, Oberlin, and Dartmouth. Cooper was committed to educating Black students and was known to say, "Not the boys less, but the girls more" (Stewart, 2013).

Cooper's intellectual prowess is showcased in her autobiography, *A Voice from the South: By a Black Woman from the South* (1892). This manuscript is considered by many to be the earliest articulation of Black feminism. In it Cooper shares her lived experiences as a Black woman in America and places Black women at the center of Black progress. She also made clear how Black women were critically conscious yet silenced by society. It is important to note that while Cooper's accomplishments and intellect were undisputed, the White power structure in Washington, DC, took offense to her bold ambitions for Black students. Because of this, her tenure at M Street was contentious, and points to the intersectional oppression(s) Black women school leaders have often endured. The opposition Cooper faced was like that experienced by other progressive Black women school leaders / instructional leaders in the pre-*Brown* era, including Nannie Helen Burroughs, Mary MacLeod Bethune, Sarah Smith, and Mary Shadd Cary. In the next section, we highlight research centered on contemporary Black women school leaders / instructional leaders.

BLACK WOMEN AS INSTRUCTIONAL LEADERS: LINKING CONTEMPORARY RESEARCH, THEORY, AND PRACTICE TO A LIBERATORY "HERSTORY"

Over the last two decades, the instructional leadership practices of Black principals, and Black women principals specifically, have become more prominent (Bloom & Erlandson, 2003; Lomotey, 2019; Peters, 2012; Tillman, 2004a, 2004b; Wilson, 2016). For example, Tillman (2004a) reviewed the literature on Black women principals post-*Brown* and found that they promoted "student achievement in both direct and indirect ways and relied on their cultural heritage and their knowledge of the cultural norms of the Black community to motivate students" (p. 130). According to Tillman, Black women principals exemplified four dimensions of Black principal leadership: (1) resistance to ideologies and individuals opposed to the education of Black students; (2) the academic and social development of Black students as a priority; (3) the importance of the cultural perspectives and epistemologies of Black principals; and (4) leadership based on interpersonal caring. Further, Wilson (2016) conducted a case study of the instructional leadership behaviors of a Black woman principal. She found that the principal facilitated teachers' professional development and encouraged collaboration, which resulted in higher student achievement.

Lomotey (2019) reviewed research on Black women principals from 1993–2017. His findings revealed that: (1) Black women most often lead in elementary schools in urban districts; (2) Black women most often lead high-poverty schools; (3) the most often cited leadership characteristic in Black women is spirituality; (4) Black women view race as a significant factor in their leadership practices; and (5) Black women often exhibit passion/othermothering/caring and servant leadership in their leadership practices. Markedly, Lomotey found that Black Feminist Thought (BFT) was used as a framework to conduct the research in the majority of the studies centered on Black women principals. He reasoned, "BFT facilitates a uniquely feminine, African-centered way of looking at the world" (p. 340). He concluded that critical frameworks such as BFT can be useful for investigating issues of race and gender, as well as traditional and new leadership theories.

Jang and Alexander (2022) applied a quantitative methodology (QuantCrit) to conduct a study of the leadership practices of Black women principals. They noted how research using quantitative methods in studies of Black women principals is limited, particularly from an intersectional perspective.[2] Additionally, they found that traditional frameworks and conceptualizations of school leadership, "which normalize Whiteness and emphasize masculinity and charisma, contradict the positionality of Black women that stems from their race or ethnicity and gender [and] may contribute to them remaining institutionally invisible" (p. 452). The authors contend that there is an "institutional silencing" (see Cooper, 1892) of Black women principals that encourages misconceptions and stereotypes about them as well as the schools and communities they serve. According to Jang and Alexander (2022), the increased use of critical frameworks such as BFT help us to better understand the lives and experiences of Black women as leaders and how the intersection of race and gender impacts their work.

Weiner, Cyr, and Burton (2022) conducted a study of 20 Black women principals who led schools during what the authors term *twin pandemics*: "COVID-19 and longstanding White supremacy and anti-Black racism" (p. 335). They sought to understand how Black women principals, who had always centered social and racial justice as a part of their leadership practices, continued to exhibit care for their students and communities during these twin pandemics. The authors pointed out that, like other Black women principals, their participants led schools in communities that were most likely to be "deeply affected by these pandemics, making their experiences particularly important to understand and share" (p. 336). Additionally, the authors made clear that while the experiences of Black women principals are not monolithic, Black women have traditionally practiced leadership behaviors that are student centered, promote an ethic of care and othermothering, and promote justice and change through tempered radicalism and servant leadership. They also noted that Black women educators are often political activists and community builders, work to empower others, and "have a deep sense of responsibility to BIPOC and vulnerable children" (p. 338).

Weiner et al. (2022) grounded their inquiry in intersectionality and BFT to facilitate the centering of Black women's experiences. According to the authors, intersectionality grounded in BFT can facilitate "counternarratives to stereotyped versions of Black womanhood, and in this case how they engage in school leadership" (p. 340). Most of the principals they surveyed led predominantly Black elementary schools and used *caring* as a part of their instructional leadership practice. Findings from the study indicate that during the twin pandemics, Black women principals: (1) continued to advocate for their students and communities;

---

2. The premises of intersectionality are: (1) race or ethnicity and gender are simultaneously present in the dynamic processes that influence Black women principals' lives (simultaneity); (2) the relationships between race or ethnicity and gender are multiplicative in shaping Black women principals' lives (multiplicity); and (3) race or ethnicity and gender establish mutually interlocking systems of power (i.e., racism and sexism) (Jang, 2018).

(2) continued to give care and grace to their staff to motivate them to keep working for children and their communities; and (3) despite the pandemics, continued to lead for equity and anti-racism.

The use of BFT as a lens to study the lives and experiences of Black women principals indicates that it is a valuable and authentic method to investigate their experiences—experiences that are distinct based on the intersection of race and gender.

As evidenced by the studies reviewed for this chapter, Black women's leadership, specifically their role as instructional leaders, is very much grounded in the principles of Black feminism. The ingenuity, forward-thinking, and deep commitment to Black education these Black women embodied was revolutionary and literally transformed the schoolhouse. Contrary to Hallinger's (2018) argument that instructional leadership has only an indirect effect on student performance and teacher behavior, research using a Black feminist lens indicates that the instructional leadership practices of Black women school leaders/principals/ instructional leaders can and do have a direct impact on teachers' motivation, school climate and culture, and student achievement. As Lomotey (2019), Jang and Alexander (2022), Weiner et al. (2022), and others have pointed out, there is a direct link between the how, what, and why of Black women principals' instructional leadership and the social, emotional, and academic achievement of students, particularly that of Black students. In the next section, we employ BFT (Collins, 2000) as a critical methodology. We engage BFT's tenets, specifically, the use of dialogue and the ethic of care to hear and listen to two Black women school leaders' praxis of instructional leadership.

BLACK WOMEN PRINCIPALS' PRAXIS OF INSTRUCTIONAL LEADERSHIP

The use of BFT as a framework for conducting research *with* Black women school/ instructional leaders adds a different and much needed dimension to education research. As noted, Black women are inherently valuable to society (Combahee River Collective, 1977) and historically have been vital to Black education (Coppin, 1913; McCluskey, 2014; Watson & McClellan, 2020). Until recently, contemporary scholarship disregarded and overlooked the contributions of Black women principals to the academic success of students in general, and Black students in particular. As Black feminism is established in Black women's lived experiences and is a process that can transform society, we employed BFT to *hear* and *listen* to Black women school leaders' praxis of instructional leadership. Culturally based perspectives such as BFT are needed to improve the academic success of Black students and address the lack of education research that considers Black women school leaders' "herstory" and praxis of instructional leadership.

Participants. We spoke with two Black women school leaders. Both women attended public schools in large urban cities for their K–12 education experience and are the first in their family to graduate from college. They also live and work in large urban cities. The first, Candice Smith,[3] is a novice school leader. She is also a Teach for America alum, who transitioned to the schoolhouse after working in nonprofit community-based organizations for nearly a decade. She began her career in education as a math teacher in a charter school, a public school that is independently run. Our second participant, Dr. Kimberly Jones, recently resigned from her position as a middle school principal. She was the founding principal of the school, City Preparatory Academy (a pseudonym), which opened in 2010 under challenging conditions. Dr. Jones made clear that while City Prep was short on material resources and physical space, it was abundant with promise.

Interview Questions. The fact that the researchers and participants identify as Black women was crucial to this study. Too often, education scholars fail to center race and gender in their research and ignore the impact of gendered sexism (hooks, 2000), as well as the benefits that come from centering issues of race and racism in the schoolhouse (Watson & Rivera-McCutchen, 2016), in school leadership (Brooks & Watson, 2018), and in leadership preparation programs (Gooden & Dantley, 2012). Accordingly, participants were asked the following open-ended questions to illuminate and understand their "how," "what," and "why," as these factors pertain to Black women's praxis of school/instructional leadership:

1. Why did you become a teacher?
2. Why did you become a school leader?
3. How would you describe your role as a school leader?
4. How would you describe your role as an instructional leader?
5. How, if at all, does race and gender impact your instructional leadership practices?

A Black Feminist Approach. BFT provides a framework that ensures Black women will be seen and heard. Two tenets of BFT, the use of dialogue and the ethics of caring, informed this study. Humanizing language was utilized throughout, as the lead author knew both women school leaders personally and professionally. The exchanges were filled with good will, warm laughter, and affirming head nods. The mutual care was tangible, even via Zoom, as the speakers "talked with one's heart" (Collins, 2000, p. 262), and the researcher listened intently while leaning in to make clear that empathy and compassion were present. This confirmed the validity during the exchange, as "emotion indicates that a speaker believes in the validity of the argument" (Collins, 2000, p. 263). Additionally, the use of a culturally sensitive research approach (Tillman, 2002) allowed the participants to express their unique, self-defined perspective about being a Black woman instructional leader. Each conversation lasted 90 minutes and was recorded and transcribed. Both researchers read the transcripts and created codes to identify

---

3. Pseudonyms are used for the participants and school names.

similar experiences and feelings. These findings were compared, and the following descriptive themes emerged: (1) In Loco Parentis; (2) I am a Teacher First; and (3) I Know You See Me. These themes were used to outline our findings. In the following section, we discuss the confirmed themes.

In Loco Parentis. The Latin term "*In loco parentis*" translates in English to "in place of the parents." This decree charges teachers and school leaders to provide young people with a duty of care. When parents entrust their children to the schoolhouse, jurisprudence has established that they have the right to expect that their child will be safe and that school officials will ensure their physical health and wellbeing. In response to the question, "Why did you become a teacher?" Ms. Smith shared how she wanted to make a difference in young people's lives. She wanted to provide her students with the same feelings of love and care she received from her former middle school English teacher, a Black woman, who is now her mentor.

During our exchange Ms. Smith recalled how her deep care for young people was a constant throughout her career. After she graduated from college, Smith was a community organizer, and from there, she explained: "I moved to running an afterschool program, housed in a local elementary school." The program supported neighborhood children and provided many extra-curricular activities, including trips to museums, the state park, and amusement parks in nearby states. Her voice became lighter as she explained:

> I was the assistant director for [community-based organization] for four and a half years. That time was really instrumental, and probably like for me, the most impactful job, because I was able to not only have over 600 program participants, who ranged in age from 5 to 21, and successfully manage a budget that was like over $600,000: I was able to coordinate meaningful initiatives like book bag drives and health fairs for families who really needed it. I was also able to create and monitor summer programs that were free to families in the community. The cool thing about that was, you know, in urban communities, parents want placements [childcare] for their children while they're at work and they want to make sure their children are safe. So, establishing the after school and summer programs was really instrumental in making sure that kids were safe between 8 am and 6 pm, and that was very important to me.

For Smith, becoming a classroom teacher was a natural progression in her professional career. Smith often shares her experience(s) of growing up in foster care with her students because many of them are in the foster care system. She does this because she wants them to know that she "sees," "hears," and "cares" for them. Teachers can never replace parents; however, they can care and support their students by being present and providing young people with the needed tools to be successful in and out of the schoolhouse. Importantly, caring must transcend race and gender in the schoolhouse if schools are to educate *all* children *effectively* and *affectively*.

The second participant was Dr. Jones, a retired middle school principal. Growing up, Dr. Jones was fortunate to have Black women teachers and school leaders who cared for her and set high academic standards. As a result, she loved going to school and at an early age was identified as "gifted." She was on the honor roll throughout her K–12 experience, and Black women educators were her role models. After college, Dr. Jones spent several years in the telecommunications industry. And after the birth of her daughter, she decided to switch careers and became a teacher. She shared, "Once I had my daughter, I was inspired to do more and wanted to have a greater impact, and education just seemed like the right place for me." However, when she returned to the schoolhouse, the Black women teachers and school leaders who had helped her to learn and grow were a distant memory. In their place were teachers and systems that were foreign to her. Dr. Jones explained how many of the instructional practices she encountered as a teacher were "very institutionalized and further marginalized our children." She also noted how "the majority of teachers were White women and how they were treating our children was indicative of why there is a school to prison pipeline." So, after a few years as a classroom teacher, Dr. Jones founded a small middle school in conjunction with the city's Department of Education. During both of these conversations it became clear that Black women school leaders act "In Loco Parentis" and work diligently to transform schools into safe and loving spaces wherein *all* students can and will learn and grow.

I am a Teacher First. In response to the question, "How would you describe your role as an instructional leader?" Dr. Jones explained,

> I am a firm believer that the only way you can be a great instructional leader is that you still have to be tied to the classroom, so you can't remove yourself from being a teacher and a student. So, the way that I approached my work was I was always in the classroom. You would not find me in my office unless there was a meeting that had to be conducted or there was a call that I had to return. I literally lived inside the classrooms for the purpose of observing how the teacher delivered instruction, but also to see how the students are engaging. I wanted to know what the scholars' experience was in the classroom, and how their needs were being met.

Based on her time as a classroom teacher, Dr. Jones knew "there were better models for effective instruction, and I wanted to exemplify that." Further, as an instructional supervisor, Dr. Jones made a point of asking teachers to record themselves in the classroom. She wanted teachers to see when they made a slam dunk—and when they missed the shot. More importantly, she wanted them to learn how to improve their pedagogy. She often reviewed tapes with teachers and had teachers review one another's tapes. This way, everyone learned together—the teachers as well as the students. Dr. Jones was a teacher, first, and she established a culture wherein every teacher was an instructional leader: they learned with and from one another to improve student learning.

As an instructional supervisor in a middle school, Ms. Smith meets with teachers individually to review student work and to help them establish learning goals for each student. During faculty meetings, she explains why it is important for teachers to know who their students are as learners and to encourage group work, a strategy she often used when she was a teacher. Ms. Smith is a still a teacher, even in her current administrative role, and is known to assist other teachers in the classroom—even when she is observing them. She requires teachers and students alike to believe in themselves and to set high standards. She also encourages teachers not to teach to the state mandated test(s). Instead, Ms. Smith helps them unpack grade-level expectations and demonstrates how they should use those concepts as the basis for instruction based on their students' sociocultural identities and lived experiences, a best practice she learned when she was in the classroom full-time.

Further, during department meetings, Ms. Smith requires teachers to work on problems based on the same state-level exam(s) that their students will take. She does this so that teachers will know what their students are expected to know. She observed, "The real work is having teachers solve [math] problems. And sometimes they get stuck ... Our math department has come together because there's so much humility." For Ms. Smith, teaching and learning are humble and communal endeavors and it shows in her approach to instructional leadership. These Black women school leaders made it clear, "I am a Teacher First" and set high academic standards for their teachers and their students.

I Know You See Me. As a school leader/instructional leader, Ms. Smith knows that being a Black woman is an important factor in how her school-community perceives her. This has made her transparent. That is, when dealing with students, teachers, and parents, she is very forthcoming. She shares what she knows as well as her limitations and makes her expectations clear. Because of this, she is trusted by all stakeholders, especially teachers. In response to the question, "How, if at all, does race and gender impact your instructional leadership practices?" Ms. Smith explained,

> When I first got to [the school], there were no Black leaders and it wasn't like an aspiration of mine; you know, in my mind, I was like, I'm gonna be a dean, because you know that's where they put all the Black women and men who can manage a class. I remember my former school leader telling me, "You're not gonna be a dean. That's where they want to put all people of color who can manage kids. Go the instructional route." And I'm forever grateful for that because I would have never thought about that ... There's a lot riding on me right now and maybe I'm putting that pressure on myself. But being a Black woman from where I'm from ... and knowing that I'm the first Black woman to lead my school since it was founded in 2002, that's super-duper important for me.

Ms. Smith is managing a great deal in her new role and knows that there are people rooting for her, especially the young teachers that she has recently hired to help change the culture of the school. She meets with them frequently to review student progress and works hard to forge relationships with all stakeholders.

Reflecting on her time as a school leader, Dr. Jones knew that her race and gender impacted how teachers, in particular, perceived her. Like Ms. Smith, Dr. Jones made it a point to be transparent. However, when she was intentional and clear with teachers, she was perceived as being "angry" by some of her White teachers and staff. She explained how her actions "came off a little bit as attitudinal." She recalled how when redirecting a White male teacher's pedagogical practice, he would always feel challenged just because she said it. Meaning, the teacher could hear and receive the same language/message from another White male and be fine with it. Yet, when Dr. Jones said the exact same thing, the teacher would be offended. She noted,

> I had to deal with a lot of White fragility . . . I had to police what I said because folks [White teachers] take things out of context; they get very emotional. Yet, when they want to say things that are very curt or undermining, they don't police what they say, especially in open forums. So, I find that there is often an unkind way of acknowledging Black women in any leadership position, and we always have to prove ourselves. We can never say we don't know.

Thus, as Lomotey (2019) has noted, Black women view race as a significant factor in their leadership. And Black women school leaders know that they must navigate racist, sexist, and other hostile environments, which results in lived experiences that are nuanced and distinct from those of other women and men.

Last, Dr. Jones shared that because of the constant pressure she faced as a school leader/instructional leader, her health suffered and she became so physically ill that she had to resign from her position in the spring of 2021. During a doctor's visit at the beginning of the year, she was faced with some hard truths. Dr. Jones shared,

> The doctors were like, okay, "So, here are your three options. You'll either have to have dialysis, a kidney transplant, or prepare for an early death. Those are your three options because at this point with your body and the work that you're doing there is no way of saving you from what's going to happen."

Upon hearing those words, Jones said she knew what she had to do. She made an "executive decision" and resigned. She had a choice to make—the schoolhouse or life—and she chose to live. Many contemporary Black women leaders exhibit some of the same leadership characteristics as pre-*Brown* Black women leaders. They also face some of the same attitudes about their ability based on race and gender. As a result, by and large, Black women school leaders remain marginalized in the schoolhouse, and the blatant disregard they experience for their person and position makes them say, "I Know You See Me!"

RECOMMENDATIONS

Despite legal mandates to desegregate schools, numerous school-reform efforts, and federal funding to close the racial achievement gap, the nation's public schools remain "separate and unequal." Black children, in particular, are not provided with an equal opportunity to learn. However, research has proven that Black women school leaders are vital to the educational success of Black students. Dr. Geneva Gay, a former high school teacher and highly recognized education professor, defines effective pedagogy as validating, comprehensive and inclusive, multidimensional, empowering, transformative, emancipatory, humanistic, normative, and ethical (2018). Gay crafted a praxis of culturally responsive teaching grounded in four critical aspects (caring, communication, curriculum, and instruction). This emancipatory framework is designed to empower both the teacher and the student. Moreover, Gay's culturally responsive teaching paradigm aligns with Collins's tenets of BFT (the lived experience; the use of dialogue to assess knowledge claims; the ethics of caring; and the ethic of personal accountability) as it builds on the personal story and centers the use of dialogue and culture in the classroom to improve instruction. Both constructs, culturally responsive teaching and BFT, are grounded in care and, as noted in the literature on Black women school / instructional leaders and in our conversation with Black women school leaders, has fueled their efficacy as instructional leaders and supervisors (see Figure 13.1).

The following recommendations reflect BFT's tenet of personal accountability that says, "you must be accountable for your knowledge claims" (Collins, 2000, p. 265) and are proffered with this in mind:

1. *In Loco Parentis.* It is important that school leaders remind teachers as well as staff members of their legal responsibility to afford *all* students with a standard of care. Schools must be safe and loving spaces if young people are to learn and grow. Educators have a legal and moral obligation to practice care, particularly with historically marginalized children and their families.
2. *I Am a Teacher First.* It is important that school / instructional leaders encourage teachers to: (a) use group work as well as individual instruction; (b) rid themselves of low expectations and deficit mental models of Black students; (c) avoid teaching to the mandated test(s);

Figure 13.1.

Gay (2018)	Collins (2000)	Findings
Caring	the lived experience	Standard of Care
Communication	the use of dialogue	Meaningful Instruction
Curriculum	the ethics of caring	Engage Black Women / Leaders
Instruction	personal accountability	Transform Leadership Preparation

rather, teachers must help students understand concepts and use culturally relevant modes of pedagogy; (d) create multiple entry points for learning and help all students to love learning; and (e) possess a passion for their subject and fill each day with care, laughter, and most importantly, learning.
3. *I Know You See Me.* Black women school leaders, because of their race and gender, face challenges in the schoolhouse that oftentimes go unaddressed. This marginalizes their trauma and is the cause of burnout, depression, and feelings of powerlessness. As a remedy, mentorship, affinity groups, and professional counseling should be offered to support and sustain Black women school leaders and to counteract the impact of racism and the hostile work environments they encounter daily in the spaces that we call schools.
4. *Engage Black mothers and othermothers in meaningful ways in the schoolhouse.* As noted, we believe the relationship between Black women and the schoolhouse is central to the academic success of Black children. Schools must recognize this fact and school leaders must build on the efficacy and cultural wealth Black women possess and engage Black mothers and othermothers in meaningful ways in the schoolhouse.
5. *Create leadership-preparation courses that highlight the praxis of Black feminism in the schoolhouse.* As noted, despite their longstanding contributions to the academic success and overall well-being of Black students, the perspectives of Black women are largely omitted from education research. Leadership-preparation courses must include the study of the lived experiences of historical and contemporary Black women school leaders and othermothers to inform and improve the preparation of school leaders, especially those future leaders who are most likely to lead in low-income, urban school districts attended predominantly by Black students.

CONCLUSION

Overall, the current discussions and research on school/instructional leadership are steeped in whiteness and obscure the lived experiences and contributions of Black women to the schoolhouse and to Black student achievement. As the nation's racial demographics continue to shift, we cannot afford to educate only *some* students. This means that new and different epistemologies for knowing, teaching, learning, and leadership for the schoolhouse are vital. Black women are essential to this needed change. Longstanding and deficit mental models of Black women in schools and society fuel an anti-Blackness that is palpable in the harsh realities that Black women principals face and evident in the harmful experiences and dismal academic outcomes of Black children in schools across the United

States. We must do and be better, and Black women/Black women school leaders can help. We must do and be better, and Black women/Black women school leaders can play a critical and much needed role. We must include Black women and Black feminist perspectives in our conversations, the schoolhouse, and in college and university leadership-preparation programs.

REFERENCES

Alston, J. A., & Jones, S. N. (2002). Carrying the torch of the Jeanes Supervisors: 21st-century African American female superintendents and servant leadership. In B. Cooper & L. Fusarelli (Eds.), *The promises and perils facing today's school superintendent* (pp. 65–75). Scarecrow Press.

Alston, J. A., & McClellan, P. A. (2011). *Herstories: Leading with the lessons of the lives of Black women activists*. Peter Lang.

Bloom, C. M., & Erlandson, D. A. (2003). African American women principals in urban schools: Realities, (re)constructions, and resolutions. *Educational Administration Quarterly, 39*, 339–369

Bolman, L. G., & Deal. T. E. (1997). *Reframing organizations: Artistry, choice, and leadership*. (2nd ed.). Jossey-Bass.

Bowers, A. J., & White, B. R. (2014). Do principal preparation and teacher qualifications influence different types of school growth trajectories in Illinois: A growth mixture model analysis. *Journal of Educational Administration, 52*(5), 705–736.

Brazer. S. D., & Bauer, S. C. (2013). Preparing instructional leaders: A model. *Educational Administration Quarterly, 49*(4), 645–684.

Brooks, J. S., & Watson, T. N. (2018). School leadership and racism: An ecological perspective. *Urban Education*, 1–25.

Brown v. Board of Education of Topeka, Shawnee County, Kansas. 347 U. S. 483, 74 S. Ct. 686 (1954).

Coleman, J. S., Campbell, E. Q., Hobson, C. J., McPartland, J., Mood, A. M., Weinfeld, F. D., & York, R. L. (1966). *Equality of educational opportunity*. U. S. Government Printing Office.

Collins, P. H. (1989). The social construction of Black feminist thought. *Signs: Journal of Women in Culture and Society, 14*(4), 745–773. https://doi.org/10.1086/494543

Collins, P. H. (2000). *Black feminist thought: Knowledge, consciousness, and the politics of empowerment*. Routledge.

Combahee River Collective. (1977). The Combahee River collective statement. In J. Ritchie & K. Ronald (Eds.), *Available means: An anthology of women's rhetoric(s)* (pp. 292–300). University of Pittsburgh Press. https://doi.org/10.2307/j.ctt5hjqnj.50

Cooper, A. J. (1988). *A voice from the South*. Oxford University Press. (Original work published 1892).

Coppin, F. J. (1913). *Reminiscences of school life, and hints of teaching*. African Methodist Episcopal Book Concern.

Cox, C. F. (2022) *Through the disciplinary looking glass: Examining the impact of the adultification of Black adolescent girls through the perspectives of New York State school administrators* [Doctoral Dissertation, St. John Fisher University]. https://fisherpub.sjf.edu/education_etd/544/

Dantley, M. E., & Tillman, L. C. (2005). Social justice and moral/transformative leadership. In C. Marshall & M. Oliva (Eds.), *Leadership for social justice: Making revolutions in education* (pp. 16–30). Allyn & Bacon.

Davis, A. Y. (1983). *Women, race, and class*. Vintage.

Dumas, M. (2014). 'Losing an arm': Schooling as a site of black suffering. *Race Ethnicity and Education, 17*(1), 1–29.

Edmonds, R. (1979). Effective schools for the urban poor. *Educational Leadership, 37*, 15–24.

Farkas, S., Johnson, J., & Duffett, A. (2003). *Rolling up their sleeves: Superintendents and principals talk about what's needed to fix public schools*. Wallace Foundation.

Franklin, V. P. (1990). "They rose and fell together": African American educators and community leadership, 1795-1954. *Journal of Education, 172*(3), 39–64.

Gay, G. (2018). *Culturally responsive teaching: Theory, research, and practice*.

Gooden, M. A., and Dantley, M. (2012). Centering race in a framework for leadership preparation. *Journal of Research on Leadership Education, 7* (2), 237–253. https://doi.org/10.1177/1942775112455266

Hallinger, P. (2018). Principal instructional leadership: From prescription to theory to practice. In G. E. Hall, L. F. Quinn, & D. M. Gollnick (Eds.), *The Wiley handbook of teaching and learning* (505–528). John Wiley & Sons.

hooks, b. (1984). *Feminist theory: From margin to center*. Pluto Press.

hooks, b. (2000). *Feminism is for everybody: Passionate politics*. South End Press

Jang, S. T., & Alexander, N. A. (2022). Black women principals in American secondary schools: Quantitative evidence of the link between their leadership and student achievement. *Educational Administration Quarterly, 58*(3). 450–486.

Justice, B. (2023). Schooling as a white good. *History of Education Quarterly, 63*(2), 154–178.

Ladson-Billings, G. (2018). The social funding of race: the role of schooling. *Peabody Journal of Education, 93*(1), 90–105.

Leithwood, K., & Duke, L. (1999). A century's quest to understand school leadership. In J. Murphy & K. Seashore Louis (Eds.), *The handbook of research on educational administration* (2nd ed., pp. 45–72). Jossey-Bass.

Leithwood, K. A., & Riehl, C. (2003). *What we know about successful school leadership*. Laboratory for Student Success, Temple University.

Lomotey, K. (2019). Research on the leadership of Black women principals: Implications for Black students. *Educational Researcher, 48*(6), pp. 336–348.

Lorde, A. (1984). *Sister outsider*. Crossing Press.

McCluskey, A. T. (2014). *A forgotten sisterhood: Pioneering Black women educators and activists in the Jim Crow south*. Rowman & Littlefield.

Morrison, T. (1987). *Beloved*. Random House.

Moynihan, D. (1965). *The Negro family. The case for national action*. Viking.

Perkins, L. (1987). *Fannie Jackson Coppin and the Institute for Colored Youth, 1865–1902*. Garland.

Peters, A. L. (2012). Leading through the challenge of change: African-American women principals on small school reform. *International Journal of Qualitative Studies in Education, 25*(1), 23–38. https://doi.org/10.1080/09518398.2011.647722

Roberts v. Boston, 59 Mass. (5 Cush.) 198. (1850).

Stewart, A. (2015). *First class: The legacy of Dunbar, America's first Black public high school*. Chicago Review Press.

Tillman, L.C. (2002). Culturally sensitive research approaches: An African American perspective. *Educational Researcher, 31*(9), 3–12.

Tillman, L. C. (2003). From rhetoric to reality? Educational administration and the lack of racial and ethnic diversity within the profession. *University Council for Educational Administration Review, 45*(3), 1–4.

Tillman, L. C. (2004a). African American parental involvement in a post-*Brown* era: Facilitating the academic achievement of African American students. *Journal of School Public Relations, 25*(2), 161–176.

Tillman, L. C. (2004b). (Un)intended Consequences?: The impact of the *Brown v. Board of Education* decision on the employment status of Black educators. *Education and Urban Society, 36*(3), 280–303.

Tillman, L. C. (2020). Has our rhetoric moved to reality? Continuing the work to achieve racial diversity and racial justice. *UCEA Review*, 1–5.

Watson, T. N., & Rivera-McCutchen, R. L. (2016). #BlackLivesMatter: A call for transformative leadership. *Journal of Cases in Educational Leadership, 19*(2), 3 11. https://doi.org/10.1177/1555458915626759

Watson, T. N., & McClellan, P. (2020). The impact of Black women leaders on student achievement. In *The Oxford research encyclopedia of education*. https://oxfordre.com/education/view/10.1093/acrefore/9780190264093.001.0001/acrefore-9780190264093-e-602

Weiner, J., Cyr, D. & Burton, L. (2022). A study of Black female principals leading through twin pandemics. *Journal of Education Human Resources, 40*(3), 335–359.

Williams, H. A. (2005). *Self-taught—African American education in slavery and freedom*. The University of North Carolina Press.

Wilson, C. M. (2016). Enacting critical care and transformative leadership in schools highly impacted by poverty: An African-American principal's counter narrative. *International Journal of Leadership in Education, 19*(5), 557–577, https://doi.org/10.1080/13603124.2015.1023360

CHAPTER 14

Supervision Redux
Leaders With Teachers Activate Culturally Responsive Practices

Lynda Tredway and Matt Militello

School leaders who supervise teachers can promote school improvement by conducting classroom observations and post-observation conversations to determine content for schoolwide professional learning and establish effective teacher evaluation processes (Grissom et al., 2021a, 2021b). To achieve these interrelated goals, school leaders need a firm grounding in research-based pedagogy, learning theory, teaching standards, curriculum, and adult coaching practices. In observing teachers, leaders wear two necessary hats: supervision (formative) and evaluation (summative). While these functions are different, principals who understand the interconnection are more effective instructional leaders (Mette et al., 2017). By grounding supervision practices in Community Learning Exchange (CLE) processes that set the necessary conditions for effective supervision and by focusing on evidence-based observations that support equitable access and rigor, leaders *with* teachers can re-shape classroom instruction. If leaders practice culturally responsive supervision and model the very practices they want to see in classrooms, they can be effective instructional leaders of equity (Radd et al., 2021).

In recent years, walkthroughs and instructional rounds (IRs) have occupied the time and attention of school and district leaders; their central purpose is to capture evidence about schoolwide instructional practices so leaders can support teacher change (City et al., 2009; Teitel, 2013). However, while school leaders may become more aware of schoolwide instructional practices (David, 2007; Marsh et al., 2005; Protheroe, 2009), walkthrough protocols and IRs typically rely on inadequate evidence for supporting individual teachers. Principals and district supervisors find the practices useful, but teachers report feelings of anxiety and judgment (Supovitz & Weathers, 2004; Valli & Buese, 2007). In particular, IRs help to de-privatize teaching and promote collaborative practices, but teachers do not tend to change their teaching practices as a result of IR feedback (Melvin, 2017). In our experience, the processes provide helicopter views of a school; however, as tools for changing individual teaching practices, they are imprecise and ineffectual because the strategies do not engage individual teachers based on their particular learning needs. To date, walkthroughs and instructional rounds have not necessarily been found to change individual teacher practices or correlate to substantial school improvement (Grissom et al., 2013).

Thus, if, in their supervisor and evaluator roles, instructional leaders establish the necessary conditions for teacher improvement, they can more effectively attend to individual teacher growth and development by implementing regular short observations and conversations that use classroom data as a primary source of improvement (Grissom & Youngs, 2016; Goldring et al., 2020; Neumerski et al., 2018). According to evidence from multiple participatory action research studies, effective school leaders used Community Learning Exchange processes to work with teachers to set up the necessary conditions for durable change in teacher practices. By attending to educator self-care and garnering relational trust with and among teachers, these leaders engaged teachers in using evidence from classrooms to improve individual practices and concurrently facilitated professional learning responsive to the needs of a particular school (Zepeda, 2017). As facilitators of schoolwide professional learning, the leaders used processes that mirrored classroom expectations (e.g., common instructional language, culturally responsive practices, equitable academic discourse, and experiential learning) to promote a climate for continuous professional learning (Yurmovsky et al., 2020).

In this chapter, we focus on the necessary conditions for schoolwide improvement and the formative tools and processes school leaders can use to maintain a steady diet of evidence-based observations and coaching conversations with teachers. Using CLE processes to build and nurture relational trust for adult learners, school leaders can establish the necessary conditions for useful supervision practices with individual teachers. Not only do the practices provide a stronger basis for evaluation and schoolwide professional learning experiences—they support leaders and teachers in reimagining organizational routines and taking charge of their individual and collective professional improvement (Spillane & Coldren, 2011; Spillane et al., 2013).

SUPERVISION REDUX: SETTING THE NECESSARY CONDITIONS

If school change is to have a lasting impact, leaders need to attend to learning for adult educators that promotes culturally responsive classroom instructional practices and supports the autonomy and authority they need to make changes. The Community Learning Exchange framework anchors our work with school and district leaders in Indigenous practices that amplify the role of the individuals closest to the work as the decisionmakers (see Figure 14.1). By coupling the CLE axioms as processes for more effective supervision practices, we have found compelling evidence that these practices show promise for achieving enduring and equitable changes in schools and communities. The axioms provide guidance

Figure 14.1. Community Learning Exchange Axioms

1. Learning and leadership are dynamic social processes.
2. Conversations are critical and central pedagogical processes.
3. The people closest to the issues are best situated to discover answers to local concerns.
4. Crossing boundaries enriches development and the educational processes.
5. Hopes and change are built on assets and dreams of locals and their communities.

Source: Adapted from Guajardo et al. (2016).

in establishing and maintaining the conditions necessary for school improvement efforts.

Thus, an effective supervision redux requires that we engage in particular processes that aid leaders in setting up the necessary conditions in which they can more effectively use classroom evidence to support teachers and bolster equity-driven culturally responsive classroom practices. By promoting self-care for social justice educators, leaders learn how to nurture a trusting climate and mutual responsibility for achieving equitable outcomes. Through storytelling, school leaders with teachers humanize the systems world of schools by articulating how their values intersect with their professional settings (Sergiovanni, 2000). Finally, school leaders themselves need supportive structures to implement practices that augment teacher responsibility for classroom changes. Just as teachers want students to take more responsibility for their learning, school leaders need to ensure that teachers have the autonomy to make decisions about self-improvement.

Self-Care for Social Justice Educators

Self-care means gathering collective resources to engage in the complex work of social justice educators. Through co-creating *espacio sano* (Velasco, 2021)—a healthy space for social justice leaders—leaders use dynamic mindfulness, personal narratives, and CLE protocols to co-create and gain strength to meet daily challenges. Dynamic mindfulness (DM) as a daily practice supports everyone in improving their abilities to interact and manage stress (Bose et al., 2017; Diamond & Ling, 2020), and personal narratives offer a storytelling space that liberates all voices (Militello et al., 2020). Through DM and personal narratives, leaders establish the conditions necessary for cultivating and sustaining trust as a critical resource for change (Grubb, 2009) and engage in culturally responsive and sustaining pedagogical practices (Paris & Alim, 2017) that help adults maintain forward motion for school improvement (Irby, 2020).

When leaders themselves experience practices and pedagogies that promote relational trust and equitable teaching and learning, they transfer the practices to support teachers—first with small teacher groups and then with the entire faculty. Our graduate students used CLE protocols to promote dialogical learning and engage teachers in collaboratively analyzing their work (Britt, 2023; James, 2023; Machado, 2019). Because of external accountability pressure, insiders' autonomy has often been compromised; we need a reset on relational trust as a crucial resource for developing practices, skills, and dispositions of instructional leaders collaborating with teachers to effect change. Only then can the leader activate the vital resources residing inside our schools—most importantly, teacher knowledge, skills, and dispositions. The power of practitioners learning and deciding together is a necessary catalyst for change in each local context (Ahn et al., 2021).

Storytelling as a Humanizing Act

Specific meeting-facilitation processes strengthen educators in using storytelling as a critical tool for activating educators' sense of purpose and possibility. Using personal narratives as a consistent process, participants articulate their beliefs about self and the power of feeling held in a community; then, they can actively co-create processes to improve their work in classrooms (Drago-Severson, 2012; Militello et al., 2020). For example, in the poem "Patience," participants identify and discuss with a partner one phrase that exemplifies their roles as leaders or teachers in "holding space" for each other to carry on the work of justice.

> *A light-giving astronomical trio*
> *Gaze at us from separate distances*
> *Cycles of day and night*
> *Far and near, embracing the daily and eternal*
>
> *Mars, the moon, and Regulus*
> *Dancing the December waltz in the night sky*
> *Ancient rhythms teaching us a trio of steps*
> *That touch the chord of memory*
>
> *Mars moments at sunup and sundown*
> *The hot mama planet of the sky*
> *Red orange fireplace poker*
> *Prodding us to share our deep secrets*
>
> *Moon friend in a blue moon month*
> *Close and luminescent*
> *With its face and phases*
> *Turning day to night and night to day*
>
> *Eighty light years away—amulet in Leo's mane*
> *The 1929 singular glow of Regulus*
> *From depression to this recession*
> *Cycle of life's economy remind us to mind our store*

Beckon us to move with the message
Grab the day and the night
Hold each other as close as breath
—Poem by Lynda Tredway (see https://education
.ecu.edu/projecti4/resources/ for other team reflections)

Personal narrative use fosters intimate and insightful conversations; as leaders and teachers learn about one other's lives and beliefs, they reconnect to their moral imperatives. As they relate their life worlds and recognize how technical school and district systems have intruded on the purposes of school (Sergiovanni, 2000), participants derive a renewed sense of organizational glue for tackling school improvement together.

Support Groups for School Leaders

In the participatory action research studies of EdD students, school leaders in communities of practice have enacted their values (Argyris & Schon, 1974; Lave, 1996). When school leaders communicate with critical friends and share dilemmas of practice with colleagues, they galvanize their principles of social justice and culturally responsive practices. For example, in a study of six Filipino-American school principals who examined Filipino cultural principles, the spirit of *bayanihan* (communalism) supported individuals in leadership roles to feel authentic, supported, and safe (Caruz, 2023). In an affinity group of White women school leaders in rural North Carolina, four women "had each other's backs" as they activated teacher improvement through equitable and culturally responsive practices observation practices (Britt, 2023; James, 2023; Morris, 2023; Mudd, 2023; Parker; 2023). Tang (2023) worked with four principals whom he supervised; through personal narratives and CLE processes, each principal enacted culturally responsive practices á la Khalifa (2018) in their schools. Payne (2023) organized K–12 school leaders in a Taiwanese international school to determine and enact appropriate culturally responsive practices.

School leaders need spaces that support critical reflection so that they can fully show up as leaders of equity and justice and institute similar practices for others. Self-care, personal narrative stories, and educator support groups offer critical tools for ensuring connection and sustenance. The practices create the necessary conditions for change. However, unless leaders change the ways they conduct and use classroom evidence *with teachers,* we do not foresee changes in teacher practice at the classroom level.

SCHOOLWIDE SHIFTS DEPEND ON CHANGING INDIVIDUAL TEACHER PRACTICE

Leaders who set up the necessary conditions for teachers can fully embody their quests to be equity-driven instructional leaders; as a result, they accelerate shifts in teacher practice by using thoughtful processes to address classroom practices (Gomell et al., 2022; Russell et al., 2017; Wong et al., 2021; Woo & Hendriksen, 2023). In our work and our framing of instructional supervision, we re-establish a central supervisory theory of action: *If a school leader establishes the necessary conditions for trusting collaboration and relies on evidence-based observation and conversations, teachers make and enact decisions about improvements that benefit individual and collective change.* However, the shift to incorporating teacher input requires a re-examination of long-standing supervision practices that often do not fully engage teachers as adult learners in making change decisions. Though it originated as "clinical supervision" (Acheson & Gall, 1980, 2003; Gall & Acheson, 2013), Cogan (1973) defined this term as "the rationale and the practice designed to improve the teacher's classroom performance" (p. 9). Multiple practitioners and researchers cultivated and used supervision practices (Glanz & Sullivan, 2000; Glickman et al., 2010; Goldhammer, 1969; Goldhammer et al., 1993; Marshall, 2009; Sergiovanni & Starratt, 2007; Sullivan & Glanz, 2013; Zepeda, 2017).

However, while Cogan (1973) maintained that "*clinical* was designed both to denote and connote the salient operational and empirical aspects of supervision in the classroom" (italics in the original, p. 9), teachers often viewed, and view, the process as inspection; and much like the documented issues with walkthroughs and instructional rounds, these practices may unwittingly signal surveillance instead of support (Ingersoll, 2003). Perhaps practitioners shied away from the clinical supervision processes because of the connotation of the term "clinical." Whatever the historical reasons, the evidence-based and research-based practices in the original forms of clinical supervision never reached the audiences that most needed them—school leaders. In fact, school leader preparation programs often reinforced the form-based, technical, regulatory, and oppressive nature of clinical supervision. By adhering to the CLE principles of democratic, locally driven dialogue, we can eliminate feelings of regulation, direction, and control that some observation tools and post-observation conversations communicate (Guajardo et al., 2016). We propose collaborative, asset-based approaches for improving practice as the supervisor observes, guides, and coaches. Then, and only then, can the school leader, with individuals and then groups of teachers, decide about and facilitate schoolwide improvement (Grissom et al., 2021a).

To do so, we need to reconsider the best attributes of clinical supervision—the formative function for supporting teacher growth. With this focus, instructional leaders using qualitative evidence for individual conversations with teachers can more effectively ensure equitable access and rigor (Drago-Severson & Blum-DeStefano, 2016; Tredway et al., 2021b). To use classroom data effectively following the tenets of adult learning theory, a collegial relationship between the teacher and supervisor is foundational so that they share joint responsibility for decisions (Drago-Severson, 2012; Glickman, 2002). Even if a supervisor has positive intentions in giving feedback, and "even if [the teacher] acts upon the supervisor's decision in good faith, [the teacher] may be unable to carry out . . . a plan of action he[/she/they] has not helped create and does not understand" (Cogan, 1973, p. 27).

Thus, we can then address two other functions of effective instructional leadership—professional learning using schoolwide evidence, and evaluation for human resource purposes—which both rest on the fundamentals of evidence-based observations and effective conversations. By relying on the humanizing philosophy and practices of CLE axioms and processes, we can change the grammar of school supervision from top-down to collaborative and from feedback to dialogical learning for leaders and teachers (Guajardo et al., 2016; Tyack & Cuban, 1998).

Re-imagining Evidence-Based Observations

Specifically, at the classroom level, school leaders should focus their instructional supervision on evidence (not perception) for conversations (not feedback), using coaching practices to guide the teacher's decisions.

- Evidence: Qualitative data using selective verbatim scripting with a coding structure that leaders and teachers collaboratively agree to use (Saldaña, 2016; Tredway et al., 2021b).
- Conversation: A reflective process in which the instructional leader discusses the observation evidence with the teacher, who chooses the improvement focus for subsequent observations (Tredway et al., 2019).
- Coaching: Using collaborative coaching techniques to co-examine evidence and guide teacher analysis and decision-making (Glickman et al., 2001; Gomell et al., 2022).

In our work with school leaders, we focus the observations and conversations on equitable access and rigor by emphasizing culturally responsive teaching and learning practices. When instructional leaders choose common tools for observation and coaching conversations, they mediate teacher learning (Wise & Jacobo, 2010; Wong et al., 2021) in which the teacher and leader engage in sensemaking and "sensegiving" (Norris, 2022). By making sense of observational data together, leaders can actively "give sense" through "utilizing data to work closely alongside teachers to build aspirational cultures" (p. 136). Evidence-based supervision practices underscore processes that build everyone's capacity for equitable vision and actions, and iterative observations and conversations provide the necessary conditions for culturally responsive supervision.

We support what Rowen and Raudenbush (2016) urge—the optimal use of information-rich observations. When a school leader uses observation tools that provide specific and actionable evidence of instructional practices, the leader can guide teachers to emphasize equitable access and active participation of all students (Fritz & Miller, 2003). As Grissom et al. (2021a) posit: to improve teaching practices, a principal should facilitate productive collaboration in professional learning communities by promoting teachers working together authentically with systems of support. By engaging in instructionally focused interactions based on specific evidence from individual classrooms, school leaders build trust and teacher agency to decide how to change and how to publicly share their practices in teacher groups (Ahn et al., 2021). To focus on instructional practice, leaders should establish a data-driven, schoolwide instructional program to facilitate interactions in professional learning communities.

Much like the charge in *Street Data* (Safir & Dugan, 2021), using normal qualitative evidence available in all classrooms ensures that school leaders and instructional coaches have the knowledge and skills to collect evidence and analyze evidence effectively with an equity lens. The Zepeda (2017) and Saphier (1993) tools are more in line with the intent of the Acheson and Gall (1992, 2003) practices that we use and support. Only by collecting selective verbatim data and coding can leaders facilitate evidence-based conversations and guide teachers to make informed choices about the next steps for improvement. As a result, school leaders can more effectively observe, model conversations that lead to improved equitable practices, and determine, with teachers, areas of professional learning for the staff.

Designing the Tools

To develop the tools for short observations, we collected and analyzed evidence from 30 PK–12 classrooms. The aggregate results included inattention to the basics of equitable access and rigor—inadequate or no "think time" after a teacher posed a question, inconsistent use of Think Pair Share (TPS), hand-raising as the primary means of calling on students—a strategy that results in inequitable participation, students blurting out responses with teachers accepting those outbursts, and low-level cognitive demand. Even when teachers used such strategies as "equity sticks," we found, students did not have adequate "think time" before teachers chose a popsicle stick with a student's name as a cold call. Rarely did teachers ask probing questions. More often than not, teachers asked a question, offered no think time, and told students to "turn and talk." Some students turned to someone or several people; some appeared to discuss the question, but many just said nothing—all of these seemingly incoherent practices contrary to advice about using TPS (Lyman et al., 2023). That advice is clear: (1) When teachers systematically prepare students to think before they participate in paired conversations, the students learn through conversation and are more willing to contribute to full class discussions; and (2) when teachers engage students in developing questions, they gain autonomy over their learning. Brain research fortifies these practices: Students who engage in dialogue process information differently, are more motivated, and are more likely to remember what they learn (Driscoll, 1994; Hammond, 2015; National Academy of Sciences, 2018; Resnick et al., 2015).

Secondly, teachers used inconsistent question forms and asked questions at a low cognitive level. They often used a yes/no question format or changed a statement to a question mid-sentence—a "fill in the blank question." They frequently began questions with "Does anybody know . . ." or ask "what is" or "who is" questions instead of "why" or "which" questions that require analysis or synthesis. The latter kind of shift to higher-order thinking is a prime equity issue.

Typically, the cognitive demand of questions at the recall or factual level required no analysis. The teachers often accepted one-word answers instead of substantial responses and did not use the student responses to ask probing questions.

Based on the classroom observations, we initially developed three equity-driven observation tools to improve more equitable and rigorous academic discourse in classrooms: Calling-On, Question Form, and Question Level. To use the tools, school leaders take selective verbatim notes in a classroom (10–12 minutes), code or name practices and tabulate the code frequency (12–15 min), then share the data with the teacher (see Tables 14.1 and 14.2). The tools seem deceptively simplistic at first glance; however, 225 school leaders who participated in a national project over 5 years used them to improve teachers' practices. When observers gain complete facility with scripting and naming students with identifiers of gender or race and tabulating the number of codes, teachers can see exactly what happened and identify what they need to shift to in their practices. As one principal remarked, "Before I was just doing what had been done to me. Now I have tools to have effective conversations with teachers" (Tredway et al., 2021b, p. 56).

Selective verbatim scripts—capturing the classroom processes and dialogue, particularly what the teacher does or says and how the students respond—provide valuable qualitative evidence. As a result, the observer codes the classroom data, and the observer and teacher have specific—and irrefutable—evidence for having a fruitful conversation—what Safir and Dugan (2021) term "street data" and Cobb et al. (2011) call "pragmatic evidence." By using evidence and engaging teachers in ongoing, constructivist professional learning, teachers decide what to change and school leaders model how to increase equitable access and rigor and organize learning democratically (Boykin & Noguera, 2011; Glickman & Mette, 2020). Neumerski et al. (2018) found that using specific processes and tools for analyzing evidence from observations is useful for the school leader and the individual teachers; in addition, tools act as social and material mediators for collective learning and action (Wise & Jacobo, 2010; Wong et al., 2021). In this way, the leader and teachers become researchers of their work, and the people closest to the work gain autonomy to make individual and collective shifts in practice.

Flipping the Post-Observation Script: Conversations Not Feedback

In the post-observation process we designed, the school leader does not provide feedback; instead, the leader uses evidence to coach teachers who together decide on specific instructional improvement goals related to the evidence. Using the collaborative structure of the supervisory behavior continuum (see Figure 14.2) is the most appropriate stance for most conversations with teachers (Glickman et al., 2001). The observer's role is to guide and coach with an eye toward equitable access, cultural responsiveness, and academic rigor.

According to the CLE axioms, leading and learning are dynamic social processes that require conversations with those closest to the issue—in this case, the leader and teacher. We know that dialogue is the backbone of effective classroom

Table 14.1. Calling on Codes

CODE	CODE NAME	Teacher Actions
R	Raising hand	calls one student with raised hand
CC	Cold Call	cold calls on a student who did not volunteer
CCD	Cold Call Discipline	cold calls on a student for discipline
B-A	Blurt-out: Accept	accepts an answer that is blurted out by a student or students
B-I	Blurt-out: Ignore	ignores a student who blurts out an answer
C&R	Call & Response	intentionally prompts students to answer in unison
ES	Equity Strategy	Uses an equity strategy (i.e., choosing a name randomly—"equity stick")
TT	ThinkTime	TT = adjusts think time to level of questions (3–10 sec.) and only calls on student after adequate
NTT	No Think Time	NTT = No ThinkTime
TR	Teacher Repeats	repeats student response verbatim
TRV	Teacher ReVoices	revoices, teacher uses a student response to paraphrase and perhaps ask other questions. (Notice difference between simple repeat and revoicing)
TPS	Think-Pair-Share	asks students to think for appropriate think time, pair, and then share

Table 14.2. Script Excerpt with Codes

Time	Selective Verbatim	Code
1:30	In this equation, who knows what operation we should use first?	NTT
	Three students call out and T. accepts response. Teacher repeats what one student says.	B-A/ TR
1:31	What if I do this first? T. shows on board. Ronnie, what happens?	NTT/CC
	Ronnie can't answer. T. calls on 1 of 4 students with hands up	R

instruction (Vella, 2008) and should be the norm in conversations among adults (Drago-Severson, 2012). Leaders who used the "Guide to Effective Conversations" (Tredway et al., 2019) reported that the collaborative conversation process was the first time in their leadership careers that they finally knew how to facilitate a meaningful post-observation conversation (Tredway et al., 2021a, 2021b). If we want to see equitable and rigorous academic discourse in classrooms, then school leaders need to model collaborative learning structures and equitable dialogue about instruction with adults.

Figure 14.2. Continuum of Supervision

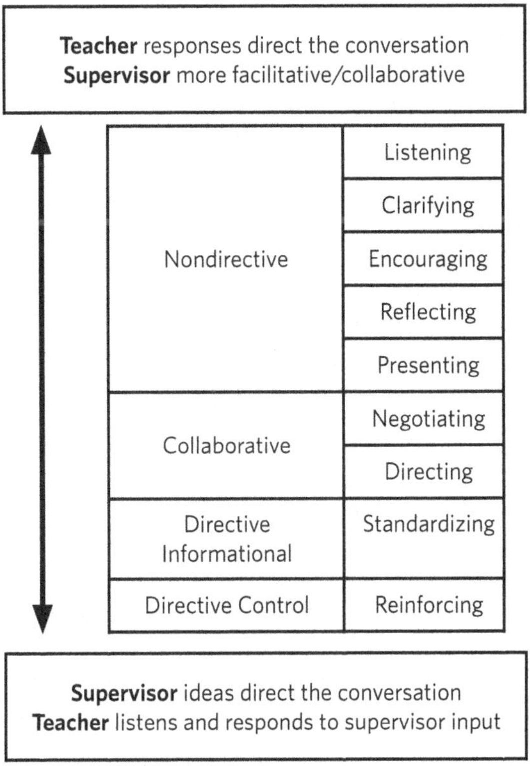

Nondirective	Listening
	Clarifying
	Encouraging
	Reflecting
	Presenting
Collaborative	Negotiating
	Directing
Directive Informational	Standardizing
Directive Control	Reinforcing

Teacher responses direct the conversation
Supervisor more facilitative/collaborative

Supervisor ideas direct the conversation
Teacher listens and responds to supervisor input

Source: Adapted from Glickman et al., 2001, pp. 126–127.

In the post-observation conversation, the school leader and teacher use the coded evidence to engage in a conversation (see Table 14.3). To prepare for the conversation, they substitute the ubiquitous and useless question about what the teacher feels about the lesson with a data-driven opening question that goes to the point of the observation. With practice and training, instructional supervisors apply coaching questions, insert suggestions about specific instructional strategies, and, if necessary, redirect responses to the evidence analysis. They periodically summarize to maintain focus on equitable access and rigor. To be clear, having nuanced conversations in which a school leader does not "give feedback" or tell the teacher what to change is not an easy shift. To effect iterative changes in the teaching practice, instructional leaders need to continue a steady set of short cycles of inquiry that include observations and conversations until teachers incorporate their decisions into their repertoire. However, following the tenets of adult learning (Drago-Severson, 2012; Knowles, 1980), each teacher needs to be in the driver's seat about deciding what to improve; however, to decide what to change, teachers need specific evidence from their classrooms. If a teacher decides on an individual improvement goal and the school leader has a plan to observe within a short period of time, iterative observations and conversations shift teacher practice.

Unlike the traditional approaches to walkthrough or instructional round feedback to staff, in which the teachers typically hear multiple ideas about what to change, an individual teacher may or may not take them to heart. As teachers in one study reported, this process was "tailormade" for their learning and improvement (Paryani, 2019). Because teachers have evidence-based realizations about their practices—including inequities—and decide what to change, the approach offers a possibility for improving equitable and culturally responsive teaching practices, and leaders have a clear process for having the equity conversations that have eluded them.

In multiple EdD participatory action research projects and studies, school leaders, with a small group of teachers, used iterative observations and gradually expanded to more staff. As a result, teachers substantially shifted their practices related to equitable access and rigor. One principal documented changes in four high school teachers as they increased equitable academic discourse over 14 months and three cycles of inquiry (Britt, 2023). She facilitated meetings using CLE protocols; she and the teachers identified equitable practices, used tools for collecting evidence on equitable access and rigor for teacher observations, and had iterative post-observation conversations. As one teacher reported, "It was very awkward to have pointed out that only the White students are talking in your class and then only White males—it was a gut punch pointed out to me." The teacher took it to heart and decided how he should organize responses so students could more equitably participate. He said: "This observation process gave me permission to fail—it has 100% changed how I reflect on my practice—I have a voice" (Britt, 2023, p. 156). Teachers openly shared observational evidence with each other and decided on practices they would try (Ahn et al., 2021); as a result, the teachers became ambassadors of change and facilitated professional learning for colleagues on equitable access and rigor.

Table 14.3. Steps of Effective Post-Observation Conversations

The following are steps **after the observation:**

STEP ONE: **Analyze the data/evidence to guide the conversation;** depending on the situation, give data to the teacher before the conversation.

STEP TWO: Decide on an **approach/coaching stance** and a location for post-observation conversation.

STEP THREE: Prepare an **opening question** related to the evidence.

STEP FOUR: Ask **coaching questions** (acknowledging, paraphrasing, clarifying, shifting, restating); summarize throughout the conversation as you move through the evidence and conversation.

STEP FIVE: **Summarize next steps** that the teacher has chosen and set a date for another observation.

James (2023) similarly worked with five teachers to effect inquiry teaching in high school classrooms by co-defining inquiry and co-developing an observation tool. Initially, teacher shifts happen slowly; however, when the school leader acts as the catalyst for change by using supervisory practices that emphasize teacher autonomy and collaboration, the change rate accelerates as teachers gain confidence in the process; then, they lead the way for colleagues. In these dissertation studies, as principals fostered culturally responsive practices, teachers experimented with the practices and made decisions about how to use them.

The process provides a window into how school leaders can crack the grammar of schooling nut, providing a rejoinder to Tyack and Cuban (1998) and to Cuban's (2012) dynamic conservatism. Through sustained attention to observation, teacher readiness, and conversations in which teachers are a part of the decisions, teachers can and do change practices (Britt, 2023; James, 2023; Ledo-Lane, 2023), and leaders can be leaders of equity across the entire school, providing what Glickman et al. (2001) call the glue of supervision. When practitioners engage in action research projects centered on equitable access and rigor, they have powerful outcomes to address systemic issues of equity perpetuated in classrooms and school systems. These improvement efforts support teachers, teacher leaders, and other administrators in their building to increase the capacity to observe instruction, code, and have conversations with teachers that lead to reflections about equitable improvements (see Table 14.4 for links to additional resources).

LEADERS WITH TEACHERS: ENSURING EQUITABLE AND CULTURALLY RESPONSIVE PRACTICES

Ensuring equitable access to the classroom dialogue and rigorous academic tasks and questions are the ultimate outcomes of culturally responsive instructional supervision practices (Ishimaru & Galloway, 2014). As teachers learn about and use practices, they push the level of cognitive demand for diverse learners. To apply theory to practice, we designed a framework of academic discourse to examine teacher and student roles across three dimensions of practice: academic tasks, protocols and questioning, and dialogue (see Table 14.5). Most classrooms, despite

Table 14.4. Tools and Protocols

Practice	Electronic Resources
Observation Tools	https://education.ecu.edu/projecti4/resources/
CLE Protocols	iel.org/protocols https://education.ecu.edu/projecti4/resources/
Conversation Guide	https://education.ecu.edu/wp-content/pv-uploads/sites/171/2019/01/Effective-Conversation-Guide_Project-I4_NOV2020_FINAL-1.pdf

Table 14.5. Developmental Academic Discourse

	ACADEMIC DISCOURSE (AD)		
	Teacher-Generated	Teacher Initiated and Facilitated	Student-Generated
Academic Task	• **Designer:** Teacher-designed, directed and controlled • **Cognitive Demand:** Typically low	• **Designer:** Teacher-initiated and facilitated • **Cognitive Demand:** Medium to high, teacher-facilitated	• **Designer:** Teacher and student collaboratively designed and facilitated • **Cognitive Demand:** High cognitive demand
Protocols and Questioning	• **Teacher Role:** Teacher-designed questions; teacher-controlled protocols • **Underlying focus:** Often compliance and behavior-driven; concerned with pacing and fidelity • **Primary interaction relationship:** Teacher-to-student; often pseudo-discourse • **Calling on strategies:** Typically raised hands; limited use of strategies for equitable access • **Level of questions:** Often recall and the application questioning levels with few questions at higher cognitive levels	• **Teacher Role:** Teacher-initiated, including encouraging student-to-student dialogue • **Underlying focus:** Student understanding and teacher use of student experiences • **Primary interaction relationship:** Teacher-to-student, with teacher encouragement of student-to-student and small groups • **Calling-on strategies:** Designed for equitable access of all students • **Level of questions:** Attention to higher cognitive level questions, including synthesis and creativity	• **Teacher Role:** Coaching students as facilitators; warm demander and strong student relationships • **Underlying focus:** Encouraging more student-facilitated groups • **Primary interaction relationship:** Student-to-student • **Calling on strategies:** Primarily student-generated questions and student-to-student interaction • **Level of questions:** Higher level questions that elicit creative responses & authentic problem-solving

| Dialogue | • **Teacher role in questioning:** All questions by teacher; posed for short responses; teacher often looking for right answers
• **Teacher-to-student dialogue:** Typically one-way dialogue and with a subset of students
• **Student responses:** Inaudible and short; often repeated by teacher or ignored if "wrong answer"; teacher often repeats student responses | • **Teacher role in questioning:** Most questions generated by teacher; questions range: recall to analysis
• **Teacher-to-student dialogue:** Focusing on extensions
  » Teacher asking for elaboration & clarification
  » Teacher requesting support for ideas
  » Student paraphrasing encouraged
  » Student questions encouraged
• **Student responses:** Often recorded by students or teachers; equitable access for student responses; complex thinking and interactions in teacher-student interchanges; multiple student ideas or solutions considered; paraphrasing of student responses encouraged | • **Teacher role in questioning:** Collaboratively generated
• **Teacher-to-student dialogue:** Primarily coaching; focusing on probing questions for deeper learning
• **Student responses:** Student-to-student dialogue, often initiated by students; student-driven conversations; built on and challenging ideas of other students; ideas supported with evidence, often co-generated |

Source: *Framework of Classroom Learning and Practice: Propelled by Equity-Driven Tools for School Change* (Tredway et al., 2019).

years of professional learning, still operate largely as teacher-generated with low cognitive demand, hand-raising as the primary call-on tool, and teachers posing all questions that mostly require recall or short responses. To shift from exclusively teacher-facilitated to students as co-generators of dialogue and questions can feel like a big ask. However, starting with small groups of teachers as collaborators changing their teaching practices has the potential for changing professional learning for all teachers (Russell et al., 2017).

Boykin and Noguera (2011) confirm that equitable access and academic rigor are two sides of the same coin. Students engage behaviorally, cognitively, and affectively, and teachers' care and cognitive demand impact the student level of engagement. As a result, promoting equitable access and rigor requires teachers to have strong relationships with students so they can facilitate high-level cognitive interactions with them. Students diminish their engagement when teachers believe them to be lacking motivation and do not engage them in rigorous tasks or questions (Skinner & Belmont, 1993). Instead, teachers as warm demanders can both establish relationships and push student rigor (Delpit, 2012; Ware, 2006).

Observation tools pinpoint interactions, detail time spent with certain students and not others, and provide concrete evidence of how students interact; thus, teachers have specific evidence that they need to activate changes in their instructional practices. Teachers change when they are clear about precisely what to change. Our schools and districts—now replete with talk about implicit bias in the abstract—could use tools that track equitable access and rigor and evidence to engage in conversations with teachers about equity and biases. By modeling culturally responsive supervision practices, school leaders use new ways of supervising teachers.

The EdD studies demonstrate that CLE axioms provided a cornerstone that guided leader decisions and actions. By concentrating on self-care, storytelling, and support groups as vehicles for cultivating and sustaining relational trust, leaders fostered the necessary conditions for engaging teachers in self-improvement. As a result, the participants consistently de-privatized their practices and together they learned in public. Starting slowly with evidence-based, nonjudgmental data, the teachers gradually accelerated their individual and group learning, willingness to change, and desire to share learning with peers.

As a result of observations across the school, a leader can ensure that the individual observation and conversation processes lead to group conversations about more equitable instructional practices for all students. Then, they build school cohesion by co-designing and facilitating equity-driven, culturally responsive professional learning in their schools (Elmore, 2004; Grubb & Tredway, 2010; Hammond, 2015). Walkthrough and instructional round goals are not wrong. However, all school leaders must improve their abilities to observe and code evidence from classrooms, to have conversations with teachers. In doing so, they provide effective supervision based on daily and real-time evidence from classrooms; then teachers better understand instruction and make daily decisions to reflect and improve. As Judith Warren Little, an advocate for teacher voice, said:

Every day is a thought experiment for teachers and leaders. We now know that leaders and teachers can be qualitative researchers of their work and gain authority and autonomy as the persons closest to the work who decide how to improve their practices. We can see inside the black box of teaching and learning!

By putting each teacher in the driver's seat to decide what to improve because of observational evidence and conversations, a school leader can fulfill multiple purposes of supervision. Re-calibrating the paradigm of perceptional data to evidence-based observations takes critical changes in leadership practices; however, the school leader, as a guide, not a regulator, is well-positioned to be an equity leader and an instructional partner for teacher improvement. Our research and work with practitioners indicates that equitable and culturally responsive leadership is rooted in supervision practices that promote trust and collaboratively engage teachers. When leaders work in systematic, humane ways that set the necessary conditions for school improvement and use the common tools for observation and conversations, school leaders with teachers can change instructional practices so that together they can foster the reality of democratic and equitable classrooms.

REFERENCES

Acheson, K. A., & Gall, M. D. (2003). *Clinical supervision and teacher development: Preservice and in-service applications.* John Wiley & Sons.

Acheson, K. A., & Gall, M. D. (1980). *Techniques in the clinical supervision of teachers: Preservice and in-service applications.* John Wiley & Sons.

Ahn, J., Campos, F., Nguyen, H., Hays, M., & Morrison, J. (2021). Co-designing for privacy, transparency, and trust in K–12 learning analytics. In *LAK21: 11th International Learning Analytics and Knowledge Conference* (pp. 55–65). doi.org/10.1145/3448139.3448145

Argyris, M., & Schön, D. (1974). *Theory in practice. Increasing professional effectiveness.* Jossey-Bass.

Bose, B. K., Ancin, D., Frank, J., & Malik, A. (2017). *Teaching transformative life skills to students: A comprehensive dynamic mindfulness curriculum.* W. W. Norton.

Boykin, A. W., & Noguera, P. (2011). *Creating the opportunity to learn: Moving from research to practice to close the achievement gap.* Association for Supervision and Curriculum Development.

Britt, L. B. (2023). *Creating a home: Promoting equitable academic discourse by establishing teacher agency and co-design* [Doctoral Dissertation, East Carolina University]. http://hdl.handle.net/10342/12819

Caruz, V. V. (2023). *Kapwa (shared identity): Filipino American perspectives and responses to educational leadership* [Doctoral Dissertation, East Carolina University]. http://hdl.handle.net/10342/12813

City, E. A., Elmore, R. F., Fiarman, S. E., & Teitel, L. (2009). *Instructional rounds in education: A network approach to improving teaching and learning.* Harvard Education Press.

Cobb, P., Jackson, K., Smith, T., Sorum, M., & Henrick, E. (2011) Designing research with educational systems: Investigating and supporting improvements in the quality of mathematics teaching at scale. *National Society for the Study of Education 112*(2), 320–349.

Cogan, M. (1973). *Clinical supervision*. Houghton Mifflin Company.
Cuban, L. (2012, August 9). Dynamic conservatism and stability in teaching. https://larrycuban.wordpress.com/2012/08/09/dynamic-conservatism-and-stability-in-teaching/
David, J. L. (2007). What research says about . . . / classroom walk-throughs. Association for Supervision and Curriculum Development. https://www.ascd.org/el/articles/classroom-walk-throughs
Delpit, L. (2012). *"Multiplication is for white people": Raising expectations of other people's children*. The New Press.
Diamond, A., & Ling, D. S. (2020). Review of the evidence on, and fundamental questions about, efforts to improve executive functions, including working memory. In J. M. Novick, M. F. Bunting, M. R. Dougherty, & R. W. Engle (Eds.), *Cognitive and working memory training: Perspectives from psychology, neuroscience, and human development* (pp. 143–431). Oxford University Press. https://doi.org/10.1093/oso/9780199974467.003.0008
Drago-Severson, E. (2012). *Helping educators grow: Strategies and practices for leadership development*. Harvard Education Press.
Drago-Severson, E., & Blum-Stefano, J. (2016). *Tell me so I can hear you: A development approach to feedback for educators*. Harvard Education Press.
Driscoll, M. P. (1994). *Psychology of learning for instruction*. Allyn and Bacon.
Elmore, R. F. (2004). *School reform from the inside out: Policy, practice, and performance*. Harvard Education Press.
Fritz, C., & Miller, G. (2003). Supervisory options for instructional leaders in education. *Journal of Leadership Education, 2*(2), 13–27. https://journalofleadershiped.org/jole_articles/supervisory-options-for-instructional-leaders-in-education/
Gall, M. D., & Acheson, K. A. (2013). *Clinical supervision and teacher development: Preservice and inservice applications*. John Wiley & Sons.
Glanz, J., & Sullivan, S. (2000). *Supervision in practice: 3 steps to improving teaching and learning*. Corwin.
Glickman, C. D., Gordon, S. P., & Ross-Gordon, J. M. (2001). *SuperVision and instructional leadership: A developmental approach* (5th ed.). Allyn & Bacon.
Glickman, C. D. (2002). *Leadership for learning: How to help teachers succeed*. Association for Supervision and Curriculum Development.
Glickman, C. D., Gordon, S. P., & Ross-Gordon, J. M. (2010). *SuperVision and instructional leadership: A developmental approach* (8th ed.). Allyn & Bacon.
Glickman, C. D., & Mette, I. M. (2020). *The essential renewal of America's schools: A Leadership guide for democratizing schools from the inside out*. Teachers College Press.
Goldhammer, R. (1969). *Clinical supervision: Special methods for the supervision of teachers*. Holt, Rinehart, and Winston.
Goldhammer, R., Anderson, R. H., & Krajewski, R. J. (1993). *Clinical supervision: Special methods for the supervision of teachers* (3rd ed.). Harcourt Brace Jovanovich College Publishers.
Goldring, E., Clark, M. A., Rubin, M., Rogers, L. K., Grissom, J. A., Gill, B., Kautz, T., McCullough, M., Neel, M., & Burnett, A. (2020). *Changing the principal supervisor role to better support principals*. Vanderbilt University/Mathematica.
Gomell, A., Hmelo-Silver, C. E., & Šabanović, S. (2022). Co-constructing professional vision: Teacher and researcher learning in co-design. *Cognition and Instruction, 40*(1), 7–2. https://doi.org/10.1080/07370008.2021.2010210

Grissom, J. A., Loeb, S., & Master, B. (2013). Effective instructional time use for school leaders: Longitudinal evidence from observations of principals. *Educational Researcher, 42*(8), 433–444.

Grissom, J. A., Egalite, A. J., & Lindsay, C. A. (2021a). *How principals affect students and schools: A systematic synthesis of two decades of research.* Wallace Foundation.

Grissom, J. A., Egalite, A. J., & Lindsay, C. A. (2021b). What great principals do. *Educational Leadership, 78*(7), 21–25.

Grissom, J. A., & Youngs, P. (Eds.) (2016). *Improving teacher evaluations systems: making the most of multiple measures.* Harker Brownlow.

Guajardo, M., Guajardo, F., Janson, C., & Militello, M. (2016). *Reframing community partnerships in education: Uniting the power of place and wisdom of people.* Routledge

Grubb, W. N. (2009). *The money myth: School resources, outcomes, and equity.* Russell Sage.

Grubb, W. N., & Tredway L. (2010). *Leading from the inside out: Expanded roles of teachers in equitable schools.* Paradigm Press.

Hammond, Z. (2015). *Culturally responsive teaching and the brain: Promoting authentic engagement and rigor among culturally and linguistically diverse students.* Corwin.

Ingersoll, R. M. (2003). *Who controls teachers' work?* Harvard University Press.

Irby, D. J. (2020). *Stuck improving: Racial equity and school leadership.* Harvard Education Press.

Ishimaru, A. M., & Galloway, M. K. (2014). Beyond individual effectiveness: Conceptualizing organizational leadership for equity. *Leadership and Policy in Schools, 13*(1), 93–146.

James, J. (2023). *Leave this place better than you found it: Facilitating inquiry-based learning experiences* [Doctoral Dissertation, East Carolina University]. http://hdl.handle.net/10342/12808

Khalifa, M. (2018). *Culturally responsive school leadership.* Harvard Education Press.

Knowles, M. S. (1980). *The modern practice of adult education: From pedagogy to andragogy.* Cambridge Adult Education.

Lave, J. (1996). Situated learning in communities of practice. In L. B. Resnick, J. M. Levine & S. D. Teasley (Eds.), *Perspectives on socially shared cognition* (pp. 63–82). American Psychological Association.

Ledo-Lane, A. (2023). *Using creative practices to foster arts integration: Supporting experiential pedagogy for teachers* [Doctoral Dissertation, East Carolina University]. http://hdl.handle.net/10342/12825

Lyman, F. T., Tredway, L., & Purser, M. (2023). Think-pair-share and Thinktrix: Standard bearers of student dialogue. In R. Gillies, N. A. Davidson, & B. Millis (Eds.), *Contemporary global perspectives on cooperative learning: Applications of CL across educational contexts* (pp. 124–143). Routledge.

Machado, M. (May 2021). *Family stories matter: Critical pedagogy of storytelling in fifth grade classrooms* [Doctoral Dissertation, East Carolina University]. The ScholarShip. http://hdl.handle.net/10342/9084

Marsh, J. A., Kerr, K. A., Ikemoto, G. S., Darilek, H., Suttorp, M., Zimmer, R. W., & Barney, H. (2005). *The role of districts in fostering instructional improvement.* Rand.

Marshall, K. (2009). *Rethinking teacher supervision and evaluation: how to work smart, build collaboration, and close the achievement gap.* John Wiley & Sons.

Melvin, J. F., Jr. (2017). *Using instructional rounds at the school level to improve classroom instruction* [Doctoral Dissertation, University of California, Berkeley]. EScholarship. escholarship.org/uc/item/1ft0s2j4

Mette, I., Anderson, J., Nieuwenhuizen, L., Range, B. G., Hvidston, D. J., & Doty, J. (2017). The wicked problem of the intersection between supervision and evaluation. *International Electronic Journal of Elementary Education, 9*(3), 709–724.

Militello, M., Tredway, L., & Argent, J. (2020). Self-care for leaders starts now. *ASCD Express 15*(23). http://www.ascd.org/ascd-express/vol15/num23/self-care-for-school-leaders-starts-now.aspx

Morris, C. L. (2023). *White women educational leaders: Embodying antiracism in eastern North Carolina* [Doctoral Dissertation, East Carolina University]. http://hdl.handle.net/10342/12807

Mudd, K. A. (2023). *Reimagining teacher induction: A framework for an asset-driven, equity-based induction process that cultivates knowledge of self, context, and professional practice* [Doctoral Dissertation, East Carolina University]. http://hdl.handle.net/10342/12812

National Academy of Sciences (2018). *How people learn II: Learners, contexts, and cultures*. The National Academies Press.

Neumerski, C. M., Grissom, J. A., Goldring, E., Drake, T. A., Rubin, M., Cannata, M., & Schermann, P. (2018). Restructuring instructional leadership: How multiple-measure teacher evaluation systems are redefining the role of school principal. *The Elementary School Journal, 199*(2), 179–350.

Norris, J. (2022). *School leaders' sensemaking and sensegiving*. Brill.

Paris, D., & Alim, H, S. (2017). *Culturally sustaining pedagogies: Teacher and learning for justice in a changing world*. Teachers College Press.

Parker, J. (2023). *Collaborative space for leaders: A participatory action research study to improve district and school leader collaboration*. [Doctoral Dissertation, East Carolina University.]

Paryani, P. (2019). *Teacher evaluation that matters: A participatory process for growth and development* [Doctoral dissertation, East Carolina University]. Retrieved from https://www.proquest.com/docview/2352654847?accountid=10639&pq-origsite=summon

Payne, B. O. (2023). *Experiential conditions for educational equity in action: Culturally responsive leadership development in an international school* [Doctoral Dissertation, East Carolina University].

Project I4. (2019). *Resources and protocols*. https://education.ecu.edu/projecti4/resources/

Protheroe, N. (2009). Using classroom walkthrough tools to improve instruction. *Principal, 88*(4), 30–34.

Radd, S., Generett, G. G., Gooden, M. A., Theoharis, G. (2021). *Five practices for equity-focused school leadership*. Association of Supervision and Curriculum Development.

Resnick, L. B., Asterhan, C. S. C., & Clarke, S. N. (Eds.) (2015). *Socializing intelligence through academic talk and dialogue*. American Education Research Association.

Rowan, B., & Raudenbush, S. (2016). Teacher evaluation in American schools. In D. H. Ditomer & C. A. Bell, (Eds.), *Handbook of research on teaching* (pp. 1159–1216). American Education Research Association.

Russell, J. L., Bryk, A. S., Dolle, J. R., Gomez, L. M., LeMahieu, P. G., & Grumow, A. (2017). A framework for the initiation of networked improvement communities. *Teachers College Record, 119* (5), 1–36.

Safir, S., & Dugan, J. (2021). *Street data: A next-generation model for equity, pedagogy, and school transformation*. Jossey-Bass.

Saldaña, J. (2016). *The coding manual for qualitative researchers*. Sage.

Saphier, J. (1993). *How to make supervision and evaluation really work: Supervision and evaluation in the context of strengthening school culture*. Research for Better Teaching.

Sergiovanni, T. J., & Starratt, R. J. (2007). *Supervision: A redefinition* (8th ed.). McGraw Hill.

Sergiovanni, T. (2000). *The lifeworld of leadership: Creating culture, community, and personal meaning in our schools*. Jossey Bass.

Skinner, E. A., & Belmont, M. J. (1993). Motivation in the classroom: Reciprocal effects of teacher behavior and student engagement across the school year. *Journal of Educational Psychology, 85*(4), 571–581. https://doi.org/10.1037/0022-0663.85.4.571

Spillane, J. P., & Coldren, A. F. (2011). *Diagnosis and design for school improvement*. Teachers College Press.

Spillane, J. P., Parise, L. M., & Sherer, J. Z. (2013). Organizational routines as coupling mechanism: Policy, school administration, and the technical core. *American Education Research Journal, 48*(3), 586–619.

Sullivan, S., & Glanz, J. (2013). *Supervision that improves teaching and learning: Strategies & techniques* (4th ed.). Corwin.

Supovitz, J. A., & Weathers, J. (2004). *Dashboard lights: Monitoring implementation of district instructional reform strategies*. Consortium for Policy Research in Education. eric.ed.gov/?id=ED493117

Tang, W. (2023). *Equity warriors: Building principal capacity to enact culturally responsive leadership* [Doctoral Dissertation, East Carolina University]. http://hdl.handle.net/10342/12803

Teitel, L. (2013). *School-based instructional rounds: Improving teaching and learning across classrooms*. Harvard Education Press.

Tredway, L., Simon, K., Militello, M., & Simon, K. (2021a). Professional development superglue. *The Learning Professional 42*(2), 52–55.

Tredway, L., Militello, M., & Simon, K. (2021b). Making classroom observations matter. *Educational Leadership 78*(7), 56–62.

Tredway, L., Militello, M., Simon, K., Argent, J., Hodgkins, L., & Morris, C. (2019). *Effective conversation guide*. East Carolina University. https://education.ecu.edu/wp-content/pv-uploads/sites/171/2019/01/Effective-Conversation-Guide_Project-I4_NOV2020_FINAL-1.pdf

Tyack, D., & Cuban, L. (1998). *Tinkering toward utopia*. Harvard University Press.

Valli, L., & Buese, D. (2007). The changing role of teachers in an era of high-stakes accountability. *American Education Research Journal, 44*(3), 519–588.

Velasco, C. (May 2021). *Espacio sano: How social justice educational leaders cultivate caring and sharing* [Doctoral Dissertation, East Carolina University]. The ScholarShip .http://hdl.handle.net/10342/9086

Vella, J. (2008). *On teaching and learning: Putting the principles and practices of dialogue education into action*. Jossey-Bass.

Ware, F. (2006). Warm demander pedagogy: Culturally responsive teaching that supports a culture of achievement for African American students. *Urban Education, 41*(4), 427–445

Wise, D., & Jacobo, A. (2010), Towards a framework for leadership coaching. *School Leadership and Management, 30*(2), 159–169. https://doi.org/10.1080/13632431003663206

Wong, C-C, Kumpulainen, K., & Kahamaa, A. (2021). Collaborative creativity among education professionals in a co-design workshop: A multidimensional analysis. *Thinking Skills and Creativity, 42* (100971), 1–17.

Woo, L. J., & Hendriksen, D. (2023). The critical role of teachers in educational design processes. *Teachers College Record.* https://www.researchgate.net/publication/367008869

Yurmovsky, M. M., Petersen, M. J., Mehta, J. D., Horwitz-Willis, R., & Frumin, K. M. (2020). Research on continuous improvement: Exploring the complexities of managing educational change. *Review of Research in Education, 44*(1), 403–433.

Zepeda, S. J. (2017). *Instructional supervision: Applying tools and* concepts (4th ed.). Routledge.

CHAPTER 15

Supervision of Guerrilla Pedagogies

Armen Álvarez and Mariela Rodríguez

The U.S. society we live in today is designed to limit the advancement of future generations of social vigilantes. One of the greatest challenges facing U.S. educators who want to help fight for greater social justice is how Guerrilla Pedagogy is perceived by the public, as well as how Guerrilla Pedagogy is defined by hegemonic structures that often reinforce deficit mindsets related to the education of culturally and intellectually diverse backgrounds. As such, guerilla pedagogues not only resist the assimilation of oppressive epistemologies, but they also ensure their instruction is liberating, transformative, and inclusive beyond the prescribed boundaries of Eurocentric education. Therefore, educators, educational leaders, and educational advocates who want to enact Guerrilla Pedagogies must be well informed by culturally responsive knowledge and praxis relating to instruction, producing tools in all possible disciplines. If developed properly, these tools will help to dismantle the logic of white supremacy and evict the settler colonizer as a producer of epistemologies that seek to erase the memory and oral history of Indigenous and Black groups.

Faced with the radical erosion of civil liberties and the unequal protection of constitutional rights, which produces social injustices, communities across the United States require instructional outcomes that can resist and deconstruct the systemic power of white supremacy. Through these instructional practices, the schoolhouse can produce justice-seeking citizens capable of governing themselves, where young people envision, enact, and renew a democracy that relies on the principles of equality and justice. It is through Guerrilla Pedagogies that education systems can empower students to seek social justice in the form of emancipation, reparation, and equity. Significant efforts to counter the history of the settler-colonizer as the "Truth" must be engaged to disrupt and dismantle the racist system to support educational reform through social justice.

In this chapter, we argue that the way to enact social justice in our communities begins with the creation of epistemologies that are consistent with a philosophy of education that produces the tools students at all levels can use to counter white supremacist ideology. Having leadership is essential, but empowering teachers to produce tools according to the canon of an emancipatory philosophy is much more critical. We say this because history informs various facets of Guerrilla Pedagogy—for example, when school segregation ended with *Brown v. Board of Education*, it also marked the time in U.S. history when the real philosophical battle began with the indoctrination of the dominant society and *epistemicide* seeking to protect the interests of the privileged (Santos, 2016, and Negrón-Montilla, 1975).

Current U.S. society is not randomly constructed, but rather is orchestrated by a system of domination that perpetuates oppression as the norm. It is from this understanding of the creation of U.S. society that instructional leaders interested in enacting social justice have to help teachers emancipate the mindset of settler-colonizer from the instructional practices that operate in the classroom, and re-imagine learning outcomes that white supremacy has tried to extinguish through *epistemicide*. In doing so, we can acknowledge how education systems are sources of knowledge, power, and control—and how through the U.S. education system white supremacy has tightly gripped the epistemologies that are preferred, taught, and reinforced in an effort to de-culturize minoritized groups.

Social justice leadership in education—and specifically culturally responsive instructional supervision (CRIS)—is effective when it resists how systems of oppression continually marginalize students and parents—all in an effort to dismantle the injustices reproduced within school systems. Yancy (2019) states that leadership is anyone who refuses to become accustomed to injustice, hatred, and bigotry. Given this definition, we must refuse all forms of forced adjustment and ignorance, including any situation that forces students to assimilate, and does not recognize their culture or lived experience as an asset. The guerrilla pedagogue is the leading philosopher in the classroom, and possibly one of the only beams of light in a community to help students resist assimilation and conformity. It is for this exact reason that instructional leaders must also be equity leaders who are able to provide feedback to ensure culturally responsive instruction occurs within the schoolhouse.

So, how can instructional supervisors awaken the critical consciousness of teachers? How can instructional supervisors counter the ongoing and harmful practices of *epistemicide* that are so often reinforced in the U.S. education system? First, it is necessary that there be leaders of social justice committed to the purpose of liberating colonized minds held captive by ignorance. Knowledge liberates the oppressed from the oppressor and gives comfort to those who are broken by injustice. Second, the pursuit of social justice makes you grow and see the world from a critical perspective. Social justice is the intrinsic knowledge that exists within your conscience. It invites you to learn more about yourself, and the relationship you have to have with the rest of the world.

As such, at the core of CRIS is a righteous indignation and outrage to being assimilated to white epistemological assumptions. School leaders need to obtain skills that assist in the interruption of subtle, vicious cycles of oppression that seem "normal" and "part of our moral values" but are only intended to protect privileged sociocultural identities and minoritize, marginalize, and otherize those deemed less privileged. Collectively or individually, CRIS can dismantle social injustices, helping teachers learn to reflect on how to think critically, face oppression, and constantly search for the knowledge of truth to unmask ignorance. It is not surprising that, as the United States faces moments of great concern over the radical erosion of civil liberties and democratic constitutional protections, we see an increased need for CRIS. But having a mentor who is focused on instructional practices and social justice outcomes can make a huge difference in the lives of students and communities that deserve the right to combat white supremacy as the norm.

GUERRILLA PEDAGOGY INFORMING AN INSTRUCTIONAL SUPERVISION STANCE

Guerrilla Pedagogy, also known as guerrilla education or educational guerrilla warfare, is a term that emerged in the field of education to describe some alternative, nontraditional approaches to teaching and learning (Norton, 1994). The origin of Guerrilla Pedagogy can be traced back to the broader concept of guerrilla warfare, which originated in military contexts. Understanding that guerrilla etymology originates from Spanish language root of *guerra* translated into English means *war*. *Guerrilla* in the Spanish language is diminutive of the original word, but in this case is used with an undertone rank connotation, meaning that it is in fact a resistance group that represents and belongs to people's well-being.

The concept of Guerrilla Pedagogy challenges the traditional educational system, which is often criticized for being rigid, hierarchical, and centered on standardized testing. Guerrilla Pedagogy advocates for a more flexible, participatory, and learner-centered approach to education that values the culture and lived experiences students bring to the classroom. It seeks to empower students, encourage critical thinking, and foster creativity by employing unconventional teaching methods and strategies. It is never an alternative approach to instruction, but rather represents the epistemology, ontology, and axiology of peoples and communities before the colonization era (Álvarez, 2023).

Although there is not a specific person or event credited with the origination of Guerrilla Pedagogy, its development can be attributed to the work of various educators, scholars, and activists who sought to challenge the status quo in education. These individuals have experimented with alternative educational models, such as Paulo Freire's critical pedagogy, Ivan Illich's ideas on deschooling, and John Holt's advocacy for unschooling. These educational thinkers and practitioners have influenced the emergence and evolution of Guerrilla Pedagogy as a philosophy and practice.

Overall, Guerrilla Pedagogy represents a response to the limitations of traditional education and the failed accountability experiment. It calls for more transformative, student-centered approaches that promote critical thinking, creativity, and social change. It emphasizes the need to adapt and innovate in education to meet the diverse needs of learners in an ever-changing world. Perhaps most importantly, it resists the efforts of settler colonialism within the education system, an approach that has been an ineffective way to bring prosperity and modernization to what humanity today calls the Americas.

COLONIALISM AND U.S. EDUCATION

The Americanization of the public school system has been a method for the United States to maintain its imperial power and colonial domination over Native Americans, African Americans, Latinos, and Puerto Ricans (Del Moral, 2013; Navarro, 2002; Negron-Montilla, 1975; Spring, 2013, 2016). The problems caused by the imposition of Americanization in schools are not isolated incidences. Rather, they are replicated and enforced over many ethnic and racialized groups across the United States by mechanisms of deculturalization and subtraction epistemologies. Santos (2016) detailed *epistemicide* as "the destruction of knowledge and cultures, their memories, ancestral links, and their manner of relating to others and nature" (p. 18). For centuries the epistemologies of Indigenous and African descents have been targeted by Eurocentric settler colonizers to erase or make invisible any other culture beyond Western and Northern European cultures (Glenn, 2015; Santos, 2014; Scheurich & Young, 1997; Smith, 2012; Tuck & Yang, 2012). It is for this exact reason that we must problematize CRIS to engage in acts of resistance.

To combat the conformity of *epistemicide*, there must be cross-race alliance groups that are developed to resist racial injustice. It is important to note that the etymology of "post-colonial" situates colonialism as a past instance; therefore it is not descriptive of the ongoing repression experienced in modern U.S. society as an uninterrupted condition of enslavement and control of peoples throughout the Americas. By examining the arguments that coincide with the use of settler colonialism as a theoretical framework, educators are able to deconstruct the logic of white supremacy that produces systems of oppression—notably the U.S. public school system that is used as an instrument to sustain the empire.

Tuck and Yang (2012) contextualize settler colonialism in the educational discourse to apply decolonization frameworks, not as a metaphor, but rather as an emancipatory framework to improve our societies, schools, and the lived experiences of students and parents. Tuck and Yang argued that settler colonialism is different from colonialism in that settlers come with the intention of making a new home on the land, a "homemaking that insists on settler sovereignty over all things in their new realm" (p. 5). This situates the settler-colonizer as a "persona," an individual or members of a group responsible for the racial disparities in the creation of epistemological tensions, and as such deserves to be studied for its relations with race and white supremacy.

Tenets of Settler Colonialism

Extracting from the principles that Smith (2012), Glenn (2015), and Tuck and Yang (2012) have constructed in their respective academic work, CRIS can help unveil the problems found in the U.S. education system, specifically as it relates to being a product of white supremacy and Eurocentric ideologies. These principles are interlaced with epistemologies that support Americanization as a direct product of the philosophy of white supremacy through the lens of settler colonialism. If these principles are to be addressed and deconstructed, it is the schoolhouse that will have to take on the initiative of reparations and emancipation to heal these outraged communities.

Smith (2012) examines the logic of white supremacy, assuming that it is neither enacted singularly nor specifically affects one racial group. Alternatively, the settler-colonizer denies the existence of racial disparities by evading it and moving toward asserting "innocence" under neutrality and color-blind notions (Tuck & Yang, 2012). Smith argues there are three pillars of white supremacy: (1) slaveability/anti-Black racism, which anchors capitalism; (2) genocide, which anchors colonialism; and (3) orientalism, which anchors war (p. 68). These can be seen throughout the U.S. school system and are pillars that CRIS can help to address in the schoolhouse.

Race as a Pillar of White Supremacy. According to Smith (2012), white supremacy is the logic that anchors the capitalist system, which maintains people of color as commodities. It uses racial hierarchy to enforce anti-Blackness, reinforcing the belief that as long as you are not Black, you have the opportunity to escape the commodification of capitalism. According to Smith (2012) and Glenn (2015), even when people do not resist Black–white binary ideas, when considering the logic of white supremacy, racial dynamics are manipulated by notions of white privilege. People of multiple ethnic and racial backgrounds, who are lighter skinned, benefit from "light-skin" privilege. Often being rewarded by adhering to the racial hierarchies imposed by white settler-colonizers, these communities become complicit perpetrators of colonialism. Smith (2012) called to move beyond the Black–white binary, which obscures the centrality of the slavery logic in the system of white supremacy (p. 75). As a result, racial tensions emerge under colorism notions and is used as a commodity to hinder decolonization and emancipation both within U.S. society and within the schoolhouse.

Genocide as a Pillar of White Supremacy. Genocide—physically and culturally—is the logic that anchors colonialism as the ultimate goal of eradicating native people and culture. Within the United States, land and natives were viewed as one entity when settler-colonizers seized, established property rights over land, and stole resources in various forms. As such, the use of direct and indirect violence to establish cultural dominance can be seen as the ultimate goal of colonization.

The white settler-colonizer came to remain in the Americas as a hegemonic power using territorial expansion as a justification for modernism. Such expansions imposed a system of political and educational structures in which existing native civilizations had only one option: to assimilate into the Eurocentric culture of the white man or to die. The assimilation of Eurocentric expectations continues to this day, giving credence to the idea of how CRIS can help students focus on the sociocultural identities and strengths they bring with them every day.

Orientalism as a Pillar of White Supremacy. Said (1994b) and Smith (2012) state that orientalism is the logic that anchors the Eurocentric academy as a structure, with the ultimate goal of defining itself as a superior civilization by positioning the East as exotic and inferior to the West (Said, 1994; Smith, 2012). The logic of Orientalism as a direct product of Western academia aims to mark as subordinate people or nations which are perceived to be a threat to the well-being of the empire and that will never be part of it. In the settler-colonizer's eyes, these are inferior and alien civilizations that coinhabit the lands that the Western empire dominates.

Glenn (2015) establishes that the settler-colonizer is perceived as more advanced; thus, other nations are already lesser beings. The superiority of Western man is central to the identity of settler-colonizers, who establish a sovereign and political government with symbols of their nationality, creating a cultural gap of superiority in the Occidental domains and inferiority throughout the Oriental domains. Similarly, Indigenous people were considered unfit to govern *terra nullius*, thus justifying the acquisition of the land. Consequently, Orientalism allows the United States to defend the logic of slavery and genocide, to stay strong enough to fight constant wars against subordinate beings threatening its existence. Therefore, for the United States to keep its hegemony, it must always be at war—against various social structures, such as legal, healthcare, and education systems.

CONTROL OF KNOWLEDGE AND KNOWING

Scheurich and Young (1997) affirm that the epistemologies existing in our educational institutions are based on the reproduction of interpretive methods that discriminate against the production of knowledge based on race, ethnicity, and other sociocultural identities. Therefore, these factors are based on how the ascendant culture built its coexisting experiences with scientific racism. This ascendant culture has as its sole purpose maintaining the dominant culture as the only "real world," and other cultures on the "margin," to satisfy its members' desire for superiority (p. 8). This is a critical problem that instructional supervisors have to encounter, where the spaces of knowledge and instruction are founded on the ontological interpretation of racist epistemologies. This epistemological racism corresponds to the experience of the creation of Eurocentric knowledge where racism is the ignition, or the primary source, for reproducing educational philosophies, curriculum, and instructional practices that are based on the racist U.S. society to which we have all been normalized.

Santos (2018) and Grosfoguel et al. (2016) add to this discourse by elaborating that the construction of these epistemologies is incomplete and must be decolonized. All educational models in the Americas are flawed where Brown and Black epistemologies are seen as being "dangerous," "uncivilized," "socialist," or belonging to "obsolete" parts of the past, making it difficult to decolonize the schoolhouse. Education systems in the Americas have actively reinforced Indigenous and Black epistemologies as being treasonous to U.S. exceptionalism. Since the Eurocentric culture brought the notion that civilization has to be modernized, this is the essential basis for which the white settler-colonizer is justified in implementing a necessary and inevitable evil—and through which the U.S. public education system operates, reinforcing deficit narratives through policy and practices. Operating within these logics, the colonizers—and U.S. educators who lack a critical perspective—are able to ferry Brown and Black epistemologies into the processes of *epistemicide*.

Spring (2013) argues that the U.S. education system positions schools as "managers" of public thought—overseers—where the distribution of knowledge in society is carefully controlled. In this process the white settler-colonizers, specifically those the U.S. empire privileges, utilizes education as an instrument to deculturalize communities of color with the objective of forcing Americanization in public schools. As such, CRIS is necessary to shift those teaching practices that view students' culture, language, and lived experiences as deficits and to instead focus on how their sociocultural identities are assets to be leveraged in their own learning.

De Facto Disenfranchisement

The purpose of educating white, affluent U.S. communities is not the same as that which exists in the neighborhoods and territories where the U.S. empire reproduces colonial subjects. The logic of white supremacy treats people of color as strangers to the educational system, where there is no purpose to their sociocultural orientations; rather, the objective of the white settler-colonizer is to apply the authoritative power that determines the moral values and outcomes of the school system. Santos (2007) explains this phenomenon where modern Western thought is an abyssal paradigm. It consists of a system of visible and invisible distinctions, the invisible ones being the foundation of the visible ones, which are what operate under the logic of white power.

In the case of disfranchisement as a problem, the white settler controls epistemological knowledge, deciding what is legal and what is illegal, who lives and who dies, what is valued and privileged and what is not valued or privileged. This directly translates to education policies that have been based on the logic of white supremacy, where colonial subjects are devoid of value since they have been, and continue to be, dehumanized. This form of oppression only adds value to white privilege. Evans-Winters (2017) asserts that "White-on-Black violence is intentional, sanctioned, and normalized by policy, institutions (e.g., media, education, religion, judiciary), and the popular imagination" (p. 20). These educational policies have historically minoritized and otherized People of Color—and exist to perpetuate a violence that seems invisible or implicit, but have been imposed specifically to manipulate, control education, and proliferate white supremacy.

Every day in the United States, the settler colonizer uses the education system as an instrument to reproduce Eurocentrism as a legitimate philosophy (Spring, 2016; Grosfoguel & Velázquez, 2016). As such, the emancipatory stories of resistance play a critical role in the discourse of confronting assimilation, giving a voice to the voiceless and fighting injustices committed by the voices of the dominating culture. Freire (1972) elaborates the "banking" concept of education, a method of teaching and learning where students simply store the information. We argue that in the Americanized context of education, students from minoritized, marginalized, and otherized families are byproducts that sustain elitism within the U.S. society at the cost of racialized individuals (Spring, 2016).

Freirean concepts of critical pedagogy greatly influence the creation of CRIS. The process of internalization of the oppressor convene the following ideas: (1) every person's ontological vocation makes you more human, where the struggle is defined in terms of one's attempt to overcome one's oppression; (2) the oppressor and the oppressed are humans but the oppressor seeks to perpetuate injustice and normalizing it; (3) through the process of conscientization, both oppressors and oppressed can understand their power; and (4) the oppressed will be able to change their circumstances only if their intentions and actions are consistent with their goal. Through a deeper understanding of critical pedagogy, instructional supervisors can learn to provide feedback about instruction that empowers classrooms to become places of liberation.

Settler Colonialism as a Form of Oppression

Settler colonialism as a theoretical framework is based on white supremacy, which serves to eradicate non-European cultures (Denoon, 1979). Wolfe (1999) developed a clearer theoretical framework in relation to the logic of settler colonialism, which is the logic of elimination. More recent academic works, which deal with discourses at an international level that have analyzed social history from the time of the Assyrians and Romans, up until the colonization of the Americas, all point to the same logic of elimination (Cavanagh & Veracini, 2017). As such, there is evidence in social, anthropological, and socio-political history that settler colonialism is a mode of oppression that thinks geopolitically.

By this logic, the United States is the empire of the greatest power and geopolitical influence today. There are other discourses that attempt to protect colonialism and settler colonialism as benefits for humanity. Two examples of these arguments are the Trump Administration's *1776 Report* and *España la primera globalizacion*, a documentary released by Hispanic scholars that attempts to justify genocide and colonization (Álvarez, 2023).

In January 2021, the Trump Administration's advisory 1776 Committee issued its *1776 Report*. This document demands a patriotic "restoration of American education," grounded on a history of the Founding Fathers' principles and the Federalist Papers (The President's Advisory 1776 Commission, 2021) and accuses utopian agendas of fostering the divisions in the United States. This argument is based on protecting whiteness and not acknowledging the role race has played in the creation of U.S. society.

In December 2021, Hispanic scholars released *España la primera globalización*, a documentary that romanticizes the Spanish Empire's horrific past of genocide, land dispossession, and *mestizaje* as a cultural exchange between two worlds. According to Álvarez (2023), the film gives the impression that Indigenous Blacks from Africa gave consent to be kidnapped and extracted from their epistemologies, ontologies, and axiology to work as slaves for capitalist societies that only supported the logics of white settler colonialism. In the same way, Indigenous people in the Americas supposedly gave permission to white settler colonialists to brutally enculturate them to European customs with acts that included the rape of our mothers and grandmothers, and the exploitation of Caribbean woman. Among many of their horrific claims, Hispanic scholars glorify the process of rape as a beneficial *mestizaje*—they call it the most important legacy of Hispanidad in the make-up of the Latin America of today (Barea & Espada, 2022; López-Linares, 2021).

These current strategies are enforcing oppression in a post-colonial period and are the very reason why Guerrilla Pedagogies are central to the idea of implementing CRIS. The etymological difference is important for educators to understand, as the phenomenon of colonialism as an event in constant transformation. The importance of these post-colonialists brings with them a very important topic directly related to decolonization.

As we noted earlier, Smith (2012), Glenn (2015), and Tuck and Yang (2012) helped create a discourse that places a white supremacist logic that goes beyond discourses in the areas of anthropology, geopolitics and international relations. These authors bring evidence that the logic of white supremacy affects social justice and brings with it oppression and violence through various social systems, including the U.S. public education system. This situates the colonizer—and if we are not aware of it, the average U.S. teacher—as the architect of an education system that serves two purposes: (1) to sustain the empire through white privilege; and (2) to continue the oppression of minoritized, marginalized, and otherized groups of individuals through de facto disenfranchisement. In this way, a Eurocentric empire has been sustained where the logic of white supremacy is to civilize and indoctrinate through the education system. And it is exactly because of these assimilation practices that principals and instructional leaders need a CRIS paradigm to help teachers engage in Guerrilla Pedagogies and practices.

GUERRILLA PEDAGOGY AS AN ACT OF RESISTANCE

Acts of resistance to the de facto disenfranchisement discussed in previous sections of this chapter include direct and intentional ways to empower students in the educational process. This includes the use of Guerrilla Pedagogy in classroom environments (Springer & Benjamin, 2019). Moving away from oppressive and hierarchical systems to inclusive and affirming spaces for learning exemplifies the valuable role of teachers. To be equity instructional leaders, they must develop and help implement instruction that is inclusive and affirming of all children in the U.S. education system.

Through Guerrilla Pedagogy, teachers and students are reciprocal learners in organic learning situations (Lavin, 2004). Teacher–student dynamics in this type of learning environment demonstrate the impact of efforts that are co-constructed. Using Guerrilla Pedagogy in classroom settings gives students opportunities for reflection and problem solving (Weems, 2013). Teachers share the teaching space with other educators and with students to approach real-world scenarios through thought-provoking discussion and critical analysis. Examples of Guerrilla Pedagogies can include language arts teachers assigning books that center the voice of the marginalized, math teachers engaging with data that highlights structural inequities, and social studies teachers unpacking historical perspectives that challenge Eurocentric norms. By operationalizing Guerrilla Pedagogy, teachers can help liberate students from an oppressive education system.

Manokore and McRae (2021) offered examples of the ways that incorporating Guerrilla Pedagogy in large classrooms within the health professions gave students time to consider applying content knowledge based on purposeful discussions and problem sets. Their findings extend those of Norton (1994) when looking at the early Guerrilla Pedagogy movement. Engaging learners in discussions about ethics and social justice in decision-making through content knowledge and understanding encourages opportunities for deeper learning of the concepts. Developing original ways of supporting student engagement requires the support of culturally responsive instructional supervisors, traditional campus principals and assistant principals, so that teachers confirm that they can try innovative teaching-learning strategies in the classroom without fear of repercussion. This requires culturally responsive instructional supervisors to reject and resist the culture of fear and repercussion embedded in the modern U.S. education system. Teacher-evaluation systems don't encourage teachers to take risks, and in fact, typically disincentivize teachers from doing so. By engaging students in nontraditional classroom practices, those responsible for the instructional supervision of teachers should also be familiar with Guerrilla Pedagogy in order to offer effective supervisory practices based on purposeful feedback.

Practicing Guerrilla Pedagogy as a form of CRIS demonstrates pro-active stances for providing feedback to teachers and students from socioculturally diverse backgrounds (Guerra et al., 2022). As such, principals and instructional leaders providing supervision can offer spaces of empowerment and growth for both teachers and students. Inviting teachers to collaborate on the type of feedback that they need will help them to glean purposeful supervision from school leaders who visit their classrooms and observe their teaching to help promote culturally responsive practices.

TIME FOR RENEWAL IN EDUCATIONAL SUPERVISION

As the tide begins to turn toward educational pedagogies that are inclusive and culturally responsive, like Guerrilla Pedagogies, the time to renew the process in educational supervision is at hand. Cormier and Pandey (2021) detail how traditional and mainstream supervision paradigms do not directly align with culturally responsive school leadership. It is difficult to ask school leaders to engage in culturally affirming practices, yet not rethink and reimagine the process of providing effective feedback to teachers who are engaging students in "nontraditional" ways, like Guerrilla Pedagogy.

An important starting point is in the curriculum found in principal preparation programs. Educational supervision courses can support incorporating strategies of Guerrilla Pedagogies in the university classroom. In this way, the dynamics of the interactions can be contextualized by aspiring school leaders. Such experiential learning lends itself to giving aspiring school leaders opportunities to actively engage in instructional leadership while addressing culturally responsive instruction. Having these experiences in the principal preparation program classrooms gives aspiring school leaders hands-on opportunities that they can share with the teachers that they will supervise in the future. Not only will this help leaders know how to engage in Guerrilla Pedagogy strategies, they will also be steeped in more critical forms of knowing.

After school leaders complete their university coursework and certification requirements, another way that they can engage in renewed efforts toward supervision is to practice "leading with" instead of "leading over" the teachers in their schools. Fritz and Miller (2003) remind us that educational leaders are first and foremost instructional leaders. Thus, instructional leaders engage in supportive ways to support teachers' creativity in the classroom. Such leaders encourage risk-taking and ingenuity to more effectively "reach" the learners of today and tomorrow.

Instructional leaders and teachers must work collectively when starting off a supervisory relationship. Like all relationships, respect and trust are at the forefront. Teachers need to feel supported by school leaders, and school leaders need to forego hierarchical impositions to offer teachers opportunities for originality in their educational spaces. Chen (2018) purported the value of co-constructing professional growth opportunities for teachers alongside school leaders. This side-by-side enrichment moves away from the standard top-down models of supervision of instruction, with the school leader as the sage imparting knowledge. A reciprocal relationship allows teachers to play more active roles in their own growth and development.

Educational advocates as guerrilla educators support student learning using similar collaborative approaches. Such teachers are not bound by the physical confines of a classroom, but engage students in ways that encourage them to become critical consumers of curriculum and their connections to global impacts.

Teachers help students understand the need to challenge some existing curricular programs, and to find ways to advocate for learning that is socially just. Then students can reflect on these inclusive and affirming learning models that they can carry with them through their educational journeys and into all places where they participate as global advocates for change. Given such a mission, the work of teachers as pedagogical experts must be fully empowered by instructional leaders who are open to collaborative supervisory practices. We reiterate the value of relationships among leaders and teachers to foster learning environments that are additive for all.

REFERENCES

Álvarez, A. (2023). *Bombazo epistemology a syllabus of survival: Dismantling settler colonialism's philosophy in the stolen land* [PhD Dissertation. Illinois State University.] https://doi.org/10.30707/ETD2023.20230711063200574735.999999

Barea, R. E., & Espada, A. (2022). *Imperiofobia y leyenda negra. Roma, Rusia, Estados Unidos y el Imperio español (Spanish ed.).* Ediciones Siruela.

Cavanagh, E., & Veracini, L. (2017). *The Routledge handbook of the history of settler colonialism.* Abingdon, United Kingdom: Routledge.

Chen, C. C. (2018). Facilitation of teachers' professional development through principals' instructional supervision and teachers' knowledge-management behaviors. In Y. Weinberger & Z. Libman (Eds.), *Contemporary pedagogies in teacher education and development* (pp. 51–64). http://dx.doi.org/10.5772/intechopen.71989.

Cormier, D. R., & Pandey, T. (2021). Semiotic analysis of a foundational textbook used widely across educational supervision. *Journal of Educational Supervision, 4*(2). https://doi.org/10.31045/jes.4.2.6

Del Moral, S. (2013). *Negotiating empire.* Amsterdam, Netherlands: Amsterdam University Press.

Denoon, D. (1979). Understanding settler societies. *Historical Studies, 18*(73), 511–527.

Evans-Winters, V. E. (2017). Necropolitics and education. In G. Sirrakos & C. Emdin (Eds.), *Between the world and the urban classroom* (pp. 19–33). Sense Publishers.

Freire, P. (1972). *Pedagogy of the oppressed.* Bloomsbury Academic.

Fritz, C., & Miller, G. (2003). Supervisory options for instructional leaders in education. *Journal of Leadership Education, 2*(2) 13–27. https://journalofleadershiped.org/wp-content/uploads/2019/02/2_2_Fritz_Miller.pdf

Glenn, E. N. (2015). Settler colonialism as structure: A framework for comparative studies of U.S. race and gender formation. *Sociology of Race and Ethnicity, 1*(1), 52–72. https://doi.org/10.1177/2332649214560440

Grosfoguel, R., Velásquez, E. R., & Hernández, R. (Eds.). (2016). *Decolonizing the Westernized university.* Adfo Books.

Guerra, P. L., Baker, A. M., & Cotman, A. (2022). Instructional supervision: Is it culturally responsive? A textbook analysis. *Journal of Educational Supervision, 5*(1), 1–26.

Lavin, J. (2004). *Guerrilla pedagogy: The discourse, ethics, and educational uses of Caribbean storytelling.*

López-Linares, J. L. (Director). (2021, December). *España, la primera globalización* (documentary). López-Li Films.

Manokore, V., & McRae, D. (2021). Revolutionizing learning environments with guerrilla pedagogy in large classes. *Journal of Practical Nurse Education and Practice, 1*(1) 31–52. https://doi.org/10.29173/jpnep7

Navarro, J. M. (2002). *Creating tropical Yankees*. Routledge.

Negrón-Montilla, A. (1975). *Americanization in Puerto Rico and the public-school system 1900–1930*. Ed. Universidad de Puerto Rico.

Norton, J. (1994). Guerrilla pedagogy: Conflicting authority and interpretation in the classroom. *College Literature, 21*(3), 136–156.

The President's Advisory 1776 Commission. (2021). *The 1776 report*. https://trumpwhitehouse.archives.gov/wp-content/uploads/2021/01/The-Presidents-Advisory-1776-Commission-Final-Report.pdf

Santos, B. S. (2007). Beyond abyssal thinking: From global lines to ecologies of knowledges. *Review* (Fernand Braudel Center), 30(1), 45–89. Retrieved from http://www.jastor.org/stabel/40241677

Santos, B. S. (2014). *Epistemologies of the south*. Macmillan Publishers.

Santos, B. S. (2016, July 16). *Epistemologies of the south and the future*. From the European South: A transdisciplinary journal of postcolonial humanities, 1, 17–29.

Scheurich, J., & Young, M. D. (1997). Coloring epistemologies: Are our research epistemologies racially biased? *Educational Researcher, 26*(4), 4–16. https://www.jstor.org/stable/1176879

Smith, A. (2012). Indigeneity, settler colonialism, white supremacy. In D. Martinez Ho-Sang, O. LaBennett, & L. Pulido (Eds.), *Racial formation in the twenty-first century* (pp. 66–101). University of California Press.

Spring, J. (2013). *The American school, A global context: From the Puritans to the Obama administration*. McGraw-Hill Education.

Spring, J. (2016). *Deculturalization and the struggle for equality*. Routledge.

Springer, D., & Benjamin, J. (2019). Groundings: A revolutionary Pan-African pedagogy for guerrilla intellectuals. In D. R. Ford (Ed.), *Keywords in radical philosophy and education: Common concepts for contemporary movements*.

Tuck, E., & Yang, K. W. (2012). Decolonization is not a metaphor. *Decolonization: Indigeneity, Education & Society*, 1(1), 1–40. Retrieved from https://jps.library.utoronto.ca/index.php/des/article/view/18630/15554

Weems, L. D. (2013). Guerilla pedagogy: On the importance of surprise and responsibility in education. *Philosophical Studies in Education, 44*(50), 50–59.

Wolfe, P. (1999). *Settler colonialism and the transformation of anthropology*. Cassell.

Yancy, G. (2019). *Educating for critical consciousness*. Taylor & Francis.

Afterword

Several messages emerge from the chapters in this volume about how to implement more effective culturally responsiveness in education and achieve better educational equity and effectiveness for ethnically, racially, and culturally diverse student populations in PK–12 schools—populations that the chapters individually and collectively refer to as marginalized, minoritized, and otherized student populations. These "lessons" are what I might refer to as guidelines for culturally responsive practice. Although they are crafted specifically within the domain of instructional supervision, they are applicable to other aspects of the educational enterprise as well, with appropriate contextualization. The lessons are apparent in individual chapters as well as among the chapters collectively. Together they create a template for implementing culturally responsive education, with the understanding that how they are actualized in practice will be affected by a wide variety of contextual variables such as school community; aspects of the educational enterprise targeted for change; and student and teacher ethnic, racial, and cultural knowledge and competencies.

The variables that shape culturally responsive practice not addressed here in the afterword since they are explicated in the various chapters, at least for their targeted foci of Culturally Responsive Instructional Supervision (CRIS). However, the thoroughness with which they are analyzed is a good model for educators involved in other aspects of the enterprise to emulate. No notions of priority should be attached to the order in which the following "lessons learned" are presented. Rather, think of them as cyclical and interactive, rather than hierarchal and sequential.

One lesson CRIS reminds educators of is the power of praxis—that is, translating theoretical ideas into possibilities for practice. It is well-founded that there are interactive relationships that exist between beliefs and behaviors. To contribute to the creation of a more equitable society, historical analyses of contemporary educational problems and efforts regarding various dimensions of sociocultural diversity are necessary. As such, thorough diagnoses of problems are necessary before solutions to bridge the theory–practice gap can be conceived and attempted.

Another lesson learned is that leadership is essential to effective culturally responsive efforts. Cultural responsiveness has transformative potential and effects, and to create a schoolhouse that is more inclusive, culturally responsive initiatives, including but not limited to CRIS, should be woven throughout the *core* of all aspects of the educational enterprise where thorough analyses of contexts and challenges should precede proposed remediations—especially through leadership decisions. Modifying existing educational paradigms to be more inclusive of different dimensions of a wider variety of sociocultural identities, groups, and experiences requires all educators to engage in becoming more culturally responsive and will not be effective without the support of formal leadership.

Related, a third lesson learned is that cultural responsiveness throughout the educational enterprise is not merely a proficiency mandate; it is a moral imperative. The educational goal for diverse students and communities should be *standardization* (high performance expectations for all students) without *homogenization* (treating all students identically at the level of action). Understanding and accepting the humanity of marginalized, minoritized, and otherized groups is the precondition for all change efforts.

This is related to yet another lesson learned—that cultural responsiveness and critical self-consciousness are interactive. Educators need to model their own messages with regards to being culturally competent and critically conscious. This requires educators to develop and refine specific skill-based competencies to be the focus of diversity reform efforts and not the nebulous and general "awareness" of differences that are often seen as performative and cursory. As such, educators must acknowledge that cultural socialization shapes and filters human attitudes, values, beliefs, and behaviors. This is true for both students and the various educators who engage in different aspects of the educational enterprise. The various manifestations and effects of these need to be addressed in culturally responsive initiatives through the ongoing development of critical self-consciousness.

A fifth lesson learned through the development of CRIS is how the salience of race, class, culture, gender, and other lived experiences (i.e., the marginalizing, minoritizing, otherizing of students) is often perpetuated in teaching and learning. Effective cultural responsiveness requires both comprehensive and task-specific efforts within individual components of teaching and learning, as well as across the many components that comprise the whole experience of school. This requires educators to decenter whiteness and other privileged sociocultural identities, norms, policies, and practices, as well as create learning and demonstrate culturally responsive skills cooperatively within job-alike communities of practice. Educators should be encouraged to differentiate instruction that is informed by, and reflective of, students' various sociocultural identities and experiences.

This connects to another lesson, which is that educators must recognize and resist diversity-evasive claims and practices. Educators need to strive to understand and resist the effects of threats of reactionary laws, policies, and practices that threaten culturally responsive initiatives. Culturally responsive efforts should be sensitive to the multidimensionality of both students' and teachers' identities, cultures, experiences, and competencies and honor the lived experiences they bring with them to the classroom every day.

The last lesson that I will offer from CRIS is the need to focus on asset-based and strengths-based reform initiatives from teachers and for students. This highlights the importance of "skill plus will" in culturally responsive change efforts. To enact this work, educators must understand claims of normalcy in the educational enterprise as acts of power, privilege, and dominance (i.e., white supremacy), and transform them into efforts that honor cultural and ethnic diversity and inclusion. For cultural responsiveness in education to be systemic and wholistic, the schoolhouse must value and employ multiple perspectives and techniques in analyzing and responding to human diversity within educational settings.

As I conclude these thoughts, I should point out that culturally responsive training for educators should focus on capacity-building and be fault-free. To know more about others, educators must also seek to know more about themselves. Educators should be deliberate about learning what they don't know about ethnic, racial, and cultural diversity and cultural responsiveness, and it is of particular importance to disrupt notions that schools are value-free and teach "objective truths." Additionally, education systems must accept the centrality of building relationships as a foundation for transforming classrooms and schools with respect to diversity, equity, and inclusion. Both intrapersonal and interpersonal development for both students and educators are imperative in coping with the challenges and evoking the benefits of ethnic, racial, and sociocultural diversity in schools and communities. This book contributes to these notions and addresses with depth how CRIS can add to the culturally responsive literature to help transform the educational enterprise.

—Dr. Geneva Gay
Professor Emerita, University of Washington, Seattle

Author Index

Aasen, P., 53
Abbott, D. J., 128, 133
Abrahamson, R. D., 18
Acheson, K. A., 179, 256, 258
Acker, J., 130
Acker-Hocewar, M., 56
Adams, M. S., 196
Adams, P., 101
Adams, S., 54
Aguilar, I., 2, 34, 37, 114, 149
Ahn, J., 254, 257, 258
Airasian, P., 106
Albert Shanker Institute, 53
Alexander, M., 84, 85, 90
Alexander, N. A., 235, 239, 240
Alexander, T., 56
Alim, H. S., 167, 168, 169, 253
Allen, R. L., 56
Al Maskari, A., 59
Alston, J. A., 236, 237
Álvarez, A., 275, 280, 281
Amanti, C., 40, 43
American Association of Colleges for Teacher Education (AACTE), 80
Ancin, D., 253
Anderson, B., 2
Anderson, J., 32, 116, 251
Anderson, J. A., 128, 133
Anderson, J. D., 52
Anderson, N. B., 151
Anderson, R. H., 256
Anderson, S., 189
Anderson, S. E., 58
Annamaa, S. A., 31, 39
Anwisye, F. S., 127
Anyon, J., 53
Apfel, N., 63
Apple, M. W., 53, 130
Archibald, T., 103, 106
Argent, J., 253, 254, 257, 260
Argyris, M., 255
Arnold, N. W., 55, 56, 59, 60, 62, 65
Asante, M. K., 126, 129
Association for Student Teaching, 81
Asterhan, C.S.C., 258

Ata, A., 182
Avci, O., 226

Bagley, W. C., 13
Baker, A., 106
Baker, A. M., 3, 14, 23, 27, 37, 39, 53, 62, 282
Baker, W., 82
Baker, W. B., 151
Ball, S., 101
Ballenger, J., 56
Banks, J. A., 14, 24, 63, 168
Banwo, B. O., 125, 127, 29, 134
Barber, L., 106
Barea, R. E., 281
Barney, H., 251
Bartanen, B., 53
Bartolomé, L., 86, 88
Bates, L. A., 58
Bauer, S. C., 235
Beach, D. M., 60
Becchio, J. A., 189
Beck, C., 82
Beckert, S., 55
Beckford, G. L., 53
Bellibaş, M. S., 188
Bellon, E. C., 179
Bellon, J. J., 179
Belmont, M. J., 264
Bencherab, A., 59
Bendixen, L. D., 31
Benjamin, J., 282
Bensimon, E. M., 16
Berger, P. L., 130
Biesta, G., 32
Blackwell, K., 151, 153
Blazer, J., 1
Bleiberg, J., 98
Block, D., 81
Bloom, C. M., 238
Blumberg, A., 102
Blum-DeStefano, J., 209, 256
Boatcă, M., 30
Bogotch, I., 171
Bolman, L. G., 234
Bonilla-Silva, E., 39

Author Index

Borders, L. D., 62
Bose, B. K., 253
Boser, U., 53
Bounsanga, J., 34, 52
Bowers, A. J., 235
Boykin, A. W., 259, 264
Bozack, A. R., 82, 83, 86
Brand, D., 67
Brandon, J., 101
Bransberger, P., 149
Brass, J., 101
Brayboy, B.M.J., 55, 188
Brazer, S. D., 235
Bristol, L., 59
Bristol, T. J., 53, 133
Britt, L. B., 254, 255, 262
Brock, J. D., 60
Brondyk, S. K., 116
Brooks, J. S., 8, 241
Brotherton, D., 62
Brouilette, L., 57
Brown, C., 57
Brown, K. M., 150
Brown, R. C., 155
Browne, S., 58, 59
Brown v. Board of Education, 235
Brunner, B., 106
Brunner, E., 98
Bryk, A. S., 256, 264
Brzustoski, P., 63
Buchanan, R., 84
Buckley, J., 103, 106
Buese, D., 251
Burden-Stelly, C., 1
Burnett, A., 101, 252
Burnham, R. M., 31
Burns, R. W., 76, 80, 82, 83, 84, 85, 86, 87
Burton, L., 239, 240
Busemeyer, M., 35
Butler, B. M., 82, 83, 81–82, 86, 90
Byrd, C. M., 215
Byrd, D. M., 83, 84

Cabral, L., 62
Caldera, A. L., 217
Calliste, A., 67
Cambone, J., 128, 132
Cambron-McCabe, N., 129
Campano, G., 61
Campbell, E. Q., 233
Campos, F., 254, 257, 258
Cannata, M., 252, 259
Capello, S., 82, 83, 84
Capodilupo, C. M., 201
Capper, C. A., 129, 150, 217, 224
Carpenter, J., 196
Carroll, R. G., 82
Carter, C., 59, 60, 62, 132, 134

Carter, H., 85
Carter, P. L., 33
Carter Andrews, D. J., 53
Caruz, V. V., 255
Carver-Thomas, D., 166
Casciola, V., 63, 76, 86, 87, 90
Castro, A. J., 19
Castro, E., 53
Causton, J., 171
Cavanagh, E., 280
Cevik, S., 120
Charner-Laird, M., 219
Chen, C. C., 283
Cheng, A., 60
Cheng, J.-J., 128
Cheng, L. C., 115
Cheng, S. L., 19
Cho, C. L., 53
Christensen, M. C., 221
Christian, A., 101
Christman, D. E., 129, 150
Chrobot-Mason, D., 67
City, E. A., 251
Clark, L. G., 56
Clark, M., 101
Clark, M. A., 252
Clark, R., 151
Clark, V. R., 151
Clarke, S. N., 258
Clayton, J. K., 37, 52
Clinton, J., 106
Cloete, N., 35
Cobb, P., 259
Coburn, C., 103
Cochran-Smith, M., 88, 90
Cogan, M. L., 32, 107, 256
Cohen, D. K., 60
Cohen, G. L., 63
Coldren, A. F., 252
Coleman, J. S., 233
Collins, G., 53, 62
Collins, P. H., 231, 232, 233, 234, 240, 241, 246
Collins, T. A., 43
Colmenares, E., 86
Colombo, M. G., 128
Combahee River Collective, 231, 232, 233, 240
Connelly, L., 205
Conrad, D. L., 62
Cook, D. A., 60, 62
Cookson, P., 168
Cooper, A. J., 237, 239
Cooper, C. W., 46
Cooper, K. S., 116
Coppin, F. J., 233, 236, 240
Corbin, B., 59
Cormier, D. R., 1, 2, 3, 4, 6, 12, 14, 16, 18, 19, 23, 27, 28, 37, 39, 63, 103, 104, 112, 113, 115, 117, 121, 150, 171, 184, 219, 283

Author Index

Cornelius, J., 58
Cortina, R., 216
Cotman, A. M., 3, 14, 23, 27, 37, 39, 53, 62, 282
Cox, C. F., 233
Cozart, S., 55
Cozzens, J. A., 54
Creswell, J. W., 60
Crockett, S. A., 43
Crutchfield, L. B., 62
Cuban, L., 57, 257, 263
Cuenca, A., 82, 83, 84, 86, 90
Cullen-Lester, K. L., 67
Currin, E., 85, 90
Curtis, R., 62
Cyert, R. M., 131
Cyr, D., 239, 240

Dana, N. F., 90, 116
Dancy, T. E., 52
Daniel, B. J., 61
Daniel, J., 57
Dantley, M. E., 12, 129, 150, 226, 234, 241
Darilek, H., 251
Darimont, C. T., 196
Darling-Hammond, L., 80, 82, 166, 218, 219, 220, 223
David, J. L., 251
Davis, A. Y., 233
Davis, B. W., 56
Davis, C., 58
Davis, J. E., 4, 12, 13, 23, 26, 36, 104, 149, 161, 162, 163, 170, 171, 173, 215, 218, 219, 221, 224, 226
Davis, S., 60
Dawson, G., 106
Deal, T. E., 234
Dee, T., 61
Dei, G., 68
Dei, G.J.S., 67
Delgado, R., 224
Delgado, R. C., 58
Delle, J. A., 58
Del Moral, S., 276
Delpit, L., 201, 264
DeMatthews, D. E., 130, 171
Denoon, D., 280
Dewey, J., 35
Diacopoulos, M. M., 81–82, 90
Diamond, A., 253
DiAngelo, R., 223
Diaz, J., 35
Diem, S., 56
Diemer, M. A., 216, 226
Dinkelman, T., 82, 83, 86, 90
DiPaola, M., 203
Dismuke, S. A., 85
Dixson, A. D., 55, 60, 62, 202, 204
Dobbs, C. L., 219

Dolle, J. R., 256, 264
Donnor, J. K., 55, 57, 62
Doty, J., 32, 116, 251
Douglas, T.M.O., 59, 63
Dowd, A. C., 16
Drago-Severson, E., 209, 254, 256, 260, 262
Drake, T. A., 252, 259
Driscoll, M. P., 257
Dron, E., 61
Drori, G., 35
Duan, C., 43
Duffett, A., 234
Dugan, J., 258, 259
Duke, L., 234
Dumas, M. J., 56, 217, 224, 233
Dupell, M., 84
Duran, B., 154
Dussel, E., 215
Dyches, J., 39

Earl Davis, J., 52
Easton-Brooks, D., 53
Eaton, A., 39
Eaton, S. E., 55
Ebbeler, J., 107
Edmonds, R., 53, 55, 234
Education Commission of the States, 61
Edwards, K. T., 52
Edwards, T., 57
Egalite, A. J., 36, 37, 53, 251, 257
Eiken, K. P., 33
Ellett, C., 99
Elmore, R. F., 188, 251, 264
Emdin, C., 205
Endy, D., 60
English, F. W., 62
Epperson, T. W., 58
Erickson, F., 18
Erickson, J. L., 197
Erlandson, D. A., 238
Espada, A., 281
Espinosa, S., 37, 62
Evans-Winters, V. F., 279
Eye of the Storm, The, 101

Fahle, E., 108
Faircloth, S. C., 191
Fanon, F., 61
Farkas, G., 234
Farley, A. N., 57, 62
Feagin, J., 52
Fear-Segal, J., 36
Feiman-Nemser, S., 82
Ferguson, A. A., 24
Ferrini-Mundy, J., 82
Fiarman, S. E., 251
Fierro, E., 129, 150
Finkelstein, I., 54

Author Index

Firestone, W. A., 180
Firth, G. R., 33
Fisher, C., 101
Fisher-Ari, T. R., 112
Fiske, S. T., 152
Fla. Stat. Section 1004.04, 81
Fletcher, E. C., Jr., 171
Floden, R. E., 53, 82
Ford, D. Y., 171
Foucault, M., 58
Frank, J., 253
Frankenberg, E., 56
Franklin, J. D., 34, 52
Franklin, V. P., 236
Frazier-Anderson, P. N., 60
Freelon, R., 63
Freire, P., 12, 14, 24, 76, 86, 87, 88, 203, 215, 216, 221, 223, 224, 226, 280
Friesen, S., 101
Fritz, C., 257, 283
Frumin, K. M., 252
Fuller, C., 170
Fusarelli, B. C., 62
Fusarelli, L. D., 62

Gage, N. A., 54
Gall, M. D., 179, 256, 258
Galloway, M. K., 263
Gamoran Sherin, M., 103
Ganon-Shiloh, S., 54
García, E., 166
Garcia, J., 63
García, S., 42, 43
Gardner, M., 218, 219, 220, 223
Garman, N. B., 53, 63, 107
Garret, M. T., 62
Gay, G., 4, 11, 12, 18, 19, 20, 21, 22, 23, 24, 25, 26, 28, 36, 43, 80, 98, 100, 102, 103, 105, 117, 118, 120, 150, 167, 168, 169, 170t, 171, 172t, 173, 208, 214, 215, 246
Generett, G. G., 251
Gerbasi, A., 67
Gershenson, S., 53
Ghiso, M. P., 61
Gibson, S., 219, 220
Gill, B., 101, 252
Givens, J. R., 24
Glanz, J., 32, 33, 37, 52, 57, 59, 256
Glasman, N. S., 101
Glatthorn, A. A., 173
Gleeter, C. E., 166
Glenn, E. N., 276, 278, 281
Glickman, C. D., 4, 14, 23, 25, 32, 33, 35, 37, 39, 40, 41, 56, 76, 119, 149, 174, 204, 208, 209, 256, 257, 259, 261, 263
Godsil, R. D., 152
Gofstede, G. J., 39
Goldenberg, B. M., 53

Goldhammer, R., 32–33, 116, 256
Goldin, C., 152
Goldring, E., 101, 252, 259
Gomell, A., 256, 257
Gomez, L. M., 256, 264
González, M. L., 129
Gonzalez, N., 40, 43
Gooden, M. A., 4, 12, 13, 23, 26, 36, 56, 104, 129, 149, 161, 162, 163, 170, 171, 173, 215, 218, 219, 221, 224, 226, 241, 251
Goodwin, M., 37
Goosby, B. J., 151
Gordon, N., 39
Gordon, S. P., 4, 13, 14, 23, 25, 32, 35, 37, 39, 40, 41, 53, 62, 76, 119, 149, 182, 256, 257, 259, 261, 263
Gorski, P. C., 33, 64
Graham, M. S., 83
Gratier, M., 41
Green, J., 217
Green, T. L., 63, 127
Greenfield, P. M., 41
Griffin, L. B., 37
Grilli, L., 128
Grissom, J. A., 36, 37, 53, 101, 189, 251, 252, 257, 259
Grosfoguel, R., 278, 280
Grosland, T., 167, 169, 171
Gross, S. J., 60
Groysberg, B., 128
Grubb, W. N., 253, 264
Grumow, A., 256, 264
Gu, Y., 34, 52
Guajardo, F., 8, 253, 256, 257
Guajardo, M., 8, 253, 256, 257
Guerra, P. L., 3, 14, 23, 27, 37, 39, 42, 43, 53, 62, 282
Gullickson, A., 106
Gummer, E., 107
Gümüs, S., 188
Gunn, K. M., 167, 169, 171

Haberlin, S., 85, 90, 154, 157
Hackmann, D. G., 62
Haddix, M., 62
Haile, H., 112
Haines, J. G., 182
Haines, N., 55
Hall, E. T., 41
Hallett, T., 55
Hallinger, P., 55, 101, 188, 234, 240
Halloran, C., 188
Hamilton, E. R., 116
Hammond, A., 211
Hammond, Z., 0
Hammond, Z. L., 19, 22, 27, 211, 215, 221, 258, 264
Hancock, B., 61

Handel, G., 127
Hanover Research, 127
Hanushek, E. A., 149
Haraway, D., 54, 60
Harbatkin, E., 98
Hargraves, M., 103, 106
Hart, C. M., 53
Harvey, D., 81
Hassan, S., 61
Hawley, W. D., 168
Hayes, R. L., 128
Hayes, S. B., 83
Hays, M., 254, 257, 258
Hazi, H. M., 54, 99, 100, 101
Heck, R., 101
Heck, R. H., 188
Heidbrink, C., 151
Heidelburg, K., 31
Helms Mills, J., 203
Hendriksen, D., 256
Henig, J., 106
Henrick, E., 259
Henry, K. L., Jr., 55, 57, 60
Hernandez, F., 129, 150
Hernandez, J., 149
Hernández, R., 278, 280
Hesbol, K. A., 171
Hesert, W. T., 63
Hesse, B., 54
Hightower, A. M., 58
Hines, E. M., 171
Hines, M. T., 33
Hitt, C., 60
Hmelo-Silver, C. E., 256, 257
Hobson, C. J., 233
Hodgkins, L., 257, 260
Hofer, B., 221
Hofman, R. H., 59
Hofstede, G. J., 39, 41, 42
Holder, I., 60
Holloway, J., 94, 101, 102
Holme, J. J., 56
Holmes Group, 82
Holquist, S. E., 56
Holt, S. B., 53
Hook, T., 54, 55, 58, 67
hooks, b., 161, 233, 241
Hoover, L. A., 76, 84
Hoover, N. L., 82
Hoppey, D. T., 83
Horsford, S. D., 62, 167, 169, 171
Horwitz-Willlis, R., 252
House, R. M., 128
Housty, J. A., 196
Howard, T. C., 17, 24
Howland, A. A., 128, 133
Hubers, M. D., 57

Hull, R. D., 58
Hung, M., 34, 52
Hunter, D., 101
Hutchins, R. M., 13
Hvidston, D. J., 32, 54, 116, 251
Hyler, M. E., 218, 219, 220, 223

Iannacone, R. M., 128, 129
Igwe, P. A., 208
Ikemoto, G. S., 251
Ilgen, D., 101
Ilies, R., 131
Ingersoll, R. M., 53, 62, 256
Ippolito, J., 219
Irby, D. J., 253
Irizarry, J., 52
Irvine, J. J., 62, 80, 168
Isaac, A., 41
Ishimaru, A. M., 63, 130, 263

Jackson, D. D., 39
Jackson, E. E., 31
Jackson, K., 259
Jacob, B., 61
Jacobo, A., 257, 259
Jacobs, J., 32, 37, 43, 62, 63, 76, 80, 82, 83, 84, 85, 86, 87, 90
James, J., 254, 255, 263
Jang, H., 108
Jang, S. T., 235, 239, 240
Janson, C., 8, 253, 256, 257
Jasper, A., 54
Jay, M., 24
Jean-Marie, G., 56, 217, 226
Jefferson, N. R., 58
Jenlink, P. M., 52
Jennings, M. E., 55
Jimenez, A. M., 182
Johnson, B., 106
Johnson, J., 234
Johnson, L., 167, 170
Jonas, R., 102
Jones, R. P., 1
Jones, S. N., 236
Joseph-Salisbury, R., 205
Justice, B., 233

Kabat-Zinn, J., 154, 158
Kafka, J., 54
Kahamaa, A., 256, 257, 259
Kanu, C., 208
Kao, K., 37
Karenga, M., 127
Katsiyannis, A., 54
Kautz, T., 101, 252
Keegan, C., 60
Kennedy, M., 104

Author Index

Kerr, K. A., 251
Khalifa, M. A., 3, 4, 11, 12, 13, 19, 21, 23, 26, 36, 39, 43, 63, 101, 126, 128, 129, 131, 142, 146, 147, 153, 157, 158, 159, 160, 164, 166, 167, 168, 170, 185, 201, 212, 215, 216, 218, 221, 223, 253
Khalil, D., 188
King, J. E., 226
Kirkland, K., 26, 150
Kisida, B., 53, 60
Klibanoff, E., 35
Knerl, L., 219
Knowles, M. S., 220, 262
Kohli, R., 31, 220, 221, 222
Kok, K., 101
Kolman, J. S., 84, 85, 90
Kosnik, C., 82
Koziol, N., 19
Kozol, J., 54
Kraft, M., 98, 101
Krajewski, R. J., 256
Krakowski, P., 105
Kuchynka, S. L., 39
Kumpulainen, K., 256, 257, 259

Lacava, P. G., 58
Ladson-Billings, G., 2, 11, 12, 21, 24, 33, 36, 43, 52, 80, 119, 131, 167, 168, 170, 202, 204, 214, 215, 217, 219, 226, 233
Lance, T., 38, 53
Lane, K. L., 129
Lanoue, P. D., 169, 171, 182
Larsen, T. J., 188
Larson, A., 85
Lassnigg, L., 35
Lave, J., 255
Lavin, J., 282
Lawrence, P., 203
Laymon, K., 114
Ledo-Lane, A., 263
Lee, J., 128
Lee, T., 188, 189
Lee, Y. A., 63
Leithwood, K. A., 58, 189, 234
Lejeune, L., 60
LeMahieu, P. G., 256, 264
Leonardi, B., 57, 62
Leonardo, Z., 13, 24, 39
Lester, D., 62
Levitt, J. I., 60
Lewis, L., 3, 53
Lieb, D. A., 1
Lieberman, M., 108
Liggett, T., 37
Lin, A. I., 201
Lindsay, C. A., 36, 37, 53, 251, 257
Lindsey, R. B., 17, 26, 119, 209

Ling, D. S., 253
Liou, D. D., 56
Lipman, P., 55
Liptak, A., 112
Little, S. J., 171
Littlefield, D. C., 61
Lloyd, C., 189
Lloyd, S. C., 58
Lochmiller, C. R., 101
Loeb, S., 189, 252
Loewen, J. W., 54
Lomotey, K., 238, 240, 245
Lopez, A. E., 56, 171, 217, 226
López, F. A., 167, 168
López-Linares, J. L., 281
Loughran, J., 90
Louis, K. S., 58, 124, 131, 189
Lourde, A., 233
Love, B. L., 24, 116, 205
Lozano, Y. E., 40
Lucas, T., 8, 11, 16, 19, 20, 21, 22, 26, 43
Lucas, T. F., 62
Lucio, W. H., 31
Luckmann, T., 130n1
Lyman, F. T., 258
Lynch, M. E., 13, 62, 80, 85, 86, 87, 89, 90, 214, 224, 226
Lytle, S., 88, 90

Mabokela, R. O., 62
Macedo, D., 203
Machado, M., 254
Mackey, H. J., 191
Macpherson, R. J., 55
Maday, T., 191
Madhlangobe, L., 163, 182
Madsen, J. A., 62
Magee, P. A., 85, 86, 90
Magee, R. V., 153, 156, 158, 159, 160, 163
Mahnkin, K., 97
Maier, A., 57
Malik, A., 253
Mandinach, E., 107
Manning, L., 13, 24, 39
Manokore, V., 282
March, J. G., 128, 131
Marchitello, M., 42
Marcoulides, G. A., 188
Marsh, J. A., 251
Marsh, T. E., 188
Marshall, K., 256
Marshall, S. L., 63
Martinez, A., 220, 221, 222
Martinez, J.G.L., 40
Martinez-Cosio, M., 128, 129
Martin-Fernandez, J., 53, 133
Marx, K., 86

Mascaluso, M., 116
Master, A., 63
Master, B., 189, 252
Mawhinney, H., 130
Maxwell, L. A., 166
May, H., 53, 62
Mayer-Smith, J., 82
McCammon, S., 112
McCarty, T., 188, 189
McClellan, P. A., 232, 233, 237, 240
McCluskey, A. T., 232, 233, 240
McCullough, M., 101, 252
McGhee, C., 62
McGhee, M. W., 62
McGinnis, C., 19
McGovern, K., 59
Mcintee, K., 59, 60, 62
McIntyre, C., 82
McIntyre, D., 82, 83, 84
McKenzie, K. B., 127, 129, 150
McKittrick, K., 53, 60, 61, 63, 67
McLeod, S., 196
McMillian, R., 55, 56, 59, 60, 65
McNamara, O., 59
McNeil, J. D., 31
McPartland, J., 233
McRae, D., 282
McVeigh-Murphy, A., 197
McWhirter, E. H., 216, 226
Mead, G. H., 130
Mehta, J. D., 252
Mehta, S., 1
Meier, J. A., 116
Melvin, J. F., Jr., 251
Menakem, R., 152, 159
Mette, I. M., 1, 2, 3, 4, 6, 12, 23, 27, 32, 34, 37, 43, 53, 54, 55, 56, 63, 112, 113, 114, 116, 117, 121, 149, 150, 251, 259
Meyers, H., 128
Mezirow, J., 115
Michael, R. S., 36
Micheaux, D. J., 56
Militello, M., 8, 253, 254, 256, 257, 259, 260
Miller, A. L., 31
Miller, G., 257, 283
Mills, C. W., 52, 117, 149
Mills, J. N., 60
Milner, H. R., IV, 3, 11, 12, 14, 23, 24, 27, 33, 40, 52, 76, 80, 115, 120, 167, 168, 207, 224
Minkov, M., 39, 41, 42
Mireles-Rio, R., 189
Mitman, G., 55
Mitra, D., 53
Mizell, H., 221
Mohatt, G., 18
Moll, L. C., 40, 43
Mombourquette, C., 101
Mong, I. K., 208

Montana Office of Public Instruction, 191
Monteiro-Ferreira, A., 126
Mood, A. M., 233
Moon, B., 82
Moore, J. L., 171
Moore, K., 223
Morewood, A., 83
Morgan, H., 35, 149
Morgan, P. D., 61
Morgeson, F. P., 131
Morris, C., 257, 260
Morris, C. L., 255
Morris, E. W., 178
Morris, M. W., 36
Morrison, D., 39
Morrison, J., 254, 257, 258
Morrison, K. L., 167, 168
Morrow, L., 55, 56, 59, 60, 65
Moule, J., 17
Moynihan, D., 233
Mudd, K. A., 255
Muhammad, G., 19, 120
Murphy, J. F., 101, 131
Murphy, M. W., 60
Murray, E., 112
Musselwhite, M., 60
Myers, K., 54, 55
Myers, S. L., Jr., 60

Nahrgang, J. D., 131
Najarro, I., 107, 208
Nally, D., 54, 55
Nardo, A. C., 36
National Academy of Sciences, 258
National Association for Professional Development Schools (NAPDS), 77
National Center for Education Statistics (NCES), 2, 34, 40, 42, 113, 166, 222
National Council for the Accreditation of Teacher Education (NCATE), 77, 83
Navarro, J. M., 276
Neale, M., 154, 155
Neasloss, D., 196
Neel, M., 101, 252
Neff, D., 40, 43
Negrón-Montilla, A., 274, 276
Nelson, S. W., 43
Neumerski, C. M., 188, 189, 252, 259
Nevarez, A., 31
Nevin, A., 128
Newton, M., 65
Ngo, H., 112
Nguyen, H., 254, 257, 258
Nichols, J. R., Jr., 82, 83, 86, 90
Nielson, C. R., 57, 58
Niemi, N. S., 82, 83, 86
Nieto, S., 168
Nieuwenhuizen, L., 32, 54, 116, 251

Author Index

Noblit, G. W., 55
No Child Left Behind (NCLB), 58, 114
Noguera, P., 259, 264
Nolan, B., 128
Nolan, J. F., Jr., 76, 81, 82, 84
Nordentoft, H. M., 67
Norris, J., 257
North Dakota Department of Public Instruction, 191
Norton, J., 275, 282
Nwosu, H. E., 208
Nyegenye, S. N., 31

Oakes, J., 57
O'Connell, H. A., 36
O'Doherty, A., 224
Ojemuyide, C. C., 208
Okolie, U. C., 208
Olafson, L., 31
Oliveras, Y., 23, 112, 113, 117, 121
Oliveras-Ortiz, Y., 1, 2, 3, 4, 6, 12, 23, 27, 63, 101
Omi, M., 52
Orfield, G., 55
Ortiz, A. A., 42
Ortiz, N., 220, 221, 222
O'Shea, C. M., 191, 197, 198
O'Shea, L. J., 82
Owens, L. R., 151, 153, 156

Pacini-Ketchabaw, V., 57
Page, T. G., 60
Paige, L., 83
Palazzolo, L., 128
Pandey, T., 3, 14, 23, 37, 39, 150, 184, 219, 283
Papageorge, N. W., 53
Paquet, P. C., 196
Paris, D., 167, 168, 169, 253
Parise, L. M., 252
Parker, J., 255
Parks, S., 62
Parsons, D., 101
Paryani, P., 262
Pateman, C., 117
Patton, L. D., 60
Paulin, P. J., 101
Payne, B. O., 255
Payne, C. M., 53, 149
Peele, C., 1
Pendharkar, E., 98
Perkins, L., 236
Petchauer, E., 53
Peters, A. L., 238
Petersen, M. J., 252
Peterson, P. E., 149
Peterson, R., 36
Peurach, D. J., 60
Pexman, P. M., 39
Phelps, C., 43

Phi Delta Kappan (PDK), 97
Picower, B., 220, 221, 222
Pierre, J., 56
Pieters, J., 107
Pinto, P. R., 54, 55
Piva, E., 128
Pizarro, M., 31
Place, A. W., 56
Plachowski, T., 31
Ponticell, J. A., 55, 180, 182, 183
Poortman, C., 107
Powell, J. A., 80
Prescott, B. T., 149
President's Advisory 1776 Commission, 280
Price, J., 128
Price-Dennis, D., 86
Protheroe, N., 251
Przybylski, R., 106
Purdie-Vaughns, V., 63
Purifoy, D. M., 55
Purser, M., 258

Qadir, R., 62

Radd, S., 251
Range, B. G., 32, 116, 251
Rapa, L. J., 216, 226
Rasheed, J. M., 203
Rasheed, M. N., 203
Ratner, C., 81
Raudenbush, S., 257
Reardon, S., 108
Reber, S., 39
Redding, C., 36, 53
Reinhard, K., 56
Reinhardt, M., 191
Rembert, A., 217
Resnick, L. B., 258
Richardson, L. S., 152
Richmond, G., 53
Riegel, L., 55
Riehl, C. J., 130, 234
RISA Framework, 226
Rivera, D. P., 201
Rivera, G. M., 169, 171
Rivera, L. M., 39
Rivera-McCutchen, R. L., 241
Robertson, P. M., 42
Roberts v. City of Boston, 237
Robins, K. N., 17, 26, 119, 209
Robinson, V., 189
Roegman, R., 63
Roehlke, H., 43
Rogers, L. K., 101, 252
Rose, H. A., 167
Rose, S. D., 36
Ross, D. J., 54
ross, k. m., 224

Ross-Gordon, J. M., 4, 14, 23, 25, 32, 35, 37, 39, 40, 41, 76, 119, 149, 256, 257, 259, 261, 263
Roth, W., 88
Rouse, C., 152
Rowan, B., 257
Rowe, K., 189
Royal, C., 219, 220
Rubin, M., 101, 252, 259
Rudasill, K. M., 19
Russell, B., 68
Russell, G., 171, 173
Russell, J. L., 256, 264

Šabanović, S., 256, 257
Safir, S., 211, 258, 259
Said, E., 278
Salazar, M., 86, 89
Saldaña, J., 257
Sampson Graner, P., 58
Sanchez, L., 61
Sandy, L., 59
Santos, B. S., 274, 276, 278, 279
Saphier, J., 258
Sarakatsannis, J., 61
Saultz, A., 59
Sawchuck, S., 56
Scanlan, M. K., 171
Schaeffer, K., 53
Scharron-Del Rio, M. R., 221
Schechter, C., 54
Schein, E. H., 142
Schermann, P., 252, 259
Scheurich, J. J., 127, 129, 150, 276, 278
Schildkamp, K., 57, 107
Schmeichel, M., 82, 83, 86, 90
Schneider, J., 59
Schober, B., 35
Schofield, J. W., 168
Schön, D., 255
Schroeder, S., 85, 90
Schroering, C., 60
Schwartz, S., 36, 61, 117
Schwartzman, S., 35
Schweisfurth, M., 35
Scribner, S., 171
Sealey-Ruiz, Y., 224, 224
Sela-Shayovitz, R., 54
Sellers, K., 58
Sensoy, Ö., 223
Serafini, A., 171
Serars, C. R., 39
Sergiovanni, T. J., 14, 76, 85, 253, 255, 256
Service, C., 196
Sexton, J., 124
Shafer, D. R., 169, 171
Shaked, H., 188, 189
Shandomo, H. M., 218, 219
Shareski, D., 196

Sharpe, C. E., 53
Shebley, S., 85
Sherer, J. Z., 252
Sherfinski, M., 103
Shields, C. M., 52, 171
Shulman, J., 102
Shulman, L. S., 99, 102, 103
Shulman, V., 57
Simon, K., 257, 259, 260
Simone, G., 155
Simpson, R. L., 58
Singleton, G. E., 211
Sirotnik, K. A., 82
Skerritt, C., 58
Skiba, R. J., 36
Skinner, E. A., 264
Skrla, L., 127
Slater, G., 68
Sleeter, C. E., 33, 63
Slick, S. K., 83
Smiley, A. D., 128, 133
Smith, A., 276, 277, 278, 281
Smith, P. A., 62
Smith, T., 259
Smith, W. A., 34, 52
Smith-Peterson, M., 58
Smyth, J., 83, 87, 88, 90
Smyth, W. J., 58
Snow, J., 85
Soder, R., 82
Sofia, M. K., 60
Soleimani, N., 221, 226
Sorum, M., 259
Soslau, E., 84, 85, 90
Speights, R., 112
Spiegelman, M., 53
Spiel, C., 35
Spillane, J. P., 60, 252
Spring, J., 53, 276, 279, 280
Springer, D., 282
Springer, M., 98
Squire, D., 54, 61
Sriprakash, A., 54, 55
Stanulis, R. N., 116
Stark, M. D., 62
Starratt, R. J., 14, 76, 256
Stefancic, J., 224
Steffy, B. E., 62
Stelmach, B., 101
Stephen, W. G., 168
Stewart, A., 237
Straume, I. S., 35
Stronge, J., 106
Sue, D. W., 201, 203
Sullivan, S., 33, 57, 256
Sun, J., 106
Sun, M., 62
Supovitz, J. A., 251

Author Index

Sutcher, L., 166
Suttorp, M., 251
Swalwell, K., 66
Swanson, C. B., 58

Taie, S., 3, 53
Talpey, L. M., 149
Tanase, M. F., 166, 215
Tang, W., 255
Tate, W. F., 24, 217, 226
Taylor, D. L., 63
Taylor, M. S., 101
Taylor, S. E., 152
Teitel, L., 251
Tennies, E., 112
Terrell, R. D., 17, 26, 119, 209
Tesfaw, T. A., 59
Tevis, T. L., 40
Theoharis, G., 62, 171, 251
Thomas, D., 39
Thomsen, R., 67
Thousand, J. S., 128
Thurlow, A., 203
Tillman, L. C., 33, 234, 236, 238, 241
Todić, J., 221
Tomich, D., 53
Tomlinson, S., 57
Torino, G. C., 201
Torres Rivera, E., 62
Totenberg, N., 112
Touloukian, C., 62
Townes, F. H., 52
Townsend, T., 56
Tredway, L., 253, 254, 257, 258, 259, 260, 264
Trinidad, J., 42
Trochim, W., 103, 106
Trujillo, T., 57
Tubbs, N., 216, 221
Tuck, E., 276, 277, 281
Tucker, P., 106
Tuitt, F., 54, 61
Turner, C.S.V., 60
Turner, D., 52
Turner, E. O., 103
Tyack, D. B., 205, 257, 263

Unsworth, S. J., 39
Urick, A., 188
U.S. Dept. of Education, 214

Valencia, R. R., 39, 43
Valian, V., 152
Valli, L., 251
Veazie, M., 112
Velasco, C., 253
Velásquez, E. R., 278, 280
Vella, J., 260
Venzant-Chambers, T., 63

Veracini, L., 280
Verma, S., 35
Versland, T. M., 197
Villa, R. A., 128
Villegas, A. M., 8, 11, 16, 18, 19, 20, 21, 22, 26, 43, 62
Vintimilla, C. D., 57
Viruleg, E., 61
Voight, A. M., 216, 226
Voss, M. W., 34, 52
Vygotsky, L. S., 87

Wagner, C. A., 203
Wahlstrom, K., 189
Wahlstrom, K. L., 58, 189
Waite, D., 53
Waite, S. R., 3, 27, 150, 215, 216, 217, 220, 222, 223, 224, 225, 226
Walls, J., 56
Walsh, M., 97, 108
Wang, W. C., 55
Ware, F., 264
Warren, C. A., 17, 26, 168
Watkins, W. H., 130
Watson, D., 37
Watson, K. T., 151
Watson, T. N., 8, 171, 232, 233, 237, 240, 241
Waxman, O. B., 1
Weathers, E., 108
Weathers, J., 251
Weems, L. D., 282
Weiner, J., 239, 240
Weinfeld, F. D., 233
Weiss, C. H., 128, 132
Weiss, E., 166
Welner, K. G., 33
Welsh, R. O., 171
Welton, A. D., 56, 63
Whitaker, M. C., 60
White, B. R., 235
Whitford, D. K., 54
Whyte, K., 193
Wichmann-Hansen, G., 67
Wickham, S. M., 204
Wideen, M., 82
Wieczorek, D., 2, 34, 37, 114, 149
Wilbon-White, T., 59, 63
Wilderson, F. B., 130
Will, M., 98, 208
Willey, C., 82, 83, 85, 86, 90
Williams, B. C., 54, 61
Williams, D. R., 151
Williams, H. A., 232
Williams, J., 59
Williams, M. E., 63
Williams, T. M., 62
Wilmot, J. M., 31
Wilson, A., 54

Wilson, C. M., 238
Wilson, S. M., 82
Wilt, C. L., 31
Winant, H., 52
Winter, M., 216
Winters, M. A., 53
Wise, D., 257, 259
Wisevoter, 6
Witherspoon, N., 59, 60, 63
Witherspoon Arnold, N., 57, 59, 63
Wittenstein, R., 58
Woessmann, L., 149
Wolfe, P., 280
Wolford, W., 54
Wong, C.-C., 256, 257, 259
Woo, L. J., 256
Woodfield, C., 171
Woods, C., 57
World Population Review, 56
Worley, L., 155
Wynter, S., 67

Xia, J., 198

Yancy, G., 274
Yang, K. W., 276, 277, 281
Yeager, D. S., 63
Yeigh, M. J., 85, 86, 90
Yendol-Hoppey, D., 76, 82, 83, 84, 85, 86, 90, 116
Yildirim, S., 120
Ylimaki, R. M., 55
York, R. L., 233
Yosso, T. J., 3, 11, 15, 40, 167
Young, M. D., 276, 278
Youngs, P., 252
Yousuf, E., 132, 134
Yurmovsky, M. M., 252

Zaker, J., 84
Zatz, N., 56
Zeichner, K., 83
Zepeda, S. J., 32, 33, 53, 55, 120, 169, 171, 173, 174, 175, 177, 182, 183, 184, 252, 256, 258
Zimmer, R. W., 251
Zuckerman, S. J., 191, 197

Subject Index

21st century skills, 197–198
1776 Report (1776 Committee), 28

Academic achievement, 19–20, 36, 41, 149, 201, 211, 240
Academic rigor, 25, 263–264
Accountability, 2, 33, 34, 53, 54, 56, 57, 105, 113, 114
African enslavement. *See* racist legacies in instruction and supervision: plantation traditions
Antidialogical professional development (APD), 220, 222
Archaeology of Self for Our Times (Sealey-Ruiz), 224
Asset-based approach, 167–168, 183, 256
Assimilation, 277–278
Authenticity, 135, 196–197

Bayanihan (communalism), 255
Biopsychosocial Model of Racism, 151
Black Feminism, 233, 247
Black Feminist Theory, 233–234, 241
Black Feminist Thought (BFT), 238, 239–240
Black Lives Matter movement, 209, 222
Black women
  as contemporary school leaders, 238–240
  educational attainment of, 232
  historical school leaders, 231, 232, 235, 236–238, 247–248
  and leadership practice: herstory, 240–245
  as mothers, 247
  scholarship on, 232, 234–236
Body scan, 157–158
Book bans, 97
Brazer and Bauer model of instructional leadership, 235
Brown v. Board of Education, 235, 274
Buddha, 154

Calling-on patterns, 178, 259, 261t
Capacity for culturally responsive praxis, 15–17, 22–23, 149–150
Care, 238, 239–240, 241, 242–243, 246
CCRI (community of culturally responsive instructors), 115–116, 120–121

Choice principle, 105–106
Classroom observation. *See* CLE (Community Learning Exchange); Culturally Responsive Framework for Classroom Observations
CLE (Community Learning Exchange)
  continuum of supervision, 261
  conversations, 259–263
  and equity, 264–265
  and evidence-based observations, 257–258
  observation tools, 258–259
  prerequisite conditions for improvement, 252–255
  school improvement, 249–250
  self-care, 253–254
  storytelling, 254–255
  supporting teacher growth, 255–257
Clinical Supervision Cycle (CSC), 32, 34, 37–38
Clinical supervision model, 32–33, 34, 256
CLS (Critical Legal Studies), 217
Cognitive dissonance, 15–16, 227
Collaborative supervision, 14, 32, 33, 127, 265, 283
Collectivism, 41, 67, 103, 255
Colonialism, 36, 188–189, 194–195, 273, 276–279, 281
Colorblindness, 35, 37–38, 40, 277
Combahee River Collective Statement, 233
Communalism (bayanihan), 255
Community Cultural Wealth, 11–12
Community Learning Exchange (CLE). *See* CLE (Community Learning Exchange)
Community mindfulness, 161–162
Community of culturally responsive instructors (CCRI). *See* CCRI (community of culturally responsive instructors)
Community relations, 129, 130, 133, 140, 159, 191
Compassion, 161–162
Conversations, 201–202, 203, 205, 206, 211, 241, 257, 259–264
Cooper, Anna Julia, 237
Cooperative correction, 236
Coppin, Frances Jackson, 236–237
Courageous Conversations, 206, 211
COVID-19, 211, 219, 237–238

301

Subject Index

CRIS (Culturally Responsive Instructional Supervision). *See also* Indigenous students and Culturally Responsive Instructional Supervision (CRIS)
   cultural capital and cognitive dissonance, 15–16
   culturally responsive praxis, 11–13, 25–27
   cultural responsiveness development, 36–37, 42–43, 44–45t, 46
   and curriculum, 23–25
   and dominant viewpoint, 39–40
   framework, 115
   and future, 28–29, 43–44, 46
   and Guerrilla Pedagogy, 274–275, 279, 280, 282
   introduction to, 13, 22–23
   key embodiments, 16–18
   leadership, 20–22
   sociocultural gaps, 18–19
   and standards, 171, 172t
   teacher capacity, 22–23, 149–150
   teacher feedback, 27–28, 114–121
   U.S. context, 28–29
   vignette, 40–42
CRISP (Culturally Responsive Instructional Supervision Practices)
   development plans, 205–208
   difficult conversations anecdote, 201–202
   supervision versus evaluation, 202–203
   supervisory behavior continuum, 203–204
   sustained progress, 209–211
   talk reliance, 203, 211
   teacher behaviors, 209–211
Critical consciousness
   critical self-reflection, 218–219
   critical theory, 215–218, 223
   as embodiment of culturally responsive pedagogy, 17–18, 214–215, 222–223
   and mindfulness, 150, 160–161
   and professional development, 219–222
   RISA Framework, 224–227
   student capacity, 226
   and teacher-level change, 119–120
Critical Legal Studies (CLS), 217
Critical place-based learning, 103–104
Critical Race Theory (CRT), 19–20, 56, 217, 226
Critical self-awareness, 129, 143, 225f
Critical self-reflection, 129, 136–137, 145, 150, 175–176, 218–219
Cross-racial alliance, 276
CRP (culturally relevant pedagogy). *See* Culturally relevant pedagogy (CRP); Culturally responsive pedagogy
CRSL (Culturally Responsive School Leadership). *See* Culturally Responsive School Leadership (CRSL)
CRT (Critical Race Theory). *See* Critical Race Theory (CRT)
Cultural bias, 42, 169, 173, 172. *See also* Implicit bias
Cultural capital, 11–12, 15–16, 21, 27–28, 105, 167

Cultural competence, 17, 100, 112–113
Cultural liaisons, 128–129, 132–135, 142–145
Culturally damaging instruction, 108, 118–119
Culturally relevant pedagogy (CRP), 131, 214–215
Culturally Responsive Curricula and Teacher Development, 129, 143–144
Culturally Responsive Framework for Classroom Observations
   data use, 180–182
   observation, 176–178
   overview, 174, 175t,182–183
   postobservation conference, 179–180
   preobservation conference, 171–176
Culturally responsive pedagogy, 3, 41, 175, 177. *See also* culturally relevant pedagogy (CRP)
Culturally Responsive School Leadership (CRSL), 11, 12, 21–23, 129–132, 170, 189, 204, 218–219, 221
Culturally Responsive School Leadership (Khalifa et al.), 170, 215
Culturally responsive teaching (CRT), 3, 11, 41, 102–106, 169, 170t,175, 177
Culturally Responsive Teaching (Gay), 2
Cultural Proficiency Continuum, 210–211
Curriculum, 23–25, 39, 129, 137, 138, 143–144, 162, 193–195, 205, 207, 279–280

Data, 12, 118, 126, 138, 141–142, 176, 180–182, 191, 252, 253
Data literacy, 106–107
Deep-level learning, 196–197
Deficit perspectives, 15, 99, 102, 105, 115, 167
Democracy and education, 34–36
Demographic trends, 52, 53, 166, 222
Developmental academic discourse, 266–267
Dialogue. *See* Conversations
Differentiated supervision, 173–174
Directive control, 206
Discipline, 36, 61–62, 132, 134
Discourse. *See* Conversations
Disenfranchisement, 279–280
Distributive leadership, 114

Educational relevance, 168
Educator workforce demographics, 28, 113, 166–167
Effective Schools Movement, 234
Effective Teacher Professional Development (Darling-Hammond), 218
Emancipation. *See* liberation
Empathy, 17, 26, 134
Empowerment, 273–274
Epistemicide, 274, 276
Epistemologies, 221, 238
Equity, 17–18, 32, 183, 211, 264
Equity audits
   background and conclusions, 124, 145
   critical responsiveness, 134–135
   cultural liason case study, 132–138

Subject Index

cultural liaison role, 128–129
focal areas, 138–142
framework application, 142–145
marginalized communities, 133–134
organizational practice, 135–136
school leadership, 125–127, 129–131
sociopolitical context, 127–128
student voice, 136–138
uncovering inequalities, 131–132
Whiteness and schools, 125
Espacio sano, 253
España la primera globalización, 280, 281
Essentialism, 13, 14–15
Ethnic/racial representation in administration, 167
Ethnic/racial representation in teaching force, 166–167
Eurocentricity, 21, 193, 213. *See also* Western beliefs
Evaluation versus supervision, 202–203
Evaluative mindset, 106, 108
Evidence-based observations. *See* CLE (Community Learning Exchange)
Exclusionary discipline, 132, 134, 136

Financial resources, 21–22
Flexible grouping principle, 105
Florida education policy, 81, 97
Formative feedback, 236
Formative process, 114, 256
Fort Abraham Lincoln activity, 194–195
Four Foundations of Mindfulness, 154
Four shifts (4 + 1), 196–197
Funding, 21–22
Funds of knowledge. *See* Cultural capital

Gender, 207, 239. *See also* Black women
Genocide, 277
"Giving sense," 257
Guerrilla education. *See* Guerrilla Pedagogy
Guerrilla Pedagogy
 about, 275–276
 and colonialism, 276–278
 and education supervision, 283–284
 and knowledge, 278–281
 as resistance, 281–282
 and social justice, 273–275
"Guide to Effective Conversations" (Tredway et al.), 26

Habits of mind development, 209
Health, 245
Hegemonic standards. *See* Whiteness centering
Herstory research, 240–245
Hierarchical structure, 34, 67, 112, 113
Higher education partnerships, 80–81
Higher-level thinking, 197–198, 223, 258–259

Implicit bias, 132–134, 137, 145, 152–153, 169, 173, 202, 205, 207

Implicit curriculum, 24–25
Inclusion, 129, 144, 162–163, 183, 211, 282
Indigenous students and Culturally Responsive Instructional Supervision (CRIS)
 colonialism, 36, 188–189, 273, 276–279, 281
 historical narratives, 193–195
 Indigenous identity, 36, 189–190
 relationships, 190–193
 Traditional Ecological Knowledge, 196–198
Individual epistemologies, 222–223, 226
Inequality regimes, 13
In loco parentis, 242–243, 246
Inner work, 156, 157, 163, 222–223
Insight capacity, 154
Instructional effectiveness assessment, 203
Instructional leadership, 25, 234–235, 236, 243–244, 244. *See also* Instructional supervision
Instructional leadership preparation, 42, 247, 283
Instructional reform, 251–252
Instructional rounds (IRs), 251
Instructional supervision. *See also* Instructional leadership
 and changing demographics, 31
 contemporary approach, 14
 critical self-examination, 42–43
 critiques, 34
 and cultural responsiveness, 3–4, 25–27, 36–37, 42–46
 and democracy, 34–36
 and dominant viewpoint, 39–42
 foundations of, 31–32
 history of, 3–4, 13–14, 32–34
 invisible culture, 40–43
 professional development, 42, 43, 46
 scholarship, 33
 and sociocultural diversity, 38–39
 SuperVision framework, 37–38
Instructional supervision education field, 11
Intention, 134, 158–159, 173–174, 245
Inventory, 67
Invisible culture, 42–43

Jeanes supervisors, 237

Knowledge control, 279–281
Knowledge creation, 233

Leaders as oppressors, 216
Learner centeredness, 275, 282
Learning organizations, 128
Learning styles, 168
Liberation, 28, 215–216, 220–221, 224–225, 233, 273, 274
Life expectancy, 151

Making a Difference (Mette et al.), 113
Measuring outcomes and teacher evaluation, 118
Mental health, 151

Mindfulness
  critical self-reflection, 153–154, 160–161
  and culturally responsive leadership, 149–150, 157
  effects of experience on the body, 151–152
  exercises, 157–160
  foundations, 154–156
  implicit bias and the body, 152–153
  inclusivity, 162–163
  social connection, 161–162
  teacher mentoring, 162
Mr. Gil vignette, 40–42
Multicultural education, 168
Myth of educational neutrality, 217

National Humanities Center, 54
Neoliberalism, 81
Neutrality, 277
No Child Left Behind (NCLB), 2, 114
Nondirective action plans, 208
Normative stance, 105

Ongoing feedback, 114
Opportunity gaps, 12, 24, 28–29, 57, 80, 149, 246
Oppression, 1–2, 125, 216, 233, 273, 280
Organizational learning, 130–131, 138, 139–140
Orientalism, 278
Othering, 97–98, 277–278

Parent and community relationships, 128, 129, 130, 140–141, 144–145
Patience (Tredway), 254–255
Pattern and trend examination, 179
Pedagogy of the Oppressed (Freire), 215
Peer-based observations, 120–121
Perennialism, 13, 14
Performativity, 101–102
Plantation futures"; 63
Plantation traditions. *See under* Racist legacies in instruction and supervision
Police murders, 214, 222
Policy analysis, 138
Postobservation conference, 179, 259–263
Power and privilege. *See* White centering and White supremacy
Pragmatic evidence of improvement, 259–261
Preobservation conference, 174–176
Prepackaged teacher evaluation systems, 115
Principals, 100–101, 169, 283
Professional Development (Kohli et al.), 22

Quantitative methodology, 239
Questioning strategies, 258–259

Race, 113, 166–167, 202, 216, 217, 223, 241, 274.
  See also Racism; Racist legacies in instruction and supervision
Racialized languages, 55–56

Racial literacy, 216–217, 224
Racial representation among educators, 53, 113, 166–167
Racism. *See also* Whiteness centering and White supremacy
  equity audits, 138, 139
  Guerrilla Pedagogies, 273, 278
  and health, 150–152, 163
  the police, 214, 222
  and segregation, 33, 108
Racist legacies in instruction and supervision
  authority and oversight, 58–59
  development and assessment, 65–66
  discipline, 36, 61–62
  inspection and surveillance, 59–60
  introduction, 52–54
  knowledge building and learning, 64–65
  labor, 60–61
  plantation traditions, 54–57, 67
  and race equity, 62–64
  race-ing instructional leadership, 63–68
  supervisory context, 66
  supervisory operations, 65
Relationships, 18, 40–41, 105, 140–141, 183, 190–193, 196–198, 264, 283
Reminiscences of School Life and Hints on Teaching (Coppin), 236
Resistance, 26, 63, 206, 238, 273–274, 276, 281
Responsiveness state, 28
RISA (Reflection Interrogation, Self-examination, Awareness) Framework, 224–227

SAMR (Substitution, Augmentation, Modification, and Redefinition) model, 197
School change, 215–217, 255–256
School climate, 20, 21, 108, 240
Self-awareness, 157
Self-care, 253–254
Self-evaluation, 106–108, 226
Sensitivity, 203
Settler colonialism, 36, 188–189, 273, 276–279, 281
Slavery. *See* Racist legacies in instruction and supervision: plantation traditions
Smith Tompkins Garnet, Sarah J., 237
Socialization, 125, 126, 127, 130, 139
Sociocultural gaps, 12, 18, 28–29, 115–116
Somali youth, 132–133, 135–136, 139, 141, 143
Somatic critical self-reflection, 153–154, 160–161
Spanish Empire, 280, 281
Storytelling, 253, 254–255
Street data, 259
Street Data (Safir & Dugan), 258
Student agency, 196–197
Student collaboration, 40, 41, 283
Student critical consciousness, 226
Student–educator relationships, 18

Subject Index

Student self-awareness, 168
Student voices, 136, 140, 141, 145
Substitution, Augmentation, Modification, and Redefinition (SAMR) model, 197
Summative feedback, 114–116
SuperVision and Instructional Leadership (Glickman et al.), 23, 37
SuperVision Framework, 37–38
Supervision in Transition (Glickman), 33
Supervision teams, 116–117, 121
Supervision versus evaluation, 202–203
Supervisory behavior continuum, 203–204
Support groups for school leaders, 255

Talk With Teachers, A (Baldwin), 224
Teacher agency, 255–256, 257–258, 262, 265, 283
Teacher autonomy, 32, 204, 208
Teacher candidate supervision
 background, 76–80
 counternarratives, 84–86, 91
 and marginalization, 81–84, 91
 praxis orientation, 87–91
 and university partnerships, 80–81
Teacher evaluation
 and administrator responsibilities, 103–104
 background, 97–98
 data use, 107–108
 limitations of, 98–99
 process, 100–102
 self-evaluation, 106–107
 system prerequisites, 102–103
 teacher responsibilities, 105–106
 tools of, 99–100
Teacher feedback, 27–28, 114–121
Teacher preparation, 162, 166, 219, 221. *See also* teacher candidate supervision
Technology infusion, 196–197
TEK4 + 1, 197–198
"Think time," 258

This work
 chapter overviews, 4–8
 and CRIS (culturally responsive instructional supervision) framework, 8–9
 terms and concepts, 34
 value of, 2–3
Time dependence, 206, 207
Traditional Ecological Knowledge (TEK), 196–198
Traditional instructional supervision, 3–4, 12–15
Trauma-informed practices, 214
Trump Administration, 28

U.S. education, 1–2, 9, 14–15, 76, 97–98, 112, 137, 278–279
U.S. Supreme Court, 112

Verbatim scripts, 259
Visibility, 171
Visualizations, 159–160
Voice From the South: By a Black Woman From the South, A (Cooper), 237–238

Western beliefs, 13, 15, 41, 125, 143, 193, 216–217, 276, 277–278
White Christian Nationalism, 1–2
White fragility, 15, 201–202, 245
Whiteness centering and White supremacy *See also* Critical consciousness; Equity audits; Guerrilla Pedagogies; Racist legacies in instruction and supervision
 contemporary frameworks, 39–40
 history of supervision, 13–14, 15, 33, 34
 importance of culturally responsive instructional supervision, 2–3, 13–14, 15
 and mindfulness, 152
 and settler colonialism, 277–278
 and the sociopolitical context of U.S. education, 1–2, 112, 113, 117, 125, 166, 222
Why Professional Development Matters (Mizell), 221

About the Editors and Contributors

Armen Álvarez, PhD, MDY, currently holds the position of assistant professor at Illinois State University, specializing in developmental math within the University College. With a dynamic professional background spanning arts administration, healthcare, education, and community engagement, Dr. Álvarez has demonstrated leadership as the associate director and program director of full-service community federal and 21st-century state grants at the Puerto Rican Arts Alliance. Additionally, Dr. Álvarez serves as a board member of Aspira Inc. in Chicago, leading initiatives related to providing alternative equitable education models. As a recent PhD graduate in leadership equity and inquiry from Illinois State University, Dr. Álvarez is actively seeking opportunities as a faculty scholar in this essential field. This pursuit combines academic excellence with practical experience, reflecting Dr. Álvarez's commitment to contributing valuable insights to the realm of educational research.

Noelle W. Arnold, PhD, is the senior associate dean and professor of educational administration at The Ohio State University. As a scholar, Dr. Arnold's work has focused on the intersections of leadership, race, gender, and community and school disparities. A former teacher and administrator at the district and state level, she also serves as a consultant throughout the United States advising districts on equity, crisis leadership, and teaching and leading in urban and rural contexts.

A. Minor Baker is an assistant professor in the elementary education program at Missouri State University. Before joining academia, Dr. Baker was a teacher and school administrator in both Minnesota and Texas. With a PhD in school improvement from Texas State University, his research interests span various areas, including school and community interactions, culturally sustaining supervision, and alternative interpretations of school leadership.

Bodunrin O. Banwo is an assistant professor in the Department of Leadership in Education at The University of Massachusetts Boston. His research focuses on the liberatory effects of communitarian programming in schools and student development. Before receiving his PhD from the University of Minnesota, Bodunrin served as a food access manager for the City of Baltimore and the Philadelphia-based nonprofit The Food Trust, a public school teacher, and a Peace Corps volunteer in

Paraguay, South America. Bodunrin looks forward to continuing his work with individuals committed to making our world a more just place.

Coy Carter Jr. is a research associate at the Center for Applied Research and Educational Improvement and a doctoral candidate at the University of Minnesota Twin Cities in the education policy and leadership program. His research focuses on neoliberal education reform and the impacts of race and racialized spaces on education policy decision making, implementation, and outcomes for racially marginalized students. His training in qualitative methods, culturally responsive pedagogy, and youth participatory action research center the experiences of community in schools. His research interests also include impacts of housing policy, gentrification, and white/reverse flight on educational opportunities for racially marginalized students.

Salih Cevik, PhD, is a UCEA Postdoctoral Research Associate at Michigan State University College of Education. He holds a PhD from the University of Georgia in educational administration and policy (EDAP). He holds graduate certificates in interdisciplinary qualitative studies and education law and policy. He has received several awards, including the Turkish Study Abroad Scholarship, EDAP Faculty Scholar Award, and the Ray E. Bruce Award. His research focuses on school leadership practices, differentiated instruction, teacher evaluation, and social justice.

Dwayne Ray Cormier, PhD, is an entrepreneur and researcher at Culturally Responsive Solutions and VSorts™ AI. His award-winning research focuses on the intersection between educators' beliefs and student and family interactions affected by the sociocultural gap. He investigates how sociocultural gaps impact educators' cultural competence, critical consciousness, relationships with students, school culture, and opportunity gaps. Using educational design research, he develops software and AI tools to assess and codify educators' sociocultural gaps, such as cultural competence and critical consciousness. The National Science Foundation Small Business Innovation Research Program funds his research and development efforts for culturally responsive software and AI tools. Dr. Cormier has been published in journals including *Educational Researcher*, *Journal of School Psychology*, *Urban Education*, and *Journal of Educational Supervision*.

Ann Marie Cotman is a postdoctoral associate in education leadership and policy at the University of Florida. Currently she teaches education leaders about the intersection of culture and education policy, though in her heart of hearts she remains a middle school teacher. Ann Marie's research seeks to expand the concept of school safety so that safety-driven policies and practices truly produce safer schools for all students.

Patricia L. Guerra is an associate professor at Texas State University. She teaches classes in educational leadership to master's and doctoral students. Prior to working in higher education, Pat worked as a teacher and school leader at Texas School for the Deaf and research associate at the Southwest Educational Development laboratory. Her research interests focus on addressing issues of equity through culturally responsive schooling, instructional supervision, and leadership.

Steve Haberlin, PhD, is an assistant professor of curriculum and instruction in the College of Community Innovation and Education at the University of Central Florida. Dr. Haberlin's research focuses on the implementation of meditation in higher education. He is the author of *Meditation in the College Classroom: A Pedagogical Tool to Help Students De-Stress, Focus, and Connect* and *Awakening to Educational Leadership: A Mindfulness-Based Approach to Supporting and Coaching Teachers*.

Helen M. Hazi, PhD, studied clinical supervision at the University of Pittsburgh under Morris Cogan and Noreen Garman, where she learned how to help teachers collect data on their performance and reflect on their practice and progress. She has been an English teacher, a curriculum specialist, a K–12 supervisor, an expert witness, and now emerita from West Virginia University. She writes about legal issues in the 50 states that have consequence for teacher evaluation and supervision and is currently exploring the role of judgment in instructional improvement. Her web page is at https://helenhazi.faculty.wvu.edu/home, and contact is always welcomed at hmhazi@verizon.net.

Muhammad Khalifa, PhD, is a professor of educational administration and executive director for urban education initiatives at The Ohio State University. His latest book, *Culturally Responsive School Leadership* (2018, Harvard Education Press), is a top-seller and is being used in leadership preparation programs across the United States and Canada. Through the Culturally Responsive School Leadership Institute, he and colleagues have developed academies, equity audits, and learning modules that will help schools and leaders and systems become culturally responsive (https://crsli.org). The advanced equity audit tool is a researched-based way to reduce achievement and discipline disparities in school. Dr. Khalifa has served as an educator and administrator in Detroit and has engaged in school leadership reform in African and Asian countries.

Megan E. Lynch, PhD, is a post-doctoral research fellow and co-principal investigator on Project PREP, a Teacher Quality Partnership grant at the University of North Florida in the College of Education and Human Services, where she studies liberatory teacher education and (critical) practitioner inquiry. She brings her experience as a teacher to multilingual learners to her work as a scholar practitioner of teacher education and supervision. Megan's research draws on sociocultural and critical theories to better understand and shape the development of socially just pedagogies and political activism alongside teacher candidates, teachers, teacher educators, and P–12 students within school–university partnerships.

About the Editors and Contributors

Hollie Mackey (Northern Cheyenne) is an associate professor of education at North Dakota State University. She recently served as the executive director of the White House Initiative on Advancing Educational Equity, Excellence, and Economic Opportunity for Native Americans and Strengthening Tribal Colleges and Universities. Her scholarship empirically examines the effects of structural inequity in Indigenous and other marginalized populations in educational leadership and public policy using multiple critical frameworks and methodologies.

Kashmeel McKoena is a PhD student in the urban education leadership and policy studies program at the University of Massachusetts Boston. His research interest is in the transition between high school and college academic help-seeking behaviors for first-generation students of color. Before beginning his doctorial study, Kashmeel served as a high school teacher in Rhode Island. Currently, he teaches first-year seminar courses and works in academic support programs at the University of Massachusetts Boston.

Rhodesia McMillian, PhD, NCSP is an assistant professor of education policy at The Ohio State University. A licensed school psychologist and former teacher, Dr. McMillian is an interdisciplinary scholar whose work examines how federal, state, and local education policies impact the educational experiences of African American students, students with disabilities, and persistent educational disparities in K–12 public education.

Ian M. Mette is an associate professor of educational leadership at the University at Buffalo. His research interests include culturally responsive instruction supervision, developing equity-oriented educational leaders in predominantly White rural spaces, and how educators, researchers, and policymakers can better inform one another to drive school improvement and reform policy. He is the founding editor of the *Journal of Educational Supervision*, and his first book, *A New Leadership Guide for Democratizing Schools from the Inside Out: The Essential Renewal of America's Schools*, was coauthored with Carl D. Glickman and was published in 2020. Dr. Mette holds a PhD in educational administration from the University of Missouri.

Matthew Militello is the Wells Fargo Distinguished Professor in Educational Leadership at East Carolina University. Before his academic career, Militello was a middle and high public school teacher, assistant principal, and principal in Michigan. Dr. Militello has over 60 publications and is currently coauthoring his sixth book on school leadership, *Leading and Learning Together: Cultivating School Change from Within*. He has been awarded over $17 million in grant funding and is the founding director of an innovative doctor of education program for ECU anchored in Bangkok, Thailand.

Yanira Oliveras is an associate professor in the School of Education at The University of Texas at Tyler. She is a former bilingual teacher, curriculum coordinator, and school principal. Dr. Oliveras's research agenda and service focus on the advancement of instructional supervision in Belize. She collaborates with the Belize Ministry of Education to build school leaders' and teacher educators' instructional supervision capacity. In 2023, she led the development of an instructional supervision sense of efficacy scale. Dr. Oliveras holds a BS in elementary education and an MEd and PhD in curriculum and instruction with a focus on supervision from Penn State University.

Cailen O'Shea is an assistant professor of educational and organizational leadership at North Dakota State University. His research interests focus on school transformation and equitable instructional leadership. Specifically, he looks at ways educational leaders can enhance instruction for all students. He utilizes both critical quantitative and qualitative research methodologies. Previously, Dr. O'Shea served as a behavior interventionist, 5th-grade teacher, and instructional technology coach in Title I schools in Lincoln, Nebraska.

Mariela A. Rodríguez, PhD, is a professor in the Department of Educational Leadership and Policy Studies at The University of Texas at San Antonio. Her primary area of research focuses on the supportive practices of school leaders working with culturally and linguistically diverse students. She has several co-edited books, and her articles have been published in journals such as *Equity & Excellence in Education* and the *Journal of School Leadership*. Dr. Rodríguez is the vice-president of Division A of the American Educational Research Association (AERA). Prior to that she served as president of the University Council for Educational Administration (UCEA).

Sashay Schettler is a citizen of the MHA Nation; her Hidatsa name is Owl Woman. Her parents are Dave and Rhonda Schettler, who are formerly of Halliday and Twin Buttes but have been residents of Bismarck for over 40 years. Ms. Schettler is the first full-time director of Indigenous education for Bismarck Public Schools, a monumental moment for Bismarck Public Schools and the state of North Dakota. In her previous role, she served as a cultural responsive coordinator for BPS. Ms. Schettler serves on a variety of community committees and boards, including but not limited to the Bismarck Human Relations Committee, Youthworks Board of Directors, and the National Johnson O'Malley Association Board of Directors. Her published scholarly writing focuses on a healthy contemporary construction of Indigenous identity and Indigenous education in PK–12 public school settings. Through her work with her established team, Sashay aims to change the narrative of Indigenous education within public school systems. She aims to close the opportunity gap for Indigenous students and empower them to be leaders within their communities and beyond.

About the Editors and Contributors

Linda C. Tillman is professor emerita of educational leadership in the School of Education at the University of North Carolina at Chapel Hill. Dr. Tillman's research and scholarship is focused on school leadership, the education African Americans in K–12 education, mentoring in higher education, and culturally sensitive research approaches. She is editor in chief of the *SAGE Handbook of African American Education* and coeditor of the *Handbook of Research on Educational Leadership for Diversity and Equity*. She is the inaugural recipient of the Linda C. Tillman Social and Racial Justice Award, which was established in her honor by the University Council for Educational Administration.

Lynda Tredway, coordinator of the international EdD program at East Carolina University, was founding director of the Principal Leadership Institute (University of California Berkeley). She teaches courses in equity, teaching and learning for school leaders, history of education, philosophy of education, and school and community. Her research interests focus on how leaders and teachers collaborate to become action and activist researchers as they take back responsibility for their professional learning. Lynda taught in DC Public Schools, coordinated a teacher residency program at George Washington University partnership with DCPS, and coauthored (with W. Norton Grubb) *Leading from the Inside out: Expanded Roles of Teachers in Equitable Schools*.

Patricia M. Virella is an assistant professor in the Department of Educational Leadership at Montclair State University. Dr. Virella's research focuses on implementing equity-oriented leadership through leader responses, organizational transformation, and preparation. Dr. Virella also studies equity-oriented crisis leadership examining how school leaders can respond to crises without further harming marginalized communities.

Shannon R. Waite, EdD, is an assistant professor in the Department of Educational Leadership and Policy Studies in the School of Education at Howard University. Her research interests include topics on diversity recruitment and pipeline programs, culturally responsive school leadership, developing critical consciousness in educational leaders and examining hyper-segregation and its connection to the school-to-prison pipeline. Dr. Waite is a former mayoral appointee on the Panel for Educational Policy in New York City Department of Education and a trustee on the Board of Education Retirement Systems (BERS).

Terri N. Watson is an associate professor of educational leadership at The City College of New York and a member of the Urban Education faculty at The City University of New York's Graduate Center. She began her career as a middle school English teacher in East Harlem. Her research examines culturally relevant school leadership and the praxis of Black women school leaders. Moreover, her scholarship is aimed to improve the educational outcomes and life chances of historically excluded and underserved children and families. She employs Critical Race Theory, Black Feminist Theory, and Motherwork as methodological frameworks.

Rebecca West Burns, PhD, is the dean of the College of Education at Kutztown University of Pennsylvania. Dr. Burns is a nationally recognized scholar of clinically based teacher education in the United States where she studies school-university partnerships, supervision, and teacher leadership. She has held several leadership positions in national organizations like the National Association for School–University Partnerships, the Council of Scholars of Instructional Supervision, and the American Educational Research Association School-University Partnership Research Special Interest Group. Dr. Burns has also designed award-winning teacher education programs and has received national recognition for her impact on urban education.

Sevda Yıldırım, PhD, is an educational policy researcher/analyst at the Ministry of National Education Presidency of Inspection Board, Turkey. She earned her master's degree in educational leadership from the University of Florida, and a doctoral degree in educational administration and policy from the University of Georgia. Her research interests focus broadly on teacher evaluation and supervision practices and policies and implementation of professional development. Other areas of interest include socially just supervision and leadership and professional development practices of school leaders. She is serving as a researcher for the Erasmus+ project called Digital Effective School Self-Assessment for Sustainable School Improvement.

Sally J. Zepeda, PhD, is a professor of educational administration and policy at the University of Georgia. She teaches courses in leadership, supervision, professional learning, and personnel evaluation. She has written widely about teacher and leader supervision and evaluation, and school and district leadership. Her scholarship has appeared in journals such as the *Review of Educational Research*, the *Journal of School Leadership*, the *Alberta Journal of Educational Research*, and the *Journal of Educational Administration*. She has collaborated with numerous national and international school systems to develop coaching and mentoring programs for teachers and leaders. She is a member of the Council of Professors of Instructional Supervision (COPIS) and received the first Master Professor Award from the University Council of Educational Administration (UCEA).